GENDER DISORDERS
AND
THE PARAPHILIAS

GENDER DISORDERS AND THE PARAPHILIAS

William B. Arndt, Jr.

International Universities Press, Inc.
Madison   Connecticut

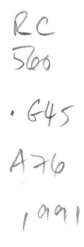
Library of Congress Cataloging-in-Publication Data

Arndt, William B.
  Gender disorders and the paraphilias / William B. Arndt, Jr.
    p. cm.
  Includes bibliographical references.
  Includes index.
  ISBN 0-8236-2150-2
  1. Gender identity disorders. 2. Sexual deviation. I. Title.
  [DNLM: 1. Identification (Psychology) 2. Paraphilias.
3. Transsexualism. WM 610 A7473g]
RC560.G45A76 1991
616.85'83—dc20
DNLM/DLC
for Library of Congress   90-4780
                                                        CIP

Manufactured in the United States of America

CONTENTS

v

TABLES

PREFACE

With ever increasing attention being paid to gender disorders and the paraphilias, it is surprising that there are so few books that give an overview of these subjects. Those that are available are written from a limited theoretical perspective. This is understandable since our information about these disorders comes from such diverse fields as endocrinology, general psychiatry, psychoanalysis, forensic medicine, psychology, sociology, and social work.

I have chosen to try to integrate this information. In this attempt I have been guided by the principle of constructive alternativism; that is, there are various perspectives from which behavior can be construed and one view does not necessarily preclude any other. Further, I have assumed that any complex behavior is multidetermined in a hierarchical developmental fashion, so that the various perspectives' major contributions are sequenced. For instance, endocrinology's impact occurs prenatally at a time when psychology and sociology are inapplicable; in childhood and later, psychological and sociological factors become operative.

My decision on which topics to include was based on several considerations. Since the *Diagnostic and Statistical Manual of Mental Disorders* (DSM-III-R) (American Psychiatric Association, 1987) represents an acknowledged standard, I have covered all the gender disorders and paraphilias mentioned there. The extent to which they are presented was determined by the available literature. In most cases I have supplemented professional sources with insights from literature, historical accounts, and publications written for the various gender disorder and paraphilia groups.

Because of my bias that not only gender disorders, but also the paraphilias, involve distortions in conceptions of masculinity and femininity, I have omitted studies using nonhuman animals. Since any behavior is, in part, culturally determined, I have limited my sources to Western cultures. Other than physical and chemical castration, the therapies used with gender disorders and paraphilias do not differ appreciably from those used with any behavior disorder. Therefore, I have not reviewed therapeutic procedures. And, since there is a scarcity of literature describing females with gender disorders and paraphilias, this book is almost exclusively about males.

Naturally, I hope that readers of this book will find it interesting, informative, and helpful. My fondest hope, however, is that this volume will serve as a source of hypotheses that will spur much needed research.

ACKNOWLEDGMENTS

I wish to express my gratitude to the following authors and publishers who have given me permission to use and reproduce material from their publications:

Academic Press and Kurt Freund

> From K. Freund (1981), Assessment of pedophilia. In: *Adult Sexual Interest in Children*, ed. M. Cook & K. Howells. London: Academic Press.

American Journal of Orthopsychiatry

> From J. Frosch & W. Bromberg (1939), The sex offender—A psychiatric study, 9:761–766; from R. Brant & V.Tisza (1977), The sexually misused child, 4:80–90. Reprinted with permission from the *American Journal of Orthopsychiatry*. Copyright 1939 and 1977 by the American Orthopsychiatric Association, Inc.

American Journal of Psychotherapy

> From D. Deutsch (1954), A case of transvestism, 8:239–242; from N. Lukianowicz (1962), A rudimentary form of transvestism, 16:655–675; from H. Benjamin (1971), Should surgery be performed on transsexuals, 25:74–82; from J. Hamilton (1972), Voyeurism: Some clinical and theoretical considerations, 26:277–287.

American Medical Association

Archives of General Psychiatry: from N. Lukianowicz (1960), Imaginary sexual partners, 3:429–449, Copyright 1960, American Medical Association; from I. Yalom (1960), Aggression and forbiddenness in voyeurism, 3:305–319, Copyright 1960, American Medical Association; from R. Vanden Bergh & J. Kelly (1964), Vampirism: A review with new observations, 11:543–547, Copyright 1964, American Medical Association; from R. Green & J. Money (1966), Stage-acting, role taking and effeminate impersonation during boyhood, 15:535–538, Copyright 1966, American Medical Association; from R. Litman & C. Swearingen (1972), Bondage and suicide, 27:80–85, Copyright, 1972, American Medical Association; from T. Van Putten & F. Fawzy (1976), Sex conversion surgery in a man with severe gender dysphoria. A tragic outcome, 33:751–753, Copyright 1976, American Medical Association; from J. Meyer & N. Reter (1979), Sex reassignment follow-up, 36:1010–1015, Copyright 1979, American Medical Association.
Journal of the American Medical Association: from C. Hamburger, G. Sturup, & E. Dahl-Iverson (1953), Transvestism, 152:391–396, Copyright 1953, American Medical Association; from M. Ostow (1953), Transvestism, 152:1553, Copyright 1953, American Medical Association; from G. Wiedman (1953), Letter, 152:1167, Copyright 1953, American Medical Association; from F. Worden & J. Marsh (1955), Psychological factors in a man seeking sex transformation: Preliminary report, 157:1292–1298, Copyright 1955, American Medical Association.

American Psychiatric Association

From *Diagnostic and Statistical Manual of Mental Disorders*, 1987, 3d ed., revised.

Archives of Sexual Behavior

From J. Randell (1971), Indications for sex reassignment surgery, 1:153–161; from P. Bentler (1976), A typology of transsexualism: Gender identity therapy and data, 5:567–584; from N. Buhrich & N. McConaghy (1977), The clinical syndrome of femmiphilic transvestism, 6:397–412; from K. MacKenzie (1978), Gender dysphoria syndrome: Towards standardized diagnostic criteria, 7:251–262; from V. Prince (1978), Transsexuals and pseudotranssexuals, 7:263–272; from N. Buhrich & N. McConaghy (1979), Three clinically discrete categories of fetishistic transvestism, 8:151–157; from M. Diamond (1982), Sexual identity, monozygotic twins reared in discordant sex roles and a BBC follow-up, 11:181–186; from S. Levine & R. Schumacher (1983), Increasingly Ruth, 12:247–261. Permission by Plenum Publishing Corp.

Louise Armstrong

From (1978), *Kiss Daddy Goodnight*. Hawthorn Books.

Basil Blackwell

From D. Laws (1984), The assessment of diverse sexual behavior and from C. Gosselin & G. Wilson, Fetishism, sadomasochism and related behaviors. In: *The Psychology of Sexual Diversity*, ed. K. Howells. Oxford, UK: Basil Blackwell.

British Journal of Psychiatry

From M. MacCulloch, P. Snowden, P. Wood, & H. Mills (1983), On the genesis of sadistic behavior: The sadistic fantasy syndrome, 143:20–29.

British Medical Journal

From W. L.-E. (1902), Book Reviews, 1:339–341.

Chevalier Publications

From V. Prince (1981), *Understanding Cross Dressing*. Tulare, CA: Chevalier Publications.

The Crown Publishing Group

From M. Martino (1977), *Emergence: A Transsexual Autobiography*. New York: Crown Publishers.

F. A. Davis

From A. von Schrenk-Notzing (1956), *Therapeutic Suggestion in Psychopathia Sexualis*. New York: The Institute for Research in Hypnosis Publication Society and The Julian Press, Inc.

Dan Cox and Reid J. Daitzman

From D. Cox & R. Daitzman, eds. (1980), *Exhibitionism: Description, Assessment, and Treatment*. New York: Garland STPM Press.

Doubleday

Excerpts from *The Silent Children* by Linda Tschirhart Sanford. Copyright © by Linda Tschirhart Sanford. Reprinted by permission of Doubleday, a division of Bantam, Doubleday, Dell Publishing Group, Inc.

E. P. Dutton and International Creative Management, Inc.

From R. Fox (1980), *The Red Lamp of Incest*. New York: Dutton. Reprinted by permission of International Creative Management and E. P. Dutton. © 1976 by Robin Fox.

Havelock Ellis Estate by Prof. Francois Lafitte, Literary Executor

From H. Ellis, *Studies in the Psychology of Sex* (1906, 1913b, 1928), Vols. 1 and 2. Copyright 1937, 1941, and 1942.

Emerson Books

From M. Hirschfeld (1940), *Sexual Pathology*. New York: Emerson Books.

The Free Press, A Division of Macmillan, Inc.

From D. Finkelhor (1979), *Sexually Victimized Children*. New York: The Free Press.

Richard Green, M.D.

From R. Green (1974), *Sexual Identity Conflict in Children and Adults*. New York: Basic Books.

Grove Press, Inc.

From The Marquis de Sade, *The Complete Justine, Philosophy in the Bedroom and Other Writings*, Copyright © 1965 by Richard Seaver and Austryn Wainhouse; *The 120 Days of Sodom and Other Writings*, Copyright © 1966 by Austryn Wainhouse and Richard Seaver; *Juliette*, Copyright © 1968 by Austryn Wainhouse. From L. Ullerstam, *The Erotic Minorities*, Copyright © 1966 by Grove Press, Inc. Reprinted by permission of Grove Press, a division of Wheatland Corporation.

Grune & Stratton, Inc.

From M. Boss (1949), *Meaning and Content of Sexual Perversions*. New York: Grune & Stratton.

Harper & Row Publishers, Inc.

From G. Henry, *Sex Variants* © 1941.

Harvard University Press

From J. Herman & L. Hirschman (1981), *Father–Daughter Incest*. Cambridge, MA: Harvard University Press.

International Journal of Psycho-Analysis

From E. Glover (1933), The relation of perversion-formation to the development of reality-sense, 14:486–504; from S. Payne (1939), Some observations of the ego development of the fetishist, 20:161–170; from M. Sperling (1947), The analysis of an exhibitionist, 28:32–45; from D. Hunter (1954), Object-relation changes in the analysis of a fetishist, 35:302–312; from R. Stoller (1964), A contribution to the study of gender identity, 45:220–226; from R. Greenson (1966), A transvestite boy and a hypothesis, 47:396–403; from M. de M'Uzan (1973), A case of masochistic perversion and an outline of the theory, 54:445–467. Copyright © Institute of Psycho-Analysis.

International Universities Press

From M. Sperling (1964), The analysis of a boy with transvestite tendencies. *The Psychoanalytic Study of the Child*, 19:470–493.

Johns Hopkins University Press

From R. Green & J. Money (1969), *Transsexualism and Sex Reassignment*. Baltimore: Johns Hopkins University Press.

Jossey-Bass, Inc., Publishers

From K. Meiselman (1978), *Incest*. San Francisco: Jossey-Bass.

Journal of Forensic Science

From W. Tuteur (1963), Child molesters and men who expose themselves—An anthropological approach. 8:515–525. Copyright ASTM. Reprinted with permission.

Journal of Nervous and Mental Disease

From N. Golosow & E. Weitzman (1969), Psychosexual and ego regression in the male transsexual, 149:328–336, © by Williams & Wilkins, 1969.

Journal of Sex Research

From V. Bullough, B. Bullough, & R. Smith (1983), A comparative study of male transvestites, male to female transsexuals, and male homosexuals, 19:238–257.

The Kinsey Institute for Research in Sex, Gender, and Reproduction

From A. Kinsey, W. Pomeroy, & C. Martin (1948), *Sexual Behavior in the Human Male*; and from A. Kinsey, W. Pomeroy, C. Martin, & P. Gebhard (1953), *Sexual Behavior in the Human Female*. Philadelphia: W. B. Saunders. Reprinted by permission of the Kinsey Institute for Research in Sex, Gender, and Reproduction, Inc.

Linacre Press

From L. London & F. Caprio (1958), *Sexual Deviations*.

Medicine, Science and the Law

From J. McGeorge (1964), Sexual assaults on children, 4:245–253.

NAL Penguin

From J. Woodbury and E. Schwartz (1971), *The Silent Sin*. Copyright © 1971. Reprinted by arrangement with NAL Penguin Inc. New York, New York.

Praeger

From G. G. Scott, *Dominant Women, Submissive Men* (1983), New York: Praeger Publishers, pp. 95, 172, 173, 176, & 201. Copyright © 1983 by Gini Graham Scott. Reprinted with permission of the publishers.

Psychiatric Quarterly

From H. Barahal (1953), Female transvestism and homosexuality, 27:390–438; from L. Shankel & A. Carr (1956), Transvestism and hanging episodes in a male adolescent, 30:478–493; from S. Nagler (1957), Fetishism: A review and a case study, 31:713–741; from "Boots" [pseud.] (1957), The feelings of a fetishist, 31:742–758; from N. Lukianowicz (1960), Two cases of transvestism, 34:517–537; from R. Zechnich (1971), Exhibitionism: Genesis, dynamics and treatment, 45:70–75.

Psychoanalytic Quarterly

From A. Brill (1932), The sense of smell in the neuroses and psychoses, 1:7–42; from E. Litin, M. Griffin, & A. Johnson (1956), Parental influence in unusual sexual behavior in children, 25:37–55; from O. Sperling (1956), Psychodynamics of group perversions, 25:56–65; from M. Sperling (1963), Fetishism in children, 32:374–392; from L. Kubie (1974), The drive to become both sexes, 43:349–426.

Psychoanalytic Review

From B. Berliner (1942), The concept of masochism, 29:386–400; from B. Karpman (1950), A case of paedophilia (legally rape) cured by psychoanalysis, 37:235–276.

Psychosomatic Medicine

Reprinted by permission of Elsevier Science Publishing Co. Inc. from H. Lief, J. Dingman, & M. Bishop (1962), Psychoendocrinologic studies in a male with cyclic changes in sexuality, 24:357–368; from E. Weitzman, C. Shamoian, & N. Golosow (1971), Family dynamics in male transsexualism, 33:289–299. Copyright 1961 and 1971 by The American Psychosomatic Society, Inc.

Putnam Publishing Group

From V. Nabokov. *Lolita.* Copyright © 1955 by Vladimir Nabokov; from *Psychopathia Sexualis* by Dr. Richard von Krafft-Ebing, Copyright © 1965 by G. P. Putnam's Sons. Reprinted by permission of the Putnam Publishing Group.

Random House, Inc.

From *The Pearl* (1968), New York: Ballantine Books.

J. Renvoize

From J. Renvoize (1982), *Incest: A Family Pattern.* London: Routledge & Kegan Paul.

Charles Slavik and Infantae Press

From *True Baby Experiences*, no. 2; *True Baby Letters and Experiences*, 1985, Books 1 and 2. Seattle, WA: Infantae Press.

Society for the Study of Social Problems

Excerpts taken from articles that originally appeared in *Social Problems*: M. Lenznoff & W. Westley (1956), The homosexual community, 3/4:257–263; C. McCaghy (1968), Drinking and deviance disavowal: The case of child molesters, 16/1:43–49; M. Weinberg, C. Williams, & C. Moser (1984), The social constituents of sadomasochism, 31/4:379–389. © 1956, 1968, 1984 by the Society for the Study of Social Problems. Used with permission.

Stein and Day Publishers

From *Incest*. Copyright © 1972 by Dr. Herbert Maisch. Reprinted with permission of Stein and Day Publishers.

Lyle Stuart, Inc.

From F. Caprio (1955), *Variations in Sexual Behavior*; from S. Weinberg (1955), *Incest Behavior*.

Robert J. Stoller, M.D.

From R. Stoller (1968), *Sex and Gender: On the Development of Masculinity and Femininity*. New York: Science House.

Charles C Thomas

From J. P. de River (1958), *Crime and the Sexual Psychopath*; from J. MacDonald (1973), *Indecent Exposure*. Courtesy of Charles C Thomas, Publisher, Springfield, IL.

Yale University Press

From R. Stoller (1985), *Presentation of Gender*; from R. Green (1987), *The "Sissy Boy Syndrome" and the Development of Homosexuality*.

PART I

INTRODUCTION

1 DEFINITIONS AND HISTORICAL TRENDS

C. P., a healthy and vigorous 38-year-old male, describes his sexual inclinations: "When I encounter a woman who very strongly attracts me and whom I very greatly admire, my desire is never that I may have sexual connection with her in the ordinary sense, but that I may lie down upon the floor on my back and be trampled upon by her" (Ellis, 1906, p. 33).

DIFFERING CONCEPTIONS

Terms referring to C. P.'s peculiar sexual preference share common meanings: *paraphilia, perverse, aberrant, anomalous, deviant, variant,* and *eccentric* all imply turning the wrong way or straying from some standard or from the center. The major problem in defining these terms is specifying what is the right way, what is the standard or center.

The simplest and most absolute standard with which to compare C. P.'s sexual behavior is the possibility of conception taking place. Using this standard, intercourse with deposit of semen in the vagina is the only normal sexual behavior. All other methods of sexual release such as masturbation, the use of contraceptive devices, and homosexuality are off-center. This

3

standard was proposed by religious leaders, but also accepted by others. While acknowledging the obvious limitations, a psychoanalyst designates perversion as sexual behavior that interferes seriously with procreation (Gillespie, 1956).

A modification of this standard is that sexual behavior must lead to heterosexual vaginal intercourse, regardless of the possibility of conception. So, those who have been sterilized or who use contraceptives would not be engaging in deviant sexual behavior. One such definition is this: "all sexual activities that deviate in object or aim from the heterosexual genital act and either lead to end pleasure or are a necessary condition for end pleasure" (Sperling, 1956, p. 56).

While the possibility of conception and vaginal intercourse give definite limits to what is normal, the statistical norm requires a range of normality. C. P.'s preferred sexual activity is unusual in that it deviates from what most people do; the indexes of the Kinsey reports contain no mention of trampling (Kinsey, Pomeroy, and Martin, 1948; Kinsey, Pomeroy, Martin, and Gebhard, 1953). Prevalence, the percentage engaging in the act, is the standard.

What about masturbation? How statistically deviant is this sexual activity in the male? The answer depends on what males we are asking about—their age, marital status, and educational level. Prevalence is a high 81 percent in single men in their early twenties and a lower 54 percent of those in their late forties. More married men in their early twenties with some college education masturbate (66%) than those with eighth grade education or less (29%) (Kinsey et al., 1948). So, for masturbation, there is no fixed statistical standard.

While masturbation is quite common, sexual contact with nonhuman animals is rare, especially among urban dwellers. Only 2 percent of urban boys who went on to college had contacts with animals, while over a fourth (28%) of rural boys had such experiences (Kinsey et al., 1948). Therefore, animal contacts are less eccentric among rural than urban youths.

Prevalence is an enticing standard to apply. It is neat, clean, based on facts, and involves no moral judgments. It might even be considered democratic in that normality is defined by what the majority do. It also does away with the idea that some sexual acts are normal and others are deviant, since there can be no definite dividing line between the two; rather, there is a continuum. Also, what is statistically normal for one group may be less so for another group.

Related to statistical norms is the cultural definition of deviancy. When sexual practices across different societies are examined, wide variations are found in what is labeled deviant, with no sexual behavior universally prohibited.

Two somewhat different conclusions are drawn from this cross-cultural data. One interpretation is that any behavior can be labeled deviant only in relation to the norms of a particular society. The other conclusion is that, since no sexual behavior is condemned across all societies, then no sexual behavior can be considered deviant. A favored example of this position is that since homosexuality in ancient Greece was supposedly encouraged, then it cannot be considered morally wrong or perverted today. But those who use this argument neglect the fact that such behavior is culturally imbedded, that it obtains its meaning and sanction from other aspects of that culture. Greek homosexuality is not an isolated fragment of behavior that can be plucked out and transported across centuries and continents.

For some sociologists, deviance is the breaking of some agreed upon rule that was created by a segment of society. Deviant behaviors are those which offend the morals of some people in a society (Goode and Troiden, 1974). Deviancy does not reside in the act itself, but in the interaction between the actor and those responding to that act (Becker, 1963).

This societal standard differs from the statistical in that it involves not what people do, but what they think ought to be done. Society's definition of an act as deviant results from an interplay of its laws, norms of behavior (mores), and actual behaviors. When these three are correlated, the deviation is pathological, as in sexual relations with a corpse, since it is against the law, a violation of norms of conduct, and has a low incidence of occurrence.

When law, mores, and behaviors are not correlated, the act is a normal deviation. While these acts are generally disapproved, they either serve useful purposes, have a high incidence, or remain secret. Masturbation is a normal deviation.

While it is disapproved, it is a high incidence act, practiced privately, and useful in relieving sexual tension (Gagnon and Simon, 1967).

Rather than studying different societies in search of sexual norms, some observe nonhuman animal behavior. They assume that since we are biological beings and sex is a biological function, then what other animals do is natural. Since nonhuman animals display themselves, watch others mating, relate sexually with the immature and with relatives, inflict pain on the female, and mount same-sex animals, then such activities cannot be deviant. Thus, Kinsey et al. (1948) conclude, "there is no scientific reason for considering particular types of sexual activity as intrinsically, in their biological origin, normal or abnormal" (p. 202).

Many of those who use the biological or cultural argument conclude that no behavior is perverse. Guyon (1933) maintains that one of nature's laws is that we use our sexual organs for pleasure and that this pleasure is independent of the manner in which it is obtained, methods used, or kind of partners. To obtain sexual pleasure, any mechanical process is as good, normal, and legitimate as any other. C. P.'s desire to be trampled upon is in tune with nature, since it brings him "keen pleasure." A similar conclusion was reached by the Marquis de Sade (1795) in his appeal to nature. He reasoned that what is pleasurable is in harmony with nature so that what gives pleasure is natural and right. If inflicting pain on others gives pleasure, then cruelty is sanctioned by nature. While certainly not advocating cruelty, Ullerstram (1966) states: "there is one thing we can be dead certain of: the 'perversions' allow considerable chances to achieve human happiness. And therefore the perversions are in themselves good, and therefore they ought to be encouraged" (p. 43).

Thus far, a particular individual's sexual behavior has been compared to the behavior and opinions of groups of humans or to activities of nonhuman animals. No attention was given to the individual involved, his motivations, or fantasies. Decades ago, Krafft-Ebing (1902) proposed that the key to diagnosis of perversion was not the act itself, but "the whole personality of the individual and the original motive leading to the perverse act" (p. 86). More recently, Bieber (1976) argues that sexuality that is the expression of disturbed parent–child relationships is deviant behavior. Such an individual has a life history sprinkled with traumatic experiences which render him incapable of maintaining close, heterosexual relations.

Rather than taking the commonplace, social acceptability, or the animalistic as standard, we will attempt to define ideal sexuality as a criterion. Ideal sexuality is an expression of the psychologically healthy person (Maslow, 1954, 1971; Erikson, 1963; May, 1969; Jourard, 1974; Wakeling, 1979).

Among other characteristics, this psychologically healthy male is confident of his masculinity. Therefore, he can either initiate or receive sexual advances, assume the kneeling or supine position in sexual intercourse without concern. He accepts his sexual impulses as natural, without anxiety or defensiveness; therefore, sex can be fun, playful, and spontaneous. He feels free to choose among many modes of sexual expression. For him, sex is an expression of love, tenderness, and respect for his partner. He chooses to have sex, rather than being driven to have sex, so he can control these impulses, suppress them, postpone gratification when the situation does not meet his standards. It is the stimulating person's personality that attracts him, not so much their physical or behavioral attributes. The partner is accepted in their own right and not as a surrogate for mother or anyone else. Needs are pooled during sex; that is, he finds as much pleasure in his partner's enjoyment as in his own. There is mutual concern for each other's feelings.

To fully appreciate an idea like ideal sexuality, it must be contrasted with its opposite, deviant sexuality. Here the man is so uncertain of his masculinity that he fears what he considers feminine traits. He equates masculinity with dominance, power, and control, and confuses passivity and the subordinate role with femininity. His penis is a weapon that conquers what it penetrates. Sexual impulses arouse anxiety, guilt, and hate. Sex is profane. J. P. Byrne, lust murderer, said it well, "I felt I ought to terrorize all women to get my own back on them for causing my nervous tension through sex" (Chesser, 1971, p. 16).

The deviant's urges are persistent and obligatory; they threaten his need to control, so they must immediately be expressed or repressed. Women are polarized into either madonnas who are asexual or harlots who sexually excite him. Moll (1906) refers to this complex of attitudes as the pornographic spirit; women are regarded as sex objects only. A man with these attitudes despises women, not realizing that he is really projecting his own self-hatred. His sexuality is an "erotic form of hatred" (Stoller, 1975). Because of insults to his formative conception of himself as a masculine being, he creates a fantasy against the hated perpetrator of the trauma. This revenge converts his trauma into the adult's triumph. His hatred and revenge are sometimes overt, but always seen in the objectification and dehumanization of the sexual object. He is egocentric, using the female for his own needs with little empathy for her feelings. She is simply an instrument for his gratification. The object is humiliated, controlled, used.

Like the statistical standard, what we have is a continuum; at one end is the ideal, at the other, the deviant. The characteristics of the two poles are summarized in Table 1.1. Basically, then, anomalous sexuality is not defined by anatomy used, object preferred, number of people practicing, or society's opinions and laws. Rather, deviant behavior is defined by the individual's motives, feelings, attitudes, and fantasies. It results from his inability to form loving relationships (Gillespie, 1956). C. P. can be labeled deviant, not simply because being trampled upon brought him to orgasm. He is deviant because he enjoyed coaxing women to tread on him so he could fantasize he was their slave and they were punishing him.

Masturbation as an act is statistically, biologically, and culturally normal. Sociologically, it is a normal deviation. Using our ideal standard, no such general statements are possible. The teenager who masturbates to the fantasy of petting his real or imagined girl friend, while not ideal, is not perverse. Another teenager whose masturbation fantasy is of chaining women to the wall of a cave and torturing them would be perverse. By most standards, having intercourse with a hog is perverse. But for many of the preadolescent boys who engage in bestiality, it is simply sexual experimentation with a creature that is readily

TABLE 1.1
Summary of Ideal and Deviant Sexuality

	Ideal	Deviant
Masculinity	Confident	Uncertain
Sexual Impulse	Accepted, controllable	Insistent, defended against
Sex Fused With	Love, tenderness, respect	Anxiety, guilt, hate
Activity	Spontaneous, experimental, enjoyable, playful	Rigid, obligatory
Partner	Accepted, respected, trusted, needs pooled, partner's enjoyment important	Treated as object, feared, despised

available (Ellis, 1906; Gebhard, Gagnon, Pomeroy, and Christenson, 1965; Gadpaille, 1975).

It is essential to distinguish between deviant acts and deviant processes which sometimes, but not always, underlie these acts. Our sexually ideal person may, from time to time, engage in acts that appear to be deviant, but they are done playfully and lovingly. By the same token, a man may seemingly relate lovingly to his partner during sexual intercourse, but is able to do so only by imagining that she is a prepubescent girl. Also, sexually deviant acts may be occasioned by a particular situation, or may be symptoms of some other pathological process such as schizophrenia or senility.

While many people engage in less than ideal sexual fantasies or acts, the term *sexual deviation* is reserved for those who are very far from the ideal. To the extent that their sexual fantasies or behaviors are obligatory, persistent, and exclusive, their sexuality is deviant. The extreme deviant has no choice, he is dominated and compelled (Gillespie, 1956; McDougall, 1972). His sexuality is an expression of a need to avoid or to dominate the feared and/or hated female.

HISTORICAL TRENDS

The study of sexual deviancy began just before the turn of this century. The taboo was beginning to lift against discussion of sexuality, as may be seen in the novels of Maupassant and Zola. Psychiatry was giving some attention to man's impulses and emotions, some of which, like sexuality, were regarded as antisocial. The early pioneers in the study of sexuality were medical men: Richard von Krafft-Ebing, Albert Moll, August Forel, Iwan Bloch, Magnus Hirschfeld, Havelock Ellis, and Sigmund Freud. Not only was their work not well accepted, but they themselves were looked upon with disdain by large segments of the medical profession and the general public (Hoenig, 1977a).

Several concepts were prominent in psychiatry at this time. First, it was a common practice to invoke "constitutional predisposition" as an explanation of disorders for which no known cause could be determined. A form of constitutional predisposition used by early students of sexual deviations was degeneration. The word *degeneration* refers in this context to an innate weakness of the nervous system, transmitted with increasing severity from one generation to another, that produces deviations from the normal human type. It is initiated or exaggerated by toxins such as alcohol, by injury, disease, or abuse of the sexual organs by masturbation or promiscuity (Hoenig, 1977a). Even today some researchers entertain the possibility that "imperative ideas," such as those seen in fetishism and transvestism, are transmitted across generations through some genetic process (Epstein, 1980).

A second much used explanation was masturbation, which was blamed for a host of diseases. A work on sexuality that expressed the authoritative opinion of the mid-1800s is William Acton's (1867) *The Functions and Disorders of the Reproductive Organs*. Acton condemned masturbation as a "scourge that seizes its victims" for it is "an habitual incontinence eminently productive of disease" (p. 83). This vice, he said, leads to insanity, suicide, self-mutilation, even tuberculosis. The process by which these dire results occur is a loss of nervous power through overexcitement and a state of enervation due to loss of semen.

Some years later, Bloch (1908) denied that moderate masturbation was the cause of insanity, believing that morbid results occur only when the masturbator was previously morbid. Excessive masturbation, however, could produce sexual perversions because the masturbator's sensibilities are blunted, so he requires stronger and more peculiar stimuli to arouse him. His ideas become more and more lascivious, finally passing over into the sphere of the perverse. Expanding on Bloch's opinions, the emphasis has shifted from the act of masturbation to those fantasies that accompany the act. It has been determined that there is a close correspondence between deviant sexual behavior and deviant masturbation fantasies in that deviant scenarios are often rehearsed in fantasy before they are manifested in behavior (McGuire, Carlisle, and Young, 1965; MacCulloch, Snowden, Wood, and Mills, 1983).

A third principle entertained by many psychiatrists of the early twentieth century was the law of the association of ideas. If two experiences occur, one just before the other, then a repetition of the first experience acquires the power to elicit the second. If a man smells roses being carried by a woman who sexually arouses him, then later the odor of roses can sexually stimulate him.

Associationism, not of ideas but of stimulus and response, is still alive as an explanation of the origin of deviant sexual behavior (McGuire et al., 1965; Rachman, 1966; Rachman and Hodgson, 1968). It is the basis of behavior modification techniques used to extinguish deviant sexual behaviors. The principles used are the same as those expressed in the late 1700s.

When base lust fills thy thoughts
Let a horrible picture rise before thy mind
Of withered dead men's bones,
So let the sensual stimulation be driven away [Bloch, 1908,
p. 421].

Kinsey et al. (1953), among many others, subscribe to the associationistic theory when they say, "the male who reacts sexually and comes to erection upon seeing a streetcar, may merely reflect some early experience in which a streetcar was associated with a desirable sexual partner" (p. 646).

While not doubting that childhood experiences may form lasting impressions, Moll, even in 1912, had his doubts when he said, "this association theory does not suffice to account for the facts" (p. 130). He questioned why only some children who experience pairings of sexual arousal with abnormal stimuli, say spankings, crave spankings as adults.

The study of abnormal sexuality began with the publication of the first edition of Richard von Krafft-Ebing's *Psychopathia Sexualis* in 1886—the first orthodox text on sexual disorders for the medical and legal professions. When psychiatry was being established as a medical specialty, Krafft-Ebing's book made sexual deviations a psychiatric speciality. This book was the first to present an inventory and classification scheme of deviant sexuality. Perversions are presented in their extreme form through the use of clinical case histories, with little space given to explanation. In an attempt to limit the audience to professionals, details of the deviant acts were in Latin as "coitus in os" and "coitus inter femora feminae." Nevertheless, the book enjoyed sufficient popularity to warrant twelve editions.

Krafft-Ebing subscribed to the idea that excessive masturbation contributed to deviant sexuality and also placed great emphasis on constitutional predisposition, especially epilepsy. In case after case, he mentions epilepsy as a contributing factor because it produces a clouding of consciousness and also induces abnormal excitation of the sexual impulses. He advised that the connection between epilepsy and deviant sexuality deserved careful study. His suggestion has been heeded. Because of frequent reports of temporal lobe abnormalities in a variety of deviants, Langevin (1985) suggests that some sexually deviant preferences may be related to abnormalities in the brain's temporal lobe.

Early reaction by the medical profession was negative. A reviewer of Krafft-Ebing's fifth edition complained about too many explicit details and worried that there was a "danger in pandering to morbid tastes" (Hoenig, 1977a). The twelfth and last edition also fared poorly at a reviewer's hands. It is, he said, "the most repulsive of a group of books of which it is the type," and "the reader is not spared the most nauseous detail." It should be "put to the most ignominious use to which paper can be applied" (W.L.-E, 1902, pp. 339–340).

To play the game of showing up Krafft-Ebing's work is easier by present-day standards than it was in the first years of this century. His views are avowedly moralistic, claiming some men to be "devoid of all moral worth" and suffering from "moral decay." Such references are considered by some to be antiscientific; they prefer to cloak their moralizing in such phrases as "weak superego" and "inability to sublimate." What little theorizing he does is clearly antiquated, resting on "deep heredity taint" and "excessive self-abuse." But, to call it "deeply damaging nonsense" and his contribution "an unmitigated disaster" (Brecher, 1969) seems an unfair use of today's knowledge to slander what was the best that could be offered decades ago.

Some contemporary reviewers do not take such a dim view of his work. One says that *Psychopathia Sexualis* is a "much maligned and neglected medical text-book" (Johnson, 1973, p. 212). Allowing for differences in terminology, the reviewer notes that one can see in Krafft-Ebing's emphasis on biological predisposition the precursor of today's search for a neuroendocrine basis for some deviations. His acceptance of associationism is seen today as the importance of the quality of early sexual experience. Although masturbation itself is no longer regarded as detrimental to sexual health, deviant masturbation fantasies have been implicated in the etiology of deviant sexual behavior.

A psychoanalyst comments that, "there would not be so much controversy about masochism had later authors paid more attention to the pioneer work of Krafft-Ebing" (Berliner, 1942, p. 392). Another expresses the opinion that, "Krafft-Ebing was . . . the most important investigator of psychosexual problems in the nineteenth century, and prepared the ground for the Freudian revolution. It is regrettable that neither Freud nor his followers gave him the recognition he deserved" (Wolff, 1977, p. 11).

Havelock Ellis, as did the other pioneers, struggled against a prudish view of sex. Not only was he a student of the psychology of sex, but also a reformer: champion of women's rights, and advocate of birth control and decriminalization of homosexuality. He studied medicine, not to practice, but to provide background for his *Studies in the Psychology of Sex* which is written with "uncommon erudition" (Hoenig, 1977b). Ellis's interest was in all aspects of sexuality from the evolution of modesty to love and pain.

Unfortunately, the first portion of his *Studies* to be published dealt with homosexuality and was on bookstore shelves only two years after the Oscar Wilde trial. Ellis was not charged, but the bookseller was arrested and tried for purveying obscene material (Bullough and Bullough, 1977).

Ellis fared no better than Krafft-Ebing in a review of his work. A 1902 reviewer concludes that the facts presented by him not only lack scientific value, but are "in themselves disgusting and nauseous," they are like a collection of "morsels of dung and scraps of offel and ordure" (W.L.-E, 1902, p. 340). Only a few decades later, his obituary read, in part, "he will remain in the memory of men as a singularly high-moulded soul, filled with a vivid sense of beauty of the world and of the potential beauty of human life in it" (Anon., 1939, p. 203).

Magnus Hirschfeld's primary interests were in homosexuality and cross-dressing. Realizing the hazards faced by those who wrote on homosexuality, he used a pseudonym on his *Sappho and Socrates*. In 1899 he founded the *Journal of Intermediate Sex Stages*. Like Ellis, Hirschfeld was also a reformer, founding the International Congress for Sexual Reform (later the World League for Sexual Reform) in 1921. The organization's first presidents were Ellis and Forel, and Sigmund Freud was a member. The group championed equal rights for women in sex and marriage, birth control, and sex education.

His Berlin Institute for Sexual Research, established in 1919, offered courses in sex education and free consultations for those with sexual problems. Through the institute he conducted surveys among college students and workers on the prevalence of homosexuality and bisexuality. The Institute was sacked by the Nazis in 1933 (Leser, 1967; Hoenig, 1977b).

Hirschfeld was impressed by the early work on the endocrine system whose secretions regulate bodily functions and he used this "sexual chemistry" to explain certain aspects of anomalous sexuality. This interest has continued in the search for differences in circulating sex hormones between homosexuals and heterosexuals. The results of these studies have been disappointing. However, current attention has shifted from peripheral hormone influences to their impact on the developing brain of the fetus.

Other early contributors to the study of deviant sexuality were Iwan Bloch, August Forel, and Albert Moll. Bloch's *Sexual Life of Our Time* (1908) was intended as an encyclopedia of the sexual sciences, including contributions from biology, anthropology, literature, and history. Moll's *The Sexual Life of the Child* was the first in-depth study of childhood sexuality, and Forel's 1905 *The Sexual Question* became a standard work (Hoenig, 1977a,b).

Sigmund Freud's psychiatric speciality was neurosis, not sexual deviations; however, he made lasting contributions to that area of study. His direct contributions include a paper on fetishism (1927), and two on masochism (1919, 1924). More importantly, his general theory of personality has been used in the explanation of almost every paraphilia.

Freud's (1916–1917) theory of perversions was based, in part, on his conception of the sexual instincts. According to his analysis, there are not one, but several partial or component instincts that emerge at various stages in the child's development. He termed childhood sexuality *polymorphous perverse* because partial instincts predispose the child to a variety of perverse sexuality. Polymorphous perversity constitutes Freud's conception of constitutional predisposition. The component instincts are paired and may be seen in either an active or a passive form. For instance, both looking at and showing the sexual parts is common among children. Another pair of component instincts is mastery and submission. In normal adult sexuality all of these components are subordinated to genital sexuality, expressed in forepleasure as a preliminary to end-pleasure of coitus and orgasm. If one of these impulses is especially strong, it not only influences later development, especially the oedipal struggle, but the impulse itself is also modified (Sachs, 1923). In perverted sexuality one or more components do not merge, rather they become autonomous, resulting in peeping, exhibitionism, sadism, or masochism.

In his idea of complemental series, Freud relates constitutional predisposition to childhood experiences. The coupling of instinctual disposition and traumatic experience causes the child to become fixated at an infantile stage of development. Some children are so predisposed that, no matter how they are protected from pathological experiences, they will succumb to some disorder. There are others, with little constitutional predisposition, who become abnormal from being exposed to heavy doses of traumatic experiences. When, in adult life, there occurs a disturbing experience, such as rejection by a loved one, there is a regression to the fixated stage and its associated partial instinct.

To understand man's sexuality, ideal as well as deviant, it is essential to trace the acquisition of his masculinity and his conceptions of women. The early investigators in sexual deviance have given us a most important principle: not only must the act be studied, but also the person. The personal roots of deviance spring from an interaction of the individual's biological nature and his early life experiences.

2 SEX, GENDER, AND SEXUALITY

SEX

Introduction

The paths to adult sexuality, straight or deviant, begin at the moment of conception. The attainment of adult sexuality involves the successive emergence of several components. During prenatal development, the male acquires the signs of his maleness, his biological sex, along with a predisposition for masculine or feminine characteristics. Sex is not an either-or distinction, but a composite of several variables that may function independently. These variables are external genitalia, internal genital apparatus, and hormonal, gonadal, and chromosomal. At birth the child receives his assigned sex— "It's a boy"—consistent with his external anatomy.

For a time after birth there is no differentiation between the newborn's body and his surroundings. Then, he gradually distinguishes between "me" and "not-me." An awareness of differences between the sexes dawn on him, he begins to establish his core gender identity, his conviction that he is a male— "I am a boy, with this body, this penis, and these sensations."

17

Around his gender identity will be elaborated his gender role—those qualities that are defined as masculine. Then later, perhaps prior to age eight, the last important gender component takes shape with the appearance of his preferred sexual partner and mode of relating to that partner— "I am me, a boy, which means that I do (sexual) things with girls" (Greenson, 1964).

For the great majority of males the various indices of sex are male, core identity is male, role is masculine, and sexual preference is heterosexual. However, these three components are complex and independent. For instance, in the homosexual, sex and gender identity are not consistent with preferred sexual partner; and in those biological males who are convinced they are really females, sex is not congruent with gender identity and role.

The guidelines for the sexual deviations are laid down in those years when these components first emerge and become solidified (Money and Ehrhardt, 1972). The long process of arriving at adult sexuality has been called the lovemap (Money, 1984b). This map does not depict a single highway for the boy to travel. Rather, routes are quite complex, with many multiple intersections and with different roads leading to the same destination. No single turn fixes the rest of the journey, but each successive turn increases the probability of arriving at a particular destination. As the boy travels over the course of his lovemap, the "choices" at intersections become fewer and fewer until he finally realizes his own particular pattern of requirements for sexual arousal, preferred partners, and modes of expressing these feelings.

For example, a boy whose prenatal development determined a somewhat female appearance and docile temperament is not bound to any particular adult sexuality pattern. Rather, the probability is increased that his mother, if she happens to be of a particular personality, will treat him as an extension of herself. This will further feminize him. But, father's role in all this must be considered. If he is withdrawn or absent, the chances of the boy's feminization are further increased; and, so it is throughout his excursion to adult sexuality. No one event, no one set of circumstances is totally determining. Adult sexuality is the product of a host of circumstances—it is multiply determined.

Biological Sex

For several weeks after conception, the embryo is sexually bipotential; that is, it has the rudimentary structures to mature as male or female depending on the presence of the male Y chromosome and associated genes on other chromosomes (autosomes). The core or medulla of the primitive gonads can become testes and the shell or cortex can become ovaries. Internal genitalia are present for both male (vas deferens, seminal vesicles, ejaculatory ducts, prostate) and female (uterus, fallopian ducts, upper vagina) in primitive wolffian and mullerian structures. The genital turbercle is capable of forming either penis and scrotum or clitoris and forward vagina.

In the second month of gestation, the Y chromosome and associated genes on autosomes trigger the synthesis of proteins responsible for male development. One such protein is the H-Y antigen that seems to be responsible for converting the gonads into testicles. Here male hormones (androgens) are manufactured that signal the bipotential structures to differentiate in the male direction. These processes are very complex. For example, an enzyme is necessary for deriving from testosterone the substance dihydrotestosterone (DHT) that is, in turn, responsible for the differentiation of penis and scrotum.

Timing here is important, for male hormones are less effective if present before or after a sensitive period—a biologically determined span of time during which the organism is set to respond to specific influences (Gadpaille, 1975). Onset and length of this sensitive period vary with the target tissue.

The chromosomal male embryo will differentiate as female if the masculinization message is sent, but the body's tissues lack androgen receptors (androgen insensitivity syndrome), or if there is a deficiency in enzymes necessary for hormone processing. The female will differentiate externally as male if androgens are supplied internally by misdirected andrenal glands or externally by mother's ingestion or production of androgens (prenatally androgenized female). Nature's default option is female; something must be added to produce maleness. Thus, errors are more probable in male than in female development (Money and Ehrhardt, 1972; Wilson, George, and Griffin, 1981).

The prenatal male sex hormones not only determine the internal and external genital structures, but also have an influence on the brain, particularly the hypothalamic region. The sensitive period for hypothalamic differentiation is between the fourth and seventh month. From the results of extensive studies, it seems likely that sex hormone levels during the sensitive period of hypothalamic differentiation may contribute to disturbances in sexual functioning later in life (Dorner, 1976).

The most obvious hypothalamic sex difference involves a portion of this area responsible for signaling the pituitary to release the gonadotropins, luteinizing hormone (LH), and follicle-stimulating hormone (FSH). These substances, in turn, notify the testes or ovaries to secrete their respective hormones. This center's default option is set on cyclic release of gonadotropins which, at puberty, results in female menstrual periods. Prenatal androgens move the setting to acyclic, producing a steady release of gonadotropins at puberty. It is conceivable that because of androgen deficiency in some males there is not a complete switch from cyclic to acyclic. These males, then, as adults will experience pseudomenstrual periods.

Male–female hypothalamic differentiation can be assessed by administering estrogen or luteinizing release hormones (LRH). In the normal female, there is an increase in LH and FSH, while in the male there is a decrease.

Other behavioral differences between the sexes that are, in all likelihood, related to prenatal hormones are that male babies are more irritable, active, cry more, and are less timid than female babies (Gadpaille, 1975).

In addition to hormones, other factors have an influence. For example, mother's ingestion of barbiturates demasculinize the fetus (Money, 1984a). A high stress level may result in prenatal demasculinization through the suppression of androgen production (Ward, 1972; Gadpaille, 1980), and homosexuality is associated with frequent and severe maternal prenatal stress (Ellis, Ames, Peckham, and Burke, 1988).

Neutrality or Biased Interaction

What is the influence of these prenatal events on subsequent gender identity and role? The environmentalists minimize any biological contribution, declaring that the newborn is gender neutral and that child-rearing practices determine identity and role. Biased interactionists, however, argue that biological forces interact with environmental events to jointly determine gender identity and role.

Neutrality

Prior to the 1950s it was generally assumed that the child's core gender identity and role were congruent with his biological sex. The expression "core gender identity" was not introduced until 1964, and the words *sex* and *gender* were often used synonomously (Stoller, 1964b). True, exceptions had been noted. Hermaphrodites, those with gonads of both sexes, and pseudohermaphrodites, individuals who display incongruity in one or more aspects of biological sex, have been recognized since antiquity. These individuals are now called intersexed. Homosexuals were often thought of as a "third sex." But it was the attention given to early transsexuals such as Christine Jorgensen that focused interest on the relation between biological sex and gender identity/role.

Environmentalists base their opinions on several studies of the intersexed. For a large majority of these individuals, gender role and partner preference are congruent with sex assignment and rearing when this assignment contradicts one or more criteria of biological sex (Money, Hampson, and Hampson, 1955; Lev-Ran, 1974). The authors of one study conclude that gender and sexual orientation have no innate basis, but are solely the products of early experiences (Money et al., 1955).

Certain conditions must be met for congruence to occur. Gender identity/role of assignment will be incorporated to the extent that: (1) the child is raised unambiguously as a boy or girl; (2) corrective surgery is initiated early; (3) gender-appropriate hormones are given at puberty; and (4) the child is gradually informed of its special condition (Money and Ehrhardt, 1972).

A case that seemingly meets many of these conditions was reported by Money and Ehrhardt in 1972. This classic study concerns one member of an identical twin pair, who, when seven months old, had his penis accidentally burned off during electrocautery circumcision. Surgical reassignment to female was begun prior to his second birthday. Mother treated the child as a female, emphasizing the feminine in clothing, jewelry, and hair style. Transformation seemed successful—the child was much tidier and cleaner than his brother, preferred dresses to slacks, took pride in his long hair, and aped mother in household activities. Mother did report some tomboyish traits of high activity level, stubbornness, and being dominant in a group of girls. At about six years, career choice was doctor or teacher with the intention of marriage. The case of this unfortunate child was heralded as evidence that masculine and feminine gender patterns are learned through appropriate parenting.

Environmentalists liken the establishment of gender identity/role to language acquisition and to the ethologists' imprinting. Like one's native language, they argue that there is a sensitive period for gender identity acquisition and that once acquired it is not subject to forgetting or extinction (Money, Hampson, and Hampson, 1957). The period begins at about eighteen months, and the gate closes at about thirty months (Money et al., 1955).

They further contend that to try to alter an established gender identity constitutes a severe threat to the personality structure. Thus, a girl gradually slipped into psychosis at age fourteen when a gynecologist told her that she might be a boy. Her breasts had not started to develop and menstruation had not begun. At age nineteen she was diagnosed as having severe ovarian deficiency caused by having only one X chromosome (Turner's Syndrome) (Stoller, 1968).

There are individuals, however, who do change gender identity later than the critical two-and-a-half years. It is said that such individuals had an ambiguous gender identity traceable to parental uncertainty and a body image that differs from others of their assigned sex (Stoller, 1968). For example, a tall, breastless "female" with an "enlarged clitoris" was never sure whether she was a boy or girl. If the child is uncertain of identity as a male or female, then a shift can occur without undue damage (Stoller, 1964a).

Biased Interaction

Decades ago, Krafft-Ebing (1902) reasoned that since the original disposition is bipotential, so there must also be two brain centers that mediate sexual life. Homosexuality was explained by the male center being too weak to override the female center. Krafft-Ebing was following Ulrichs, who wrote in defense of homosexuals from 1864 onwards. He proposed that congenital homosexuals, while physically males, were mentally and emotionally females, describing them as having a "female soul enclosed in a male body" (Carpenter, 1908).

Freud (1932–1936), too, concluded that each individual, whether male or female, is both masculine and feminine in varying degrees. Using biology as his reference, he noted that sperm is active, while the ovum is passive. Therefore, in the mental sphere masculinity is the preference for active aims, femininity for passive aims. This is Freud's bisexuality hypothesis—an innate predisposition to develop in a masculine or feminine direction. His bisexuality hypothesis has been criticized as lacking definite meaning (Fenichel, 1945), and as a misgeneralization from the original bipotentiality of the embryo to a presumed brain/psychological bipotentiality (Rado, 1940).

In 1965, Diamond, citing evidence from animal and human studies, proposed a built-in bias that predisposes the newborn toward a masculine or feminine identity and role. A follow-up of the twin whose penis was burned off and was raised as a girl supports Diamond's views. When she was thirteen years old, her new psychiatrists reported that she was having major psychological problems with the feminine role. She had a masculine gait and appearance and was teased by peers as "cavewoman." The psychiatrists were doubtful that she would be able to adjust as a female. Learning of this, Diamond (1982) asserted that nature imposes "limits to sexual identity and partner preference and that it is within these limits that social forces interact and gender roles are formulated" (p. 183).

The way little boys were reared some years ago has been cited as evidence against radical environmental views. It was customary to let their hair grow and even dress them like little girls. They still became masculine because being treated like a girl was at odds with their constitution. If such feminine treatment had jibed with a more female constitution, then they would have developed along feminine lines (Benjamin, 1954).

The notion of a sensitive period for establishing gender identity has also been questioned on the basis of cases in which changes took place as late as puberty. Biased interactionists see these changes as resulting from some biological force that can, when potent, override child rearing practices. Biological force refers to "energy from biological sources (such as endocrine or CNS systems), which influences gender identity formation and behavior" (Stoller, 1968, pp. 65–66).

Reports began to appear claiming successful changes in gender identity/role well after the supposed thirty-month gate (Dewhurst and Gordon, 1963). One research team was "amazed at Mary's willingness to discard feminine things and adopt male dress" after a change of assigned sex at puberty (Berg, Nixon, and MacMahon, 1963).

An illustration of the influence of biological force is the case of a child who had female genitalia at birth and was raised as a girl. At fourteen, it was discovered she was a chromosomal male. Mother describes her own frustration:

> The child ate so fast. It wasn't like a little girl. . . . As a tiny baby she moved too fast. She did everything crash! bang! nothing gentle. . . . [At age one] when she was put out to play on the sidewalk with the other children, she played with a neighbor boy and they played very much alike. . . . It dissatisfied me. I wanted a girl—but here she was a— [Stoller, 1964b, p. 221].

Another such case is an eighteen-year-old, labeled "girl" at birth, who had an enlarged "clitoris" which was called a "growth." He was raised as a girl in a family of nine sisters and one brother. He was cared for by a "matriarchical" older sister who gave him instructions, prior to puberty, about menstruation and bust development. He started to doubt his sex when these events did not take place and when he compared his "growth" with his baby nephew's penis. At fifteen he was attracted to girls and had a nocturnal emission while dreaming of seducing a girl. He decided to change to a male (Barton and Ware, 1966).

The influence of prenatal hormones is seen in genetic females who have been prenatally androgenized either congenitally or by mother's taking an adrogenizing hormone to protect the pregnancy. By and large, these girls, aged four to sixteen years at the time of the study, considered themselves tomboys. They showed high energy output in their athletic interests and skills and in their preference for boy playmates. Functional, rather than feminine dress was preferred, and they were indifferent to doll play and tending infants. Life goals centered on careers rather than marriage. Thus, the masculinizing effects on the brain were demonstrated. At the time of this study, there was no evidence that sexual orientation had been influenced (Money and Ehrhardt, 1972). However, in another series of twenty-six early treated cases of prenatally androgynized females, dating behavior was markedly delayed; for example, by age seventeen only three had had a date. In addition, there was some evidence of bisexual experiences and fantasy (Schwartz, 1976).

In some cases, diabetic mothers were given estrogen and progesterone to prevent pregnancy complications. Data were gathered by interview and psychological testing of their sixteen-year-old sons. Compared to sons of nonmedicated diabetic and nondiabetic mothers, the treatment boys were less aggressive, assertive, and athletic. Similar groups of six-year-olds were studied, with the only difference being that teachers rated the treatment boys as less assertive and athletic. Comparison of the six- with the sixteen-year-olds is difficult since different hormones were administered (Yalom, Green, and Fisk, 1973), and, it has been determined that the balance of estrogen and progestin prescribed influences behavioral outcomes (Reinisch and Karow, 1977).

Other studies comparing children whose mothers were administered hormones during pregnancy with nontreatment groups have found only minimal effects, such as increased TV watching time (Kester, 1984), and a decrease in self-ratings of athletic skills (Ehrhardt, Meyer-Bahlburg, Feldman, and Ince, 1984).

That this masculinizing effect is attributable to androgens and not simply to the presence of the Y chromosome is evident in development of genetic males who are androgen insensitive. These chromosomal males differentiate as females with respect to gender and sexuality, although libido is depressed (Masica, Money, and Ehrhardt, 1971). At puberty, they express a preference for being wives, with desires to raise families over having careers. Most are sexually attracted exclusively to males. In general, they are strongly feminine and content in their feminine role (Money and Ehrhardt, 1972; Lewis, 1976).

In mountain villages of the Dominican Republic eighteen males were studied who had been born with severe ambiguity of the external genitals, but with normal prenatal, neonatal, and pubertal testerone levels. Their condition was due to a deficiency in the enzyme needed to convert testosterone into DHT, so that their penises and scrotums did not differentiate. Without these external structures, they were identified and raised unambiguously as girls in communities where gender role differentiation was pronounced. Because of normal testosterone levels, virilization occurred at puberty. Seventeen of the eighteen changed to masculine identity and sixteen assumed masculine roles, such as living with females, despite ridicule from some villagers. Their masculine gender identity evolved over several years as they noticed male pubertal changes (Imperato-McGinley, Peterson, Gautier, and Sturla, 1979).

Investigators who studied two brothers with the same enzyme deficiency as the Dominican subjects conclude that fetal androgen exposure of the brain seems to have a greater effect on gender identity than does the sex of rearing (Savage, Preece, Jeffcoate, Ransley, Rumsby, Mansfield, and Williams, 1980). However, a different conclusion was reached from observations of similar cases in Papua New Guinea. Here boys who were reared as girls switched gender after puberty only under public pressure (Herdt and Davidson, 1988).

Of course, any natural experiment is subject to the criticism of lack of controls. There is insufficient information on others' reaction to the childrens' abnormal looking genitals. Also, since testosterone levels were normal, it is expected that they behaved as boys and this might have influenced the children's certainty of their gender identity (Rubin, Reinish, and Haskett, 1981).

Contemporary investigation of biological force has been freed from the natural experiment method. For example, researchers assayed five sex hormones from neonates' umbilical cords at birth. These children were evaluated at six, nine, twelve, and eighteen months of age. Timidity was rated by their reaction to toys that ranged from benign (soft fuzzy dog) to fear provoking (mechanical monkey). Boys' timidity was positively related to umbilical estrodial and negatively related to progesterone and testosterone. There were no such hormonal relations for girls, but overall, girls were somewhat more timid than boys (Jacklin, Maccoby, and Doering, 1983).

Studies such as this, when added to naturally occurring cases, lend solid support to the idea that prenatal hormones bend the child toward either masculine or feminine development. Since masculinization of the brain is not an all or nothing process, it is possible to be partially masculinized and partially defeminized (Money, 1984a).

GENDER IDENTITY/ROLE

Definitions

At the center of one's gender conception is gender identity, one's conviction of being a male or a female (Greenson, 1964; Stoller, 1968). It is expressed by the young child labeling himself and others as boy or girl. Around this core gender identity there develops one's gender role, the definition of what it means to be manly or womanly, concepts of masculinity and femininity.

While masculinity and femininity are not manifest until later, processes are operative during the early months of life that influence the direction of gender development. Gender identity is derived from three sources: the already discussed biological force; assigned label of "boy" or "girl," and related attitudes and behaviors of parents and significant others; and body image, particularly the awareness of the anatomy and sensations of the genitals, including differences between the sexes (Greenson, 1964; Stoller, 1964b).

The route on the lovemap from gender identity to gender role for boys is more precarious than for girls. Not only are boys more prone to gender disturbances, they also have a greater prevalence of psychiatric disorders, such as antisocial behavior, neurosis, and psychoses (Eme, 1979).

Early Mother–Child Interaction

Shortly after birth, the child becomes emotionally attached to mother. There is more to this attachment than simply a dependence for closeness and physical well-being. There is an emotional tie between the two, a symbiotic union. At this early stage, the baby has no idea of "myself" and "herself." He is at one with mother, he is merged with her, there is a fusion of tactile, visual, and auditory perceptions (Greenson, 1968).

Some theorists assume this merger implies becoming like mother, taking in, incorporating her qualities. That is, during this very early symbiotic phase of development, the baby boy identifies with his mother, since being one with mother is to be like her (Lichtenstein, 1961).

While there is some disagreement as to whether or not attachment implies identification (Heilbrun, 1973), there is evidence that boys' early gender behavior is largely feminine. Both boy and girl are protofeminine prior to establishment of core gender identity because both are originally fused to mother (Stoller, 1968). This poses no problem for the girl. But for the boy, it means that if he is to become masculine, he must overcome this protofemininity.

Mahler (1972) has identified several phases in the child's psychological separation from mother so that he can become an individual. Biological birth is a dramatic, clearly observable event. Psychological "hatching," however, is a prolonged process of developing concepts of one's own body and of significant people in the child's world.

Differentiation begins at about four to five months when the infant begins to shift his attention from mother to other objects, including his own body. Practicing comes next, at about seven to ten months, as he moves away physically from mother, but never too far. He becomes interested in inanimate objects, which at first she gives him. These are explored with all his senses—visual, smell, touch, taste, and sound. Still, mother takes precedence over all. She is his home base to which he returns for emotional "refueling." When he attains an upright posture at about ten to twelve months, he begins a love affair with his own blooming abilities and with the world about him. Now he moves farther and farther away from mother.

In the next phase of the separation–individuation process, rapproachment, he attempts to share his interest in his world with mother. This phase begins anywhere from sixteen to twenty-five months with his ability to toddle, and continues into the third year. Now he is more aware of his separateness and takes greater advantage of it. He discovers the anatomical differences between the sexes. Emotional life becomes differentiated, and separation anxiety may increase; language and symbolic play begins.

During early infancy, mother is the first "it" to separate out from his diffuse experience. She is the "not me," and becomes the ground for all experiences of other people. Later, she is the one to separate from, but also the one to return to. To continue separation or to return to mother is one of the earliest conflicts faced by the growing boy. The urge to remerge, to return to the warmth of union with mother, is a strong and perhaps a permanent wish. But, to return means giving up individuality. Mother, and for some men, females, become not only a symbol of a blissful state, but also a symbol of nonindependence, the "main menace to autonomy" (Dinnerstein, 1976).

To overcome his protofemininity and acquire his masculine identity and role, the little boy must not only inhibit his urge to remerge with mother (Stoller and Herdt, 1982), but he must also disidentify with her (Greenson, 1968). Giving up his feeling of being like her is not easy, since he confuses loving someone with being like someone. If he fails to do this, he will retain his protofeminine identity, leaving himself liable to later gender disorders (Stoller, 1968). For boys at risk for deviant sexuality, separation results in rage at having to leave the blissful closeness with mother, fear of returning to this Eden with consequent loss of individuality, and hatred toward mother for placing him in this conflict situation (Stoller, 1975). These boys develop "merger fantasies" of being incorporated and swallowed by females (Ovesey and Person, 1973).

Separation is facilitated by mother's ability to gradually release her son. For healthy development, she must strike a delicate balance between her wish to hold onto her child and her desire to let him grow (Schad-Somers, 1982). If mother views her child as an extension of herself and is able to stifle his acquiring a sense of self as a separate being, he feels possessed and has fears of being rejected. The particular deviation that emerges later is partly determined by mother's specific behavior toward the child at this time of separation (Lihn, 1971).

Not only is father an important agent in interrupting this union, so is teddy bear, acting as transitional object. This object is selected by the child during his first year of life as a representation of mother. It is soft, durable, has an odor; it is the giver and recipient of tenderness. As he gains independence from mother, the need for this transitional object fades.

To aid themselves in disengaging from mother, some boys use the sour grapes approach of disparaging mother and things feminine, but underneath this expressed contempt, they may carry a secret adoration of mother (Greenson, 1968). If carried too far, this disparagement–adoration attitude leads, in later life, to the harlot–madonna conception of women.

The remerging or separating conflict is less difficult for the little girl. If she fails to completely separate from mother, she will lose her independence, possibly become neurotic, but experience no damage to her sense of being feminine (Stoller, 1968). Retaining her early protofeminine identity, she becomes feminine to the extent that mother is feminine (Gershman, 1970).

Body Image

In the attachment phase and continuing during separation, the boy is forming his self identity—a sense of his continuing oneness and a sense that he is unique, different from others (Green-acre, 1958). The first aspect of this self identity to emerge is body image—the conception of what our body is like, how it appears, how it feels, and our evaluation of it. The infant begins to experience that his body belongs to him, that he can control it, that it and he are the same from day to day.

He comes to know his body from sensations arising from within, from sensations he produces, and from what other people do to it, especially mother, who is the important agent for the organization of body image. She does this by her mothering behavior of feeding, burping, cleansing, all with some emotional involvement. She communicates her feelings toward his body, particularly his genitals, by the quality of her contact. This influences his valuation of his body as pleasurable or unpleasurable, good or bad. Later in development, more complex feelings of pride, disgust, and shame will evolve and various body parts will gain their own meaning (Meyer, 1980).

Especially important to gender identity is the penis and sensations emanating from it (Greenacre, 1958). One source of stimulation is genital toying that begins around the end of the first year. Between sixteen and twenty-four months, when gender identity is emerging, there is a normal surge of sexual interest with increased genital play and curiosity about anatomical sex differences (Galenson and Roiphe, 1971). The boy is developing the idea that: "I am a boy with this toy and I am different from those others—girls." Genital play is a reflection of the quality of the mother–child relation. Where relations with adults are minimal, as in a foundling home, genital play does not occur even in the fourth year (Spitz, 1962).

While having a penis and scrotum with testicles facilitates male identity, they are not necessary. A boy was born with no penis, a scrotum that resembled the lips of a vagina, and bilateral testes. He was raised unambiguously as a male and developed a masculine identity and role. His mother reports,

"He likes to wrestle and box. He likes all kinds of sports—likes to watch sports on television, and he told me that he wants to be a wrestler—big and fat—when he is big. . . . He dislikes anything that looks girlish to him—any kind of shirt that even looks like it might belong to a girl—he wants everything boy's" [Stoller, 1968, pp. 41–42].

The Oedipus Complex and Castration Anxiety

When experiencing a build-up of anxiety, a man would seek out a barber. He would request a shave, feel his face, and complain that the shave was not close enough. The barber would reshave him with some annoyance. As the razor was drawn over his neck, the man would ejaculate.

This rare paraphilia illustrates the reenactment of the Oedipus complex and castration anxiety. Being under the barber's sheet represented being in his parents' bed. This rekindled his incestuous wish and consequent fear of castration. But, in his recreation, he triumphs over his castrator, he annoys the barber. To celebrate his escape from castration, he ejaculates (Freedman, 1978).

For Freudian psychoanalysis, the Oedipus complex and castration anxiety are indispensable for the explanation of abnormal behavior. The basic observation is that after separation–individuation, at about three years, some boys still cling to their mothers and act like little suitors. These boys appear estranged from their fathers and seem to be fearful of them.

Few would disagree with these observations, but Freud's interpretations have stimulated much controversy, because he declared that it occurs in every boy's life and because he sexualized the boy's attraction toward his mother.

Freud's version of these events is that between ages two and three, the boy begins to take great pleasure in the sensations from his penis (phallic stage). Since mother has been arousing intense sensations in him, he wishes to share with her these new and wonderful feelings. He wants to become her lover, he wants to displace his father in her life. But, this strong and powerful rival stands in the way of his possessing mother. The little boy becomes concerned that his rival will take away his prized penis. If he has already noticed that women lack penises and assumes they have been castrated, then the idea of losing his penis becomes starkly realistic. Concern becomes terror and his situation intolerable. He attempts to resolve this threat by renouncing his claim on his mother and by repressing all sexual feelings.

In the positive Oedipus resolution, the boy identifies with

his father, attempts to be like him, internalizes his qualities, thus strengthening his masculinity. In the negative resolution, he assumes a passive attitude toward father and identifies to a considerable degree with mother; that is, he tries to be like her in relation to father, which leaves him with some feminine qualities (Freud, 1940).

Freud (1923) invokes biological force to explain why there is a positive or negative resolution. It is the relative strength of constitutional masculinity and femininity that influences the resolution of the Oedipus situation in terms of identification with either father or mother.

Deviations are explained as means of coping with castration anxiety. The boy may identify with the penisless mother and want to be like her (transsexualism), or dress like her (transvestism). Displacement of mother's imagined penis onto an inanimate object results in fetishism. Evoking others' reaction to one's penis to reaffirm its power is seen in exhibitionism. Seeking a mother replacement is the peeper's aim (Rubins, 1969).

Castration anxiety has been used so routinely as an explanation of deviations, that it becomes a monotonous nonexplanation; since it is used to explain everything, it explains nothing (Glover, 1933; Christoffel, 1936; Gillespie, 1952).

Let us attempt a reinterpretation of this Oedipus situation. First of all, it is not a universal experience, but is a symptom of the boy who is still in the throes of the remerging separation conflict with mother. On the one hand, he is still clinging to a union with mother that is too satisfying, with accompanying fears of venturing out on his own. On the other hand, he fears losing what little autonomy, independence, and masculinity he has achieved.

Second, his basic fear is not that he will lose his penis. His penis is not only a pleasurable toy; it is the symbol of his maleness, it represents his masculinity. Therefore, any real or imagined threat to his manliness, whether from being told that his penis will fall off to being dressed as a girl, is traumatic and may leave its mark on his gender development (Stoller, 1975). Not castration anxiety, but the fear of losing his masculine identity is a central feature in the major deviations (Gershman, 1970).

And third, it is not father, but mother that he fears will deprive him of his masculinity (Stoller, 1974). In the Oedipus myth itself, father was not the castrator; it was Oedipus who symbolically castrated himself by poking out his eyes with a pin from Jocasta's garments. And, evidence from myths of many lands and times indicates that it is not father, but mother who is the threatening castrator (Lederer, 1968).

In addition to this pathological relation with mother, many boys who have consolidated their separation and begun to establish their masculinity playfully rehearse relations with women with their mothers.

Gender Role Acquisition

Gender identity acquisition coincides with the emergence of language at about eighteen months and, like language development, it is a gradual acquisition. Consolidation of gender identity occurs in later phases of separation–individuation about the same time as weaning and toilet training (Meyer, 1980). Up to this point, we have spoken of gender identity as a simple, unitary concept, but it is, in fact, composed of several successive aspects. While a boy of two may have some knowledge of gender identity, it will take a year or more for him to fully understand the implications of this knowledge. A full grasp of gender identity results from the evolution of several aspects. First to appear is gender identity labeling ("I am a boy"); next, stability ("I probably could not become a girl"); then, motivation ("Even if I really wanted to, I couldn't become a girl"); and finally, constancy ("Even if I wanted to, and if I wore girl's clothes, I could never be a girl") (Eaton and von Bargen, 1981).

Gender labeling itself takes about a year to develop. While two-year-olds are able to correctly noun label pictures of males and females, they cannot place their own pictures with the appropriate sex, nor can they correctly answer the question, "Are you a boy or a girl?" By thirty months, most are able to identify their own sex, and by thirty-six months, all children use labels appropriately (Thompson, 1975; Marcus and Overton, 1978).

While gender labeling is being learned, knowledge is acquired about gender roles; that is, gender appropriate activities.

Two- and three-year-olds display considerable knowledge of gender role, which is related to their degree of gender identity and gender constancy. Also, as gender constancy firms up, children are gradually forming their gender role preference, that is, their positive valuation of activities considered appropriate to their gender identity, and they tend to devalue the opposite gender (Kuhn, Nash, and Brucken, 1978).

Appropriate gender role behavior involves not only the adoption of congruent behaviors, but also avoidance of behaviors associated with the opposite gender role. Roles not only specify "do's," but also "don't's." In support of the contention of an early protofeminine orientation, it has been found that initially boys do show a preference for the feminine, that they have many don't's to learn.

Boys are more ambivalent in their gender preference than are girls. When asked to choose their most wanted gender role objects (necktie, screwdriver, women's hosiery, dustpan), two-and-a-half- to eleven-year-old boys choose fewer same-gender objects than do girls and the younger boys make more feminine than masculine choices (Verner and Snyder, 1966).

As masculine role adoption increases from age three to late childhood, most boys defeminize; that is, they avoid feminine behaviors (Hartup and Zook, 1960; Hartup, Moore, and Sager, 1963; Bates and Bentler, 1973; Bates, Bentler, and Thompson, 1973). For example, not only do they choose increasingly more masculine toys, but movement away from protofemininity is also evident in boys' relations to adults. Both boys and girls often seek body contact with teacher. But, at about age four, boys desist while girls continue. Boys apparently channel their desire for closeness away from feminine physical contact with teacher to the more masculine playful fighting (Gunderson, Melas, and Skar, 1981).

Boys differ in their ability to put aside femininity and adopt masculinity. Gender role ability is probably a function of the biological force and degree of separation from mother. Male homosexuals display a delayed defeminization. Asked to recall whether they were "sissies," 42 percent so labeled themselves in childhood, 33 percent considered themselves sissies as adolescents, but by adulthood, only 3 percent saw themselves as sissies (Harry, 1983).

Some of these boys who have feminine longings may overcompensate by becoming exaggeratedly masculine. Only later will this disturbance in masculinity become manifest when they experience failure in masculine performance, such as perceived failures in power struggles and in self-assertion. This may result in pseudohomosexuality by the formula: "I am a failure as a man" = "I am castrated" = "I am effeminate" = "I am a homosexual" (Ovesey, 1969; Person and Ovesey, 1978, 1983).

Many studies of gender role acquisition are based on a unidirectional model that assumes that the child is a blank slate on which parents write their gender role scripts. The bidirectional model corrects this by recognizing that not only do parents influence the child, but that parental behavior is, in part, a function of the child. One source of the child's influence on parents is the biological force that predisposes a masculine or feminine direction and determines gender role ability. Thus, the same parent will react differently toward the assertive and person-oriented child than toward the placid and socially unresponsive child (Bell, 1968).

Parental contribution to gender role acquisition begins early, since parents hold differing expectations for the two sexes. These expectations will be enhanced or frustrated by the child's ability to conform to them. And this, in turn, may alter parents' attitudes and behaviors toward the child.

Parents rated their sons, compared to their daughters, as firm rather than soft, large rather than fine featured, bigger, and more attentive. Fathers gave more extreme ratings of sons and daughters than did mothers (Rubin, Provenzano, and Lurie, 1974). At six months, mothers engage in less touching of boys than of girls. By thirteen months, children are behaving differently toward mother. Boys are less reluctant to leave her, return to her less often, and vocalize to her less than do girls. When frustrated, boys engage in less crying and help-seeking from mother than do girls (Goldberg and Lewis, 1969).

This differential treatment of boys and girls need not be deliberate. Gender role adoption is a subtle process and parents are not fully aware of what they are doing. Mother–father pairs who had children of both sexes interacted with a six-month-old female who was presented and dressed as either a boy or girl. Despite the fact that a majority of these adults avered that there should be no differential treatment of boys and girls, they reacted differently. As a girl, the child received more verbal interaction, and as a boy, more direct gaze (Culp, Cook, and Housley, 1983).

Parents who denied that they treat their own children differently on the basis of sex did, in fact, react differently. They gave more praise to and were more critical of girls than boys, and they joined in play more with boys than girls (Fagot, 1974). They responded positively when the child engaged in gender appropriate play and negatively when the child behaved in cross-gender ways (Fagot, 1978).

Mother is less concerned with gender appropriate behavior than is father. Feminine play was more likely for four-year-old boys when with mother than with father (Jacklin, DiPietro, and Maccoby, 1984). Mothers of three- and five-year-olds were more affectionate toward their sons when they were playing with girls' toys rather than with boys' toys, whereas for fathers this was reversed (Langlois and Downs, 1980). And, with eight-year-olds, mothers behaved the same toward boys and girls, but fathers related differently (Tauber, 1979). Mothers seem to inhibit defeminization in their sons, while fathers encourage masculinization.

There is more to parental influence on gender role adoption than simply encouraging or discouraging certain behaviors. The emotional climate surrounding the child is also important. Kindergarten boys' masculinity was related to degree of affection between fathers and sons, fathers' warmth and nurturance, and to the degree to which fathers took an active part in their sons' upbringing (Mussen and Distler, 1960; Mussen and Rutherford, 1963).

Boys' gender role corresponds to the parent who is more dominant and affectionate, whether mother or father (Moulton, Burnstein, Liberty, and Altucher, 1966). If mother is more dominant than father, then the boy is lower in masculine gender preference than when parental dominance is reversed (Hetherington, 1965).

Masculine role adoption is further complicated if father is absent or weak, or cruel and harsh (Brown, 1957). Father absence, especially if it occurs during preschool years, is associated with early feminized behavior, but this often gives way to compensating masculine behavior later in childhood (Hetherington and Deur, 1971; Drake and McDougall, 1977).

It is noteworthy that several studies report little relationship between boys' and fathers' masculinity. It is not so much father's modeling of masculinity that influences the son's masculinity, but rather his dominant position in the family and his nurturant attitudes toward his son (Hartup, 1962; Mussen and Rutherford, 1963; Lynn, 1974). It appears that father's functions are to encourge defeminization and, where necessary, to disrupt mother's feminization. Such actions by father then serve to free the boy to adopt masculinity from many sources.

What are the processes by which the child acquires knowledge of gender relevant behaviors? The simplest process is by giving or withholding rewards for certain responses. Reinforcements not only increase the chances that the response will recur, they also provide the child with information about what it means to be a boy, especially when they are in the form: "You're acting like a young man" or "Girls do that, boys don't."

Modeling is another way by which components of gender role are learned. As he views people in his world that he has categorized as male and female, he notices that certain behaviors are sex-linked; that crying, for example, is frequent in females and infrequent in males. He also notes that women are often rewarded for their crying, whereas men are not. It is as if he reasons, "Since I am a male and males cry only infrequently, whereas the other ones, females, cry frequently, I do not cry." In contrast, he sees no sex link in smiling since both males and females smile at about the same rate. Smiling, therefore, does not become connected with his gender representation because it is not gender relevant.

The child acquires both masculine and feminine behaviors, but performs those he considers gender appropriate because he anticipates more reward for them than for cross-gender behaviors. Before he can code a behavior as masculine or feminine, he must identify himself as male, see that he is subject to expectations and rewards similar to other males, and see that the behavior is gender relevant (Perry and Bussey, 1979).

Why does he mold himself after males and not females? Since his thinking at this early age is concrete, tied to physical appearances, he defines being like a boy and not being like a girl in physical terms, as sex differences. He labels himself as boy and, since he values himself, he values that which is congruent with his male identity. In addition to being reinforced for doing boy things, he does boy things because they are valuable, to do them is rewarding in itself (Kohlberg, 1969).

This gender relevant information does not remain as lists of do's and don't's. He assimilates this information, builds with it mental representations (schemas) of what it means to be masculine and feminine. He is not simply a passive recipient, but is an active seeker of gender relevant information. We have already seen him acting as if he were a scientist, scanning male and female models, "calculating" differences in frequency of behavior between the two. Also, like the scientist, sometime between sixteen and twenty-eight months, he begins to generate a naive theory that organizes this incoming information. These gender theories or representations, like the scientist's theories, guide his behavior and allow him to make inferences, and to interpret and anticipate future events (Markus, 1977; Martin and Halverson, 1981).

Gender representations regulate his behavior by allowing him to anticipate the future so that he can engage in gender appropriate behaviors. They organize gender related information and bring about selective attention and memory so that schema-consistent input is rendered salient and remembered while inconsistent input is ignored or forgotten. On a memory recognition task, first and second grade boys with high gender role adoption were able to better recognize traditional masculine role pictures (male fire fighter) than nontraditional gender role pictures (man sewing). There was no such difference for low gender role adoption boys (Liben and Signorella, 1980).

The boy's conception of masculinity increases in rigidity from two to seven years as gender constancy progresses. Exceptions to his gender rules are not allowed— "Boys never wear dresses" and "They never wash dishes." But around age seven, when he begins to realize that superficial changes do not alter one's gender, this rigidity decreases (Huston, 1983).

We have seen that much of the boy's role learning consists more of what not to do than what to do (Lynn, 1969). Consequently, the boy not only builds a representation of the masculine with which he identifies, but he also develops a representation of the feminine that complements the masculine (Markus, Crane, Bernstein, and Saladi, 1982). Money and Ehrhardt (1972) refer to these two processes as identification—the process of learning to behave like members of one's own sex; and complementation—the process of learning to reciprocate behavior of the other sex. These two processes begin in early playful role-taking behaviors and are coded separately, one is primary and "like me," the other secondary and "not like me." It is possible that the boy may overvalue the masculine, devalue the feminine, and feel negatively about his own preverbal protofeminine residue.

These two representations, masculine and feminine, are similar to Jung's animus and anima. If the male is outwardly oriented in the masculine direction, then his unconscious orientation is feminine (anima). His anima is complementary to his masculinity. It is the image of the female, his own Eve. His anima is projected onto females and influences his perceptions of them (Jacobi, 1973).

Two types of psychological scales are used to assess degree of masculinity and femininity (M and F) in adults. One is based on the assumption that these two characteristics are inversely related, so that the more questions answered in the masculine direction, the lower the femininity score. The other type of scale assumes that masculinity and femininity are independent, that individuals have different quantities of both and therefore the scales yield both an M and F score.

Summary

Despite several decades of researching and theorizing, the processes by which gender identity/role are acquired are still not well understood (Pleck, 1981). However, some tentative propositions can be derived from the literature.

There is a biological force that facilitates or interferes with the acquisition of masculinity. This force interacts with the boy's early protofemininity. Where the masculinizing force is weak, the boy will have more difficulty defeminizing than where the force is strong. Further, if early attachment to mother is defective or if mother does not encourage separation–individuation, the chances of later interpersonal and sexual difficulties are enhanced.

Even an "adequate" mother may not encourage her son to defeminize, a task often left to father. If father is absent or, probably worse, present, but psychologically distant, masculinization is weakened or delayed.

Through parental reinforcement and example, and with the boy's own cognitive abilities, knowledge of masculinity and femininity are acquired. From these sources, the boy constructs his masculine and feminine representations and his evaluation of them. These, in turn, influence his sexuality.

SEXUALITY

Components of Sexual Behavior

Sexual behavior involves a complex sequence of components, many of which are multidetermined. This sequence can be divided into two segments—arousal and gratification. Behaviorally, arousal begins with locating an arousing partner (object). After finding a partner, there is pretactile looking, smiling, and mutual eye contact. Then there is tactile contact including light touching, petting, and kissing. This is followed by genital contact. Finally there is gratification with orgasm. At some point in the arousal phase tumescence begins, erection in the male. And after orgasm, detumescence sets in (Freund, Scher, and Hucker, 1983).

Arousal

For the sequence to be activated, it is necessary that the person label his sensations as sexual. The experience of sexual arousal, like any other emotion, requires both physiological activation and labeling of those physiological responses as sexual (Schachter and Singer, 1962). Especially during the initial phases of arousal, mislabeling is likely, since the physiological changes are similar to other arousal states. In later stages, increasing tumescence of the penis is a salient cue to the sexual nature of the experience. Mislabeling occurs when sensations are experienced as nonsexual when, in fact, the source is sexual. Such mislabeling can occur in a severely sexually inhibited person who must deny his sexual impulses. Another type of mislabeling takes place when nonsexual sensations, such as building fear or rage, are labeled sexual. Since the source of arousal is seldom purely sexual, sensations from nonsexual emotions fuse with the sexual, with the whole compound of physiological changes experienced as sexual (Rook and Hammen, 1977).

Sexual arousal is probably more subject to mislabeling than other emotional or motivational states because parents usually either fail to label or negatively label their child's sexual activities and sex organs. This creates an aura of mystery and fear, depriving the child of accurate verbal symbols with which to rationally deal with his sexuality. As a consequence, a vacuum is created where confusion and fantasy reign. For instance, it is quite common for four-year-olds to fail to differentiate between urination and sexuality (Gagnon, 1967; Rutter, 1971).

The sexuality of many children is interfered with from infancy on by prohibition and punishment. The infant is discouraged, sometimes with heroic efforts, from manipulating his penis. This interference serves to attach anxiety to sexual arousal, because sexual stimuli become cues for expected punishment. This fused anxiety is augmented by an unfavorable oedipal situation where the boy's sexual expression is threatened. In adult relations, sensations of sex, anger, and anxiety will form a compound. He may be unable to label the anger and anxiety components, yet feel hostile and as if he were in danger. For some, the anger and anxiety are so great that they cannot relate sexually without some defensive maneuvers (Reik, 1941; Bieber, 1953).

Arousal creates a state of high excitement, but does not of

itself often lead to discharge. The gratifying end pleasure is obtained through direct stimulation of the penis, and orgasm.

Developmentally, sexually exciting stimuli proceed from physical to psychological and from diffuse to focal stimuli. For pre- and early adolescent boys, erection and orgasm are easily induced by a variety of stimuli, such as taking a shower, bicycle riding, being scared or angry, band music, seeing or thinking about girls, and physical contact with girls. However, by the late teens, the range of effective stimuli has narrowed considerably to genital manipulation and sexual thoughts, and by early adulthood, the physical without being accompanied by the mental seldom gives rise to erection (Kinsey, Pomeroy, and Martin, 1948).

At the physiological level, circulating androgens, particularly testosterone, can energize sexual desire. Psychologically, a host of nonsexual factors enter into the complex of urges leading to sexual activity, such as aggression, power motives, passive–dependent wishes, overcoming loneliness, and generalized tension relief. In some men, sexuality is fused with pride and doubts about masculinity so that insults to their maleness prod them to compensate by making sexual conquests (Kardiner, 1954). So, rather than a single sex drive, there are a host of factors prompting an individual to sexual activity.

Partner Preference

The qualities of the partner that are sexually stimulating are almost as varied as the number of sexually active males. Most men have not one preferred or ideal sexual partner, but a hierarchy of preferences. Some are able to describe their ideal partner in minute detail, often from fantasies rather than reality. Others do not have a particularly well-developed preference. The criteria used may be physical and/or psychological; rooted in the past as a symbol of mother and/or refer to the partner in her own right.

There are differences among men as to what are considered suitable substitutes for their ideal. When the ideal is unavailable, others lower on the hierarchy, but still within the range of acceptability, may be sufficiently arousing to initiate the sexual sequence. So, a man may prefer a certain type of adult female but readily accept an early adolescent female as his partner, or, under certain circumstances, he may use another male as a substitute.

The qualities of the most preferred sexual partners and suitable substitutes are multiply determined. The relation of currently circulating hormones has been studied to determine differences between homosexuals and heterosexuals. Results have been contradictory, but predominately negative (Meyer-Bahlburg, 1977; Storms, 1980). Rather than current hormones influencing partner preference, it is more likely that their effect, if any, is prenatal. And, rather than a direct influence, prenatal hormones would increase the probability of specific sexual learning either through an effect on the brain, and/or on body build and gender related behaviors (Meyer-Bahlburg, 1977, 1980).

There is some evidence that the prenatal biological force may set in motion the likelihood of a path of psychosexual development leading to a same-sex partner choice. This is seen in the choice of a group of prenatally androgenized genetic females. Most were early treated with surgery and cortisone to prevent further masculinization. When they were seventeen years or older, over a third, in varying degrees, indicated a preference for a female partner (Money, Schwartz, and Lewis, 1984).

Sexual preferences may be assessed by simply asking the person to state his choices. A more sophisticated technique is to show him pictures of nude males and females of various ages while he is wearing a gadget on his penis that measures changes in tumescence. If he has a strong preference for adult females, greatest tumescence will occur in response to pictures of adult females, with smaller or no tumescence to young females and males.

Modes of Relating

Modes of relating to sexual partners are influenced by one's evaluation of masculinity, conception of females and femininity, and attitudes toward sexuality. In the ideal, loving relationship,

the man will identify with and be convinced of his own masculinity and accept his sexuality. He will also value the feminine,
not only within himself, but in females. Therefore, he will be
able to relate to females in a positive, egalitarian mode.

However, where he identifies with, but doubts his own
masculinity, denigrates the feminine, and considers sexual acts
as aggressive, his mode of relating sexually will be hostile. Or,
where he is unsure of his masculinity and fears the feminine,
he may place himself in a subservient role to females. Other,
less than ideal combinations of identifications, evaluations, and
negative feelings about sexuality serve to increase the chances
of dysfunctional modes of relating.

Childhood Sexuality

Masturbation

Genital toying is seen from seven to ten months and again from
fifteen to nineteen months, with signs of erotic arousal such as
flushing and increased respiration rate (Galenson, 1980). Aside
from early childhood genital toying, masturbation begins in
boys at age six to seven, but not all achieve orgasm (Langfeldt,
1981). From year five or six to puberty, there is a gradual
increase in sexual activity. Incidences of masturbation and heterosexual play increase, and there is a gradual rise in homosexual play (Rutter, 1971).

Sex Play with Others

Sex play, like other play of children, is a rehearsal for adult
roles. Boys are practicing and testing their masculine and complementary feminine representations with girls and other boys.
Uninhibited sex play is associated with uncomplicated adult
heterosexuality (Money, 1984b). Sex play with mutual exploration is seen in four-year-olds (Rutter, 1971), and by ages five
and six is even more explicit. Boys especially seem to be interested in their own genitals, handling them and showing them
to others (Gunderson, Melas, and Sklar, 1981).

Primal Scene and Parental Seduction

Two specific childhood experiences have been indicted as precursors of later deviant sexuality—observing the primal scene and parental seduction. The child's observation of sexual intercourse, especially between his parents, is supposed by some to inevitably have a pathological effect on his personality. It is said to be invariably interpreted as a sadistic, aggressive attack. Damage is caused, not only by witnessing the primal scene, but also by fantasizing about the scene. However, the effects of observing the primal scene are not necessarily pathological, but depend on the child's level of development and the entire family dynamics. Sadistic conceptions are largely determined by aggressive scenes between parents outside the bedroom (Esman, 1973).

Parental seduction involves imposing on the young child, often under the guise of affection, forms of sexuality totally inappropriate to his age. It includes sleeping with him into late childhood, bathing him when he is fully capable of cleansing himself, administering unnecessary enemas, lack of modesty in the home, and permission to engage in abnormal sexual behaviors (Litin, Griffin, and Johnson, 1956).

One parent, often with the tacit approval of the other, fosters the child's sexual acting out because it provides that parent with some (unconscious) gratification for his or her own forbidden impulses. The parent of the sensually aroused child does not allow him a genital outlet, but deflects his excitement to other channels. For example, it is suggested that in fetishism, mother arouses her son, refuses him gratification, and encourages his use of an object as a substitute for her body (Litin et al., 1956).

The parent may use equivocation by sending the double message that, "You shouldn't do that, but do it anyway." A mother, finding her son wearing her soiled underwear, said, "For heaven's sake, if you must do that, at least take some of my clean things." Father's complicity is seen in his remark when he saw the boy, "Teddy, you would have made a pretty girl" (Litin et al., 1956, p. 40). Parents may model deviant sexuality by engaging in hostile, sadistic sex play in front of the child.

Sometimes, seduction is by permission. An example is the mother who allowed her son to touch her breasts until he was twelve years old. Then, she told him his breast touching must stop, remarking that, "Boys like you go around attacking women when they grow up" (Johnson and Robinson, 1957, p. 1652).

It is likely that parental seduction has a long-term influence on the child's conception of sexuality. For instance, a mother who was so depressed that she could not relate to her son as an individual used him as an object because the body contact made her come alive. In her relations with her son, she focused on the external and superficial. The son adopted this mode of relating, considering himself an irresistible seducer, but felt used and exploited (Coen, 1981).

In addition, the "choice" of a particular paraphilia is influenced by specific organizing or triggering experiences. Examples are witnessing another child being spanked, being dressed as a girl, and being unexpectedly observed while urinating. These experiences are sexually arousing to the boy because they are consistent with his personal sexual mythology (Socarides, 1988).

Despite all the handicaps placed on childhood sexuality, incidence of referrals for persistent, inappropriate sexual behavior appears to be rather slight. Of 516 prepubescent children seen at a child psychiatry department, only six boys evidenced such behavior. Onset of this behavior was about eight years and their behavior was similar to that of aggressive boys: they were sexually aggressive with peers, for example, forcing a girl to undress and fondling female classmates, and demonstrated exhibitionism and homosexuality (Pomeroy, Behar, and Stewart, 1981).

Adolescent Sexuality

The boy's already established gender identity and role precedes and organizes his sexuality (Person and Ovesey, 1983). At puberty, the surge of sex hormones does not determine the course of adult sexuality, rather it activates the already established patterns. The lovemap, already sketched out in childhood, charts the person's sexual fantasies and related behaviors. It first appears in wet dreams or in masturbation fantasies. It is personal and stable (Money and Ehrhardt, 1972; Money, 1984a,b).

Early and Late Puberty

Average age of onset of puberty is about thirteen years, six months, with a range of from eight years to fifteen and older. Average onset of first ejaculation is thirteen years, ten months. There are marked differences in sexuality between boys with early and late onset. While younger boys begin some sort of sexual activity shortly after onset, older boys delay such activity from one to two years. Almost three-quarters of the younger boys' first ejaculation is achieved by masturbation, while only half of the older boys bring on their own first ejaculation. Total number of orgasms for the younger boys is twice that of older boys. Even thirty to forty years later, those with earlier onset have higher rates of orgasm than those with later onset (Kinsey, Pomeroy, and Martin, 1948).

Socially, early maturers tend to live in harmony with social expectations—they make a good impression, conform, and display social consciousness. These attributes persist into adulthood. As new impulses are thrust upon them rather suddenly, initially they have difficulty in managing them. Their sexual impulses are strong, but so is their overcontrol of impulses. They express more aggressive fantasy themes and also more themes of being coerced than late maturers.

For a time, late maturers feel left behind, frustrated, and somewhat concerned about their masculinity. They have more time to integrate pubertal changes into their self-concept and to organize their sexuality and abilities. They tend to be uninhibited and expressive, more insightful and flexible than early maturers (Peskin, 1967). They are attention seekers, and are less popular, confident, and assertive than earlier maturing boys (Rutter, 1971).

Masturbation and Sexual Fantasy

Adolescence is a time not only for loosening family ties, but also a second chance for resolution of infantile conflicts and emotional ties. It has been called the second individuation phase (Blos, 1967). It is a time when gender roles are irreversibly integrated and final sexual patterns are organized. Although the central masturbation fantasy theme is being determined throughout the preadolescent period, it becomes integrated in the final sexual pattern (Laufer, 1976). Because of the major physical changes experienced at puberty, body image must be reorganized.

For two-thirds of preadolescent boys, masturbation leads to their first ejaculation (Kinsey et al., 1948). From ages seven to thirteen incidence of masturbation rises from 10 to 80 percent (Rutter, 1971), and by age thirteen between 40 to 60 percent of males are masturbating (Kinsey et al., 1948; Sorensen, 1973; Hunt, 1974; Hass, 1979). Frequency ranges from zero to two or three times a day (Kinsey et al., 1948).

While the incidence of masturbation fantasy in the preadolescent is very low, it is usually an accompaniment of adolescent and later masturbation (Kinsey et al., 1948; Seghir and Robbins, 1973). Only about 10 percent of boys that masturbate report never fantasizing (Sorensen, 1973; Hass, 1979).

Masturbation is sexual play whereby the boy learns to master his sexual impulses and to rehearse in fantasy his adult role. Along with accompanying fantasies, masturbation is a bridge between childhood and adult sexuality, serving to abolish and/or integrate infantile sexual modes into more adult modes of sexual expression (Laufer, 1968; Francis and Marcus, 1975).

As if he were scanning the final paths of his lovemap, the boy tests various fantasy themes during masturbation for their arousal value. Some are found unacceptable and dropped from the repertoire; others are continued and elaborated upon (Laufer, 1976). These fantasies are more than day dreams since they involve action with associated sensations of mounting sexual arousal (Bonime, 1969). The masturbator is acting on himself, without interference from others. He is in charge of the production (Nydes, 1950), which is acclaimed at its ending by the rewarding orgasm.

As with other sources of sexual arousal, there is a funneling trend in the evolution of masturbation fantasies—the range of fantasy themes decreases with age (Hunt, 1974). Initially, bizarre fantasy themes are not uncommon, but are often transitory (Francis and Marcus, 1975). Some popular themes are: forcing someone or being forced to have sex; sex with more than one person; and varying degrees of violence (Sorensen, 1973). Sadistic themes are more common than usually thought (Lukianowicz, 1960b).

By ages eight to twelve, many boys regard their homosexual and incestuous fantasies as "dirty minded" (Langfeldt, 1981). Incest fantasies that do intrude during masturbation may induce loss of erection. An alternate fantasy is substituted which, while it inhibits the incestuous fantasy, is at the same time symbolic of incest.

Almost half the boys who masturbate experience guilt sometimes (Sorensen, 1973). Guilt and anxiety over masturbation stem from several sources. One is the feeling of loss of control, the idea that one's body is an alien force that cannot be controlled. Perhaps a more important source is the regressive fantasies that occur during self-gratification. These may be recognized as "perverted," "disgusting," and "shameful" (Laufer, 1968; Stoller, 1985a). Freud (1919) notes that masturbation guilt is not generated by the act itself, but by the fantasies that accompany the act. It may be that the antimasturbation crusades, while directed at the overt act, really stemmed from the fear of deviant sexual fantasies.

As early as 1895, the relation of masturbation fantasies to deviant sexuality was recognized when Schrenck-Notzing remarked that: "The memory-pictures cultivated by onanism may become imperative conceptions, and force the individual's sexual impulse into a perverse direction" (p. 25).

In the various sexual deviations, the type of masturbatory fantasy characteristically conforms to the individual's sexual preferences, and the visualized love object serves to gratify his deviated sexual desire (Lukianowicz, 1960b). Almost every deviation, fantasized or acted out, is an aid to masturbation, since it is necessary for sexual arousal (Karpman, 1954). Indeed, Stoller (1975) defines perversion as the acting out of a fantasy that has evolved over the years to preserve the individual's erotic pleasure.

Sex Play with Others

Somewhere between 60 and 70 percent of boys aged eight to thirteen are involved in sex play ranging from display of genitals to genital contact (Kinsey et al., 1948). Between ages ten and twelve, the majority of children would choose an opposite sex partner, but most of their friends are of the same sex. Consequently, in early adolescence, sex play with other boys is more common than with girls, with 50 to 60 percent of boys involved. Sexual exploration among chums is probably the least anxiety provoking and is usually a rehearsal for relations with girls. Most same-sex sexuality is simply a way to satisfy curiosity and to experiment with techniques (Gadpaille, 1969). Display of the penis is most common, with manipulation of genitals, anal or femoral insertion, and oral contacts following in frequency (Kinsey et al., 1948). For those boys who are concerned with penis size and ejaculation, it is natural that they would seek reassurance from their age mates. Transient putting on of women's garments in early adolescent may parallel this adolescent homosexual experimentation (Person and Ovesey, 1978).

Frank sex play with girls begins at about nine years, with about 40 percent reporting contacts. At puberty there is a sharp rise in heterosexual interest and activities (Rutter, 1971). Activities are similar to play with boys with display of genitals most common, and manipulation of the female's genitals, attempts at coitus, finger insertion into vagina, and oral contacts following in that order (Kinsey et al., 1948).

If a firm sense of masculinity has been acquired and if women are viewed as equals, deserving of respect, then the individual can proceed in the direction of ideal sexual relationships. If, however, his sense of masculinity has been stunted and his feelings about women permeated with adoration, fear, and hate, then he is probably headed for one of the several sexual bypaths.

PART II

THE GENDER IDENTITY/ROLE DISORDERS

The great majority of heterosexual and homosexual men have a core gender identity that is consistent with their biological sex; that is, they unambiguously experience themselves as males and are comfortable with that identity. Also, most men behave, think, and feel in ways they consider masculine; in other words, their gender role is congruent with their maleness and gender identity.

There are some, however, who either occasionally or continuously feel as if they were women, and when they do, they assume feminine role behaviors, particularly feminine attire. Such men are diagnosed as having gender identity/role disorders.

There is a spectrum of these disorders, even though only two or three discrete points have been defined. An individual is not fixed at one point on this spectrum, but may move to and fro. At the least severe end is the man, a partial or fetishistic transvestite, who is sexually aroused by wearing one or two pieces of feminine clothing. Next is the complete transvestite who, as regularly as possible, dresses fully as a woman, apes feminine mannerisms, and fantasizes himself as a woman. Further along the spectrum is the transgenderist (Kane, 1975), or gynemimesist (female mimicker) (Money and Lamacz, 1984). He goes further than occasional cross-dressing and feels as if he were a woman even when not cross-dressed. However, he does not want to be a female, just to look and feel like one. The advanced transgenderist has himself depilitated, dosed with female hormones, and fitted with breast implants so he can live as a woman while retaining his male organs. Finally, at the most severe end is the individual who experiences himself as a female all the time, and can no longer live with himself because of the presence of a penis and absence of breasts and vagina. This is the transsexual.

Several entwined threads run across this spectrum of disorders: stability, extent, and preferred sexual partner (Freund, Steiner, and Chan, 1982; Blanchard, 1985a). Stability of cross-gender identity varies from episodic to continuous fantasies and feelings of being women. Many transvestites feel as if they were women when they are cross-dressed and, perhaps occasionally when not en femme. Transgenderists and transsexuals experience cross-gender identity most to all the time.

Extent of feminization varies from wearing a few pieces of feminine clothing to actually undergoing transformation of the body. Differing feelings accompany these physical changes. When dressed as a woman, some transvestites experience sexual excitement. Other transvestites and also transgenderists and transsexuals have feelings of being at ease and a sense that being garbed as a woman is appropriate because of their feminine identity.

The preferred sexual partner of the transvestite is female, while the transsexual wants a male partner. Using the terms *heterosexual* and *homosexual* complicates the situation, at least from the gender disordered person's perspective. For, when in his female mode, he may well insist that, in having sex with a male, he is heterosexual; sex with a female would to him be homosexual. To maintain his heterosexuality when with a female, he imagines her to be a male.

Note: The classification scheme used here is not the same as that prescribed by the American Psychiatric Association's 1987 *Diagnostic and Statistical Manual*, Third Edition Revised (DSM-III-R). There is an implicit assumption in this manual that gender dysphoria precludes cross-dressing which is sexually arousing. Therefore, transvestites who cross-dress to become sexually aroused are classed as paraphiliacs, while those whose purpose is to ease tension or relieve gender discomfort are classed under gender identity disorder of adolescence or adulthood, nontranssexual type (GIDAANT). There is evidence that runs counter to the above assumption; that is, one half of strongly gender dysphoric men are, at least occasionally, sexually aroused when cross-dressed even though they are disturbed by this (Blanchard and Clemmensen, 1988).

DSM-III-R's term is *gender identity disorders* and does not include incongruent gender behavior as such. Three diagnoses are included: transsexualism, gender identity disorders of childhood, and GIDAANT, all of which involve a sense of inappropriateness of gender identity. The latter includes former fetishistic transvestites who are no longer sexually aroused by cross-dressing, and homosexuals who cross-dress, especially some female impersonators. In the present discussion, gender role is included, as a result transvestites are included; that is, men who are sexually aroused and/or who experience feelings of contentment by cross-dressing.

3 CHILDHOOD GENDER IDENTITY DISORDER

INTRODUCTION

A five-year-old boy repeatedly wears his mother's pantyhose and bra, uses her lipstick and perfume, has feminine mannerisms, and plays with dolls. Is this behavior pathological? Professionals who attempt to modify feminine behavior in boys believe so. But, there are those who question the pathology of such behavior and the ethics of altering it.

Reasons given for lessening feminine and increasing masculine behavior are to alleviate the intense unhappiness of these children and the turmoil in their families, make them more acceptable to their peers who are cruel to them, and prevent adult homosexuality, transvestism, and transsexualism (Bates, Skilbeck, Smith, and Bentler, 1974).

Those opposed to attempts to defeminize boys contend that gender norms should be shunned as a basis for defining pathology because there is controversy over the healthfulness of these changing norms. Some feminine behaviors may be positive—playing with dolls can be rehearsal for parenting. What is labeled feminine by society may not be so labeled by the boy; for example, his concern with beautiful objects may presage artistic talents. And, it is difficult to differentiate between gender role nonconformity and disturbance (Wolfe, 1979).

Those who feel that traditional gender roles are not in the best interest of the individual or of society criticize efforts to alter feminine behavior in boys. They see such therapists as bowing to social and parental pressure, forcing the child to abandon his femininity for the sake of adjustment. Their suggested alternative is to alter parents' behavior so that they are accepting of feminine behavior, and to train the boys in assertiveness so they, in turn, can modify behavior of those who are unaccepting of them (Nordyke, Baer, Etzel, and LeBlanc, 1977; Winkler, 1977).

Others view attempts to alter feminine behavior in boys as yet another effort of psychological institutions' "insidious attempt to stamp out gay identity in young children." They proclaim the right of all growing people to develop an adult homosexual identity (Morin and Schultz, 1978, p. 142).

Prevalence of childhood gender identity disturbance is a rare one in one hundred thousand, with a sex ratio of fifteen boys to one girl (Rekers, Bentler, Rosen, and Lovaas, 1978).

DEFINITION

In childhood gender disorders, either gender identity and/or gender role may be involved. The major definitional problem is whether children with cross-gender identity ("I not only enjoy being girlish, but also want to be a girl") constitute a separate group, or whether they are simply more disturbed than those with only cross-gender role behavior and appropriate gender identity ("I enjoy being girlish, but I do not want to be a girl") (Bradley, 1985). Because it was assumed that boys with cross-gender identity would, as adults, want a sex-change operation, they were called childhood transsexuals. This name has been dropped because of difficulty in testing the assumption.

Some have proposed that there are two overlapping syndromes: gender behavior and gender identity disturbances. Behavior disturbances consist of chronic cross-dressing, use of cosmetics, feminine mannerisms, gestures, gait, speech, and voice. While these boys avoid anything masculine, they do not express a desire to be girls. In identity disturbances, also called cross-gender identification, the boys say they want to be or fantasize being girls. They want to grow up to be mothers, breast-feed, and/or have their penises removed (Rosen, Rekers, and Friar, 1977).

In 1968 Stoller made a qualitative distinction between childhood cross-dressing or transvestism and childhood transsexualism; that is, cross-gender identity. Cross-dressing, he argued, occurs after masculine gender identity is established, while cross-gender identity is formed prior to masculine gender identity. More recently, however, he (1985b) views gender disorders as a continuum. In extreme cases of cross-gender identity, the boys experienced too much gratification in symbiotic union with mother, did not adequately separate, and so do not suffer from conflict or anxiety. In less extreme cases, there is evidence of conflict and anxiety.

To test this two-syndrome hypothesis, gender disturbed boys were rated on both degree of masculine–feminine identity and behavior. Since the degree of relationship between identity and behavior was only moderately high, the investigators concluded that the two syndromes are related, but not synonymous (Bentler, Rekers, and Rosen, 1979). However, when the unreliability of the rating scales is accounted for, the relationship between identity and behavior is nearly perfect. This reanalysis indicates that not only are identity and behavior related, but also synonymous.

Degree of cross-gender behavior is related to gender identity. A common measure of identity is the sex of the figure first drawn when the child is asked to draw a person. More gender disturbed children draw the opposite sex figure first than do nondisturbed children. And, those gender disturbed children who do draw the opposite sex figure first are more likely to play with opposite gender toys and engage in cross-dressing than those who draw the same-sex figure first (Zucker, Finegan, Doering, and Bradley, 1983).

Feminine behavior in cross-gender identity boys is constant, occurring each day. Not only do these young boys dress in girls' clothes, but their walk, gestures, voice inflection, and topics of conversation are feminine. They are pretty, sensitive, and intelligent.

Simply because a boy does not display masculine behaviors does not imply that he is feminine. The behaviors that best define feminine boys are, in order: cross-dressing; avoidance of rough-and-tumble play; wish to be a girl; not wanting to be like father; attention to mother's fashion; and girl-type doll play (Green, 1987).

Two grades of gender disturbed boys have been suggested—major and minor. To qualify for a major disorder, the boy must display at least one of these behaviors: cross-dressing; expressed wish to be a girl or grow up to be a woman; assume a female role in fantasy games; and imitate feminine mannerisms. Minor behaviors are: dislike for rough play and boys' toys; preference for artistic pursuits; playing primarily with girls; graceful movement; and being teased as a sissy (Newman, 1976).

For an official DSM-III-R diagnosis of gender identity disorder of childhood, the child must demonstrate the wish to be the opposite sex. Other necessary features are an anatomically normal prepubertal child who experiences intense distress over belonging to their assigned sex, and either an aversion toward their gender-appropriate activities and/or repudiation of their sexual anatomy (American Psychiatric Association, 1987).

THE BEHAVIOR

Onset

Onset of cross-gender behavior ranges from eighteen months to six years, with a median age of five years (Green, 1987), and most mothers know by age six that their sons' behavior differs from that of other boys (Zuger, 1984). Incidence of feminine behaviors in normal second grade boys is low, where mothers report 6 percent desiring to be female, 13 percent dressing as girls, 7 percent wearing lipstick, 15 percent playing with dolls, and 3 percent being averse to boys' games (Zuger and Taylor, 1969).

Wanting to Be a Girl and Aversion to Penis

In severe cases the boy expresses a desire to be a girl and displays a disdain for his penis, as this mother reports: " 'he's standing in front of the mirror, and he took his penis and he folded it under, and he said, "Look, Mommy, I'm a girl" ' " (Green, 1987, p. 3). It is safe to assume that those boys who dislike their penises have seen the female genitals, perhaps mother's (Lukianowicz, 1959).

Cross-Dressing and Playacting

The boy's early toys are mother's clothing and accessories— " 'He has put on my bathrobe, my nightgown, and things like that. . . . I've caught him in a slip every once in a while—you know, a half slip that looks like a skirt. He puts on my shoes' " (Green, 1987, p. 137). The earlier and more regularly cross-dressing occurs, the more severe the gender disturbance (Rosen, Rekers, and Friar, 1977). Modal onset of cross-dressing is two to three years. There is another peak in onset between eleven and sixteen (Lebovitz, 1972), probably reflecting a retreat from impending manhood.

Dressing includes a variety of garments, with high-heeled shoes the most common item— " 'And he just didn't want to wear high heels quite frequently, but all the time' " (Green, 1974, p. 159). The child uses these clothes as a defense against separation anxiety. Mother's clothes may be a substitute for her skin, so they are "what the pouch of the kangaroo is to the baby kangaroo" (Greenson, 1966, p. 402).

Another and intense interest is in acting and feminine role taking (Rekers and Varni, 1977) that is facilitated by high verbal ability (Money and Epstein, 1967). His feminine role taking is indicative of a hunger for identification, where the mechanism "If I imitate, I become" is operative (Greenson, 1966). The mother of a seven-year-old reports, " 'when he dresses up he sort of parades around and puts on a show with modeling and that sort of thing as if he were imitating a woman. He plays to the audience' " (Green and Money, 1966, p. 537). There is much improvisation, such as using a felt marker for lipstick and father's T-shirt for a dress— " 'He can come up with a complete costume out of little or nothing' " (Green, 1974, p. 162). Many of these boys later aspire to be actors (Green, 1987).

Because cross-dressing may be situational, it is important that at least one other sign be present for a diagnosis of gender disturbance. For instance, an eight-year-old boy would put on his mother's under and outer garments, but showed no other signs of femininity. Although his parents wanted and loved him, they let it be known that they had hoped for a daughter. At the time of his cross-dressing, they were not paying much attention to him. His dressing was an attempt to make himself into a girl to obtain his parents' acceptance. Cross-dressing ceased when the parents stopped talking about wanting a daughter and assured him that he was loved (Dupont, 1968).

Cross-Gender Play

Cross-gender play is especially diagnostic if engaged in after age five (Rosen et al., 1977). Examples of these play interests are taking the feminine role in "house" and in story-telling, and preferring Barbie Doll to Ken Doll— " 'His favorite characters are Cinderella, Snow White, and he loves the Wizard of Oz and copies the girl' " (Green, 1987, p. 136); " 'He likes to play house, and he's the mama when he plays house' " (Green, 1974, p. 155). Gender disturbed preschool boys engage in more feminine play activities (painting, jump rope, putting on plays), fewer masculine nonathletic play (building forts, toy guns, using tools), and fewer masculine athletics (basketball, foot races, wrestling) than do non-gender-disturbed boys (Bates and Bentler, 1973).

Compared to their siblings and psychiatric cases, seven-year-old gender disturbed boys spend a larger proportion of time playing with girls' toys (dolls, purses, lipstick) than with boy's toys (plastic cowboys and Indians, handcuffs) (Zucker, Doering, Bradley, and Finegan, 1982). And, in a family doll play situation, seven-year-old feminine boys and normal girls spend more time with mother and infant dolls than normal boys (Green and Fuller, 1973a).

This cross-gender play is situation specific. When alone, they play mainly with feminine (lipstick, dolls) rather than with masculine (rubber knife, toy electric razor) objects. However, feminine play and some masculine play occurs in certain situations for each child. For instance, Kraig engaged in feminine play in the presence of mother and a male stranger, but play was masculine with father present (Rekers and Lovaas, 1974; Rekers, 1975). Kraig's masculine behavior in father's presence illustrates father's inhibitory influence on the boy's femininity.

Feminine Mannerisms

" 'He usually puts his hands on his hips and starts walking like a girl, or starts moving his behind real sissylike. He does that quite often, too' " (Green, 1987, p. 149).

Motor behavior of feminine boys was compared with that of conventionally masculine boys and feminine girls aged from four to ten. They were videotaped, all similarly dressed, walking, running, throwing a ball, and telling a story. Judges rated the feminine boys halfway between the boys and girls on degree of masculinity–femininity (Green, Neuberg, and Finch, 1983). The feminine boys are more uncoordinated than boys with adjustment problems and normal control boys (Bates, Bentler, and Thompson, 1979).

THE BOY

Biological Basis

Because of the early onset and extreme nature of his behavior, it is easy to assume that there must be some constitutional predisposition. However, evidence for this assumption is sketchy and circumstantial. One piece of evidence is the often reported beauty and female appearance of these boys. Another hint of some biological factor comes from the pattern of intellectual skills. While not differing from other children in overall IQ, feminine boys are better at verbal tasks than perceptual organization (Money and Epstein, 1967). Compared to other children, there is some deficiency in spatial relations, and the more severe the femininity, the greater the deficit (Zucker et al., 1984). Because girls demonstrate greater verbal than perceptual or performance abilities, it is conceivable that some biological factor is in play (Finegan, Zucker, Bradley, and Doering, 1982).

Parental Contribution

The families of feminine boys do not differ from those of masculine boys in pattern of siblings, ethnicity, or religious affiliation (Green, 1987). Generally, the family is intact (Green, 1985), but father has little interaction with his son and is far less significant to him than is mother. In a group of gender-disturbed children, either there was no male role model present in the home, or if present, he was psychologically remote, uninvolved in making decisions, and not affectionate or nurturant toward the boy (Rekers, Mead, Rosen, and Brigham, 1983). Forceful paternal dominance is infrequent (Green and Money, 1961); rather, fathers are passive, distant, and physically absent much of the time. They fail to interrupt the too close tie between mother and son and do not interfere with their wives feminizing their sons (Stoller, 1968, 1979, 1985b).

Fathers' interests are outside the home rather than within the family (Rosen and Teague, 1974; Bradley, 1985). They are ambitious, set high personal standards, and are concerned with orderliness and cleanliness (Rosen and Teague, 1974). The father of a boy in treatment explained feebly: " 'Well, I'm very busy myself. I'm forming a complete new thing in my business, as a matter of fact. I've been very, very busy, and I should spend more time with him . . . but my intention is good, and I think that maybe in another four or five weeks' " (Green and Fuller, 1973b, p. 64).

Father has doubts about his own gender identity/role and is described as "soft" and "effeminate" (Rosen and Teague, 1974). He is seemingly indifferent to his son's cross-gender behavior, often rationalizing it as a phase. Perhaps a masculine son would threaten his own shaky masculinity. He may even covertly court his son as a substitute for what he finds lacking in his wife. In turn, the son may comply and actively solicit father's interest as a means of preventing him from leaving the dysfunctional family (Money, 1984a). For example, the step-father of a ten-year-old reports, " 'he comes straight out and says, 'Would you go to bed with me?" ' " (Green, 1974, p. 163).

His son's definite preference for mother and for feminine activities eventually alienates father. The boy senses this rejection and this moves him deeper into his feminine pattern, as a mother describes:

> "His father was more proud of the oldest boy and his interest in sports. He would stop and listen to him because they talked on the same level. His father would make comments like 'That's going to be my All American. This will be my drum majorette'. . . . I'll say, 'Go to your father now. . . . Talk about the game he is watching,' and because it's interrupting my husband's visual end of it, and he can't concentrate on the game, my son recognizes it, and he'll soon leave. . . . He'll come back to me" [Green, 1974, pp. 223–224].

The boy's view of father, manifest at about four years of age, is built on his mother's evaluations. Father is seen as a person who frustrates and angers mother, is worthless, and certainly not one to emulate (Stoller, 1979). When he is older he perceives his father as masculine, but thinks of him in negative terms, as "a lousy father," "a drunkard," and "spending little time with me" (Lebovitz, 1972).

Whether father is passive or aggressive, his son senses him as weak, seeing even aggressiveness as a sign of powerlessness. He turns to omnipotent mother, since his desire to be feminine is an expression of his wish to be powerful (Fischoff, 1964). Sometimes hatred for father gives rise to homicidal fantasies. Billy, age six, fantasized his father being run over by an auto, and asked his mother whether she thought he could trick his father into going into the furnace where he would be burned up (Bender and Pester, 1941).

Mother is not necessarily the dominant parent, but she is so in the eyes of her son: " 'My husband makes a lot of decisions, but they are not decisions the boy sees. I wouldn't say I run the whole show. I run the show that my boy sees' " (Green, 1987, pp. 180–181).

Mothers are described as feminine but boyish; for example,

hair short but stylish. According to Stoller (1969a), as children, they acted and dressed like boys, their friends were boys, and they played boys' games. While Green (1987) found no evidence of tomboyishness, he did confirm Stoller's contention of mothers' disinterest in dating and premarital sexual activity. As an adult she believes that females, including herself, are inferior and worthless, and is envious and angry toward men. She complains of a sense of emptiness and hopelessness and has a history of psychiatric problems (Friend, Schiddel, Klein, and Dunaeff, 1954; Rekers et al., 1983). Long periods of moderate to severe depression are common (Bradley, 1985; Stoller, 1985b).

Some mothers hope for a girl baby. When it is a boy, they attempt to feminize him. " 'I wanted a girl so bad that I prayed every night so hard for a girl. Even when he was a boy, everybody said he looked just like a girl. . . . I used to dress him like a little girl. I wanted a girl so bad' " (Green, 1987, p. 153).

Others have a desperate desire for a male child, feeling at some level that he will fill the emptiness in their lives. " 'It was great. It was just a fantastic experience. I wanted a boy. I think I would have killed myself if I hadn't had a boy. . . . I don't have any idea why. But it was just absolutely perfect for me. I wanted him to be little so he would stay little longer and be more babylike' " (Stoller, 1985b, p. 91).

Mother sees her baby boy as attractive, graceful, charming, delicate, and reports that often he is mistaken for a girl (Green and Money, 1961; Rosen et al., 1977; Stoller, 1985b). " 'He was a beautiful child. He had the body and the face—everything—of a little girl, very dainty' " (Green, 1974, p. 216); and, " 'up until the time when he was about three, people kept mistaking him for a girl, and I was kind of pleased by it' " (Green, 1987, p. 221).

Mother experiences "overflowing love and concern" for her son that is triggered by his beauty and responsivity to her. Other sons in the family are not as dear to her and develop masculinity. She uses the feminine boy to compensate for her sense of emptiness and her regret at not being male. She binds him to herself by fostering an intimate union, and treats him as if he is an extension of her own body. It is not the amount of time she spends with him that is crucial, but the quality of the contact, as one mother describes: " 'Very close, but I don't think excessive. . . . He loved to be cuddled. I loved to give him a bath. I loved to put oil on him. I used to massage him. I used to stretch his body out. I got pleasure from it' " (Green, 1987, p. 180).

Distortion of the child's gender identity is not due to this physical contact as such, but to mother's desire to deter his separation. She is solicitous and permissive to the extreme—no weaning, no toilet training, no frustration. The child is provided with a close to tensionless, uterine state that blurs the boundary between his body and her own (Greenson, 1966). While similar maternal closeness has been reported in homosexuals and transvestites, there are fewer conditions attached to mother's overprotectiveness in gender disturbed boys (Stoller, 1969a).

While mother may be either neutral or encouraging of her son's femininity, she does discourage any signs of masculinity. She fails to provide sufficient positive regard for him to feel self-worth. He reacts to any withdrawal or hostility on her part with a sense that there is something wrong with him, with his masculinity, and seeks ways to enhance his standing in mother's eyes. Cross-gender behavior provides him with a solution, and one that is not discouraged (Bradley, 1985).

When the boy is several years old, the relation is still one of intimate physical and psychological contact (Rosen et al., 1977). For instance, the boy uses "We" rather than "Mother and I" (Greenson, 1966). He clearly prefers mother to father (Green and Money, 1961), goes to her for sympathy, and is more likely to object to separation from her than from father (Rekers et al., 1983). Mother is his constant companion.

Sometime during his second year, the boy begins to manifest his feminine orientation. Often he does this on his own, without mother's active participation. Few parents see anything wrong with their sons' effeminate behavior (Rosen et al., 1977). A minority of mothers and even fewer fathers express strong negative reactions to the boys' femininity (Green and Money, 1961; Zuger, 1970). Possibly, as a reaction to the thought that he has failed his son, father denies there is a problem (Green, 1974). Mother may be amused and think it is cute, denying that these behaviors are feminine. For instance, she may rationalize his play with girls as a sign that he is a ladies' man. Or, she may disapprove, but ignore his behavior: " 'I used to get real disgusted with him the way he would act and everything, but all the time I'd just ignore it. I never thought there was anything really to worry about' " (Green, 1974, p. 213).

Father may not approve, but does not interfere. Reporting on her husband's reaction to their son wearing girl's clothes, a mother says: " 'he didn't like it at all, even the first few times that the boy would wear this dress. But he didn't do anything about it. He would blame me for it that I shouldn't allow him to wear the dress' " (Stoller, 1985b, p. 47). Another remarks, " 'I'm sure my husband has noticed it, but he has chosen to ignore it. I spoke to him several years ago about it, and he didn't react in any way except to say that he'll outgrow it; there's nothing wrong' " (Green, 1974, p. 215).

If there is a necessary condition for producing a feminine boy, it is the failure of parents to discourage cross-gender activities (Green, 1974). Often, subtle approval is given through equivocation. " 'One time he got my lipstick—and it was brand new lipstick; I hadn't even used it—and he tried to use it, and instead of rolling it back and putting the lid on it, he just shoved the lid on it, and it crushed on the top, and it really made me mad. I told him "I haven't even used it. Couldn't you use an old one?" ' " (Green, 1974, p. 157).

Frequently, it takes some outsider—friend or nursery school teacher—to convince parents that their child's behavior is deviant. This mother's son would dress in his sister's clothes. " 'Joan, my friend, kept suggesting that maybe he shouldn't do that when he was little. . . . Joan suggested that [it] was a little strange. It began to bother me' " (Stoller, 1985b, p. 80).

While the family relations just described are fairly well established, there are a few investigators who have been unable to find any consistent family pattern (Bakwin, 1960, 1968), or any peculiarities in families of feminine boys. Comparing families of feminine and nonfeminine boys, no differences were found in satisfaction with marital relationship, whether the child was desired, or parents wanted a boy or a girl, or affect expressed toward the child. There was a slight tendency for mothers of feminine boys to be the dominant parent (Zuger,

1970). Between feminine boys and ambulatory psychiatric boys, no differences were found in parental age, course of pregnancy, delivery, or birth weight (Zuger, 1974).

Peer Relations

The gender-disturbed child is deficient in interpersonal skills (Zucker, 1985). Accompanying his excessive dependency on mother is an unwillingness to make friends (Bakwin, 1968). He plays with fewer boys than do boys with other adjustment problems (Bates, Bentler, and Thompson, 1979), and abhors their rough and tumble activities. His early peer relations are with girls. " 'The boys at school and the boys after school have picked on him, and then he either plays by himself or with girls. And the kids in the neighborhood are rougher than he is and won't have anything to do with him' " (Green, 1974, pp. 263–264).

In free-play situations, three- and four-year-old moderately feminine boys (those who were drawing, playing kitchen, and who dress up) receive more negative and less positive feedback from peers than do straight children. These boys play alone three times as often as other children. While not considering cross-gender behavior "wrong," children do see it as "weird" and "strange," and most say they would punish such behavior, with older children being more negative than younger ones (Carter and McCloskey, 1984). Girls are given more leeway. Those engaging in cross-gender play are not given negative feedback by their peers (Fagot, 1977), and children report less negativity toward such behavior in girls than in boys (Carter and McCloskey, 1984).

Later, in school, the feminine boy does not relate to other boys and is teased by them: " 'And the kids at school pull him down and pull his shirt off to see if he's got 'chi-chis' or if he's built like a woman' " (Green, 1974, p. 166). Peer rejection results either in attempts to defeminize or in further alienation (Harry, 1982) that drives him away from the masculine and toward the feminine. As feminine affectation increases, so does social isolation and stigmatization. This isolation adds to his psychopathology (Rekers, 1977).

Some feminine boys are hostile and aggressive, and have

more behavior disturbances, such as defiance of authority, lying to mother, disobedience, and pouting than non-gender-disturbed boys (Bates et al., 1973, 1979; Bates, Skilbeck, Smith, and Bentler, 1975). One boy, considered a "sweet child" by his mother, when at school was cruel to other children and tried to harm them. He was later referred because he put on his mother's lingerie while masturbating (Waggoner and Boyd, 1941).

In 1938, MacDonald reported on criminally aggressive behavior in passive, effeminate boys who had been referred for a long history of attacks on other children, stoning, hitting with baseball bats, and sexual assaults on both boys and girls. They manifested this behavior only when with boys. In contrast, when in the presence of females, they assisted in housework, and with girls they dressed in girls' clothes, wore hair ribbons, and played with dolls. These boys had minimal relations with their fathers, who were inactive in rearing them. They were in the charge of women who were aggressive, dominant, rejecting, and despising of adult males. The boys were fearful of attacks from other boys. Perhaps their aggressiveness and fear of attack stemmed from a confusion of aggression with masculinity (Lim and Bottomley, 1983).

When they do play with other boys, they are bossy in an unpleasant and ineffective way and are resistant to other children's play suggestions: " 'My son wanted to play house and the other boy didn't want to play house, and my son got very obnoxious and almost forced him into playing house, and they finally did' " (Green, 1987, pp. 218–219).

Sissiness in third to sixth grade boys is related to a host of socially negative behaviors, such as getting angry, making fun of others, breaking rules, uncooperativeness, intolerance of others, and going along with others. These sissy boys lack traditional feminine qualities of nurturance and supportiveness (Hemmer and Kleiber, 1981). For some, this antisocial acting out behavior persists into adulthood. Personality test profiles of young adults who had been effeminate in childhood indicate social maladjustment and a disregard for social standards (Lebovitz, 1972).

Conflict Free or Disturbed

As a young child with limited social contacts, he may not show any maladjusted behavior other than his effeminacy. Later, however, when he comes into contact with his peers, he suffers from their rejection. To escape this rejection and ridicule, he withdraws from social contacts, and maintains his isolation and detachment (Rosen et al., 1977; Rekers et al., 1978). In addition to his reaction to interpersonal difficulties, he is especially sensitive to the feelings of others and is therefore more prone than other children to become disturbed by family tensions. Also, he tolerates anxiety poorly and becomes flooded with emotion easily, which, in turn, interferes with his cognitive functioning (Bradley, 1985). Little wonder, then, that he is a miserable child who suffers from anger, hostility, and depression.

An important theoretical question is whether his psychic disturbance results solely from his interpersonal difficulties or whether he suffers from conflict over his feminine identity. Stoller (1985b) proposes that, having never separated from mother, he adopts a feminine identity without conflict. Further, because the markedly feminine boy remains so closely tied to her and because father does not encourage separation, he does not experience the normal oedipal conflict and castration anxiety. Other theorists, however, find "significant intrapsychic turmoil" over his desire to become female (Pruett and Dahl, 1982; Meyer and Dupkin, 1985) and that his feminine behavior masks his core conflict, which is the desire for and the dread of re-merging into mother–child oneness (Loeb and Shane, 1982).

Outcome of Femininity

Over the years, there is a change in many feminine boys' behavior. Cross-gender activities are most pronounced in their early years up to about age seven. Thereafter, there is a lessening of feminine behavior (Bakwin, 1968).

This trend is similar to the defeminization of homosexuals over time, where the more blatant feminine behaviors drop out, while subtle traces remain. From a fifth to a third of homosexuals recall wanting to be a girl during childhood, but by adolescence, the prevalence reduced to around a tenth. Similarly, cross-dressing incidence went from about 40 to 15 percent (Harry, 1982).

Treatment of feminine boys from five to twelve years old is effective in reducing feminine behaviors and alleviating conflicts (Newman, 1976; Green, 1987). However, for those who do not respond or who do not defeminize, gender aberrations crystallize during puberty and from then on are resistant to intervention. In one follow-up study, a third displayed serious gender disturbances, with the earlier the onset, the more serious the adult disturbance (Lebovitz, 1972).

Since, in extreme cases, the boy wants to be a girl, an expected outcome of a feminine boyhood is adult transsexualism. This expectation is difficult to test. Because the prevalence of transsexualism is so very low, the probability of finding it in a follow-up study of feminine boys is slight (Weinrich, 1985). This is especially so since the number of cases in most follow-up studies is small.

Even for those who did receive therapy, the most probable outcome is homosexuality. In several studies, where feminine boys were reexamined in their early twenties, 60 to 70 percent were homosexual, 20 to 30 percent were heterosexual, and only a few were either transvestites or transsexuals (Zuger, 1966, 1978, 1984, 1988; Money and Russo, 1981; Green, 1985; Zucker, 1985; Davenport, 1986). Children used in follow-up studies have been treated for gender disorders and they may not be representative of those not seen; that is, their natural history has been disrupted and their parents may differ from those of nonreferred children with similar disturbances.

That the effeminate boy is at high risk for homosexuality is born out by retrospective studies. Forty-seven percent of exclusively homosexual men cross-dressed more than other boys they knew, while none of the heterosexuals reported this. Twenty-nine percent had been labeled "sissy," compared to 2 percent of exclusive heterosexuals. And, inbetween groups of nonexclusive homosexuals and heterosexuals report decreasing effeminate behaviors (Whitam, 1977). Twenty-seven percent of homosexual and only 3 percent of heterosexual males recalled a persistent desire to become females in their earlier years (Saghir and Robbins, 1973).

4 TRANSVESTISM

INTRODUCTION

Occasional cross-dressing in childhood is not uncommon and is not, by itself, considered deviant. Twenty-three percent of unmarried males reported cross-dressing less than once a month in childhood and adolescence, usually for school plays or on Halloween (Saghir and Robins, 1973).

Cross-dressing was common at some medieval carnivals and festivals (Henriques, 1960; Partridge, 1960). In ancient and medieval times only men acted in the theater, so dressing for female parts was necessary. Many plays in the current repertoire call for men to dress as women, such as *Some Like It Hot, Charlie's Aunt,* and *As You Like It.* The list of male actors who have occasionally cross-dressed in performance is extensive—from Fatty Arbuckle to Mickey Rooney. Some male performers, though not female impersonators, regularly cross-dress, for instance, Benny Hill, Flip Wilson, David Bowie, and Boy George.

Attitudes and Support Groups

Psychiatrists consider transvestites and transsexuals more as ill or disabled than as sexual criminals, while psychologists and social workers see them as peculiar and difficult to understand (Brierly, 1979).

Transvestites can find acceptance in several organizations. The Beaumont Society in Great Britain, founded about 1969, has some five hundred members. In Australia and New Zealand are the Seahorse Clubs (Brierly, 1979). Perhaps the oldest and best known is the Society for the Second Self (Tri-Ess), founded by Virginia (Charles) Prince. Tri-Ess publishes *Transvestia,* and serves as an information source. Those into bondage, discipline, rubber or leather fetish, and homosexuals and transsexuals are excluded from membership (Prince, 1981). Club members' ages range from twenty-one to seventy-one, with a mean of thirty-nine years (Buhrich and McConaghy, 1976).

Tri-Ess not only attempts to negate the image of the transvestite as a sick, perverted individual, but also promotes a positive self-image, providing members with a convenient rationalization.

> We are a few steps closer to the real human who hopefully will someday walk this earth—the person . . . who will have access to all their human potentials, to be used and enjoyed under appropriate circumstances; who, while acknowledging the possession of one or the other type of reproductive equipment, accepts that fact with detachment and doesn't build his/her whole self-structure around it [Prince, 1981, p. 51].

At local chapter meetings, men arrive in male appropriate garb and change at the host member's house, where they discuss issues related to their cross-dressing. There is no sexual activity. Transvestite conventions, such as "Be All You Can Be Weekend" and "Fantasia Fair," feature fashion shows, dinners, seminars on medical and legal matters, and consultations in makeup and dress.

Prevalence

Cross-dressers are rarely seen in the consulting room, not because the actual prevalence is low, but because therapists do not probe and because patients are ashamed to volunteer such information (Pomeroy, 1975). Estimates place the number of transvestites at about one million in the United States (Oppenheim and Robin, 1974) and 30,000 in the British Isles (Randell, 1975). Four percent of pornographic magazine covers depict transvestites or transsexuals (Dietz and Evans, 1982).

In a study of forty-seven societies, it was found that the more stress placed on gender distinctions, the lower the frequency of sanctioned cross-dressing for boys unable to meet the demands of the masculine role (Munroe, Whiting, and Hally, 1969).

Cross-Dressing in Women

Transvestism is comparatively rare in women; those who dress as males are frank homosexuals or transsexuals (Feinbloom, 1976). Estimates of the sex ratio vary from two to six females per one hundred males (Kinsey, Pomeroy, Martin, and Gebhard, 1953). This ratio is reversed in the U.S.S.R., where crossdressing is rare in men and found almost always in women. This is attributed to the inferior status of women and the elevated status of men (Stern, 1979).

In 1968, Stoller flatly maintained that there are no female transvestites. Those who do cross-dress, he said, were homosexual or transsexual. But by 1982, he had found three cases of female transvestism; that is, women who experience sexual excitement by wearing men's clothing. Like the female transsexual, they had been markedly masculine since childhood. They differ from female transsexuals in that they possess some feminine qualities and are not put off by frankly homosexual relations.

DEFINITION

Differing Conceptions

In 1838 Esquirol considered cross-dressing a manifestation of schizophrenia. Westphal, in 1876, described a young man who was arrested in feminine clothes and had frequently stolen clothing and other feminine articles. While not homosexual, Westphal described him as somewhat feminine in appearance. A few years later in 1881 there was published the case of a happily married man of high moral character who became sexually excited when wearing a corset and high-heeled boots (Ellis, 1928).

It was not until 1910 that Hirschfeld differentiated transvestism from other conditions, especially homosexuality, as "the impulse to appear in the outward trappings of the sex to which a person, according to the visible sexual organs, does not belong" (1938, p. 187). Other literal definitions are "the morbid impulse to dress in the clothing of the opposite sex" (Peabody, Rowe, and Wall, 1953, p. 399) and the "desire to look like the other sex by wearing the clothing of that sex" (Brown, 1960, p. 218). The problem with these literal definitions is that they do not clearly distinguish transvestism from the cross-dressing of transsexuals, effeminate homosexuals, and female impersonators.

Ellis (1928) labels the condition eonism, after the Chevalier D'Eon, a noted cross-dresser of the 1700s (Nixon, 1964). The eonist is a person who is so attracted to and admiring of women that he wishes to be one of them, not simply in garb, but also in interests and attitudes. However, he does not care to emulate women in their sexual partner choice, and remains asexual or heterosexual. Similarly, Prince (1981) introduced the term *femmiphile*, lover of the feminine.

More recent conceptions attempt to describe the purpose of cross-dressing. Stoller (1968) defines transvestism as pleasurable cross-dressing by a man who has a firm male core gender identity. One source of his pleasure is his knowledge that he possesses a penis.

Sexual arousal is central to several definitions (Benjamin, 1954). According to DSM-III-R criteria, transvestism is diagnosed when there are "recurrent, intense sexual urges and sexually arousing fantasies . . . involving cross-dressing," notably in heterosexual males (American Psychiatric Association, 1987, p. 288). Excluded from the diagnosis are those who cross-dress to relieve gender discomfort with no sexual arousal, and homosexuals and transsexuals who cross-dress.

It is questionable whether transvestism should be limited to sexual stimulation. There is a large group for whom cross-dressing does not have sexual meaning, but who find pleasure in the "gender switch" or in the easing of the tension of their gender discomfort (Person and Ovesey, 1978; Prince, 1981).

A definition of transvestites that combines both of these components is, "subjects who gain emotional relief by cross-dressing and show or have shown fetishistic arousal to cross-dressing" (Buhrich and McConaghy, 1979, p. 152).

Homosexual Cross-Dressers

Before continuing the discussion of transvestites proper, we will describe the cross-dressing of homosexual drag queens and female impersonators, who do not qualify for a diagnosis of transvestism.

In homosexual drag the person cross-dresses to mimic females. He is not sexually aroused by the clothing. It is a mockery and parody of the female rather than an attempt to duplicate her. The costume is often quickly improvised. It is used for satire to imitate the petty faults of females; it is meant to be silly and is acted out outrageously. Those imitated are usually already caricatures of femininity such as Marilyn Monroe, Mae West, Marlene Dietrich, and Carmen Miranda (Baker, 1968).

If the masquerade is too good, the homosexual will be repelled, since the male appears too much like a sexy female. A homosexual's description of his reaction to one man in drag illustrates this.

> Another one, very slim, put on a pair of falsies, a turban hat to hide short hair, and a dress with a wide flair skirt. Other than hair on the chest which showed, the effect of femininity was so convincing (even his heels) that I promptly lost interest. Actually produced a beautiful effect—the kind of woman I would like if I could [Lenznoff and Westley, 1956, p. 259].

Sometimes cross-dressing is used to attract other males. About 5 percent of homosexuals are extremely effeminate in manner and style of dress. Their feminine dress is a form of narcissistic adornment and is used as a means of sexual enticement. Except when costumed for a beauty contest or drag ball, their sex is obvious to the knowledgeable viewer (Feinbloom, 1976).

Some male prostitutes dress as women. They are more outlandish than their female counterparts—clothes are tighter and skirts shorter, and they are more forceful and aggressive in solicitation. Many have breasts augmented by hormones or implants. Most (83%) are black males, as compared to about 50 percent black females. Understandably, many of their clients who are seeking females become hostile when their partner's true sex is discovered (Cohen, 1980).

Female impersonators earn their living by masquerading as females in theaters and night clubs. They are both "performing homosexuals and homosexual performers." To homosexuals who consider themselves no different from heterosexuals except for sexual partner choice, the female impersonator represents the stigma of the gay world, conforming to the stereotype of the homosexual as effeminate, as a man who acts like a woman.

There are important differences between the transvestite and the female impersonator. The transvestite dresses for himself or for his sexual partner, whereas the impersonator demands an audience. The transvestite prizes feminine underclothing, often wearing these items under his male outer clothing. The impersonator, while donning the outer clothing and makeup of the female, wears men's shorts and T-shirts underneath (Newton, 1972).

Most transvestites are overtly heterosexual. However, some theorists, delving into the unconscious, find evidence of latent homosexuality (Gutheil, 1930). The homosexual identifies with his mother. The fetishist denies she lacks a penis. The transvestite combines the two in his identification with the phallic mother (Fenichel, 1930). Homosexuals and transvestites differ in their relation to males and females. Homosexuals eliminate women from their lives, while transvestites eliminate men (Ovesey and Person, 1976).

Some homosexuals do wear articles of other men's clothing for sexual arousal, such as athletic supporters (Freud, 1927; Gillespie, 1940; Bak, 1953). This homovestism does not represent mother's penis, rather it symbolizes father's penis (Zavitzianos, 1977).

Types of Transvestites

Hirschfeld identified four types on the basis of sexual partner choice. From the data he collected in one of the first surveys of sexual behavior, he estimated that a third of those who cross-dress are heterosexual, a third homosexual, and about a tenth bisexual. The rest were either asexual or automonosexual meaning narcissists who engage in masturbation as their sole sexual outlet. Since transsexualism was not identified until the early 1940s, years after Hirschfeld's studies, some unknown percentage of his sample would now be called transsexual.

Ellis (1928) defined two main types, with transitional stages between them. In the first type, effeminization is confined to female clothing and articles of adornment and the sexual partner is female. In the second, less common type, the desire to be female is more pervasive and extends to a desire to assume the psychological and physical attributes of the female. Today, this second type would be called transgenderist or transsexual.

Transvestites differ in the degree they desire to assume the feminine role. The true or nuclear transvestite is satisfied with wearing feminine attire. He has no desire to alter his bodily appearance and may be content to wear a single or a few feminine garments throughout his life. Transgenderists or marginal transvestites assume more of the feminine role and physical appearance than simply by dressing in women's clothes. These transgenderists, compared to true transvestites, have more fantasies of being women, began full cross-dressing earlier in life, more have cross-dressed in public, their feminine gender identity is more intense, and heterosexual interest is weaker.

Relation to Fetishism and Transsexualism

Transvestism is on a spectrum from clothes fetishism to transsexuality, bridging the gap between the two (Person and Ovesey, 1978; Brown, 1983). It has been called an amalgam of just about everything—homosexuality, castration anxiety, sadomasochism, narcissism, scoptophilia, exhibitionism, and fetishism (Gutheil, 1954).

Fetishism

The clothes fetishist achieves sexual arousal by seeing, touching, and sometimes by putting on articles of feminine attire. The question of whether the clothes fetishist evolves into the transvestite or whether all transvestites begin as clothes fetishists is unresolved (Benjamin, 1954; Grant, 1960; Taylor and McLachlan, 1962; Friedemann, 1966). While fetishism and transvestism may be closely allied in their origins (Peabody, Rowe, and Wall, 1953), the two may still be independent of one another (Brierly, 1979).

Unlike most clothes fetishists, the transvestite wants new clothes that appeal to him and are felt to be consonant with at least part of his character (Hirschfeld, 1938). While desire for new clothes is true of the adult transvestite, it is not true of the beginner, who usually borrows clothes belonging to his mother or sister. Using a relative's clothes could be a matter of convenience, since the youngster is ashamed to buy women's clothes. But, it has been suggested that there is an olfactory factor involved—he wants clothes that have been worn because they have retained the odor of the wearer (Fenichel, 1930). It may happen that when transvestite urges are suppressed, nasal congestion occurs, which serves as a deodorant against this olfactory factor in transvestism (Wilson, 1948).

Transsexualism

The transsexual wishes to assume the entire role of the female with clothes being only one aspect of that role, whereas for the transvestite, cross-dressing is a hobby to be indulged in for a couple of evenings a week (Feinbloom, 1976).

While some investigators see no sharp distinction between transvestism and transsexuality other than degree of femininity (Benjamin, 1954; Lukianowicz, 1959), others consider them to be completely separate (Baker, 1968; Hoenig, Kenna, and Youd, 1970; Stoller, 1971; Buhrich and McConaghy, 1977a). They argue that the transsexual desires to be and believes he is a female and that his cross-dressing is not sexually arousing. He wants to be rid of his penis. The transvestite does not want to be a female and his cross-dressing is arousing. He prizes his penis. However, some transvestites are not disinterested in sex change: 20 percent have looked into it, but rejected the idea, and 25 percent are or have been on female hormones. This contrasts with 96 percent of male homosexuals who were not at all interested in sex change (Bullough, Bullough, and Smith, 1983).

Transsexuals, compared to transvestites, are more intense in their feminine gender identity/role, more interested in a male than a female sexual partner. They also have a lower incidence of sexual arousal with clothes, fewer sadomasochistic fantasies, and are more likely to dress permanently as women. Since the two groups do not differ in age, it is concluded they are "separate clinical entities" (Buhrich and McConaghy, 1977b). However, another group of investigators found "few clinical differences in personality" between transvestites and transsexuals (Steiner, Sanders, and Langevin, 1985).

Evaluation of the Literature

Some of the information about transvestism comes from psychotherapists' reports. Such studies are based on a very select group of transvestites. A survey of over five hundred transvestites revealed that only a third had ever visited a therapist, and of these, only a third went more than once. So, less than 10 percent ever had a chance of being represented in the clinical literature (Prince and Bentler, 1972).

Fortunately, there are other sources of information. The existence of support groups and publications produced by transvestites allows researchers to sample from nonpatient groups. Of course, there is still some selectivity, since only those who have "come out" are affiliated with such organizations. Characteristics of nonpatient transvestites have been obtained through social networking (Talamini, 1982) and by direct observation of club meetings (Feinbloom, 1976).

THE ACT

Precipitating Events

The impetus to cross-dress may come from anxiety and depression concerning demands to be assertive that are felt to test the individual's masculinity (Ovesey and Person, 1976). Thus a twenty-one-year-old had the urge to cross-dress when he experienced tension from examinations and athletic events (Lewis, 1963). Frustration of dependency needs, such as separation from a needed person, may precipitate the urge (Berman, 1953; Segal, 1965; Ovesey and Person, 1976). If this anxiety is chronic, women's undergarments may be worn daily (Ovesey and Person, 1973), which is a rather common practice (Buhrich and Beaumont, 1981). Other precipitators are conflict, boredom, and desire for sexual arousal (Croughan, Saghir, Cohen, and Robins, 1981). Sometimes the urge arises simply from seeing feminine clothing or a well-dressed woman: "When I see a beautifully dressed woman, I try to imagine myself in her position" (Buhrich, 1978, p. 148).

Dressing-Up

The transvestite may begin his career with a single item of clothing, heels for example, curious to find out what it feels like to put them on. But the visual effect is marred by his bare and hairy legs, so he shaves and puts on hose. To hold up the hose, he needs a garter belt, all of which is appealing, with the exception of his chest, so he needs a bra, and so on. The effect of the shoe has radiated to other articles of feminine clothing (Kane, 1975). About 90 percent of adult transvestites at first cross-dressed only partially (Buhrich and Beaumont, 1981; Docter, 1988).

This radiation is described by a transvestite who, at about twelve years, rubbed his mother's underclothing on his penis. He put them on. Then,

> I began to want just more than women's panties. I started putting more and more articles on every time I masturbated. I would put everything on—that is the underclothes, the dress, the shoes, and would also put lipstick on, a bandanna over my head so you couldn't see that I had

short hair. In other words I looked exactly like a woman. I would stand
in front of the mirror and look at myself. I would say that I wouldn't
make such a bad looking woman [Peabody et al., 1953, p. 345].

The transvestite usually has a complete wardrobe and supply of accessories: underwear, dresses, skirts, cosmetics, wigs,
and jewelry (Brown, 1960). Obviously, the type of clothing preferred depends, in part, on the particular societal norms of
feminine dress. While Americans might consider the Scottish
kilt a bit feminine, one Highlander transvestite dislikes wearing
them, much preferring a skirt (Brierly, 1979). Often the clothes
are out of date, reminiscent of those that mother wore during
the transvestite's early childhood (Ovesey and Person, 1976).

Subscribers to a transvestite magazine give their preferences for female garments while engaging in coitus. These are
listed in Table 4.1. Other than during sexual intercourse, 85
percent prefer to dress completely (Prince and Bentler, 1972).

Anywhere from a fourth to two-thirds dress partially or
totally en femme at least once a week (Buhrich and Beaumont,
1981; Croughan, Sagher, Cohen, and Robins, 1981). A large
majority take one hour or more to dress, and the entire cross-
dressed session lasts an average of five hours (Docter, 1988).
Most have photos of themselves cross-dressed, sometimes more
than fifty (Buhrich, 1978). Because they are so concerned about
how they look, spend so much time in dressing up and in admiring the results, transvestites have been called narcissistic
(Fenichel, 1930; Edelstein, 1960). Some indeed may be narcis-

TABLE 4.1
Garments Worn by Transvestites During Coitus

Garments	Percent (N = 504)
Nightgown	27
Panties	20
Padded Bra	18
Hose	17
High Heels	11
Full Costume	20

Source: V. Prince & P. M. Bentler (1972), Survey of 504 cases of transvestism. *Psychological Reports*, 31:903–917.

sistic, but these behaviors are true of almost everyone who costumes themselves.

Learning to dress up properly, especially the use of makeup, is difficult to master alone. Some men are fortunate to have wives or female friends who will teach them. Others can resort to transvestite fashion houses: "We can make you the lady you want to be—makeup lessons by appointment."

The essence of transvestism is not the wearing of women's clothes as such, but what they signify; that is, the wearer's own conception of what it means to be feminine. It can signify identification with women, because they are considered superior to men; humiliation, since women are conceived as inferior beings; and/or narcissistic admiration of the feminine side of one's self (Steiner, Sanders, and Langevin, 1985).

It is not only what women wear, but what they do, what interests them, and how they feel that is important (Fairchild, 1975). The transvestite strives to become the kind of woman that his masculine self finds most attractive (Brown, 1960). He is perceptive in that he sees in clothes something consonant with his own feminine aspect. He is sensitive in that his clothes have an impact on him, they make him feel a host of emotions—"panicky, exciting, thrilling, threatening, marvelous, uplifting, dangerous, fearful." He has discovered the "girl within" (Prince, 1981, p. 17).

Two Components of Cross-Dressing

There are two components in transvestism—fetishistic and nonfetishistic. The fetishistic component gives rise to sexual arousal. It may be a transitional stage to the second, nonfetishistic component (Ellis, 1928; Benjamin, 1966). The second component provides relief from gender tension and a sense of being at ease (Ovesey and Person, 1973; Pomeroy, 1975). Even though there is a moderate negative correlation between these two components (Blanchard and Clemmensen, 1988), they may be present in the same person (Segal, 1965). If anxiety and tension are inimical to sexual arousal, then the feeling of being at ease allows the transvestite to become sexually potent (Oppenheim and Robin, 1974). Also, the release of sexual excitement, achieved by wearing women's clothes, can produce relaxation and tension reduction.

The relative importance of these two components often changes over time as the individual practices his habit (Docter, 1988). If, at first, there was little sexual arousal, women's clothes and the act of dressing probably becomes eroticized at puberty (Buhrich and McConaghy, 1976; Ovesey and Person, 1976). If, in the beginning, there were erotic feelings and a sense of adventure, the novelty often wears off and eroticism wanes. Other rewarding experiences take their place.

When cross-dressing is a sexually exciting experience, it gives rise to the urge to masturbate. It may even be necessary for sexual potency. Transvestites report a decrease in this sexual arousal from the late teens to early thirties (Buhrich and McConaghy, 1976). Forty-two percent of a group of transvestites, mean age thirty-nine, recalled such arousal during adolescence, but only 12 percent reported current arousal, and 41 percent reported a decrease in arousal (Buhrich and Beaumont, 1981).

One man, after dressing in women's clothes with a silk garment touching his inner thighs, would straddle a chair and by friction induce orgasm. At first, this practice was used for sex alone. However, he discovered that this act also lessened anxiety over school examinations and then anxiety from a wide variety of sources (Cooper, 1963).

The feeling of being at ease, a relief from tension, and being able to relax while en femme was reported by over half of transvestites (Buhrich, 1978). Such feelings increase with continued use of women's clothes. For some gender disordered adolescent boys, cross-dressing allayed separation anxiety resulting from loss or changes in relationships (Lothstein, 1980b). Almost half report currently feeling less masculine demands and less competitive when cross-dressed, but only a few report these feelings during their adolescence. Other shifts in feelings are mentioned. One is an increase in feeling sensual, elegant, beautiful ("I feel soft and silky all over") from 18 percent in adolescence to 48 percent in adulthood. There is also a lessening of guilt and anxiety that accompanied dressing up in adolescence (Buhrich, 1978).

A transvestite describes his feeling of being at ease: "I feel much gender comfort when I cross dress. I feel at ease—very passive and warm. Actually, I'm a very aggressive person when acting out my male role. When I dress as a woman I feel this offsets the other side of my personality" (Talamini, 1982, p. 23).

Men who experience this comfortable feeling may be those who overly strive to live up to their masculine ideal, but who cannot attain this goal without undue tension. They find release from the tensions of being a man and dealing with masculine responsibilities, and living up to the masculine stereotype (Kane, 1975). Cross-dressing is extremely popular with politicians who visit prostitutes (Janus, Bess, and Saltus, 1977). For such men, leaving masculinity by cross-dressing enables them to experience femininity as they define it: "passive, accepting, non-demanding" and to accept the feminine within along with the masculine and thereby attain wholeness and inner understanding (Prince, 1981).

A deeper root of this feeling of comfort may be that cross-dressing symbolically represents reestablishing the symbiotic mother–son fusion along with passive wishes toward father. This reunion eases feelings of loneliness, emptiness, and tension (Segal, 1965). The basic conflict is the desire for fusion with mother versus the wish to be independent and masculine. Cross-dressing is a compromise solution since at once one is a male and is also mother.

Mirror Ritual and Altered Awareness

The transvestite does not wish to be a female, rather he wants to be seen as a woman by himself and possibly others. This often leads to what is called the mirror complex (Gutheil, 1954); that is, being aroused by viewing his mirror image (Buhrich and Beaumont, 1981). He experiences a fusion of himself as a man with the woman in the mirror. Thus he achieves his desire to merge with a woman without giving up his masculinity—a "blissful union" with a woman who cannot reject him (Friedmann, 1966). He admires both his penis and his image as a beautiful woman (Fenichel, 1930).

A twelve-year-old painted his lips with red ink. " 'Then without any premeditation, I put on some of my mother's clothes and glanced at myself in the mirror. I looked like a girl . . . I had an erection and began to masturbate' " (Lukianowicz, 1962, p. 666).

Some transvestites imagine having sexual intercourse with the female in the mirror: "I dress up as Sharon and by looking in the mirror, imagine I am having sexual intercourse with her . . . I like to screw the girl in the mirror" (Buhrich and McConaghy, 1977a, p. 407).

Others do not use mirrors, but fantasize themselves a woman being aroused by a man. "I don't look at myself when I masturbate. I put my hands under the dress, which of course covers the penis. Sometimes on such occasions I feel as if I am taking the part of the woman—making myself believe that someone is putting his penis into me" (Karpman, 1947, p. 308).

The transvestite may enter a trancelike, dissociated state of a dual sex nature during masturbatory fantasy. The following occurs to a single, forty-three-year-old when dressed for his daily ritual:

> I see myself dressed up as a woman, and I feel as if I was a woman. And then I see "him" stepping out of the mirror, with his penis stiff and erect, trying to embrace me. . . . It is a sort of a sweet intoxication, a sort of half-dream, during which I do everything almost unconsciously. . . . Somewhere at the back of my mind there is a vague notion that I then masturbate, but at the same time I see him bending over me and pushing his big stiff penis into my body, as if I were a real woman [Lukianowicz, 1960b, p. 437].

During intercourse, it is not uncommon for the transvestite to imagine that his penis and his partner's vagina merge, so that there is an exchange of penis and vagina, that is, his partner puts her penis in his vagina (Oppenheim and Robin, 1974).

Asphyxia is sometimes used to induce blurring of consciousness. A thirty-nine-year-old was found hanged in the closet of a cheap hotel room. In a note he describes his anticipation of coming events. He first details his cross-dressing and other preparations for his own hanging. Then:

> Quivering with excitement, I just stand and swish the lovely skirts about

my legs. I know what I'm doing next, I'm really terrified by sadistic thrill. It is 9:35 Sunday night and in three minutes I will be dead. I strike the match, reach down and set fire to the gossamer edge of the black nylon slip. Quickly I wrap the chain around my wrists and snap the padlock firmly. In a frenzy of passion, I kick the chair over and my body is spasming at the end of the chain noose. I come wildly, madly. The pain is intense as my clothes start burning my legs. My eyes bulge and I try to reach the keys, knowing I have finally found the courage to end a horrible nightmare life dangerously [Litman and Swearingen, 1972, p. 81].

A young man combined symbolic strangulation and incest. Dressed in his mother's clothes, he would tie a string around his penis. This string passed through a ring in the ceiling and he would rhythmically pull at it to gain erection. While masturbating, he fantasized having sexual relations with the Holy Virgin, uttering "Mary, Mary" (symbolic incest) (Lukianowicz, 1965).

Passing

Of interest is the audience for whom the transvestite dresses. There are those who dress for themselves only, as Hirschfeld's automonosexuals. Others, who perhaps have overcome their guilt and shame, wish to pass as women in public. From a third to two-thirds of transvestites report having been dressed-up in public (Prince and Bentler, 1972; Buhrich and Beaumont, 1981). Here there may be an element of exhibitionism, to fool people, to be admired as a woman. A rare case of a transvestite exhibitionist is a married forty-five-year-old who becomes sexually aroused when exposing himself to males when cross-dressed (Rosen and Kople, 1977). Some have no interest in the admiration of other men, but want to be accepted as a woman by women. Still others may go public as an act of defiance against what they consider to be absurd gender stereotypes (Ackroyd, 1979). Also, the risk involved may be enjoyable (Ovesey and Person, 1976). Perhaps, in an odd sort of way, the courage to go public validates their masculinity.

Since the goal of many is to feel feminine in all respects, it is to be expected that they would find it exciting, even exhilarating, to be taken for a female without being "read," that is, identified as a male dressed as a female (Fairchild, 1975). If done successfully, it is proof of the genuineness of the feminine side and of the man's ability to present this side (Beigel, 1969). This desire to pass is akin to an actor's wish to be completely accepted in the role.

Adverse Consequences

Transvestism is not without negative consequences. Ninety-five percent of one sample had either been arrested for cross-dressing or experienced interference with occupation and social relations as a result of it (Croughan et al., 1981). However, only one-half of another group of transvestites report that their cross-dressing has had harmful effects on themselves or others (Docter, 1988). The heavy impact of cross-dressing on marriage is considered later.

Transvestite Literature

Two themes are prominent in transvestite literature (Beigel and Feldman, 1963; Stoller, 1970, 1975; Buhrich and McConaghy, 1976): coercion and persuasion. One features a frightened young man who never wanted to wear feminine clothing, trapped by powerful women. These women, dressed in black undergarments and spiked-heel boots, are usually buxom and womanly.

They force him into women's clothes. When dressed up, he makes a fine, even beautiful girl, but underneath it all he is still a man. After his initial humiliation and in spite of their warnings, the sign of his sexual arousal becomes visible.

The women are harsh in their training in feminine ways. Soon he feels his masculinity waning, his submission increasing. From then on, he lives as a female slave.

The coercion in these stories helps relieve the reader from guilt over his own cross-dressing, since the character struggles against being feminized. The force used symbolizes for him not external coercion, but his own urgent, irresistible desire to cross-dress.

In the other theme the male dresses as a female out of

curiosity or as a disguise. He may be persuaded to cross-dress by a woman, but never forced. This kind, understanding woman helps him perfect his dressing, makeup, and feminine mannerisms.

By and large, these two themes are found in different publications and appeal to different audiences. The dominated transvestite stories are found in adult bookstores with titles such as *Stud Sissy* and *Cross Dressed Submissive*. Such stories have little appeal for a large segment of transvestites. In a survey of *Transvestia* readers, only 40 percent approved of stories with masochistic elements, while 90 percent approved of stories without such themes (Prince, 1981). Of these same readers, only 5 percent enjoyed being dominated by a female (Prince and Bentler, 1972). Perhaps this sample represents those who have accepted their cross-dressing without guilt, and do not need the rationalization of being forced.

The idyllic theme appears primarily in magazines published by transvestite clubs and have such titles as *From Martin to Marion* and *Jennifer: Women by Choice*. Perhaps those who prefer the stories with the humiliated hero are those who were treated cruelly in childhood (Stoller, 1970) and who are still sexually aroused by their cross-dressing. The idyllic stories appeal to those who currently use cross-dressing to ease gender tensions and whose mothers were warm, seductive, and supportive of their feminine ways.

In addition to these two themes, other elements are found in these stories. Incest is often present, with sister originally dressing him as a girl or engaging in sexual play with him during adolescence. Also, scenes with female homosexual activity are common (Ovesey and Person, 1976). Readers of this material want to be loved as women by women; they want to be the woman's little girl (Fenichel, 1930).

THE PERSON

Current Status

Marital Status and Wives

Often the transvestite marries with the fallacious expectation that this will cure him of his affliction and will shore up his fragile sense of masculinity (Lukianowicz, 1959; Bentler, 1976). From two-thirds to four-fifths of transvestites are or have been married (Buchner, 1970; Prince and Bentler, 1972; Buhrich, 1978; Buhrich and Beaumont, 1981; Crougham et al., 1981; Talamini, 1982; Docter, 1988). Of those who were married, two-thirds have children (Buchner, 1970).

Despite a report of good marital adjustment (Fookes, 1969), the husband's cross-dressing often puts a strain on the relationship. Over a third of those who were divorced placed the blame on their cross-dressing (Prince and Bentler, 1972). Most (60–70%) do not tell their wives of their habit prior to marriage (Talamini, 1982; Docter, 1988) and a fourth of their wives are unaware that they cross-dress (Prince and Bentler, 1972). Reasons husbands give for not informing their wives are that they were too embarrassed and they thought that marriage would cure them. One half of the wives found out by chance, and of these, a majority (60%) were accepting of their husband's peculiarity. There appears to be no effect on the offspring as none cross-dressed and the male children engaged in rough-and-tumble play (Talamini, 1982).

Occupation and Interests

Apart from their dress-up sessions, transvestites appear more masculine than feminine. They are overly aggressive, competitive, and have hypermasculine jobs and hobbies. Compared to general population figures, transvestites are overrepresented in high-prestige occupations such as employer, manager, scientist, engineer, and professional, and are virtually absent in personal service jobs (Brierly, 1979; Bullough et al., 1983; Docter, 1988). Because of their difficulty in relating to other males and their engaging in power struggles with them, many seek self-employment (Ovesey and Person, 1976; Person and Ovesey, 1978).

Their favorite hobby is sports (Talamini, 1982). They also express interest in mechanics and photography, and quite a few pursue such sports as skydiving, scuba diving, and sports car racing (Feinbloom, 1976).

Politically, they tend to be conservative and somewhat racially prejudiced (Feinbloom, 1976). In all, they attempt to project an image of "responsible male citizens" and wear "breastplates of righteousness."

Personality

On personality tests, transvestites do not show psychotic trends (Bentler and Prince, 1970), but do have higher neurotic and introversion scores than others (Gosselin and Eysenck, 1980; Gosselin and Wilson, 1980). One study does report test profiles indicating passive–aggressive personality with paranoid features (Beatrice, 1985).

There is some evidence that they are intellectually competent and even superior (Fookes, 1969; Bentler, Sherman, and Prince, 1970). However, they may not be able to take full advantage of their intellectual abilities because of a certain amount of irrationality, constricted and rigid perceptions, and preoccupation with body features (Bentler et al., 1970). Compared to other males, they have adequate impulse control, a tendency to withdraw from social involvement, a dislike of being the center of attention, and are less approval seeking (Bentler and Prince, 1969).

Biological Basis

Early writers proposed vague constitutional bases for transvestism, most often some "special bisexual disposition" (Ellis, 1928; Fenichel, 1930; Benjamin, 1954; Gutheil, 1954). It has also been claimed that tranvestites lack virility and robustness (Ellis, 1928; de River, 1958). There is no evidence to support these assertions.

Only a few cases have been reported where there are indications of temporal lobe involvement. A thirty-six-year-old had cross-dressed for three years. His urge to do so was preceded by an epileptic aura of epigastric pain and tension in his jaws. With female underwear on, he felt completely calm, but then revulsion set in. Heterosexual desires began to diminish. Evidence pointed to calcified cysts in his right temporal lobe (Davies and Morgenstern, 1960). In another case, both epileptic attacks and cross-dressing ceased after temporal lobe surgery (Hunter, Logue, and McMenemy, 1963).

In one case transvestism was linked with manic–depressive psychosis. A twenty-four-year-old male experienced wide mood swings for over four years and had been practicing sexually arousing cross-dressing for two years. Lithium carbonate led to remission not only of his psychotic symptoms, but also of his transvestism (Ward, 1975).

A few cases of familial transvestism have been reported. In one father–son case, the boy did not know of his father's cross-dressing until he admitted his own habit (Buhrich, 1977). In another, two brothers both stole women's underwear and the father was a pedophile (Liakos, 1967).

Some slight evidence has been offered of a possible heredity factor. Identical and fraternal twins' responses to the fantasy item "Wearing clothes of the opposite sex" were compared. There was a stronger association for identicals than for fraternals (Gosselin and Wilson, 1980).

Early Life

Mother

More transvestites' mothers were housewives than were the mothers of transsexuals and homosexuals (Bullough et al., 1983). About half were the dominant parent (Prince, 1981).

Two types of mothers have been identified. The symbiote (Stoller, 1967) is warm and supportive; her son becomes a non-masochistic transvestite. Seductively, she turns for gratification from her distant and threatening husband to her son. She either approves of or does not object to her son's cross-dressing. The boy interprets her approval as her wish to disguise him as a girl in order to placate his theatening father. Feminine clothes protect him by serving as a transitional object symbolizing mother and thus perpetuate his dependency on her. Also, by covering up his masculinity he takes a submissive stance to his father and other male competitors, thus disarming these rivals (Ovesey and Person, 1973, 1976).

The symbiotic-hostile mother is angry, destructive, and domineering. She rears the masochistic transvestite. She both demasculinizes and erotically arouses her son, so that he remains dependent on this phallic woman with whom he identifies. She was close to and protective of her son in his early years, but with subtle hostility directed toward his masculinity. Her encouragement of his cross-dressing varies from subtle to punitively dressing him as a girl. Father is passive, distant, and emotionally uninvolved. In addition to threats from competitive males, the boy is also threatened by his dominating mother. He hopes that by dressing like a girl, he becomes a girl, and consequently mother's hostility will decrease and acceptance increase (Spensley and Barter, 1971; Ovesey and Person, 1973, 1976). Mother's seductiveness and her hostility toward her son's masculinity is evident in a man's recollection that when he was a boy his mother would dress him as a girl, put her hand under his skirt and tell him that he was not a boy, but rather a girl, that boys are bad (Oppenheim and Robin, 1974).

Stoller (1968, 1980) emphasizes mother's punitive dressing of her son as a girl. Because of her strong envy of men, she humiliates her little boy by dressing him occasionally as a little girl. In response to this treatment, he creates his transvestite fantasy in which he triumphs over his humiliating mother. Initially, he feels no sexual arousal. When, as an adult, he cross-dresses, it is as if he were saying to her, "You thought you were punishing me by threatening my masculinity. See what you have accomplished? Look at my erect penis. I have turned your punishment into my pleasure."

While it is reported, especially by Stoller that, as a child, the transvestite was cross-dressed by a woman, very few report being treated as a girl when they were children (Beigel and Feldman, 1963; Talamini, 1982). And, only 4 percent report punishment by being dressed as a girl, being brought up in a feminine way, or having a mother who wanted a girl (Prince, 1981). When punitive cross-dressing does occur, it may be that both mother and son conspire to bring on such punishment (Oppenheim and Robin, 1974).

Sister

While mother is the usual model for her son's femininity, not uncommonly it is his sister who serves this role. Sister may initiate the boy into cross-dressing. A twenty-one-year-old, when a boy, was dressed like a doll by his sister. They engaged in sex play, but when his penis became erect, she would playfully hit him saying, "You're a girl." It was at this time that he began tucking his penis between his legs and thinking of himself as a girl. Later, standing in front of a mirror, he would put on his sister's clothes, place a tight belt around his waist, tuck his penis away, and masturbate. Both sister and mother collaborated to feminize this boy. He recalls the tingle in his penis when, dressed in sister's clothes, they both looked fondly at him (Lewis, 1963). Other cases of sisters being involved in their brothers' cross-dressing are reported by Fenichel (1930), Karpman (1947), and Lukianowicz (1960a).

Many report envying their sister because parents treated her tenderly and did not expect as much from her as from them (Oppenheim and Robin, 1974). In their early years they are typically not only dressed and undressed by mother, but also allowed to be with her when she dressed. Later, perhaps when the child's curiosity about sex was aroused, he is banned from mother's dressing room. The dependent child experiences this as a loss of love and substitutes for it by touching and fondling mother's underwear. The presence of a sister who is allowed to continue being with mother at these times leads him to believe that he could continue being close to mother if he were a girl (Beigel and Feldman, 1963).

The budding transvestite starts from gender envy, not sex envy (Prince, 1981). Preference for daughter over son was seen in a group of adolescent transvestites. The boys' sisters were admired and preferred by mothers who were warm and giving to their daughters, but not to their sons (Spensley and Barter, 1971). For instance, Frank, age six, was masculine in appearance and dress. Father was abusive and seldom home. When he was two, his sister was born. Grandmother gave all her affection to the baby, and none to Frank. He became incorrigible and aggressive, started dressing as a girl, shunned boys, and played solely with girls (Bender and Pester, 1941).

Father

More so than others, parents of transvestites reverse conventional gender roles, with mother being more dominant, independent, and aggressive than father (Taylor and McLachlan, 1964; Newcomb, 1985). A crucial element is a psychologically absent father who does not interrupt mother's feminization of their son. If present, father is passive and detached (Stoller, 1968) or is verbally or physically abusive (Ovesey and Person, 1976). Having little positive interaction with his son, he is less significant to him than is mother. While father and son may do things together, they never really know one another (Fairchild, 1975). But, almost three-fourths of transvestite magazine readers report that father had provided them with a good masculine image (Prince and Bentler, 1972).

In some cases, father serves as a model for the boy's cross-dressing. One father began cross-dressing when he was sixteen years old. His continued cross-dressing was maintained by threats to his masculinity, such as a boss critical of him, fights with his wife, and sexual impotence. Three of his sons, who had seen him dressed as a woman, modeled themselves after him in job choice, mannerisms, and cross-dressing, which they did when stressed, especially by their dominant mother (Krueger, 1978). Similarly, several cases are reported in which boys had warm relations with homosexual fathers and they themselves engaged in prepubescent homosexual behavior (Bender and Pester, 1941).

Onset and Career Pattern

A transvestite's earliest recollection is: "I found a fur collar belonging to my mother. She let me wear it and walked with me down the alley. Mother and another woman smiled at me and I felt a pleasant sensation from the soft fur and from the approval" (Deutsch, 1954, p. 240).

Transvestites trace the origin of their condition to early

childhood (Ackroyd, 1979) or before puberty (Gebhard et al., 1965). Cross-dressing becomes more pronounced with practice (Ellis, 1928; Benjamin, 1966; Docter, 1988). Information on first occurrence of cross-dressing as reported by transvestite magazine subscribers is presented in Table 4.2.

These figures are similar to those found among groups of Australian and American club members (Buhrich and Beaumont, 1981). From one-half to three-fourths had cross-dressed by age ten (Bullough et al., 1983; Docter, 1988). Age of onset is not related to parental characteristics, homosexual experiences, or to transsexual tendencies (Prince and Bentler, 1972). For half of adult transvestites, first sexual arousal with cross-dressing occurred after onset of cross-dressing (Buhrich and Beaumont, 1981), and for two-thirds, first orgasm was not associated with any kind of cross-dressing (Docter, 1988). If we can rely on their memory, this means that for many, initial cross-dressing was not associated with sexuality and was continued for several years through some other form of gratification.

At the time of his first fascination with women's clothing, the transvestite is ready for the experience—he is already curious about women. Sexual curiosity was prohibited and punished during childhood. Thus, he became interested in clothing that hid those female parts that most interested him (Beigel and Feldman, 1963). Then, some trigger episode occurred: costuming for Halloween, a school play, or seeing mother's or sister's underthings and wondering what it would feel like to put them

TABLE 4.2
Onset of Cross-Dressing

Age	Percent (N = 504)
Before 5	14
5 to 10	40
10 to 18	37
After 18	8

Source: V. Prince & P. M. Bentler (1972), Survey of 504 cases of transvestism. *Psychological Reports*, 31:903–917.

on (Prince, 1981). The experience is somehow gratifying and he begins to cross-dress in secret.

During adolescence the boy's goals are conventional heterosexual relations and marriage, but he encounters difficulties in establishing intimate relations with girls because of excessive shyness, low self-esteem, and a feeling of inadequacy in his masculine role (Docter, 1988).

He does not take the homosexual route, either from aversion to such relations, or, if willing, from a lack of contacts or unattractiveness to homosexuals. So he returns to or continues his earlier method of sexual gratification—using feminine objects. If he stays at this stage, he remains a clothes fetishist. But, the future transvestite is committed to achieve social and sexual relations with girls, so he elaborates in fantasy a female image with whom he interacts. For instance, a transvestite's early masturbation fantasies involved clutching a piece of fur or silk, and imagining he was holding a girl in his arms (Deutsch, 1954).

His fantasy female is gradually internalized and fused with his feminine representation, with which he partially identifies. He may label himself as a transvestite, adopt a feminine name for his feminine representation, and from transvestite publications learn techniques of neutralizing his shame and guilt. This whole process requires great facility in fantasy life. He may exit the pattern at this stage if he is successful in heterosexual relations.

The longer he continues relating to his feminine image, the more fixed the pattern becomes. His idealized girl within becomes a part of him, and provides him with an internal relationship with a female that other men act out in reality. He gives himself gifts of feminine garb, he becomes his own nurturant mother and wife. This fixation occurs by eighteen to twenty years. Marriage might interrupt the process, but he finds relations with his wife unsatisfactory compared to his fantasy relationship (Buchner, 1970).

Sexuality

Transvestites' sexual desire is said to be weak (Ellis, 1928; Benjamin, 1954; Guitheil, 1954; Lukianowicz, 1959; Beigel and

Feldman, 1963; Gebhard et al., 1965). While arousal by femi-nine clothing is often intense, arousal by women is minimal. Transvestites have experienced little variety in sexual behaviors (Fagan, Wise, Derogatis, and Schmit, 1988), have had few sexual partners (Person and Ovesey, 1978), or have confined them-selves to prostitutes or elderly women (Gebhard et al., 1965). Compared with transsexuals, transvestites engage in more sex-ually deviant behavior, such as peeping, exposing, frottage, and contacts with immature females (Steiner, Sanders, and Lan-gevin, 1985).

However, this is not the way they describe themselves. Only a few report any difficulty dating in adolescence. Most say they petted, had crushes, and engaged in sexual intercourse (Tal-amini, 1982). Two-thirds claim average sexual interest in women, and a fourth say they have above average interest (Prince and Bentler, 1972). Four-fifths report masturbating while cross-dressed and half have engaged in heterosexual coi-tus while cross-dressed (Croughan et al., 1981). In sexual re-lations, they prefer to assume the inferior position (Hirschfeld, 1938; Oppenheim and Robin, 1974).

The vast majority report being mostly or totally heterosex-ual (Prince and Bentler, 1972; Pomeroy, 1975; Randell, 1975; Buhrich, 1978; Bullough et al., 1983). Their heterosexuality has been confirmed by phallometric testing where they show a stronger arousal to females than to males (Buhrich, 1978).

Transvestites have a negative attitude toward homosexuals, and some have an overpowering disgust for homosexual activ-ities (Lukianowicz, 1962). Both the Beaumont Society and Tri-Ess Sorority actively exclude homosexuals from membership (Ackroyd, 1979). A transvestite expresses his sentiments about homosexuals: "I can't really warm up to homosexuals. . . . As long as they leave me alone, I'll let them be. But if my kid ever said, 'I'm gay, Daddy,' I think I'd die. I still think of homosexuals as fags, queers, and fruits" (Feinbloom, 1976, p. 105).

Despite this negative attitude and the concern that they may be mistaken for homosexuals when cross-dressed, some transvestites frequent homosexual bars and drag dances. They even have photo collections of homosexual cross-dressers (Fein-bloom, 1976).

Masculinity/Femininity

The seed of transvestism is planted after core gender identity that "I am a man" is established, so what becomes distorted is gender role, or what it means to be masculine. Most transvestites were not effeminate as boys, rather they engaged in boyish activities, valued the masculine, and did not play with girls (Ovesey and Person, 1976; Person and Ovesey, 1978). From 17 to 29 percent were called "sissy" when boys and from 14 percent to 42 percent had wishes of being a girl (Buhrich and Beaumont, 1981). Asking whether sports were important in adolescent life as a gender marker, transvestites and a control group did not differ in their answers, whereas transsexuals and homosexuals did not consider it important (Bullough et al., 1983).

Perhaps, as children, they alternated between masculine activities and feminine dressing (Brown, 1960), as did one twenty-one-year-old who tried to loosen his ties to mother and sister by emphasizing masculine behaviors—black leather jacket, motorcycle driven recklessly. But, also at this time he would admire himself before a mirror dressed as a girl, thinking, "I am my own beautiful girl." Anxious about being surpassed by men, he strove to outdo them. But, then he withdrew from competition for fear he could not keep up. In school he had the urge to shout, "I'm only a girl; don't ask me questions." He was plagued with concern over the smallness of his penis, which was relieved only when he cross-dressed. His behavior was interpreted as an obvious "defense against castration," but a more likely interpretation is a flight to femininity to preserve his masculinity (Lewis, 1963).

A simple explanation of transvestism is that the man identifies with the female. But, one should be cautious with such a sweeping and loose use of the term *identification*. With what aspect of femininity does he identify, or better, what is it about women he prefers for himself? Three different aspects have been defined: sexuality, attitudes and emotions, and social role. The man who identifies with female sexuality is the passive homosexual; with her attitudes and emotions, the transsexual; and with the social, the transvestite (Prince, 1957). Since he is envious of and in love with women, he may employ the mechanism of introjective identification, whereby he takes unto himself desirable characteristics that he has attributed to women, for to him, loving is becoming (Ovesey and Person, 1976). However, the idea of identification with the female has been questioned. Rather, the transvestite may be imitative, a person who has failed to develop adequate gender role representations and who is adept at acting as if he were a woman (Sperber, 1973).

One method of assessing degrees of masculinity and femininity is to administer any of the many gender role inventories. In one study of transvestites, elevated femininity scores were noted (Beatrice, 1985), and another sample scored more feminine than homosexuals and other males, but not different from females (Brierly, 1979). However, they do not score as feminine as do transsexuals (Steiner et al., 1985). Transvestites were given Bem's Sex Role Inventory, a scale which yields masculine, feminine, and androgyny scores. Compared to nontransvestites, somewhat fewer were classed as masculine and more as androgynous (Talamini, 1982; Docter, 1988).

Gender role can also be measured by using personality inventory scales that tap traits on which the sexes differ. Transvestites score lower in dominance and aggression, but higher on rebellious and self-reliant scales than a control group (Bentler and Prince, 1969). As a reaction to their uncertainty about their masculinity, many present an overemphasized masculine front (Benjamin, 1954; Beigel and Feldman, 1963).

Gender Role Concepts

We have already seen that mothers of transvestites were either hostile or seductively close-binding, and women depicted in transvestite literature were similarly domineering or succoring. Here we will examine other women: the woman the transvestite wants to appear to be when dressed up and the woman with whom he would like to have a relationship. Also considered is his own feminine representation, the woman within.

There is a wide variety of feminine roles chosen including servant, governess, or maid of a distinguished lady, or he may fantasize being a respectable middle-class woman or glamour girl. The woman he would like to be is patterned after the kind he admires and envies (Ackroyd, 1979).

The hostile mother is said to produce the masochistic transvestite who glories in serving as a maid, or practices bondage and discipline with a dominant woman, either in fantasy or in fact (Person and Ovesey, 1978). From almost a third to two-fifths have bondage fantasies when cross-dressed (Buhrich and McConaghy, 1977b; Buhrich and Beaumont, 1981). If a man considers males to be superior to females, then in order to feel feminine, he must also feel degraded. In addition, if he experiences guilt over his superior role, he requires punishment to assuage this feeling. Being submissive to a female leads to a more complete role reversal for him. In addition, being forced to wear feminine clothing can absolve him of responsibility for not being masculine (Prince, 1981). If dressing as a female is symbolic of flight from an exaggerated conception of masculinity to passive, helpless femininity, then being bound, or treated as a servant is an additional way of saying that, as a girl, he is helpless and cannot compete as a male (Oppenheim and Robin, 1974).

In his actual or fantasized dealings with women, the transvestite is attracted to a particular type (Stoller, 1967, 1968). These types are similar to those found in transvestite literature. One is the "malicious male-hater" who dresses men in women's clothes to humiliate them. Valerie hated men and was bent on destroying their masculinity. Leaving her homosexual husband for a gender confused man, she encouraged him to buy feminine articles and taught him to use makeup. Valerie asked him to assume the supine position in coitus. To suit her whim, she would order him to appear in public dressed as either a strong male, an effeminate male, or as a girl. He "deliciously permitted this domination and fell completely in love with her—'I wanted to be her . . . to mingle with her and unite into one' " (Weitzman, Shamoian, and Golosow, 1970, p. 300). In an attenuated case, a man's wife teased him about being unmasculine and "forced" him into a feminine role by having him purchase her tampons and other toilet articles (Calogera, 1987).

The other type of woman sought is the "succorer," feminine, gentle, warm, and affectionate, who at the beginning of the relationship, lovingly supports the man who is already into cross-dressing. This type of woman is desired by the son of a seductive, close-binding mother. She is idealized as one concerned with the beautiful, the good, and the true. She likes pretty and fashionable clothing, is passive, gentle, artistic, and maternal (Feinbloom, 1976). When cross-dressed, he identifies with this idolized creature and partakes of her "goodness" and "virtue" (Prince, 1981). Speaking of women, one transvestite says: "I felt things in their moods that were delectable to me. I had a desire to experience the life of a woman. Their gay social movements were simple and serene. There was grace in their postures. There seemed to be a sort of music about women" (Henry, 1955, p. 97).

The relation between the woman within and the woman without is seen in a man who had two women in his fantasies—"Little Girl" and "Amazon." The little girl symbolized his sister in whose clothes he had dressed as a child. The Amazon represented his stern, dominant stepmother. He, as the little girl, wished to be dominated by the Amazon (Fenichel, 1930).

The classical psychoanalytic interpretation of the transvestite is that as a little boy he wanted to possess his mother sexually, but feared castration as punishment for these urges. He removes this threat by identifying with mother or sister and by believing in the phallic woman (Fenichel, 1930). By unconsciously accepting the existence of phallic women, he denies the possibility of castration. This is illustrated by a transvestite's dream:

> "Suddenly she started to take off her clothing as if very angry. She stood in front of me only clad in some underwear that was very beautiful. She reached under them and in her hand she held a small penis and shook it before me laughing. . . . As she stood there holding the penis, I became very passionate and pulled her down on the couch with me" [Karpman, 1947, pp. 311–312].

He dresses like a woman, not because he wants to be a female, but to obtain the power that he feels is possessed by the phallic woman (Storr, 1957). Another interpretation involves the unconscious drive to be both sexes—a variation of Freud's bisexuality hypothesis. The transvestite, believing in the phallic woman, struggles to achieve two mutually contradictory identities, to become both male and female (Kubie, 1974).

He has sex, not with a woman, but with her clothes, which represent her penis, and he himself represents the phallic woman (Fenichel, 1930). Also, feminine clothes represent mother (Person and Ovesey, 1978). His incest strivings are disguised by his cross-dressing, since wearing feminine clothing means being inside mother's clothes, that is, inside his mother, to have sexual relations with her (Hora, 1953). Clothes being a mother representation explains why those worn by transvestites are so often out of date, like mother used to wear.

His early partial identification with his feminine representation, coupled with his striving to be masculine, has left him with two independent conceptions of himself. Rather than integrating masculine and feminine components, the transvestite views the two components as antithetical. They are sequenced rather than combined (Brown, 1960). His exaggerated conception of masculinity is one of strength and dominance (Oppenheim and Robin, 1974; Feinbloom, 1976). His conception of femininity is a mixture of the dominant aggressor and the passive succorer.

This split or dissociation in his gender representations is akin to that seen in double personality except the transvestite is aware of both roles (Ellis, 1928; Hirschfeld, 1938; Brown, 1960; Oppenheim and Robin, 1974). The concept of dissociation has been replaced by ego splitting, but perhaps the double personality model is still applicable to gender conceptions of the transvestite (Van Kammen and Money, 1977). The masculine component is personified as "my brother," and the feminine as "my sister."

A large group, almost four-fifths (78%) by one estimate, describe themselves as "split personalities" with feelings, interests, and personalities change according to how they are dressed (Prince and Bentler, 1972; Person and Ovesey, 1978). These personalities may have equal or unequal strength, they may be in equilibrium or the feminine may assume ascendancy, and this feminine ascendancy may be episodic or continuous. He may cope with his feminine side by alternating masculinity with femininity. When feminine, he is assured of masculinity by his knowledge of his penis under feminine clothing (Prince, 1981).

When there is alternation, resulting role behaviors tend to

be exaggerated as highly aggressive, dominant masculine to gentle, tender feminine (Money and Lamacz, 1984). A transvestite describes this change: "When I cast off everything male and put on the outward trappings of a woman I can perceive almost physically how falseness and violence rushes out of me and disperses like fog" (Hirschfeld, 1938, p. 188).

In another case, the masculine component, Desmond, is a soldier of fortune, highly macho, with a history of extreme cruelty to his enemies, such as castrating them with wire. The feminine component, Marie, is a whimpering, little girl type, sfraid of men, sad, and alone (Money, 1974).

A twenty-three-year-old college student had been having cyclic alternations of masculine and feminine. His roommate describes his feminine phase. "I can tell when [Paul] 'goes across'; his total attitude changes, the way he walks; his voice gets higher; he starts to sweep, to mop, to clean out the tub. On the feminine side he is highly excitable; he is very sensitive to disturbing stimuli" (Lief, Dingman, and Bishop, 1962, p. 358).

Paul showed signs of a deficiency in androgenic hormone secretion which probably accentuated his childhood feminine pattern. At age twenty, he entered a "second puberty" with an increase in male hormone that masculinized his physique and the cyclic alternation began to abate. His sex drive was low and he had definite homosexual leanings. Similar shifts have been reported by Randell (1959).

Transvestites took a personality test when in their masculine mode and again when dressed as women. In their feminine role they scored lower on neuroticism and higher on extroversion. Dressing up seemed to allay their anxiety and reduce their shyness (Gosselin and Eysenck, 1980).

For some there is also an alternation in heterosexual and homosexual feelings. When dressed as males, almost all (90%) true transvestites considered themselves exclusively heterosexual; dressed as females, only two-thirds felt exclusively heterosexual. The abandonment of heterosexuality was more pronounced in transgenderists—from three-quarters when dressed as a male to less than half when attired as a woman (Buhrich and Beaumont, 1981).

This alternation of gender role may stem from a fear of being unequivocally either masculine or feminine. Feeling that he is neither man nor woman, he finds himself in a limbo between the two worlds (Kubie, 1974).

If the feminine component finally gains ascendancy, transvestism shades off into transgenderism and transsexuality. He can no longer live with himself because of the presence of his male physical attributes and may consider feminizing his body. There is a range of options from facial cosmetic surgery, breast augmentation, hormone treatment, to the whole package including genital surgery. About a fifth have looked into but rejected the idea (Bullough et al., 1983) and two-fifths report wishes or fantasies of being physical females (Buhrich, 1978). About a third express a desire to have breast and/or nose surgery only, while another third would like to have genital surgery (Buhrich and Beaumont, 1981). A fourth were or had been on female hormones (Bullough et al., 1983). Those who do ask for sex alteration surgery tend to be in the forty to sixty-five age bracket (Steiner, Satterberg, and Muir, 1978). Transvestites' interest in such procedures contrasts sharply with the 96 percent of male homosexuals who were not at all interested in sex change (Bullough et al., 1983). It may be that some seriously disturbed transvestites, stimulated by stories of sex change operations, seek such alternation for themselves in times of personal crisis (Housden, 1965).

Six transvestites have been studied who initially alternated between assuming masculine and then feminine roles. All had tried being husbands and fathers and had chosen masculine occupations. Their two roles were exaggerated and stereotypic. Feminine clothing produced a calm, contented feeling. Finally masculine–feminine alternation became increasingly difficult, and they eventually considered total assumption of the feminine role (Higham, 1976).

Reaction to Deviancy

While the initial experience of cross-dressing was peculiar, exciting, strange, and somehow pleasant, shame and guilt were also felt since they knew men are not supposed to be interested in that sort of thing (Prince, 1981).

Feelings about their cross-dressing vary from a sense of relief and contentment to "omnipresent torture" (Randell, 1959). Less than a fourth were currently trying to restrict or stop their cross-dressing, but two-thirds or more had at one time gotten rid of their costumes (Prince and Bentler, 1972; Buhrich, 1978), usually only once (Croughan et al., 1981). This effort to desist most often occurs in adolescence out of a conflict between pleasure and guilt (Buhrich, 1978).

From a fourth (Prince and Bentler, 1972) to a half have consulted a mental health professional (Croughan et al., 1981). Those who sought consultation, compared to those who did not, were more feminine, with more imagining themselves as females while cross-dressed in adolescence and as adults (Croughan et al., 1981).

In explaining their deviation to themselves and others some attribute it to hormones and heredity. Others blame their mothers for cross-dressing them as children, or wishing that they had been a girl. Some cite the official Tri-Ess view that they are getting in touch with the girl within (Feinbloom, 1976).

Others place the ultimate blame with society that exaggerates the difference between the sexes. In a society where both sexes dressed alike cross-dressing would not exist (Prince, 1981). However, it is probable that transvestites would engage in some other deviant behavior, because "doing something unacceptable" is an important constituent of their gratification (Feinbloom, 1976).

5 TRANSSEXUALISM

INTRODUCTION

The Transsexual Phenomenon

Prior to the 1950s, there were only scattered reports of individuals who thought they belonged to the opposite sex. First mention of the delusion of being a woman was in 1830 by Friedreich who noted that it was not a rare disorder. In 1870 Westphal described a woman's preference for the male role. Thought to be effeminate homosexuals, transsexual males were described in negative terms, as for example, in this 1886 portrait by Tarnowsky:

> [A]ctuated by the desire to appear feminine, loves to put on female attire, to wear his hair long, and to go about with open neck and laced waist; he likes to perfume and powder himself, and to paint and pencil the eyebrows . . . he is whimsical to the verge of hysteria, cowardly, pusillanimous, vindictive and willful [cited by Schrenk-Notzing, 1895, pp. 118–119].

Kraft-Ebing (1902) diagnosed such people as "metamorphosis sexualis paranoia" and described cases of both men and women who felt they had changed sex. The term *psychopathia transsexualis* was introduced by Cauldwell in 1949 to describe a girl who wanted to become a boy. Later, Benjamin used the term *transsexualism.*

The title of "First Sex Conversion Surgeon" belongs to F. Z. Abraham, who reported his procedures in 1931. And the first popularized account of transsexual surgery goes to "Man into Woman," about a Danish painter transformed into Lile Elbe. For the next twenty years there were only occasional reports of transsexual surgery, principally in non-English-language journals.

In 1951 the Christine Jorgensen story made headlines: "Ex-GI Becomes Blond Beauty, Operation Transforms Bronx Youth." This transformation was effected in Denmark with hormones and surgery by a team headed by Christian Hamburger.

The vast majority of the one thousand letters Hamburger (1953) received in less than a year following his treatment of Jorgensen were from people with a genuine desire to have their sex altered. In an article in the *Journal of the American Medical Association* he pleaded with his colleagues to show compassion for these people by easing their plight through surgery. "The object of the medical profession, therefore, is to bring about—as extensively as possible—conditions that may contribute toward the patient's mental balance and a certain sense of 'purpose of life' " (Hamburger, Sturup, and Dahl-Iverson, 1953, p. 393).

His appeal met with immediate opposition, particularly from psychoanalysts. One declared that Hamburger's patient was neurotic, a condition that cannot be cured by emasculating surgery simply because the patient requests it. "If a patient has a wish to die, should the physician actively comply with the patient's wish or even condone his suicide?" he asked (Ostow, 1953, p. 1553). Another remarked, "with all due respect for the surgical skill of Dr. Hamburger and his associates, one can hardly maintain that psychiatric indication for this procedure was sound" (Wiedman, 1953, p. 1167).

Not all ears were so deaf. One who listened was Harry Benjamin, New York endocrinologist. Since his first meeting with Christine Jorgensen, Benjamin had become the champion of the transsexual's plight; treating and referring hundreds for surgery. His 1966 book, *The Transsexual Phenomenon,* was the first in-depth study of transsexualism.

Because the demand was there, operating rooms were opened in Casablanca, Tokyo, Tijuana, Mexico City, and Rome. In some of these, surgery was provided on demand. Later, gender identity clinics were established at medical centers in the United States, the first of which was at Johns Hopkins in 1966. By 1979 surgical procedures were routine in at least a dozen centers (Restak, 1979) in the United States and forty in the Western hemisphere (Harry Benjamin Association, 1985). Foundations, referral, and information centers were established, such as the Harry Benjamin and Erikson Educational Foundations to sponsor medical meetings and workshops, disseminate information, and provide patient advocacy and grants for research (Billings and Urban, 1982).

Medical procedures and a psychological rationale were in place by the time these clinics opened. Hormone therapy and genital reconstruction had been used in treating intersexed individuals. The 1955 study of the intersexed by Money and the Hampsons led to the conclusion that socialization, not biology, is the basis for core gender identity. So, it was argued, when physical sex and gender identity are in conflict, the person's self identity should be the determining consideration (Edgerton, Knorr, and Callison, 1970). If sex is self-defined, then even a preoperative male transsexual must be referred to as a woman. So when "she" is in a sexual relation with another woman, "she" is a lesbian, even though male genitals are intact (Feinbloom, Fleming, Kijewski, Schulter, 1976): Thus, "the thought of holding her penis to urinate was repulsive to her" (Sabalis, Frances, Appenzeller, and Moseley, 1974, p. 907).

Despite the acceptance of medical treatment of transsexuals by prestigious medical schools and hospitals, criticism continued. It was argued that those applying for sex alteration were purely psychiatric patients demanding to be mutilated (Cappon, 1970); that transsexualism is not a diagnosis, but a wish voiced by homosexuals whose delusion that they are females frees them from guilt; that it is a wish of certain transvestites who want to change their playacting of a feminine role into a reality, and by schizophrenics with chaotic sexual identities (Socarides, 1969).

Critics maintained that transsexual surgery was a "drastic nonsolution" akin to prefrontal lobotomy (Restak, 1979), performed by the "innocently ignorant" and motivated by "misguided compassion" (Cappon, 1970). It "has led to the most tragic betrayal of human expectation in which medicine and modern endocrinology and surgery have ever engaged" (Kubie, 1974, p. 382). Surgery leaves unaltered a disturbed sense of self and only adds to the deep conflicts by sanctioning distorted yearnings (Meerloo, 1967; Socarides, 1969; Eber, 1980). It is "only a painful, expensive, dangerous, and misguided attempt to achieve between the legs what must eventually and inevitably be achieved between the ears" (Prince, 1978, p. 266).

Early, superficial follow-up studies reported successful outcomes with few complications (Billings and Urban, 1982; Lothstein, 1982b). Negative outcomes, such as the man hospitalized with severe depression fifteen months after surgery (Golosow and Weitzman, 1969), seemed to have been ignored by those advocating medical treatment of transsexuals.

In a 1969 article titled "A Biased View of Sex Transformation Operations" Stoller (1969b) expressed concern over the easy availability of surgery and the lack of carefully controlled follow-up studies. Ten years later, he maintained that this radical, irreversible surgery should be reserved for only the most feminine males, but that, "working with the encouragement of the news media, patients and physicians have created a circus atmosphere that has inflated and distorted the diagnostic, treatment, and social issues . . . a fad to which the medical profession has pandered" (Stoller, 1980, p. 1698).

Attitudes Toward Transsexuals

In a study of physicians' attitudes published in 1966, those in several specialities were loathe to recommend or perform sex alteration procedures, but expressed acceptance toward those patients who had already obtained such procedures (Green, Stoller, and McAndrew, 1966). College students were more liberal, with only about a fourth expressing negative attitudes (Kando, 1973; Leitenberg and Slavin, 1983).

Prevalence and Sex Ratio

Estimates of prevalence of transsexuals vary widely. For males they run from 1/100,000 to 1/37,000. Female prevalence is lower, ranging from 1/400,000 to 1/100,000 (Hoenig and Kenna, 1974a; Pauly, 1974b; Roberto, 1983). In countries where transsexualism is relatively less stigmatized, such as Singapore and the Netherlands, prevalence for males is a high 1/29,000 (Tsoi, 1988) and 1/18,000 respectively (Eklund, Goorem, and Bezmer, 1988). It is estimated that in 1979 there were 3,000 to 6,000 reassigned individuals in the United States, with as many as 60,000 who consider themselves candidates for reassignment (Harry Benjamin Association, 1985). Increases in reported cases over the years may be attributed to publicity given to the condition, availability of treatment centers, and to a broadening of the definition of transsexualism (Dolan, 1987). It appears that the prevalence is higher in societies with stricter gender role distinctions and antihomosexual attitudes than in more sexually liberal societies (Ross, Walinder, Lundstrom, and Thuwe, 1981).

Of those who wrote letters to Hamburger (1953) requesting help, men outnumbered women three to one. Estimated ratios of males to females vary from ten to one to one to one (Hoenig, Kenna, and Youd, 1970; Benjamin, 1971; Hyde, 1979; Roberto, 1983; Eklund et al., 1988; Tsoi, 1988), with about three-fourths of applicants to gender identity clinics being male (Meyer, Knorr, and Blumer, 1971; Lothstein, 1979b). There may be relatively more women in Europe (Hyde, 1979) and there is evidence that this sex ratio has been evening out over the years (Walinder, 1971; Walinder and Thuwe, 1976; Sorensen and Hertoft, 1980b). In one clinic in Poland, the ratio of diagnosed transsexuals is one male to five-and-a-half females (Godlewski, 1988).

There are several reasons for the prevalence of males. While there are more male than female applicants, about the same number are accepted for surgical treatment. This is because males other than true transsexuals seek treatment, whereas females who apply are usually true transsexuals (Lundstrom, 1981). Male to female surgery is more effective and less costly than female to male. Also, while men are freer today than they once were to experiment with changing life-styles, the gender disturbed male's choice is by and large limited to surgery. Women, however, having a greater latitude in dress and behavior, can stabilize without surgery. And, according to a feminist commentator, even in a patriarchical society, men envy the creative powers of women, symbolized by, but not limited to the ability to bear children. Such men attempt to gain possession of these powers by superficially looking like women (Raymond, 1979).

DEFINITION

Differing Conceptions

Controversy over the nature of those who desire to shed their anatomical sex and assigned gender identity has produced a variety of definitions. The broadest are those that focus on the request for sex change surgery—"a biologically normal person who insistently requests hormonal and surgical sex reassignment" (Ovesey and Person, 1973, p. 63).

Other definitions stress the felt incongruity between sexual equipment and gender identity: "A condition wherein one's gender identity and anatomy are perceived as incongruous. . . . The desire of these persons to negate and change the biological sex and pass into, become, and be accepted in the opposite gender role is a very strong and overwhelming one" (Feinbloom, 1976, pp. 148–149).

Official DSM-III-R criteria are discomfort with and a feeling of inappropriateness of one's assigned sex, coupled with a desire to have these organs removed, and a desire to live as a member of the opposite sex. This is not a reaction to stress, but has persisted for at least two years. Excluded from the diagnosis are the physically intersexed and schizophrenics with cross-sex delusions.

In addition to the standard transsexual, a wide variety of people have been applying for sex reassignment, such as transvestites, nonobligatory homosexual masochists, stigmatized and polymorphous perverse homosexuals, and schizoid personalities (Meyer, 1974a). In 1971 the name *gender dysphoria syndrome* was introduced, meaning biologically normal individuals requesting reassignment (Laub and Fisk, 1974). The name changed, but the definition remained the same. "A person who believes himself or herself to properly belong to the opposite sex and who, while not denying his or her sexual anatomy, attempts to live in the chosen social role and seeks out sex reassignment procedures" (MacKenzie, 1978, p. 251).

Varieties

Since it is claimed that female transsexuals are more homogeneous than males (Lundstrom, 1981), types of transsexuals refer primarily to males. Several criteria have been used to define various typologies. Two varieties differ in their social adjustment. The first displays defective moral and social judgment as evidenced by a history of antisocial behavior, general unreliability, and passive homosexual behavior. Presentation of the feminine is theatrical, exaggerated, and seductive. Many want to be entertainers. After surgery one patient went from room to room in the hospital displaying his naked body to other patients, some of whom reacted with near panic (Martino, 1977). In the second group are those who have tried unsuccessfully to assume the masculine role, have been married and have children. There is no history of antisocial behavior and they are less demanding and more cooperative than other sex reassignment patients. They report considerable depression and contemplation of suicide. Often they have attained considerable vocational success (Wolf, Knorr, Hoopes, and Meyer, 1968; Knorr, Wolf, and Meyer, 1969). A variation of the socially adjusted type is the career oriented person, who does not aspire to housewifery or to flaunt sexuality, but seeks respectability in the business or professional world (Kando, 1973).

Another grouping is based on feelings about genitals. Those who dread their own genitals are anxious, impulsive, wish to be penetrated, and are given to self-mutilation. They want not so much to be a woman as not to be a man (Hyde, 1975).

The gender envy group's main concern is to have opposite sex genitals, being indifferent to their own genitals. A majority of applicants ranked getting female genitals as more important than having their penises removed (Freund, Langevin, Zajac, Steiner, and Zajac, 1974). They are less anxious and impulsive than the gender dread group. Their attention is focused on superficial aspects of femaleness (Lothstein, 1979b). Too great a craving for a vagina may be a sign that a homosexual wants sexual relations with heterosexual men (Benjamin, 1971). Ruth expresses his gender envy. "My sexual awakening made me painfully aware that I did not have a vagina. What was happening to young women in my peer group was not happening to me. I was very envious of their outward appearances, but, most of all, it was the vagina which symbolized the lack in my own body" (Levine and Shumaker, 1983, p. 252).

A widely accepted, threefold classification based on prior sexual history (Bentler, 1976; American Psychiatric Association, 1987) is presented in Table 5.1. The homosexual transsexual's preferred partners are other males and he asserts that "Before surgery, I was homosexual," while the standard (asexual) and heterosexual deny this. The heterosexual type, usually a transvestite, has had an active sex life with females, is separated from the standard transsexual by reporting "Pleasant and successful intercourse with females." The standard type reports low sexual interest and activity with little gratification from his genitals. The most important reason for surgery for the homosexual is to have sex with men as a woman, while for standard and heterosexual it is to avoid masculine expectations.

Heterosexual—Gender Dysphoric Transvestites

A diagnostic problem that arises is whether those who have ever been sexually aroused by their cross-dressing should be considered transsexual. After studying a group of transsexuals with a history of fetishistic cross-dressing, Buhrich and McConaghy

TABLE 5.1
Bentler's Three Types of Transsexuals

"Before surgery, I was homosexual."

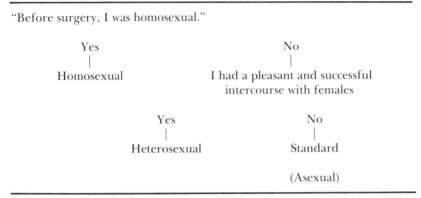

Source: P. M. Bentler (1976), A typology of transsexualism: Gender identity therapy
and data. *Archives of Sexual Behavior*, 5:567–584.

(1977c) conclude that those whose cross-dressing was sexually
arousing can be accepted as transsexuals.

Eighty percent of the heterosexuals applying for conversion have been erotically aroused by cross-dressing (Blanchard,
Clemmensen, and Steiner, 1987). Their core gender identity
is more unequivocally male than the other two types. Under
stress, principally threats to masculinity, defenses against separation anxiety crumble and the transsexual wish emerges (Person and Ovesey, 1974a,b). They tend to be older than other
transsexuals, are more often married, have had more heterosexual experiences, and penile volume changes indicate heterosexual arousal (Buhrich and McConaghy, 1979).

Two groups of gender dysphoric transvestite transsexuals
have been identified—aging, with a mean age of fifty-one, and
younger, mean age thirty-six. Neither group has a history of
childhood gender identity/role disorder, just an attachment to
feminine clothes. The aging type has clear masculine identification, with active heterosexuality, fantasies about women, and
no homosexual experiences. They are married and often have
children. The women they seek are succorers. Transvestite behavior is long-standing and private, with sexual arousal being
replaced by feelings of being at ease. They are mildly to severely

depressed, guilty about their cross-dressing, anxious, perhaps suicidal, and may attempt self-castration. Marital difficulties, illness, retirement, and separation are typical events that may lead them to seek alteration. They see becoming a woman as an escape from depression, life's stresses, and difficulty in maintaining their transvestite existence (Meyer, 1974a; Steiner, Satterberg, and Muir, 1978; Wise and Meyer, 1980).

The younger transvestite transsexuals are married and have masculine occupations. Covert dressing started in childhood or early adolescence. They have had homosexual experiences with passive longings toward men. Relations with wives are dependent and hollow. Precipitating events are conflictual marriages and male children reaching the oedipal stage. They identify with their sons and seem to relive their own childhood, separate from their wives (mother surrogate), abandon masculinity, and attempt to repair this loss by escaping to the feminine. Thus, the major difference between the aging and those in the younger age group lies in those stressful situations that send them into seeking sex alteration (Wise and Meyer, 1980).

Effeminate Homosexuals

The homosexual type fears engulfment and displaces his dependency to male figures, with his partner's penis symbolizing mother's breast. Mothers were either symbiotic and clinging or intrusive, overpowering, and physically and emotionally hostile. The transsexual wish occurs when homosexual adaptation fails, as when their lover leaves them. They are willing to sacrifice their penises for the security of dependency. They may be either effeminate-passive or effeminate-aggressive (Person and Ovesey, 1974a,b).

Standard Transsexual: Primary–Secondary Distinction

There are those who claim there is pure, true, or primary transsexualism (Benjamin, 1967; Person and Ovesey, 1974a,b; Stoller, 1980). One of the most influential and restrictive diagnoses of primary male transsexualism is that of Stoller (1980) who describes them as the most feminine of all males; men who have never been able to live with a normal appearance in the male role. A "blissful symbiosis" with mother left them with a conflict-free female core gender identity. Others seeking conversion, secondary transsexuals, include transvestites and effeminate homosexuals whose core gender identity is ambiguous rather than female. DSM-III-R's definition includes both primary and secondary transsexualism (Dolan, 1987).

Person and Ovesey (1974a,b) offer another view of the primary transsexual. They trace the problem of all transsexuals to the separation stage of separation–individuation, with each type attempting to resolve separation anxiety at different developmental levels. Person and Ovesey's primary transsexual's solution is the primitive fantasy of symbiotic fusion with mother. He is confused about gender identity rather than convinced of his female identity. In secondary transsexualism, the wish to be female arises only after periods of homosexuality or transvestite living. Person and Ovesey view Stoller's primary type as confused, not unambiguous, in gender identity, while to Stoller their primary transsexual is his secondary one.

Because of this disagreement over primary or true transsexuals, we will use the term *standard,* and put aside the question of either stable or confused gender identity. This standard male transsexual is one who claims a lifelong conviction of being female, while acknowledging that he is a biological male. Thus, he is not delusional. From childhood on, he dressed as a female whenever possible. Generally, cross-dressing was not sexually arousing, ruling out fetishistic transvestites; it simply felt right. Childhood play and fantasies were predominately feminine, and he hoped he would become a woman when he grew up and relate sexually to a heterosexual male. He has difficulty living as a man and believes he would be better adjusted in the opposite gender role. He may be passing as a female on his own and can do this convincingly. Ultimately, he desires sex reassignment surgery (Pauly, 1969a; Stoller, 1969a; Meyer, 1974b; Meyer and Hoopes, 1974).

Relation to Transvestism

An important difference between transvestite and transsexual lies in feelings toward the penis. For the transsexual his penis, especially when erect, is looked upon with disgust, whereas the transvestite needs his penis as a sign of masculinity (Oppenheim and Robin, 1974). Even those transvestites who take estrogens draw the line at having their penises removed, although they may fantasize being a complete woman. Another difference is attitude toward homosexuality. Transvestites shun homosexuals, while transsexuals may be preoccupied with men, but as a woman relating to heterosexual men. They will have nothing to do with men who are interested in their penises (Stoller, 1968).

Transvestism is amenable to psychotherapy, whereas transsexuality is extremely resistant (Barker, 1966). Transsexuals, compared to transvestites, are more intense in their cross-gender identity and role, and are interested in a male rather than a female sexual partner. They have a lower incidence of sexual arousal with feminine clothing, fewer sadomasochistic fantasies, and are more likely to dress continuously as women. Since the two groups do not differ in age, it has been concluded they are "separate clinical entities" (Buhrich and McConaghy, 1977b). However, another group of investigators found few personality differences between the two (Steiner, Sanders, and Langevin, 1985).

MALE TO FEMALE TRANSSEXUAL

The Act

Precipitating Events

Requests for reassignment by standard transsexuals occur after the individuals learn of the possibility. Today, such information is common knowledge so the adult needs only the motivation and money to make an appointment.

For the effeminate homosexual and transvestite, desire for alteration is often of short duration and is requested as an escape from some specific, acute emotional life crisis (Newman and Stoller, 1974; Wojdowski and Tebor, 1976). This crisis is precipitated by events such as abandonment by a significant other, parenthood, their child entering oedipal age, inability to meet masculine expectations, and loss experienced as gender related (Kirkpatrick and Friedman, 1976; Meyer, 1982).

Cross-Dressing

Some studies report that early cross-dressing is prevalent among standard transsexuals, especially for outer garments, since underwear has a sexual meaning (Person and Ovesey, 1974a). There are reports that almost all screened transsexuals recall a prepubertal urge to cross-dress between the ages of six and ten (Lutz, Roback, and Hart, 1984; Beatrice, 1985), with only a very few ever trying to discard their feminine garments (Buhrich, 1978). Other studies, however, have found low prevalence of cross-dressing in standard transsexuals (Wojdowski and Tebor, 1976; Bullough, Bullough, and Smith, 1983).

Estimates of those who have experienced sexual arousal in dressing as a female vary from none to 80 percent (Hamburger et al., 1953; Hoenig and Kenna, 1974b; Sorensen and Hertoft, 1982). One who was not erotically aroused by female clothing is Canary Conn (1974), who, at age six, dressed as a female. "This was new to me, a me I hadn't really had time to understand. The clothes were just an expression of feelings that didn't seem to match those of other boys my age, but I loved the feelings and I loved the girl who was me when I was alone" (p. 34).

For transvestite–transsexuals, feminine clothes represent mother and thereby confer protection and also act as a defense against their incest wishes (Person and Ovesey, 1974b). In a group of aging gender dysphorics, cross-dressing was episodic, secretive, and alternated between being sexually arousing and anxiety allaying (Lothstein, 1979a).

To one patient, a belt used in cross-dressing was of particular importance, perhaps symbolic of his effort to separate his feminine mind from his male genitals: "I tied in my waist with a belt; it was like cutting myself in half" (Weitzman, Shamoian, and Golosow, 1970, p. 297).

Pseudomenstruation and the Wish to Have Children

" 'I am experiencing menstrual periods in the form of splitting headaches, sleepless nights, very trying days' " (Olkon and Sherman, 1944, p. 161). Some report cramps and even rectal bleeding (Pauly, 1965). It has been suggested that fantasies of menstruation, usually from the rectum, derive from envy of women, psychological emasculation, and from the infantile cloacal theory that babies are born through the anus (Faegerman, 1955). Some fantasize giving birth after having been impregnated anally (Greenberg, Rosenwald, and Nielson, 1960).

Self-Mutilation

Forty-four cases of self-castration have been reported in the English-language literature from 1900 to the late 1970s, while only seven cases of eye extirpation were reported for about the same period (MacLean and Robertson, 1976). While self-castration is most common in schizophrenics, it has been reported in a number of distraught transsexuals, from 3 to 18 percent of whom have attempted or accomplished mutilation of their genitals (Pauly, 1965, 1968; Hoopes, Knorr, and Wolf, 1968). One way for transsexuals to convince physicians of their sincerity is to attempt self-mutilation (Benjamin, 1966).

While it may appear to be an impulsive act, there is often evidence of premeditation. One man obtained a job as a male nurse in a urology unit to prepare himself for his own surgery (Lowy and Kolivakis, 1971). Mutilation is preceded by a long history of repudiation and dissociation of genital organs from the body image. In over a dozen cases there was a history of dependent relations with a dominant mother and absent or distant father. Gender identity was confused, there was dissatisfaction with the masculine role, and relations with women tended to be submissive (Cleveland, 1956; Blacker and Wong, 1963; Schneider, Harrison, and Siegel, 1965; Lowy and Kolivakis, 1971).

One man managed to remove a testicle without undue pain. He placed a sanitary napkin over the wound, dressed as a woman, and gained entry to a hospital in this guise (Grotjahn, 1948). Another who felt he was "half man and half women," sought to cure himself by two attempts at excising his testicles, neither of which was successful. He decided to practice the operation on a "loafer," but the intended anesthetizing blow to his proposed victim's head proved fatal (Yawger, 1940). Finding the cost prohibitive, a twenty-five-year-old, after studying surgical texts, removed both testicles and flushed them down the toilet. He boasted, "no one can call me a man now" (Haberman and Michael, 1979). Prior to successful self-surgery and while drunk, a forty-four-year-old merchant seaman requested, "I want to be loved . . . I want to be more like a girl. I want to have my penis and scrotum cut off" (Esman, 1954, p. 80). Other cases of self-mutilation by the gender disturbed have been reported (Bowman and Engle, 1957; Money and DePriest, 1976).

The Experience of Passing

Successful passing by transsexuals who have undergone surgery is related to younger age at surgery, geographical mobility, and successful surgery. Of course, such physical variables as looking, sounding, and acting like a female are related to the ability to pass (Kando, 1973). After the transsexual has assumed a feminine name, it is necessary to secure a new set of identification papers. Filling out job application forms presents difficulties, since there are no college transcripts in the new name, no letters of reference, no employment or medical history, in fact, no history at all (Feinbloom, 1976).

While most adopt a traditional feminine gender role, an exception is the male to female lesbian-feminist who breaks with the feminine stereotype. Not totally adopting the feminine, he preserves much of the masculine. He renounces his male body but not his masculinity or his sexual orientation. In intruding himself into the feminist and homosexual ranks, he attempts to assume a leadership role not unlike some eunuchs of old who were in charge of women of the harem. In one feminist's opinion, these "constructed lesbian-feminists not only colonize female bodies but appropriate a feminist 'soul' " (Raymond, 1979, p. xix).

Transsexual Subculture

In the late 1970s, about one hundred preoperative transsexuals formed a network throughout New York City. All were on public assistance and receiving psychiatric consultation. Two or more live together and they meet in small groups. They mutually reinforced one another's beliefs of being women (Siegel and Zitrin, 1978).

Resistance to Gender Identity Change

Psychotherapy aimed at altering transsexuals' gender identity is said to be "ineffective" (Randell, 1971), "a waste of time" (Benjamin, 1954), have "no long term effect" (Sorensen, 1981a), be "totally" and "uniformly unsuccessful" (Baker, 1969; Edgerton et al., 1970), "not proven helpful" (Pauly, 1968), and "of no avail" (Vogt, 1968). In 1980, Stoller observed that there was no treatment that could make a primary transsexual masculine.

Efforts to change cross-sex identity are said to be not only difficult, but dangerous (Lothstein, 1979b); some have been pushed into psychosis (Pauly, 1968). Transsexuals view psychotherapy that focuses on their gender discomfort as an obstacle to what they themselves have prescribed—sex reassignment surgery (Roberto, 1983).

One source of difficulty in psychotherapy is the transsexual's lack of insight; he does not readily relate dreams, and associations are meager (Person and Ovesey, 1974a). Rapport is difficult to establish. He blocks, manipulates, and tries to control the therapeutic situation, perhaps challenging the therapist's authority because of his own feelings toward his father (Forester and Swiller, 1972). The therapist finds him disturbing to work with, perhaps because he awakens the therapist's own gender concerns (Lothstein, 1977). In the face of all these problems, psychotherapists are apt to accept the thesis of irreversibility of the transsexual's feminine identity (Eber, 1982).

At one gender identity clinic where group psychotherapy is a routine part of evaluation and preparation for further treatment, almost half the patients elected nonsurgical solutions to their gender identity disturbances (Keller, Althof, and Lothstein, 1982). Good candidates for psychotherapy rather than surgery are alienated homosexuals who can be helped to accept their homosexuality, and the sexually ambiguous and inadequate personalities who have arrived at the conclusion that a sex change will relieve them of their problems (Dallaert and Kunke, 1969; Forester and Swiller, 1972; Morgan, 1978; Lothstein and Levine, 1981).

Despite the prevailing view that nonmedical therapy is useless, there are reports of successes. An unusual case of a "cure" by exorcism is that of a twenty-two-year-old who was conservatively and independently diagnosed as a transsexual. He began using makeup and dressing up when he was four years old, and took estrogens in his teens. On his way to a medical center for surgery, he was told by a fundamentalist physician that he was possessed by evil spirits. This physician undertook to exorcise them, after which the patient announced that he was a "man." In a two-year follow-up there was solid evidence of a gender identity reversal. He claimed to be dating and experiencing heterosexual arousal (Barlow, Abel, and Blanchard, 1977).

While electric aversion treatments were ineffective in one case (Marks, Gelder, and Bancroft, 1970), in another, electric aversion, modeling, and praise was successful. Piece by piece, feminine behavior was dismantled and masculine behavior erected. However, rejection of the feminine role occurred only after direct modification of fantasies of being a woman having sex with a man (Barlow, Reynolds, and Agras, 1973). Six years later the patient reported a heterosexual orientation and his motor behavior was almost completely masculine (Barlow, Abel, and Blanchard, 1979).

Stages of Alteration

Only one in nine applicants to established gender identity clinics is accepted for surgery (Bentler, 1976). Of course, an untold number of rejectees and dropouts simply go to clinics where surgery is performed on demand.

The first step in the process is an initial evaluation to determine the appropriateness of sex reassignment. Several criteria are used to determine acceptance. Motivation must be authentic, not transient and situational. For example, excluded would be an effeminate homosexual who has just suffered disappointment in an affair, or a homosexual who views transformation as an escape from anxiety and guilt. The applicant must show a degree of psychological stability, thus excluding gender confused schizophrenics. Also unsuitable for surgery are homosexuals and transvestites whose penises are necessary for sexual pleasure (Stoller, 1969b).

One of the problems faced by those who screen transsexuals is that many candidates know the correct answers for acceptance (Benjamin, 1971). They have familiarized themselves with the literature, are "unreliable historians," and "inclined to distort" (Lukianowicz, 1959; Pauly, 1965; Knorr, Wolf, and Meyer, 1968; Stoller, 1973; Levine, 1980). They give "excellently memorized reconstructions of their childhood," and are able to present the facade of a well-adjusted person (Worden and Marsh, 1955). Some are coached in what to say by other transsexuals (Lothstein and Levine, 1981).

Their memory is selective for early feminine behavior and exclusive male partner choice. For instance, one patient denied any heterosexual activity, yet later mentioned having sired children (Keller, Althof, and Lothstein, 1982). In fact, it is claimed that the high incidence of textbook cases may be due to the ability of well-informed patients to deceive interviewers (Billings and Urban, 1982).

The view that they distort their histories is not shared by all (Pomeroy, 1975). "I do not share the view that patients do not tell the truth. I think I have been practicing psychiatry long enough to know when a patient is deceptive" (Randell, 1971, p. 155).

The second step is counseling to explore stability of gender identity, deal with emotional problems and family relations, explain procedures, and correct misconceptions and extravagant expectations like becoming a "gorgeous sexpot pursued and ravished by young Marines" (Van Putten and Fawzy, 1976, p. 752). In order to proceed, prognosis must be poor for psychotherapeutic amelioration of gender discomfort (Knorr et al., 1969; Baker and Green, 1970; Roberto, 1983).

Third, some secondary sex characteristics are altered by depilitation of hair and hormone treatment. Depilitation by electrolysis is a long, costly, and uncomfortable process. It takes from 100 to 200 hours to remove an average beard. Estrogens can lower plasma testosterone levels to those found in women (Migeon, Rivarola, and Forest, 1968), resulting in reduced sexual drive, fewer orgasms, and loss of spontaneous erections (Kwan, Van Maasdam, and Davidson, 1985). Not all changes reverse with cessation of administration; for example, augmented breast tissue and testicular atrophy (Morgan, 1978). Effects of female hormones are described by Jane Fry. "I was more at peace with myself. . . . My male sex drive was nil, and I was much happier; I had just a very good reaction to them—I felt good. My breast size increased a little, but not all that much, and my fat distribution changed" (Brogden, 1974, p. 131).

Voice is most resistant to change, especially for males. Frequency can be raised, but the fundamental male quality is retained (Coleman, 1983). The most salient clue of sex, even in an attractive, cross-dressed transsexual, is the sound of his voice (Franzini, Magy, and Litrownik, 1977).

The fourth step is a test of the applicant's ability to live as a female for a year or more. The purpose of this period, the passing phase, is to achieve gender reorientation by assuming the status of the opposite sex (Blanchard and Steiner, 1983). This involves living as a female at work, socially, and at home, and having female documents. Often this trial period requirement is resented (Randell, 1969). At this point, some candidates are undecided about having surgery. These men tend to be older, about forty years, more are married and have children (57%) than other candidates (Kockott and Fahrner, 1987).

The final step is reconstructive surgery. A prominent reason given for wanting surgery is "to make my body more like my mind, as a woman" (Bentler, 1976, p. 569). Body characteristics that arouse the most dissatisfaction are penis, testes, scrotum, body and facial hair, and lack of breasts (Lindgren and Pauly, 1975; Kuiper and Cohen-Kettenis, 1988). Additional reasons for requesting castration and amputation of the penis are revulsion over these male symbols, fear of detection, and feelings of incompleteness. For most, the desire for a vagina relates to the wish to be a complete woman rather than for coitus (Pauley, 1965; Hastings and Markland, 1978).

Acquiring a social role as a woman is often more important than having sex as a woman (Bentler, 1976). When asked why they sought surgery, a majority of applicants said it was for their own satisfaction rather than to please men (Freund, Langevin, Zajac, Steiner, and Zajac, 1974). They want the operation to confirm their fantasy of being female, they want reality made congruent with their mythology (Sorensen and Hertoft, 1980a).

A feminist (Raymond, 1979) observes that there is a fetishistic quality to this desire for sex change, in that female "artifacts" take the place of real, total femaleness: "If I have the external genitalia of a female, then I am a woman." Females are objectified as breasts and vaginas, things to be appended. The detested penis is a thing to be discarded. Related to objectification of the body is the conception of one's self as an object to be surrendered to the transsexual experts.

Patients are often demanding in the extreme and any delay in surgery is an intolerable frustration, responded to with depression and suicide threats. One patient entered the psychiatrist's office almost in shock, having made an incision at the base of his penis just before his appointment in order to force approval of sex reassignment (Stoller, 1973). This sense of urgency is not specific to surgery, but occurs even over trivial matters. Impulsivity, urgent time sense, and low frustration tolerance were found in adolescents and adults (Worden and Marsh, 1955; Lothstein, 1980b; Beatrice, 1985).

Prior to surgery a group of carefully screened applicants were optimistic, mildly euphoric, used massive denial and isolation of affect, and lacked fear of surgery. Their dress was exaggerated and their behavior seductive (Lothstein, 1978). Despite this eagerness, analysis of dreams reveals ambivalence and indecision regarding whether to be male or female (Volkan and Bhatti, 1973; Volkan and Berent, 1976).

The aim of surgery is twofold—removal of male features and construction of female ones. This involves amputation of the penis, removal of testicles, construction of a vagina, breast augmentation, silicone injections to round out buttocks and thighs, and cosmetic surgery to feminize facial features; for example, nose remodeling and surgical reduction of the Adam's Apple.

Some are surprised at the amount of pain they experience after surgery (Hastings and Markland, 1978), which challenges defenses, and may result in depression and second thoughts about surgery (Lothstein, 1978). Despite the pain, most are joyful that they are "women" (Wolf et al., 1968; Hastings and Markland, 1978), experiencing a "riddance" phenomenon as the offending penis and testicles are gone (Meyer, 1982).

Many have been called "surgical junkies" because of their "endless pursuit" of an impossible goal (Pauly, 1965). The homosexual type seems to pursue further alteration more than others (Bentler, 1976). Only a few days after initial surgery, they are requesting additional cosmetic surgery. In keeping with their superficial conception of women, they equate breast size with degree of femininity (Hastings and Markland, 1978). Some even request uterine implants so they can have babies (Lothstein, 1980a).

After a two- to five-year postsurgical elation phase, many realize that nothing has really changed, they are simulated, not real females (Meyer and Hoopes, 1974). Patients reporting some dissatisfaction complain of inadequate vaginas (Edgerton et al., 1970), surgical complications (Hore, Nicolle, and Calnan, 1975), and the need for more cosmetic surgery (Sorensen, 1981a).

There are more complications in sex reassignment surgery than in many other surgical procedures. Half to two-thirds experience some surgical complication (Laub and Fisk, 1974; Lindemalm, Korlin, and Uddenberg, 1986). Part of this may be attributed to the patient's failure to comply with postsurgery care. Complications include breast cancer from hormone treatment, loss of vaginal lining, vaginal stenosis and need for repeated vaginal reconstruction, infections, hemorrhaging, loss of skin grafts, rectovaginal fistulas, vascular complications, and chronic postoperative depression (Jayaram, Stuteville, and Bush, 1978; Sorensen, 1981a; Billings and Urban, 1982).

Adjustment Before and After Alteration

Follow-up studies in the 1960s and early 1970s reported satisfactory and even "dramatic" improvements after surgery (Benjamin, 1964; Edgerton et al., 1970; Hoenig, Kenna, and Youd, 1971; Money, 1971; Hore et al., 1975). These early studies used impressionistic and anecdotal evidence from patients' self-reports, presented brief case descriptions (Hertz, Tillinger, and Westman, 1961; Sturup, 1976), and used rough categories such as good, satisfactory, and unsatisfactory. More recently, rather sophisticated rating scales have been developed (Hunt and Hampson, 1980a).

The inadequacy of relying solely on patients' reports of satisfaction is demonstrated by a follow-up study of ten males, all of whom expressed satisfaction— "It was the right thing to do." Six experienced difficulty in forming stable relationships, social withdrawal, paranoid reaction, and depression; at least one worked as a prostitute; one was living as a male; and one was delusional and suicidal (Sturup, 1976). The meaning of "satisfactory outcome" was stretched beyond limits; for instance, a satisfactory outcome was reported in a six-year follow-up for a male who was a probable drug addict, an admitted prostitute, and "slightly depressed" (Hertz et al., 1961). Others expressing "no regrets" were troubled with depression, suicidal thoughts, and with only moderate improvement in social and sexual functioning (Lothstein, 1980a). Small wonder, then, that reviews of these early studies found about a 66 percent satisfactory outcome rate (Pauly, 1965, 1968).

As the design of follow-up studies improved, a more realistic picture emerged. For example, although overall adjustment increased from pre- to postsurgery for two-thirds, there was either no change or a decline in psychological adjustment. Economic adjustment did not change, but there was improvement in social and sexual adjustment (Laub and Fisk, 1974). In a long-term follow-up, the majority were unchanged in both sexual and global psychosocial adjustment (Lindemalm et al., 1986).

A Danish study, with an average follow-up time of six years, found no improvement in social adjustment—half were unemployed, and the number on disability pensions increased. Yet, most said their economic condition was good. A majority were living alone in social isolation, and one-fifth had attempted suicide (Sorensen, 1981a).

More meaningful than percentage improvement is information on those aspects of life that change for better or worse

and differences between those who do and do not show improvement. Such information could yield data that would increase prediction of surgical outcomes. Differential improvement
in various areas of life was determined for carefully screened
applicants. Overall psychopathology did not change, there was
only modest improvement in financial self-sufficiency and interpersonal relations, and notable gains in sexual adjustment
and family acceptance (Hunt and Hampson, 1980b).

Factors associated with failure are poor surgical results and
patients over thirty years of age. Other contraindications are
alcoholism and drug use, inadequate family support, having
completed military service, and heterosexual experiences (Walinder, Lundstrom, and Thuwe, 1978; Lundstrom, Pauly, and
Walinder, 1984).

Results regarding different outcomes for effeminate homosexuals, gender disturbed transvestites, and standard transsexuals are equivocal. Some investigators conclude that
satisfactory presurgical passing as a woman is more important
than the patient's diagnostic category. In one study, effeminate
homosexuals showed overall improvement (Laub and Fisk,
1974) and in another there were "spectacular" results in five
patients who were initially judged as poor candidates, but who
demonstrated they could live responsibly as women (Fisk, 1978).
Degree of adoption of social feminization, that is, living as a
woman at home, work, and socially, is related to lower levels
of tension and depression (Blanchard, Clemmensen, and Steiner, 1983).

Other studies, however, indicate that improvement is related to type of transsexualism. In one series, standard transsexuals fared somewhat better than others, being better off
economically, more satisfied, and having fewer complications
(Sorensen, 1981a). These different outcomes led to the conclusion that differential diagnosis should be given maximum attention when considering reassignment surgery (Lundstrom,
et al., 1984).

In support of the importance of considering type of applicant is the finding that of those who were refused treatment,
the standard transsexual faired less well than troubled transvestites and effeminate homosexuals. Effeminate homosexuals

who cross-dressed were more satisfied with their functioning without treatment (Lundstrom, 1981).

The 1979 study of Johns Hopkins' reassignment patients was, in part, responsible for the cessation of transsexual surgery at that institution. Operated patients were compared to unoperated patients. The unoperated group were those who had not successfully completed the required term of cross-living. Adjustment scores were determined using arrests, economic level, gender-appropriate cohabitation or marriage, and psychiatric problems. Since the operated and unoperated groups did not differ in adjustment scores, the researchers concluded that, "Sex reassignment surgery confers no objective advantage in terms of social rehabilitation, although it remains subjectively satisfying to those who have rigorously pursued a trial period and who have undergone it" (Meyer and Reter, 1979, p. 1015).

This study has been criticized for arbitrary scoring weights, use of an unoperated-on group as a comparison, and using objective measures to the exclusion of subjective feelings and fantasies (Fleming, Steinman, and Bocknek, 1980).

Transsexual outcome studies are plagued with a host of deficiencies and difficulties (Lothstein, 1982b). Many reports fail to provide basic data such as age, socioeconomic status, and ethnic origin. One of the most glaring problems is that the individuals studied are only a small fraction of those who have been treated (Hunt and Hampson, 1980b). Dropouts contaminate before and after comparisons, and many postsurgical patients refuse to participate: "I don't want to be reminded. I have a new and happier life now. I want to forget the past" (Benjamin, 1971, p. 82).

While there are standards of care for gender dysphorics, it is doubtful that they are universally used for diagnosis or for recommendation of surgery (MacKenzie, 1978; Harry Benjamin Association, 1985). Consequently, comparison across studies is almost impossible. Criteria for change are gross psychological or sociological ratings or are impressionistic and subjective.

The "transsexual experiment" involves, in addition to surgery, hormone administration, gender reorientation through a trial living period, and counseling. Findings of no change after surgery may be due to the preoperative success of these nonsurgical procedures (Lothstein, 1980b; Blanchard and Steiner, 1983). In addition, simply being accepted into a treatment program with the expectation of surgery relieves gender dysphoria (Kuiper and Cohen-Kettenis, 1988).

Seldom is there any control of these other procedures, such as the effects of hormone treatment. While most clinics administer opposite sex hormones pre- and postsurgery, they vary widely in types of hormones and doses used (Meyer, Walker, and Suplee, 1981). The importance of hormone treatment is seen by the finding that those who had self-administered hormones had less deviant scores on a personality inventory than those who had not taken hormones, and length of time on hormones was associated with lower deviant scores (Leavitt, Berger, Hoepner, and Northrop, 1980).

It is a sad commentary that with so many published studies "little is actually known" of the medical and psychological effects of surgery (Lothstein, 1982b).

The Person

Current Status

Age and onset. During the early 1960s in Sweden only about a third of the applicants for reassignment were under twenty-five (Akesson and Walinder, 1969). More recently, in England and Wales (Hoenig and Kenna, 1974a) and in Singapore (Tsoi et al., 1977, 1988) about two-thirds are from fifteen to twenty-four years old. Modal age at time of request in the United States is in the twenties (Hore et al., 1975). Probably the oldest to have complete reassignment surgery was seventy-four-year-old Marty/Mary Ann (Docter, 1985).

The desire to be a girl since early childhood is commonly reported by standard transsexuals. Others began believing they were girls at about six years of age (Beatrice, 1985).

Ethnic origin. Evidence that blacks are overrepresented is contradictory. In some studies, a third to a half of the applicants were black (Lothstein, 1978, 1979b). But of about five hundred applicants at the Stanford clinic, only 8 percent were black and less than 5 percent were Asian (Dixen, Maddever, Van Maasdam, and Edwards, 1984). In New Zealand, nine of ten preoperative transsexual prostitutes are Maori, whereas they account for only one of ten in the general population (MacFarlane, 1984).

Marital status. Overall incidence of marriage depends, in part, on how many heterosexual transvestite applicants are included in the sample. Estimates of those who have been married vary from a fourth to a half (Pauley, 1965; Hoenig et al., 1970; Meyer et al., 1971; Randell, 1971; Verschoor and Poortinga, 1988). About a fourth had lived or had a stable relationship with another male (Hoenig, Kenna, and Youd, 1970; Meyer et al., 1971; Kockett and Fahrner, 1988; Verschoor and Poortinga, 1988). In Singapore, all male applicants were single, and 60 percent had steady boyfriends (Tsoi et al., 1977). Incidence of involvement with a male partner, more common for the homosexual than the heterosexual transsexual, increases with education and degree of physical feminization, indicating perhaps that male partners see femininity as physical rather than behavioral (Blanchard, 1985b).

Occupation/social dependency. Employment is usually in traditionally feminine occupations such as clerical and beauty operator (Hoopes et al., 1968; Bullough et al., 1983). Homosexual applicants tend to be on public assistance and work as prostitutes, while nonhomosexuals have more education and are steadily employed (Levine, Gruenwald, and Shaiova, 1976; Blanchard et al., 1987). In England and Wales, a high incidence of educational and work maladjustment, unemployment, and low socioeconomic standing were noted.

Biological Basis

Early researchers have proposed some prenatal neuroendocrine abnormality as the basis of transsexualism (Hamburger et al., 1953; Benjamin, 1954, 1971; Bentler, 1976). Others have suggested that there is a "schizotaxic nervous syndrome" predisposing individuals to a spectrum of disorders including transsexualism (Hyde and Kenna, 1977), or a cerebral abnormality resulting in a learning disorder (Hoenig and Duggan,

1974). These are still speculations, since little evidence has been advanced.

The search for abnormal levels of circulating androgens has, for the most part, yielded negative results (Kupperman, 1967; Migeon, Rivarola, and Forest, 1968; Aiman and Boyar, 1982). There is at least one report, however, of lower circulating androgens in gender disturbed than in normal males (Starka, Sipova, and Hynie, 1975), and sperm count is low in some transsexuals (Aiman and Boyar, 1982).

A not uncommon problem with hormone studies is that some patients take female hormones on the quiet. For example, in one case testosterone metabolism was comparable to that found in women, and it was discovered later that the subject had been secretly taking estrogen (Philbert, 1971).

Current interest is in the prenatal influence of H-Y antigen, since it is thought that this antigen may somehow affect the sexual center in the hypothalamus. The complexity of the procedures for identifying H-Y antigen negative individuals is attested to by conflicting results. Several investigators have reported over half of transsexuals studied were H-Y antigen negative (Eicher, Spoljar, Cleve, Murken, Richter, and Stangel-Rutkowski, 1979; Engel, Pfafflin, and Weideking, 1980) and some abnormality in the hypothalamic-pituitary neuroendocrine function has been suggested (Boyar and Aiman, 1982). But, other investigators have found no evidence of H-Y antigen abnormality (Wachtel, Green, Simon, Reichart, Cahill, Hall, Nakamura, Wachtel, Futterweit, Biber, and Ihlenfelt, 1986). Supporting the case for some prenatal hormone influence is the finding that nine of twelve homosexual transsexuals gave a positive LH response to estrogen priming, whereas all of the heterosexual and bisexual transsexuals responded negatively (Dorner, 1988).

A higher than usual rate of diabetes mellitus has been reported in transsexuals and their relatives. It is supposed that the lessening of sexual urges associated with diabetes is, in some way, related to transsexualism (Koranyi, 1980). A diabetic and epileptic patient had been cross-dressing since he was five years old. At fourteen, he was wearing women's clothes, lipstick, and rouge, and he was feminine in appearance and interests. He said he felt more "at ease" in women's clothes. He had neither heterosexual nor homosexual interests. It was concluded that his epilepsy, hormone dysfunction, and femininity were somehow related (Petritzer and Foster, 1955).

The search for chromosomal abnormalities has been mostly fruitless (Hoenig and Torr, 1964), although occasionally a case is reported (Videla and Prigoshin, 1976). A few monozygotic twin transsexuals have been described (Benjamin, 1971). One pair played like girls when children, avoided sports, and later fell in love with heterosexual men (Anchersen, 1956). Several transsexuals were found in the maternal side of the same family, along with considerable incidence of other gender disturbances and seizure disorders. Although a recessive gene effect cannot be excluded, no cases of cousin marriages were found in families of transsexuals (Walinder and Thuwe, 1977).

Gender disturbances in twins and nontwin brothers may be explained by early environment as well as by heredity. Two male triplets suffered severe deprivation during their first three years, like not using eating utensils. Later their mother substitutes showered them with attention. Both were extremely effeminate and requested sex conversion (McKee, Roback, and Hollender, 1976). There are at least two reports of transsexual brothers, but they are readily explained by manner of upbringing. In one case, the brothers were raised by a grandmother; their other male siblings reared by natural parents were not transsexual (Hore, Nicolle, and Calnan, 1973). In the other case, the home situation duplicated Stoller's transsexual family (Stoller and Baker, 1973).

Electroencephalograph (EEG) abnormalities have been reported in about half of a group of transsexuals, with another fourth showing borderline abnormalities (Hoenig and Kenna, 1979). And, amphetamine use has been related to gender disturbances, perhaps due to the drug's disinhibitory action. One patient experienced the wish to be female with cross-dressing after injections of meta-amphetamine (Lothstein, 1982a).

Early Life

Consistent with the two definitions of primary transsexuality, there are two different descriptions of development —conflict-

free and conflict-defense—producing either stable female identity or confused gender identity. While these descriptions are
presented longitudinally, they were not derived from longitu-
dinal studies. For example, Stoller's position is based on observation of very effeminate boys and retrospective accounts of
adult transsexuals (Eber, 1982).

Parents. Transsexuals do not differ from others in parental
age or in birth order (Walinder, 1969).

According to Stoller's conflict-free position, the transsexual's maternal grandmother was cold, distant, and stern, and
did not give her daughter a sense of worth. The daughter, in
turn, concluded that being a girl was of no value. She did have
good relations with her father and shared his masculine interests, but he abandoned her before puberty. Pubertal changes
dashed her hopes of growing up to be a male, leaving her with
a strong bigender orientation.

She married a passive, distant man whose masculinity she
did not need to envy. When she gave birth to a beautiful, love-
able, cuddly male, she was overjoyed. Mother maintained extreme physical closeness with her son, as described in the
chapter "Childhood Gender Disorders." Pleased with her son's
graceful and appealing nature, a close and loving "blissful symbiosis" was formed. His early protofemininity was uninter-
rupted and he did not acquire a masculine identity or role.
While mother encouraged his feminine behaviors he, not
mother, instituted cross-dressing and girls' roles in play. Between three and five years of age, he talked of being a girl. The
oedipal situation failed to modify his femininity; it was free of
conflict and fear of castration. In fact, he wanted to be rid of
his penis. He was not like an oedipal girl, for he did not long
for his father (Newman and Stoller, 1971). Later, under pressure from peers and others, he may have tried to defeminize
by hiding his feminine nature. Resulting sadness and loneliness
seemed neurotic, but he was reacting to a painful environment,
not to inner conflict. When he learned of transsexualism, he
single-mindedly sought conversion (Stoller, 1980).

Consistent with Stoller's opinion that primary transsexualism is rare, efforts to find those who meet his criteria have been
disappointing (Meyer, 1982), but a few cases have been de-

scribed. Three brothers, all transsexuals, were raised by a "Stoller mother": she was confused about her gender identity, discouraging the children's separation from her; father, rarely home, was seen by the boys as a "romantic stranger" (Sabalis et al., 1974).

The conflict-defense position denies "blissful symbiosis" and conflict-free female gender identity. These theorists propose instead that conflict and defense are at the heart of transsexualism. Forming the basis of gender identity confusion is a strong desire for reuniting with mother together with a fear of and defense against engulfment (Lothstein, 1979b).

Those who advocate this position find, as does Stoller, that mother's own gender identity is confused and she unconsciously denies differences between the sexes. Relations with her male child are ambivalent. They are positive when seen as her phallus; negative when the child tried to separate, at which point she retaliates by becoming distant and by disparaging his genitals. Having adopted his mother's lack of sex distinctions, he later tries to convert this fantasy into reality and confirm the transmutability of the sexes (Meyer, 1982).

Some mothers, rather than being close, were emotionally distant. While providing routine care, they neglected their sons' emotional needs (Person and Ovesey, 1974a; Meyer, 1982), often because of their own physical illness, helplessness, or irresponsibility (Halle, Schmidt, and Meyer, 1980). Whether mother was close or distant, engulfing or hostile, she provoked the boy's attachment to her and his later strong yearning to reunite with her. She allowed separation in gender unrelated areas but inhibited formation of a stable masculine gender identity.

According to this conflict-defense view, transsexuals do not have a female, but an ambiguous core gender identity, and their view of themselves as female trapped in a male body is an attempt to resolve this ambiguity. Gender identity ambiguity impairs acquisition of masculinity, so they do not develop the usual range of masculine feelings and behaviors. The scales are eventually tipped from ambiguous identity toward feminine identity and a loathing for their maleness. In childhood and adolescence there were cross-sex wishes, not cross-sex convictions. The source of this gender disturbance is severe separation anxiety occurring before object differentiation. The child uses a fantasy of fusion with mother to alleviate this anxiety. He becomes mother and seeks to adopt a feminine core gender identity (Ovesey and Person, 1973). Later in life, he regresses from a fragile gender identity to a primitive fusion with mother, based on the infantile belief that in acting like mother, one becomes like mother (Weitzman et al., 1970).

Studies of adult transsexuals' feelings toward their mothers do not resolve the conflict-free versus conflict-defense controversy. About half of a group of adult transsexuals reported very good childhood contact with mother and unsatisfactory contact with father. While nontranssexuals' closeness to mother lessens over the years, transsexuals maintain close ties with her (Uddenberg, Welinder, and Hojerback, 1979). A group of screened transsexuals reported a preference for mothers during their adolescence, although they described them as domineering. Most were ambivalent toward mother, with both close contact and also dread of her domineering quality (Sorensen and Hertoft, 1982). No difference was found between screened transsexuals and controls on mothers' care or overprotection (Parker and Barr, 1982), but unsatisfactory relations with both parents from childhood to adulthood is reported (Uddenberg et al., 1979).

Maternal grandmothers played a significant part in raising almost a third of one sample. These grandmothers were loving and accepting of the boys' feminine behaviors (Halle, Schmidt, and Meyer, 1980). A boy was raised by a "Stoller grandmother" until she died when he was six years old. She kept him physically close—they slept and used the bathroom together. She was permissive toward his cross-dressing and feminine interests. From age seventeen he lived and worked as a woman and underwent reassignment surgery in his early twenties. A few days after surgery he was hospitalized with "acute symbiotic psychosis" with agitated grief, panic, hallucinations, and insatiable demands for bodily contact. Because surgery did not magically reunite him with grandmother, he experienced several days of psychosis, which then abated (Childs, 1977).

Feelings toward fathers range from neutral and distant

(Sorensen and Hertoft, 1982) to outright hatred. Screened transsexuals view their fathers as less caring and somewhat more overprotective (not granting freedom, invading privacy) than do other males (Parker and Barr, 1982). There was no difference in unreplaced father loss between applicants for reassignment and regular homosexuals. It is not physical absence that is influential, but psychological distance (Freund, Langevin, Zajac, and Steiner, 1974). Loss of father during adolescence precipitates a gender shift in many transsexuals, for father often inhibits expression of femininity (Bernstein, Steiner, Glaister, and Muir, 1981).

In one case there was extreme emotional and physical closeness to father and mother, both of whom were initially totally permissive. Father's closeness, lasting until the boy was fourteen, was coupled with strong negative feelings. The son recalls, "I was so attached to my father. Time and time again my father would come into bed with me, hugging and kissing me. . . . He would put on a record and he'd bounce around and dance with me and we'd dance together." But father also became so enraged at his son's femininity and closeness to his mother that he would slap and derogate him as an incompetent boy. Later, the boy was able to express his rage at father, yelling, "I'll kill you, I'll kill you" (Weitzman, Shamoian, and Golosow, 1971, p. 292). Another expressed his hatred for his father— "He has a heart problem. Maybe if I have surgery, it will finally make him kick off" (Wojdowski and Terbor, 1976, p. 198).

Gender acquisition. Part of the controversy between the conflict-free and conflict-defense positions involves the transsexual's acquisition of feminine identity. Stoller's conflict-free view posits early adoption of a feminine identity. Those espousing the conflict-defense position maintain that the boy was neither effeminate, theatrical, nor identified as a sissy. He did engage in boys' play, but with an unspoken sense of distaste. While envious of girls, he did not mimic them. He did experience a growing awareness of marked differences between himself and other boys (Person and Ovesey, 1974a). His later "I am a female" contention is an adaptive maneuver to resolve the ambiguity of his gender identity.

Was the transsexual, as a child, overtly feminine, or was he neither clearly masculine or feminine? Retrospective reports do not provide a definite answer. Nonmasculine behavior during childhood is evident. Physical aggressiveness, such as fighting and skill and interest in athletics, was lower in transsexuals than in regular homosexuals, who were lower than heterosexuals (Blanchard, McConkey, Roper, and Steiner, 1983). Almost two-thirds (64%) said they had no interest in sports as children compared to one-fourth of a comparison group (Bullough et al., 1983).

Some investigators have reported not only nonmasculinity as in aversion to fighting, boys' games, and rough, outdoor activities, but also frank childhood femininity (Hamburger et al., 1953; Sorensen and Hertoft, 1982). Two-thirds of trans-sexuals claim that by age five they felt they were females, had a greater childhood preference for girls' games (Lutz, Roback, and Hart, 1984), and that they were more feminine than regular homosexuals (Hellman, Green, Gray, and Williams, 1981). Pre-pubertally, 37 percent were cross-dressing, 63 percent played exclusively with girls, 60 percent were embarrassed by disrobing in front of boys, and 90 percent felt they were females. After puberty, 50 percent were cross-dressing occasionally, and 43 percent consistently (Pauly, 1968). Many were called "sissies" by their age mates (Money and Primrose, 1969).

Some of the confusion in the literature regarding child-hood effeminacy is due to failure to specify the type of gender dysphoria. At least three-fourths of standard and effeminate homosexual transsexuals considered themselves effeminate as children, whereas not more than one-fourth of transvestite transsexuals reported being childhood sissies (Lundstrom, 1981; Blanchard, 1985a).

Those who see transsexuality as a defense against homo-sexuality, in partial agreement with the conflict-defense posi-tion, deny there is a firm sense of feminine identity. During childhood, they maintain, femininity was expressed as a wish— "I want to be a girl," or "I feel like a girl." However, by the time they reached adolescence, screened males report fantasies of actually being females (Sorensen and Hertoft, 1982). A shift takes place from a wish to a belief that they are girls: "I am really a woman." When this shift is made, it is no longer a gender disorder, rather it is a delusional idea, based on an illogical deduction that "I am sexually attracted to males; A female is sexually attracted to males; Therefore, I am a female" (Siomopoulous, 1974, p. 57).

Before forming a clear conception of cross-gender identity, many do feel that they might be homosexuals— "Maybe I was a queer and just hadn't accepted it. But I'd never felt like a queer. I'd never called myself a queer. I always assumed I was a girl" (Conn, 1974, p. 57).

For whatever reason, the homosexual route is not open.

> Would you like to be homosexual?
> No, because that means being a fairy. The idea of playing with another man's penis disgusts me. If I could be a woman it would be different.
> Would you like to be surgically converted into a woman?
> Yes. That would make it all right, and I would not be a fairy [Shankel and Carr, 1956, p. 487].

The adolescent gender dysphoric, sexually attracted to men, is vehemently antihomosexual (Lothstein, 1980b). The adult, even though sexually attracted to males, cannot accept that he is homosexual for that would mean he is male (Ovesey and Person, 1973). His declaration that he is a female avoids the stigma of homosexuality and defends against his passive homosexual desires (Anchersen, 1956; Socarides, 1969). A transsexual, who after surgery was "immersed in delusions," reports, "I had the surgery so that they could no longer call me a fag. I wanted to remove that onus" (Van Putten and Fawzy, 1976, p. 752).

One possible explanation of why the homosexual route is not taken is suggested by the finding that, during childhood, a majority of transsexuals were either devoutly religious or regular church attenders (Pomeroy, 1967). Perhaps there is a difference in early religiosity between transsexuals and homosexuals. Strong religious background might lead to fear and denial of homosexuality in the transsexual, and weak religious upbringing would lead to a degree of acceptance of same sex partners. Comparing groups of Catholic transsexuals and homosexuals, it was found that their parents' religiosity, but not their own childhood devoutness, was greater in transsexuals than in homosexuals (Hellman et al., 1981).

The transsexual may attempt to overcome his gender dysphoria by striving to assume a masculine role (Hamburger et al., 1953). Compensatory masculinity refers to discomfort from an unfavorable comparison of one's self with a polarized conception of masculinity and femininity, resulting in exaggerated displays of masculinity. This has been demonstrated experimentally by threatening participants' masculinity. This threat resulted in increased levels of expressed masculinity for high masculine males, but lower levels for androgynous males (Bahl, 1979). Unfortunately, we do not know the effect of threat on gender ambiguous individuals.

In postadolescence, there may be one last attempt to express masculinity (Person and Ovesey, 1974a) by joining the military, engaging in heterosexual intercourse, and getting married. Military service serves the purpose of getting out of an intolerable home situation, provides an opportunity to develop a sex congruent role, and denigrates the feminine (Wojdowski and Terbor, 1976; Brown, 1988).

Eventually, the transsexual solves his problem when he hits upon the "magical idea" of achieving satisfying relations with others by changing his sex (Lothstein, 1979b). Discovery of the transsexual solution often occurs suddenly. "That December, while reading Masters and Johnson, I suddenly realized, on a gut level, that if I were female everything else would make more sense" (Feinbloom et al., 1976, p. 66).

This contention becomes crystalized when he hears of sex transformation operations. While persons presenting themselves for surgical transformation may claim that they have always wanted to be female, conflict-defense theorists maintain that, in fact, they discovered this desire after learning about a sex change operation (Ovesey and Person, 1973). They often wishfully falsify memory (Lukianowicz, 1959).

Homosexual transsexual. The career path of the homosexual transsexual is different from that of other transsexuals. He was raised by a dominant female who encouraged his femininity. Father was emotionally or physically absent. He was confused and ambivalent about gender identity, and has been effeminate since early childhood, feeling like a girl since about the age of five. He avoided boys' activities, preferring girls as playmates, and so was teased for being a "sissy." Early interest in wearing women's clothes was an enactment of transformation fantasies; that is, imagining being an admired and envied person (Person and Ovesey, 1974b, 1984).

At first, he considered himself homosexual, assuming the insertee role in anal intercourse. Family ties were severed and he moved into the homosexual world where he openly cross-dressed. Here he hoped to find a place where he could be open about one aspect of his problem—same sex preference. He may have sought homosexual relations, but eventually found it difficult to adapt and so withdrew from relations with homosexuals. Doubts set in about being a homosexual, since he considered himself and wanted to be treated as a female. But, homosexuals reacted to him as if he were a male or did not relate to him because he was too feminine.

Although growing alienated from the homosexual world, he continued to frequent bars, principally to meet other transsexuals or bisexual males. Attempts to move in the heterosexual world proved unsuccessful. He became dependent on public assistance, worked as a prostitute, passing as a female. He may have found a bisexual lover who relieved his feelings of loneliness, confirmed his sense of femaleness, and on whom he became dependent. Female sexual equipment is desired in order to attract heterosexual males (Levine, Shaiova, and Mihailovic, 1975; Levine, 1976).

Personality and Relations with Others

Compared to regular homosexuals, male applicants have poorer self-concept and adjustment, are less self-accepting, and have more severe psychopathological signs (Roback, Strassberg, McKee, and Cunningham, 1977). Interviews with applicants revealed that four-fifths had some psychiatric disturbance, and of these, two-thirds were diagnosed as personality disorder, and a few as schizophrenic. Psychometric testing showed an even more serious disturbance rate (Levine, 1980). The MMPI schizophrenia scale is often elevated (Langevin, Paitich, and Steiner,

1977; Tsoi et al., 1977; Fleming, Cohen, Salt, Jones, and Jenkins, 1981; Beatrice, 1985), indicating unusual thoughts and behaviors.

Transsexuals often receive diagnoses of personality disorder that include schizoid, paranoid, and borderline personality. Some show conversion disorder (hysterical neurosis) features of repression, denial, selective memory, and coy flirtatiousness (Finney, Brandsma, Tondow, and Lamaestre, 1975).

The behavior of many transsexuals fits with the diagnosis of borderline personality disorder whose main feature is instability in many areas of life (Volkan and Berent, 1976). Borderline personality features seen in transsexuals include an inability to deal with ambiguity and stress, sense of emptiness and aloneness, externalization of problems, superficiality expressed as avoidance of intimate relations, low tolerance for emotions, poor sense of continuity of self, and substance dependence. These borderline symptoms appear to abate with the assumption of the opposite gender identity/role (Meyer, 1982).

Depression is common in adult (Randell, 1971; Langevin, Paitich, and Steiner, 1977; Tsoi et al., 1977) and notable in adolescent gender dysphorics (Lothstein, 1980b), and in aging transvestites who request surgical alteration as their last chance for happiness (Steiner et al., 1978; Lothstein, 1979a). Transsexuals report more phobias, anxiety, depression, and thoughts of hopelessness and suicide than male heterosexuals (Derogatis, Meyer, and Vazquez, 1978). Both suicide threats and attempts are common, with about a third threatening and a fourth reporting attempts (Pauly, 1965; Hoopes et al., 1968; Dixen et al., 1984; Kockott and Fahrner, 1988). Their depression is "empty" in that there is no anger or guilt (Person and Ovesey, 1974a), rather it is sensed as loneliness. How much of this depression is secondary to gender identity problems is difficult to determine.

They are not only unaccepting of society's prescribed gender roles, but also of other social norms as seen by their high unconventionality scores on the MMPI (Rosen, 1974; Langevin et al., 1977; Tsushima and Wedding, 1979; Lothstein, 1980b; Fleming, Cohen, Salt, Jones, and Jenkins, 1981; Hunt, Carr, and Hampson, 1981; Beatrice, 1985), coupled with lack of responsibility and low frustration tolerance (Sadoughi, Jayaram, and Bush, 1978). Standard transsexuals are more committed to conventions of society than are other types (Wojdowski and Tebor, 1976).

Criminal and antisocial behavior is not uncommon (Hoenig et al., 1970; Hoenig and Kenna, 1973). Three-fourths of one sample admitted having been in trouble with the law; however, some of the difficulty involved passing as a female (Meyer et al., 1971). From 17 (Dixen et al., 1984) to 30 percent (Hoenig et al., 1970) have worked as prostitutes. In Singapore, over 80 percent were full- or part-time prostitutes (Tsoi et al., 1977). Reasons given for working as prostitutes include difficulty in gaining employment because of their transsexuality, need of money for surgery, and the satisfaction of having sex with a heterosexual male (Levine, Gruenwald, and Shaiova, 1976).

As teenagers, they were unable to form close relationships, and interactions with peers were superficial, most having no male companions in early adolescence (Pomeroy, 1967). A sense of isolation was pervasive during these years (Sorensen and Hertoft, 1982), as they withdrew into still more isolated living (Lothstein, 1979b). Feelings of being different were augmented by other boys' interest in girls and their own low sexual interest in either sex (Person and Ovesey, 1974a). Only 16 percent said they had a happy childhood compared to 60 percent of a comparison group (Bullough et al., 1983).

Frustrated dependency needs result in feelings of low self-worth and unacceptableness. Transsexuals, like hypochondriacs rationalize their discomfort in concrete terms; the hypochondriac by imaginary physical ailments, the transsexual by claiming to have the wrong body (Shave, 1976).

Feelings of being empty result from early losses and physical separations, such as the child's hospitalization (Person and Ovesey, 1974a). Blunted emotions were noted in homosexual transsexuals and suppression of genuine emotions in nonhomosexual transsexuals. However, they are able to simulate affect (Levine et al., 1976), which probably contributes to their air of superficiality.

Ruth, a male transsexual, describes his feelings of alienation. " 'In my adolescence there was much conflict between my personal mythology and reality. I believe there were many times when it was difficult for me to keep contact with the real world. I was a loner, an alien. I had a sense of not belonging to the world in which other people lived' " (Levine and Shumacher, 1983, p. 253).

Withdrawal can spiral into further alienation: "I was being tormented by the kids for being feminine so I withdrew, but the more I tried to withdraw the odder I became, and the more they tormented me the more I withdrew" (Brodgan, 1974, p. 41).

Not unexpectedly, much interest is centered on themselves to the detriment of close interpersonal relations. This self-centeredness is not narcissism; they are not more aroused by their own bodies than by the sight of other people's bodies (Freund et al., 1974).

Their idea of interpersonal relations is limited to being admired by others (Worden and Marsh, 1955) and therefore, such relations are superficial, not intimate (Person and Ovesey, 1974a). Other men serve as props for transsexual convictions: "I was never attracted to men per se . . . they were just tools for my fantasy . . . it put me in a position of power . . . they wanted me to be like a girl in the sex act" (Weitzman et al., 1970, p. 299).

Sexuality and Partner Preference

Especially in the standard transsexual, sexual urge is weak pre-operatively (Hamburger, 1953; Benjamin, 1954; Pauly, 1968; Sorensen and Hertoft, 1980a) and masturbation is infrequent (Freund, Langevin, Zajac, Steiner, and Zajac, 1974; Hoenig and Kenna, 1974b). When they do masturbate it may be without fantasies and in order to rid themselves of offending erections (Worden and Marsh, 1955). Hardly any sexual satisfaction is gained from what little genital contact they have. They have had fewer heterosexual experiences than homosexuals (Freund, Langevin, Zajac, Steiner, and Zajac, 1974). And, compared to heterosexual males, they report much less variety in sexual behaviors and their attitudes toward sex are more conservative. There is a minority of from 10 to 20 percent, probably homosexual, who were rated high in activities leading to orgasm (Derogatis et al., 1978), and sexual contacts with men were extensive with many different partners (Pomeroy, 1967).

The causes of this low sexual urge and outlet are varied. For some, it may be due to ingestion of female hormones (Pomeroy, 1967). For others, there may be repression of sexuality rather than simply low sex drive (McCully, 1963). And, those who loathe their penises as symbols of their hated maleness avoid any stimulation of that organ (Ovesey and Person, 1973).

In sexual contact with males they take the receptor role, primarily anal (Pomeroy, 1967; Sorensen and Hertoft, 1982). Many do not seek erection and do not regret losing potency after estrogen treatment (Money and Primrose, 1969). However, after vaginoplasty, about half reported orgasmic experiences (Lindemalm et al., 1986).

They do have a rich sexual fantasy life (Pomeroy, 1967), but little interest in erotica. Most of those who were exposed to erotica in their preadolescent years were with a family member at the time, rather than alone or with peers. This exposure was not followed by sexual activity. Low incidence of exposure continues into adolescence. What erotic material they do see tends to feature homosexual activity, but there is little desire to act out these scenes. Erotica is not as arousing as feminine objects, such as clothing or as their own fantasies (Goldstein and Kant, 1973).

While reporting the same number of sexual fantasy themes as heterosexuals, transsexuals' fantasies contain role reversal—cross-dressing, imagining themselves as women, being submissive (bondage, forced to submit) (Derogatis et al., 1978), and being females having sex with a male (Pomeroy, 1967; Freund, Langevin, Zajac, Steiner, and Zajac, 1974; Person and Ovesey, 1974a). Role reversal fantasies are especially common in standard transsexuals (Sorensen and Hertoft, 1982).

Fantasies reveal a highly idealized concept of love and marriage, with romance more important than sex (Doorbar, 1969; Person and Ovesey, 1974a) and emotional gratification more satisfying than orgasm (Edgerton et al., 1970). Responsiveness is not always accompanied by erection (Pomeroy, 1967).

Jan Morris (1974) reports that his sexual fantasies centered more on "caresses than copulation."

The majority, as many as 80 percent, prefer male sexual partners (Pomeroy, 1967; Hoenig et al., 1970; Barr, Raphael, and Hennessey, 1974; Hoenig and Kenna, 1974b; Hore et al., 1975; Sorensen and Hertoft, 1980a; Bullough et al., 1983). They are attracted to heterosexual men (Freund, Langevin, Zajac, Steiner, and Zajac, 1974); homosexuals disgust them (Hamburger et al., 1953). Using penile volume change, it was found that those requesting surgery were more aroused to male stimuli than were homosexuals. Perhaps, as an index of their interest in the feminine, transsexuals' galvanic skin response was stronger to pictures of females than was that of homosexuals (Barr, 1973; Barr and Blaszczynski, 1976).

A small group of from 4 to 25 percent, probably gender dysphoric transvestites, want a female sex partner (Barr et al., 1974; Feinbloom et al., 1976; Sorensen and Hertoft, 1980a; Bullough et al., 1983) and a few are bisexual. Others are uncertain of their sexual orientation, like one postoperative transsexual who was so attractive that he became a successful topless dancer and received several marriage proposals. Yet, a year after surgery he gave up sexual relations with men and formed a stable relationship with a woman (Gottlieb, 1978). Partner preferences of transsexuals, transvestites, and homosexuals are shown in Table 5.2.

Interviews with male partners of transsexuals reveal that all were heterosexually experienced and some had had no contact with the homosexual community. When they met their transsexual partners, most assumed that they were women (Money and Brennan, 1970).

Gender Role Conceptions

Other than those few transsexuals who are "profoundly and naturally" feminine, there is an absence of consolidated gender identity/role. Rather than being feminine, they are simulating femininity (Meyer and Hoopes, 1974). As a defense against ambiguous gender identity, they have assumed a pseudofemi-

TABLE 5.2
Partner Preferences of Transsexuals (TS),
Transvestites (TV), and Homosexuals

Percent	TS	TV	Homosexual
Partner			
Female	24	82	2
Male	52	6	80
Both	17	12	17
Neither	6	2	2
Number of subjects	33	65	57

From: V. Bullough, B. Bullough, and R. Smith (1983), A comparative study of male transvestites, male to female transsexuals, and male homosexuals. *Journal of Sex Research*, 19:260.

nine narcissism, with low genital interest (Sorensen and Hertoft, 1980).

Simulation is not difficult on masculinity–femininity scales. On these scales, transsexuals score in the extreme feminine range, indicating either conformity to the traditional feminine stereotype or disavowal of the masculine (Rosen, 1974; Roback, Mckee, Webb, Abramowitz, and Abramowitz, 1976; Langevin, Paitich, and Steiner, 1977; Tsoi et al., 1977; Lothstein, 1979a; Fleming et al., 1981; Hunt, Carr, and Hampson, 1981; Beatrice, 1985).

On scales that yield both masculinity and femininity scores, such as Bem's Sex Role Inventory, most transsexuals score more feminine and less masculine than either females or males (Skrapec and MacKenzie, 1981). Masculinity scores are lower than those of homosexuals (Freund, Langevin, Zajac, and Steiner, 1974). Denial of masculinity, rather than adoption of femininity, is seen in one study where transsexuals and heterosexual males were only three points apart on femininity, but transsexuals were twelve points lower on masculinity (Derogatis, Meyer, and Vazquez, 1978). For some, masculinity and femininity scores are equal, placing them in the androgynous category (Fleming, Jenkins, and Bugarin, 1980; Skrapec and MacKenzie, 1981).

In the cognitive realm, gender dysphorics' verbal IQ scores are higher than their perceptual organization scores, a finding supposedly characteristic of females (Money and Epstein, 1967). They talk more and use fewer evaluative phrases (good–bad) than heterosexual males, indicating that they are selective in judging their own behavior (Money and Block, 1971). On a vocabulary test designed to differentiate between the sexes, transsexuals knew as many feminine as masculine words, whereas control males knew twice as many masculine as feminine words (Kenna and Hoenig, 1978). Similarly, diagnosed preoperatives emitted more sex-typed behaviors, both feminine and masculine, than control females. This may account for the impression that they are more feminine than females (Barlow, Mills, Agras, and Steinman, 1980).

None of these gender role studies answer the question of stable or confused gender identity. A few do indicate that transsexuals are eschewing masculinity more than they are affirming femininity.

Some (Sorensen and Hertoft, 1980a) see transsexuals as similar to Reich's passive feminine character who covers up his sadistic–aggressive urges, incestuous longings, and castration fears by a feminine submissive attitude toward life, anal interests, and passive, masochistic homosexuality (Reich, 1949). However, no evidence of sexual masochism was found in transsexual applicants (Freund, Langevin, Zajac, Steiner, and Zajac, 1974).

The desire for reassignment on the part of those who loathe their maleness is more of a rejection of male identity than a quest for female identity (Sabalis, Staton, and Appenzeller, 1977). They see males as aggressive and destructive creatures (Guze, 1969): "Men are lustful gorillas, viscious destroying . . . the man is just a penis, a nothing . . . they perform to satisfy women and then have to be grateful to them" (Weitzman et al., 1970, p. 299).

The preoperative transsexual suffers from gender role strain; that is, the feeling of difficulty in fulfilling his masculine role obligations. This role strain is augmented by his exaggerated conception of masculinity, and so, in comparing himself with it, he becomes convinced of his own unworthiness. If not truly masculine, a conception that he both loves and fears, then he must be feminine, which means to him, female (Guze, 1969). Jan Morris's (1974) concept of manhood was molded in the military tradition of courage, loyalty, self-discipline, and being in charge of things. Yet, Morris did not share this unquestioned sense of manhood, and resented being identified with the male sex, even by close friends.

A feeling of disgust is evoked by pubertal body changes, especially toward penis enlargement (Lothstein, 1980b) and, by late adolescence, all male physical characteristics are loathed (Pauly, 1968). Perhaps, as a focus of his own self-loathing, his penis is singled out for special hatred since it symbolizes manliness and negates his being a woman (Person and Ovesey, 1974a). The penis becomes a separate entity, an alien being, a depersonalized portion of the body, a thing that does not belong (Guze, 1969). It is a source of disgust and contempt and is regarded as ugly (Benjamin, 1954; Worden and Marsh, 1955): "I just want to get rid of those awful things between my legs" (Randell, 1969, p. 356).

A postsurgical patient remarks: " 'My sex urge whored everything . . . I resented the continuous pressure of sex, I had too many erections in one day . . . my penis got the better of me, I wanted freedom from it . . . I failed as a man. Now I am a woman' " (Weitzman et al., 1970, p. 300).

One source of this loathing may be hatred toward father. Rage against father is displaced onto that part of himself symbolizing father and maleness, as this father reports: "He would get angry with me and say: 'I'll kill you, I'll kill you, I'll cut my balls out and throw them in your face' " (Weitzman et al., 1971, p. 294).

After psychotherapy, another young man, whose alcoholic father mistreated both his son and his wife, said: "Now I can see how I turned my negative feelings for my father into negative feelings about men in general and how that has developed into positive desires not to be a man but to be totally a woman. Maybe then I would be treated better or something" (Forester and Swiller, 1972, p. 349).

Shortly after surgery, gender role strain is lower in transsexuals than in males or females. They endorse more traditional feminine traits than females and see themselves as matching those traits (Kando, 1972). After amputation, the negative genital attitude is replaced by an appreciation of the penis's absence. In sexual terms, there is a dislike for the aggressive, insertor sexual role, and a desire to experience the insertee role (Prince, 1981). Jan Morris (1974) attributes some of his personality change from activity to passivity to removal of his penis which symbolized maleness, thrust, and strength. After its removal, he felt his body was made to "yield and accept."

If the penis is depersonalized, then perhaps there would be a low incidence of phantom penis after amputation. Some report that this experience is indeed rare (Money and Primrose, 1969; Hastings and Markland, 1978), while others find the phantom experience not at all uncommon (Wolf et al., 1968; Guze, 1969; Lothstein, 1980). In one series, about a third experienced phantom penis (Sorensen, 1981a). Of course, if some penile tissue is left after amputation to form an artificial vagina, then phantom sensations are to be expected (Kubie and MacKie, 1968).

Insecure gender identity is resolved by escaping from the masculine to the feminine which is seen as nonaggressive and idyllic (Sorensen, 1981a). The perceived passivity of women affords an escape from the fear of their own aggressiveness (Volkan and Berent, 1976), and of being aggressed against: "I'm really a woman—don't hurt me. I'll do what you want" (Guze, 1969, p. 174).

Females are seen as being loved, admired, and dependent (Lothstein, 1979b). Womanhood is glorified as is female anatomy. For the most part the concept of sex differences is focused on appearances, not substance (McCully, 1963; Bentler, 1976). "[I picture myself] as a female with beautiful long hair and with my features changed so that I would be attractive so that people would notice me" (Worden and Marsh, 1955). Vaginas are described as "marvels and beauties that are beyond description" (Morgan, 1978). Others feel disgust and horror for women's vaginas, but still want one for themselves: "I would like it on me, but I find it repulsive on another woman's body and would prefer to see men's organs" (Worden and Marsh, 1955, p. 1296).

Women may be viewed as powerful and controlling. While

they are loving, protecting, and beautiful, they "have the power, the control . . . they dominate and emasculate men" (Weitzman et al., 1970, p. 298).

Other than those rare transsexuals who have been female identified since childhood, most have both masculine and feminine identities and associated roles, and there may be instability in the strength of the two dissociated (split) representations (Volkan and Berent, 1976). The feminine encompasses tenderness, concern for others. It is positively evaluated and identified with. In the masculine representation there is activity and aggressive striving. The difference between transsexuality and multiple personality is that the transsexual is aware of both unintegrated aspects (Meyer, 1982).

One preoperative transsexual experienced difficulty in separating his feminine and masculine roles, like leaving "her" lipstick in "his" trenchcoat. He had to think twice before greeting friends, unsure of whether they were "her" or "his" acquaintances. He even had to check in a mirror to find out whether he was her or him (Feinbloom, 1976). Another had three wardrobes and personas to match: Ed, the aggressive male; Edward, a "handsome, smooth-cheeked prince" on the effeminate side; and his favorite, Maria, an "innocent and beautiful virgin" (Weitzman et al., 1970).

In another case, a young transvestite who received reassignment surgery felt the presence of and acted out masculine and feminine roles; one portion of his personality being dominant at a time. There was yet a third portion, with the unisexed name Sandy, who was able to respond as either male or female (Money and Wolff, 1973).

Usually "brother" is actively disliked: "I hated George, and by having surgery I killed him." George's maleness had been condensed on the penis, even though this person lived for some time after surgery as a male (Prince, 1981, p. 47). Conn (1974) reveals that, "it was as if I had become obsessed with the virtual elimination of everything masculine from my life; as though I were afraid in a tight moment I might step back over the line [back to masculinity]" (pp. 175–176).

In some cases, the compartmentalized masculine identity may suddenly reemerge (Eber, 1980). A twenty-five-year-old's referral request was "to look like a man again" (p. 33). He had self-administered estrogens, and, without funds for surgery, "I did it myself." At twenty-one, he had a vagina installed. As a successful fashion model, he earned as much as $300 a day. He was married to a heterosexual male, but sex was not enjoyable because "deep inside I knew I was really a man" (p. 33). Later he became involved with a girl, and assumed a masculine role. But, he vacillated between wanting to be, and dressing like, male and female.

Gender identity/role weakness and instability is seen in a twenty-two-year-old who had been living as a female for over two years. Several days before surgery, the hospital decided to stop doing sex reassignment. Both frustrated and relieved, he said that if he had had surgery, he would have continued to live as a female, but felt happier now in the masculine role. However, after five years in that role, he was again contemplating reassignment (Shore, 1984).

One patient's desire to be a woman was cyclic, accompanied by a cramping feeling he thought was spurious menstruation. He recollects this desire to be a female from earliest childhood. Cross-dressing began at nine years of age and was accompanied by sexual arousal. Several times he had thought of mutilating himself and sought psychiatric help for depression and anxiety. The administration of phrenotropic drugs (nialamide, clorpromazine, meprobamate) relieved him of his desire to be a woman (Pennington, 1960).

FEMALE TO MALE TRANSSEXUAL

The Act

Stages of Alteration

In reputable gender identity programs, the female applicant is required to pass through the same screening, orientation, and counseling procedures as the male. Lothstein (1983) believes that long-term psychotherapy, not surgery, is the initial treatment of choice. One of the few reports of successful gender identity change involves an adolescent female who underwent two years of individual and milieu therapy. Since nursery school she had wanted to wear boy's clothes. She had early sought affection from her mother who did not reciprocate. There was evidence of denied homosexuality (Davenport and Harrison, 1977).

Bodily characteristics with which preoperative females are most dissatisfied are having ovaries, uterus, clitoris, vagina, and breasts, and lack of facial hair (Lingren and Pauly, 1975; Kuiper and Cohen-Kettenis, 1988).

As with males, a good number of females take hormones prior to coming to a gender identity clinic. Behind her stated purpose of wanting to masculinize her body, there are other unstated, fanciful motives. Some of these are beliefs that androgens will remove her breasts, enable her to grow a penis, give her strength and courage, and make her less vulnerable (Lothstein, 1983).

Some effects of androgen are reversible when hormone administration is discontinued: enlargement of the clitoris of up to a three-inch length, cessation of menstruation, increased sex drive, coarsening of the skin, and acne. Irreversible effects include thickening of vocal cords which deepens the voice, growth of beard and body hair, and potential loss of fertility (Benjamin and Ihlenfeld, 1973; Meyer, Finkelstein, Stuart, Webb, Smith, Payer, and Walker, 1981; Lothstein, 1983).

If she proceeds satisfactorily through the program and does not respond to psychotherapy, then sex alteration surgery can be recommended. Surgery is usually a several step procedure. First is breast tissue removal, which may leave considerable scarring. Phantom breast experiences after mastectomy are extremely rare (Money and Brennan, 1969; Lothstein, 1983). Next, uterus, fallopian tubes, and ovaries are removed. The final step, not elected by all, is construction of a scrotum with plastic testicles and a penislike appendage (phalloplasty). The major reason for wanting a penis is fear of being discovered as a female (Hoopes, 1969). Phalloplasty is not as yet a perfected technique and may require repeated surgical repair. Many postsurgical fears and dissatisfactions revolve around the grafted penis (Lothstein, 1983). Surgical complications occur in one-quarter of the cases (Laub and Fisk, 1974).

Before and After Adjustment

Most females express satisfaction with the outcome of surgery (Hertz et al., 1961; Money, 1971). In a review of outcome studies, a trend was noted for females to have more favorable outcomes than men (Lundstrom, Pauly, and Walinder, 1984). It appears that they are better able to adjust to the masculine role than males can to the feminine role (Pauly, 1969b). Suicide attempts decreased, many had a female partner, and more were sexually active than before surgery (Sorensen, 1981b). However, about half reported ideas of suicide after surgery (Lothstein, 1980a).

Successful assumption of the masculine role is related to psychosocial adjustment, lowered depression and tension, and living with a partner. Adjustment showed a stronger relation with taking male hormones than with surgery, but it may have been the expectation of surgery that had a salutory effect (Blanchard and Steiner, 1983).

The factor leading to unsatisfactory outcomes is failure to achieve an adequate artificial penis (Money, 1971; Randell, 1971; Sorensen, 1981b; Lundstrom et al., 1984). Those who have only a mastectomy fare better than those who also have phalloplasty. It may be that those who elect phalloplasty are the gender envious type who have unrealistic expectations about their artificial penises, making them especially prone to fear and depression when results do not measure up (Lothstein, 1980a).

The Person

Current Status

Age and onset. Typical age at which female transsexuals register at a clinic is the early twenties (Akesson and Walinder, 1969; Pauly, 1974a; Lothstein, 1983; Tsoi, 1988). Their decision to seek alteration is often in response to some personal loss or abandonment, such as the death of their father (Lothstein, 1983).

Most female transsexuals report wishes of being a boy when

they were about six to seven years old (Pauly, 1974a; Blanchard et al., 1987) and almost all had cross-dressing urges prior to puberty (Sorensen and Hertoft, 1982; Lothstein, 1983). Actual cross-dressing began earlier and they were more consistent about it than males (Pauly, 1969b; Verschoor and Poortinga, 1988).

Ethnic origin. Black female applicants are rare (Lothstein, 1979b). In a review of studies throughout the world, only one female was not Caucasian (Pauly, 1974a). At the Stanford Clinic, the ethnic distribution of applicants was 93 percent Caucasian, 3 percent black, and 4 percent Asian (Dixen et al., 1984).

Marital status. A fifth or less have been married to males, but a third to a half have lived or had a stable relationship with a woman (Hoenig, Kenna, and Youd, 1970; Meyer et al., 1971; Pauly, 1974a; Lothstein, 1983; Kockott and Fahrner, 1988; Verschoor and Poortinga, 1988). They and their female partners are no more conformist, rule-bound, or concerned with appearances than control couples (Fleming, Castos, and Mc-Gowan, 1984). Their relationships are as stable and satisfying as those of comparable nontranssexual couples (Fleming, MacGowan, and Castos, 1985).

Involvement with a female partner is related to degree to which she is regarded by others as a male. An important aspect of the relationship is the extent to which the partner shares her conviction that she is a man (Huxley, Kenna, and Brandan, 1981b). It may be that female partners see masculinity as more behavioral than physical (Blanchard, 1985b). Those with partners, compared to those without, had less time unemployed, more stable ratings by psychiatrists, knew more male words on a vocabulary test, and were more persistent in pursuing their transsexual aims (Huxley, Kenna, and Brandan, 1981a).

Biological Basis

Abnormally large plasma testosterone values have been reported (Pauly, 1974b), some almost double the concentration for control females. As a consequence, menstrual cycles are longer with less frequent strong bleeding. It has been suggested that transsexualism in the female is associated with androgen overproduction (Sipova and Starka, 1977). Other studies, however, report that circulating testosterone is within the normal range for women (Jones and Samimy, 1973).

Because of atypical reactions to luetenizing releasing hormones, it is speculated that there was an abnormal hormone situation during the sensitive period of brain development, especially in hypothalamic-pituitary gonadotropin regulation (Seyler, Canalis, Spare, and Reichlin, 1978). Studies on small samples of transsexual women have found over half were H-Y antigen positive (Eicher et al., 1979; Engel, Pfafflin, and Wiedeking, 1980). Also, one-third showed evidence of ovarian disease that interfered with normal hormone production (Futterweit, Weiss, and Fagerstrom, 1986).

An early study reported no cases of chromosomal abnormality (Hoenig and Torr, 1964), but occasionally cases of complex chromosomal abnormality do appear (Videla and Prigoshin, 1976). Monozygotic twin studies do not support the idea of an inherited, genetic factor. One female of a monozygotic pair was exceedingly masculine, and the other feminine (Green and Stoller, 1971).

Abnormal EEGs have been reported in a third to a half of cases studied (Pauly, 1974b; Hoenig and Kenna, 1979), but the causal link, if any, to transsexualism is unknown.

Early Life

Parents. Two-thirds were raised in a rural setting (Pauly, 1974a). Family life was chaotic, with a half suffering abuse, neglect, losses, and separations (Lothstein, 1983). Contact with both parents was more unsatisfactory than in a comparison group of pregnant women (Uddenberg et al., 1979).

This strong, vigorous infant of an unlovely appearance will learn, very early in life that being a girl is bad and being a boy is good. Mother, although present, was too depressed or too physically ill to provide mothering (Stoller, 1972, 1980). Her own lack of a cohesive sense of self was communicated to her daughter. Mother was emotionally disturbed, cool and rejecting, and the nondominant partner in marriage. Since mother disliked her own femininity and was envious of males, she wanted a male child of her own. But, a daughter was born and she disparaged the little girl's femininity, yet she also felt a kinship as between miserable females (Lothstein, 1983): "My mother always made me feel that to be a woman is bad. I remember her always telling me that she wanted a boy instead of a girl" (Barahal, 1953, p. 403).

Perceiving mother's hostility and her own hostility toward her mother, the girl defensively shifts to a tentative masculine identity (Lothstein, 1979b). Not only was mother unable to accept her daughter's femaleness, she also impressed her with the dangers of relying on males, the enemy. The little girl accepted mother's negative feelings toward her female genitals, and observed the advantages of being a boy. For instance, one little girl's brother came home after a long hospitalization to be showered with mother's affection. Shortly thereafter, the girl decided to be a boy (Warner and Lahn, 1970). Mother, either alone or in conjunction with father or grandparents, supported boyish behaviors and masculine identity (Lothstein, 1983).

As happens with heterosexual males, female transsexuals' contact with mother decreased from childhood to adulthood, whereas contact with mother increased for a group of pregnant women (Uddenberg et al., 1979). In adolescence transsexual women were ambivalent toward their mothers, seeing them as weak and in need of protection, but also fearing their authority (Sorensen and Hertoft, 1982).

Martino (1977) describes her father as a "man's man in the Italian tradition, feared by almost everyone who knew him, loved by few, respected by all" (p. 4). Fathers are reported to be very masculine, physically abusive, emotionally disturbed, and alcoholic (Redmount, 1953; McCully, 1963; Pauly, 1969b, 1974a). Their physical absence from the home when their daughters were young served to enhance their standing in the daughters' eyes when they were present.

Father did not take over the mothering role abandoned by his wife, but assigned those responsibilities to his daughter and encouraged her masculinization. He did not give support to his emotionally distant wife, but sent his daughter in to fulfill that role. Mother is seen by her daughter as being in need of her protection from the father (Redmount, 1953; Pauly, 1969b,

1974a; Stoller, 1972, 1980): "She made me promise when I was about 10 years old that, when I grew up, I would take care of her" (Barahal, 1953, p. 395). In such a situation, the girl fears being like her vulnerable and abused mother (Lothstein, 1983).

Not only is there a strong prepubertal attachment to father (Simon, 1967; Pauly, 1974a) but also a need to repair the separation from her mother (Meyer, 1982). A twenty-two-year-old, a tomboy in childhood, wore her hair short, and dressed as a man. She had numerous homosexual relationships, especially with married women. She saw men as those who make women suffer as her father had made her mother miserable. Her love of women served as a substitute for the love she sought but was denied by her mother. "I frequently brought girls home and kissed them in front of my mother just to make her jealous, as if to say, 'You see you don't love me, but I can get others to do so' " (Barahal, 1953, p. 406).

Gender development. As children, they were extremely active, engaging in fighting, playing boys' games, and wearing boys' clothes (Vogt, 1968; Stoller, 1972; Pauly, 1974a). They were clearly different from other girls and often labeled "tomboys" (Money and Brennan, 1969). Compared to male transsexuals, females suffered less teasing and social isolation because of their cross-gender behaviors. Desires to dress as boys could be satisfied by wearing unisex clothes. They had clear fantasies of being boys when they were as young as five years old (Lothstein, 1983) and by about eight years they had invented boys' names for themselves (Stoller, 1972). In childhood they associated primarily with boys, but in adolescence shifted their preference to girls because they were sexually attracted to them. In adolescence, they were rather extroverted (Sorensen and Hertoft, 1982).

Personality

There appears to one major variety of gender disturbed females (Blanchard, 1985a). She is the most masculine of females and has been so since childhood. According to Stoller (1980), she is unlike the male primary transsexual in that her cross-gender identity is a product of trauma. Rather, she is the ultimate outcome of active female homosexuality (Anchersen, 1956).

There is the impression that the female transsexual is more of a "solid citizen" than the male, holding a respectable and responsible job, and achievement oriented in a traditionally male occupation. There is an absence of exhibitionistic behavior that is noted in some males. She is more businesslike in her approach to surgery and has more reasonable expectations of its outcome than do males. She sees transformation as a necessary step in being successful in the masculine role (Hoopes, 1969). Life goals are to pursue education or vocational careers, seek marriage, home, and children (Martino, 1977). Above all, she wants to appear active, potent, and dominant (Sorensen and Hertoft, 1980a).

An often cited finding is that female transsexuals are not especially psychopathological (Rosen, 1974; Roback et al., 1976; Derogatis, Meyer, and Boland, 1981). However, physical self-concept, self-esteem, and psychological adjustment are lower in transsexuals than in either homosexuals or heterosexual females. In all, from one-fourth to one-third are seriously disturbed (Strassberg, Roback, Cunningham, McKee, and Larson, 1979). One-half are given psychiatric diagnoses in addition to gender identity disorder (Levine, 1980), and three-quarters of gender disturbed adolescents have severe personality disorders (Lothstein, 1980b). Depression ranges from mild to severe, and about a half have been suicidal but only a few (5%) have actually attempted suicide (Huxley, Kenna, and Brandon, 1981a; Lothstein, 1983; Kockott and Fahrner, 1988).

Those who dread their breasts and long to be rid of them display more pathology than other women seeking sex change. Gender envy females are anxious to have phalloplasty and are caricatures of masculinity (Lothstein, 1979b).

Compared to male applicants, females report fewer criminal convictions, a more stable work history, more stable sexual relationships, fewer suicide attempts, and fewer attempts at self-mutilation (Pauly, 1974a; Dixen et al., 1984). Still, there is personality test and behavioral evidence of unconventional attitudes and acting out—theft, robbery, and alcoholism (Pauly, 1974a; Roback et al., 1976; Lothstein, 1980). Drug dependence is reported to be higher in female than in male transsexuals (Meyer, 1982).

Sexuality and Partner Preference

Breast development, onset of menstruation, and other pubertal sex changes were loathed and recalled as disturbing, disgusting, and humiliating (Benjamin, 1966; Stoller, 1972; Pauly, 1974a; Lothstein, 1980b). Some bound their breasts tightly to give a flat-chested appearance. Many were convinced they had hidden testes (Pauly, 1974b). Menstrual flow was reported as scant.

Transsexual females have had fewer sexual experiences with men than heterosexual females, with a half to two-thirds having such encounters (Derogatis et al., 1981; Lothstein, 1983). Only a few of these were long-term relationships. They had sexual relations earlier in adolescence than did a group of female homosexuals (McCauley and Ehrhardt, 1977). Eighty percent had their first sexual relationship with a female before they were eighteen years old, compared to only 40 percent of female homosexuals (McCauley and Ehrhardt, 1980).

Incest occupies a prominent place in their histories, with almost a fourth reporting instances of sexual misuse by male relatives (Lothstein, 1983). One woman had been seduced by her stepfather and two of her uncles when she was about twelve years old (Barahal, 1953).

Sex drive is lower than in heterosexual females, but they are not asexual (Derogatis et al., 1981). Sexual responsivity is low in masturbation and in heterosexual or homosexual relations. Disliking their female parts, they do not allow contact with their breasts or vagina, rather they masturbate their partners (Money and Brennan, 1969; Sorensen and Hertoft, 1980a). One-half do find pleasure in clitoral stimulation and some report orgasm from indirect stimulation from women (Pauly, 1974a; McCauley and Ehrhardt, 1980) and they report more variety in sexual techniques than do male transsexuals (Dulko, 1988).

She must be the initiator of sex, the dominant, active one, and her partner must be receptive (Pauly, 1974a; Sorensen and Hertoft, 1982). She seeks a female partner who is a highly feminine heterosexual who likes male bodies, longs for pregnancy and motherhood, and who responds to her as if she were a man (Stoller, 1972, 1980; Pauly, 1974a). Her attachment to her female partner is sentimental and romantic rather than genital (Money and Brennan, 1969)— "I am desperately and hopelessly in love with the most wonderful girl in the world" (Hamburger, 1953, p. 369).

They report the same number of sexual fantasies as heterosexual women, but they are more cross-sexed and more conservative (Derogatis et al., 1981). Virtually all have same sex partner choice (Hamburger, 1953; Randall, 1959; Sorensen and Hertoft, 1980a) of which they became aware between ages six to twenty-two. In her fantasies, she is a male, without breasts and with a penis, having sexual relations with a woman (Money and Brennan, 1969; Hoenig, Kenna, and Youd, 1970; McCauley and Ehrhardt, 1980; Verschoor and Poortinga, 1988). A rare exception to this is a girl who wanted to be a male ballet dancer and have a "homosexual" relationship with a man (Lothstein, 1983).

Early in her sexual awakening, she probably considered herself homosexual, and was initially confused and disturbed by this (Pauly, 1974a; Lothstein, 1983). Eventually, homosexuality is denied: "You and I are not lesbians. We relate as man to woman, woman to man. I'm not sure of all the differences now—but there are differences" (Martino, 1977, p. 132). Homosexual females are disliked because they define the transsexual as female and want to touch them (Stoller, 1972).

There are many similarities, but also important differences between transsexual and homosexual women. No differences in parental background were found. Both groups were labeled tomboys, preferred boys' toys, and had little maternal interest in fantasy or play. But, more transsexuals than homosexuals wanted boys for friends and playmates, wanted to be boys, had stronger negative feelings to wearing girls' clothes, menarche, and breast development (Ehrhardt, Grisanti, and McCauley, 1979). Transsexuals feel more friendly and positive toward males, and are less competitive with them than are female homosexuals (Stoller, 1972; McCauley and Ehrhardt, 1980).

Masculinity–Femininity

The female transsexual lacks a consolidated sense of self as female, fearing femaleness she equates it with being helpless, dependent, and vulnerable. Maleness, being strong and aggressive, is safe (Volkan and Berent, 1976). At some level of consciousness, the penis is felt to be an amulet that will protect her from separation and loss, and allay her fears of being penetrated (Lothstein, 1979b, 1983). She sees men as making women suffer and as untrustworty, yet she wants men to love and protect her (Barahal, 1953). The masculine role she adopts is stereotyped and caricatured (Sorensen, 1981b). Her personality has been likened to Reich's phallic narcissistic character who finds satisfaction in action, who reacts to gender identity uncertainty by working on the environment (alloplastic), trying to convince herself and others of her masculinity (Sorensen and Hertoft, 1980).

Masculinity–femininity scale scores indicate that transsexual women, while not feminine as females, are not overly masculine when compared to males (Money and Brennan, 1969; Pauly, 1974a; Roback et al., 1976; McCauley and Ehrhardt, 1977; Lothstein, 1980; Derogatis et al., 1981; Fleming et al., 1981; Fleming, MacGowan, and Salt, 1984). About a third scored in the androgynous range, with masculinity and femininity scores about equal (Fleming, Jenkins, and Bugarin, 1980). When asked to draw the picture of a person, 92 percent of transsexuals compared to 13 percent of female homosexuals, drew the male figure first. This supposedly indicates that female transsexuals are more identified with males than are homosexuals.

PART III

THE PARAPHILIAS

Paraphilia is the current term for what previously had been called sexual perversion or deviation. The term was introduced to avoid the negative connotations attached to the older labels. Literally, paraphilia means misplaced attraction, emphasizing that deviations are disturbances in the arousal phase of sexuality. Paraphilias are roundabout ways to sexual stimulation, detours to the final activity—manipulation of the penis through intercourse or masturbation (Balint, 1956).

According to the *Diagnostic and Statistical Manual of Mental Disorders* (DSM-III-R), the essential feature is "recurrent intense sexual urges and sexually arousing fantasies generally involving either (1) nonhuman objects, (2) the suffering or humiliation of oneself or one's partner (not merely simulated), or (3) children or other nonconsenting persons. [Further] the diagnosis is made only if the person has acted on these urges, or is markedly distressed by them" (American Psychiatric Association, 1987, p. 279). Even if an individual persistently engages in and enjoys his own paraphiliac fantasies and related pornography, but has not acted out these urges, then he does not merit a DSM-III-R diagnosis of paraphilia. This requirement, that the individual act out his urges, is a significant change from the earlier DSM-III definition that included "unusual or bizarre imagery or acts" (American Psychiatric Association, 1980, p. 266).

The sexually ideal male not only is certain of his masculinity, he is also attracted to a person to whom he can relate as an equal in a warm and loving way. The paraphiliac, however, is attracted either to something or someone other than an adult and/or relates to his partner in an incomplete or nonegalitarian fashion.

There are two general types of paraphilias—disturbances in partner preference and distortions in mode of relating to that partner. Degree of deviance in partner preference is assessed by the distance from the ideal partner, varying from an object (fetishism) to an immature human (pedophilia and incest). Modes of relating may focus on preliminary stages of the sexual encounter such as exposing one's penis (exhibitionism) and merely looking at another (peeping). Or, the interaction may progress to actual or fantasized contact with the partner in a controlling (sadistic) or subservient (masochistic) manner.

These two types of paraphilias are similar to those defined by Freud (1905) in his distinction between the object and aim of the sexual impulse. He considered any partner other than a mature female a deviation of object, and any act that did not culminate in genital union a deviation of aim.

6 FETISHISM

INTRODUCTION

It is not uncommon to find attractive certain physical attributes, forms of dress, odors, and a host of other details. These attributes exert a charm, we are drawn to the person because of them. However, the emphasis is on the person possessing the quality, not on the quality itself. It is also the case that many are put off by a particular quality. In an otherwise attractive person, one quality—facial hair, a small blemish, an accent—may totally override attractive forces and result in distaste.

The line from commonplace to deviant is crossed when it is not the person as a whole, but a single part that is attractive, when a part is displaced from the person and becomes a sexual object in itself (Krafft-Ebing, 1902; Romm, 1949). Often in fetishism, sexual arousal is triggered by a part that has no obvious or direct relation to sexuality, such as hand, nose, or foot. The line is surely crossed when that which is desired is not a part of a person, but an object, such as an article of clothing, hairbrush, or some kind of material as rubber, leather, or fur. The situation becomes pathological when the part or object takes precedence over the person, when one aspect becomes the focus of the individual's sex life, and when it substitutes for a lover (Stekel, 1930a; Hirschfeld, 1940).

175

While the normal lover overestimates the person who possesses certain special qualities that make her more valuable, the fetishist depreciates the woman and exhalts the fetish. He may be so alienated from women that he is repelled by the nude female and especially by the sight of her genitals (Romm, 1949). What is a means to an end for the normal lover becomes an end in itself to the fetishist, who thereby makes himself independent of women (Stekel, 1930a).

Fetishism has certain advantages over other deviations. So long as he does not steal the object of his affection, his problem is easily concealed, so that he is not subject to ridicule or harassment. The fetish frees the fetishist from dependence on other people. And, he need not compete with other males for the possession of his adored and easily obtainable object (Freud, 1927; Romm, 1949).

He need not be alone in worshiping his fetish. Publications that cater to various fetish lovers, while not numerous, are available. In a survey of pornographic magazines, less than 1 percent each featured leather, rubber, and boots and shoes (Dietz and Evans, 1982). If he chooses, he can seek out like-minded fellows. The Macintosh Society is a social and self-help group based in England with over one thousand members from twenty-three countries. Also in England, there is a correspondence club for leather lovers with two hundred members (Gosselin and Wilson, 1980).

DEFINITION

The Meaning of Fetishism

Fifteenth-century Portuguese explorers told of carved objects revered by West Africans. Their worship not only brought benefits, but also warded off evil. Their power was so strong that it was dangerous to touch or even approach them. They were idealized, potent, dangerous, magical symbols. The term *fetish* was introduced in 1760 by the French anthropologist Charles de Brosses to refer to these images (Nagler, 1957). It derives from the Portuguese *fetisso* meaning an object signifying something that it does not resemble, yet produces feelings associated with its referent. In turn *fetisso* is thought to come from the Latin *facere,* meaning to make; that is, artificial.

Alfred Binet, of intelligence test fame, was the first to use the term *fetish* to refer to an unusual, sexually arousing stimulus. In 1888 he reported an incident that involved one of his students. While in a public park, this student noticed he had become sexually aroused to the point of erection. Looking about, he saw that next to him was a woman who emitted a strong, but pleasant body odor, which he realized was the cause of his sexual arousal (Haire, 1934).

A satisfactory definition of fetishism must detail the degree to which the person is attracted to the fetish and the nature of the fetish object. Degree of attraction poses no problem, as most definitions require that the fetish be either the most preferred or the exclusive means of sexual arousal. However, there are problems in defining the fetish object. Some definitions specify that the fetish be a nongenital object (Greenacre, 1968), thus possibly ruling out pubic hair. Other definitions require that the fetish be an inanimate object, and use the term *partialism* when erotic interest is centered on a part of the human body (Karpman, 1954). In DSM-III-R partialism is classed as a paraphilia not otherwise specified.

The official DSM-III-R criterion is, "recurrent, intense, sexual urges and sexually arousing fantasies . . . involving the use of nonliving objects (fetishes) (American Psychiatric Association, 1987, p. 282). The definition rules out articles worn in cross-dressing and objects that are specifically designed for sexual arousal, such as vibrators and pornographic playing cards.

The least restrictive definition is the best: "Fetishism may be defined as a form of behavior wherein sexual activity and sexual fantasy focuses to an unusual extent upon a body part or an inanimate object rather than on a person as a whole" (Gosselin and Wilson, 1984, p. 90).

In negative fetishism, it is the absence of some quality that is demanded. For example, an intelligent, educated man had a fetish for one-legged women. Impotent with two-legged women, he became quite passionate with one-legged women. Through extensive correspondence with one-legged women, he found himself a wife (Ellis, 1906). Related to negative fetishism is antifetishism, an aversion to a quality arising from the absence of the positive fetish. One who has a fetish for red hair, may also be repelled by any other hair colors (Hirschfeld, 1940).

Differing Conceptions

Does the fetish object gain some of its power because it is a symbol of something else or is the original pairing between fetish and sexual arousal purely an accidental association? Freud declared in his 1927 paper that the fetish is a substitute for the woman's, usually mother's, missing penis. Even though the fetish is not always a conventional phallic symbol, it acquires phallic meaning and thus gains power to attract. Its phallic significance is often acquired by accident as it is the thing seen by the child just prior to his discovery that mother lacks a penis. This explains the prevalence of feet, shoes, and undergarments as fetishes; fur represents pubic hair. Freud's theory also accounts for the rarity of female fetishists, since their discovery that mother lacks a penis comes as no big surprise.

From Binet to contemporary learning theorists, associationists have stressed the random association between fetish and sexual arousal and have not sought for any symbolism in the connection. Studies have shown that penile tumescence can be associated with pictures of women's boots by pairing boot pictures with pictures of a naked woman (Rachman, 1966; Rachman and Hodgson, 1968).

This viewpoint gives rise to some difficult questions. If fetishism is based solely on a chance pairing of an object and sexual excitation, then why is it not more common? Why are some fetish objects, such as shoes, feet, and rubber, so common, while pillow cases and coffee cups are extremely rare fetishes? Since sexual arousal often occurs when the male has his pants on, why are men's pants so seldom found as fetishes (Grant, 1954)?

To be sure, there is an association of ideas, but it is much richer than simply fetish paired with lust. A man who described himself as mild and timid has a fetish for women wearing heeled boots, since such boots "symbolize to me above all the idea of womanly energy and decision" (Hirschfeld, 1940, p. 41).

Another question receiving varying answers is the nature of the person who succumbs to fetishism. Binet gives little attention to the person, explaining the origin of this condition as an "accident acting on a predisposed subject." By predisposition he means a "general nervous hypersthesia"—excessive sensitivity of all the senses.

Hirschfeld (1938) considers the predisposition to be rather specific. He attributes the peculiar disposition of the subject to "sexual chemistry," that is, the balance of the sex hormones, a popular conception in his day. The fetishist is predisposed to "reach to certain categories and experiences and not to others" (p. 539). He is not arguing that the disposition to reach is as specific as a readiness for shoe or hair, but rather, the individual is pretuned to a particular class of objects and experiences. For example, one who has a strong need for tenderness would be more likely to acquire fur or hair fetishism than an attraction for rubber or leather.

Relation to Other Deviations

Fetishism has been associated with peeping, sadistic practices, bisexuality, homosexuality, and transvestism (Greenacre, 1953, 1955). Kleptomania and transvestism are seen as emerging from the same basis as fetishism; kleptomania emphasizes the seizing, and transvestism, the putting on of the object (Balint, 1935). An intimate relation between fetishism and sadomasochism has been proposed (Karpman, 1954), where leather, rubber, shoes, boots, and chains are standard fare in sadomasochistic scenes.

Homosexuality and Fetishism

Fetishism and homosexuality are often linked (Bak, 1953; Nagler, 1957). One view of this close relation is that they both stem from the early discovery that women lack penises, but the two differ in the person's reaction to this discovery and in the degree of postoedipal identification with mother and father (Lorand, 1930; Bak, 1953). It is thought that the fetish is formed earlier in development than homosexuality (Katan, 1964).

In the healthy, heterosexual orientation there is an acceptance of the penisless female and a masculine identification with the father. The homosexual accepts mother as she is, lacking a penis, and he identifies completely with her. Acknowledging women's castration, he avoids them, and turns to the penis of another man (Katan, 1964). The fetishist, however, denies that women have been castrated. The development of a fetish saves him from homosexuality, but prevents a healthy sexual adjustment. He is saved from homosexuality because he has endowed the female with a penis which makes her less fearsome and therefore tolerable as a sexual object (Freud, 1927; Gillespie, 1940; Katan, 1964). Both the homosexual and fetishist share a fear of the masculine role due to a sense of inadequacy and low self-esteem (Nagler, 1957; Storr, 1957). The homosexual fetishist may wear a same-sex fetish, such as jockstrap or male boots. This has been called "homovestism" and the fetish is said to represent father's penis (Zavitzianos, 1977).

Transvestism

Clothes fetishism and transvestism are closely allied in that both overvalue women's clothing and in both the fantasy of the phallic woman is preserved (Peabody, Rowe, and Wall, 1953). They are also strongly related in that the symbol, female clothing, is dominant over the person, and pleasure is obtained from the symbol. In both, there was a strong attachment to mother and a desire to be united with her through clothing, since clothes represent mother.

But there are important differences. Ejaculation is easy for the fetishist, but not so for the transvestite. For the fetishist, the sexual symbolism is not obvious so that much meaning condenses onto the fetish, whereas women's clothes are clearly symbolic of the opposite sex (Epstein, 1961). An interesting combination of fetishism and transvestism is the man who cross-dressed with a fantasy of one-legged women engaging in sexual acts with him (Woody, 1973). He played the role of a female with a penis having sex with a woman who had lost a limb.

In fetishism, the female is dispensed with and symbols,

articles of feminine clothing, are substituted. In transvestism, the desire is to play, in part, the role of the female, but often with a woman (London, 1957). Both the fetishist and transvestite overestimate the feminine, but only when the clothing is brought into relation to the person do we have transvestism (Fenichel, 1930). The fetishist does not wear the article for any period of time, rather, the fetish is petted, fondled, squeezed, kissed, and caressed. Finally, it is brought into contact with the genitals so that orgasm can be obtained. However, if the object is worn for long periods of time, then clothes fetishism shades into transvestism (Stekel, 1930a; Hirschfeld, 1940).

Fetishism in Women

It is generally agreed that extreme fetishism is very rare in women (Krafft-Ebing, 1902; Ellis, 1906; Forel, 1905; Kinsey, Pomeroy, and Martin, 1953; Chesser, 1971). However, in its milder forms, such as attraction to men with beards, men dressed in military uniforms, tall men, and athletic men, fetishism is not uncommon.

According to standard psychoanalytic theory the fetish represents a penis. Fear of losing the organ is, of course, not operative here; rather the fetish represents a wish for a penis. By virtue of identification with her father, the woman wants to possess a penis (Fenichel, 1945). Consequently, the full-fledged female fetishist has strong masculine strivings (Socarides, 1988), and behaves toward the fetish as if it were a male; for example, a female handkerchief fetishist puts her nose in the handkerchief (Balint, 1935).

In the case of a female vibrator fetishist, it was concluded that her vibrator represented her father's penis. Using the vibrator, with which she chatted, allayed her castration anxiety since she did not have to touch her genitals to achieve orgasm (Zavitzianos, 1982).

Another woman was troubled with transient fetishism—she needed to read a book while she masturbated, the book represented father's penis and was used to deny her lack of a penis. The book also stood for a breast (Zavitzianos, 1971).

Evaluation of the Literature

Since Binet's time, contributions to the understanding of fetishism have come from two groups—psychoanalysts and learning theorists. Freud's 1927 paper "Fetishism" initiated rather intense interest in this deviation and numerous reports from psychoanalysts. However, this interest seems to have peaked in the 1950s and has waned since then. Despite the many psychoanalytic publications on fetishism, one reviewer remarks that "the meagerness of the literature basic to the prevailing psychoanalytic concepts of fetishism is noteworthy" (Nagler, 1957, p. 713).

However, interest in fetishism by psychoanalysts seems to have occurred in the 1950s, this time by those practicing behavior modification. It was thought that fetishes, unreasonable attraction to objects, should be as amenable to treatment as phobias, unreasonable fear of objects. However, in these articles more attention is devoted to techniques of symptom removal than to the personality of the fetishists.

Almost all our knowledge about the dynamics of fetishism comes from psychotherapists, mostly with a psychoanalytic orientation. The shining advantage of such studies is that they can provide an in-depth look into one individual, an individual who trusts the therapist and therefore is apt to reveal all. But, for this advantage a price is paid. There is an obvious sampling problem, not only because the number of patients seen is small, but also since those who seek professional help are only a segment of the population of interest, the segment that is troubled. It may well be that the mental abnormality associated with sexual deviates is the reason they seek psychotherapy and are thereby identified as deviant, rather than the cause of their deviation (Bejke, 1953).

Another disadvantage of clinical studies is the selective attention of the therapist. For instance, if the analyst is convinced that the fetish is a symbol of mother's missing penis, then he may overlook or fail to probe for other meanings. These shortcomings are not confined to the study of fetishism, but apply to any paraphilia where the bulk of our information comes from therapists' consulting rooms.

THE ACT

Fetish Objects

While virtually any body part, item of clothing, or article of daily use can become a fetish, there are relatively few classes of objects that do become fetishes. For decades, feet and shoes have been the most common of all fetishes (Ellis, 1906; Stekel, 1930a; Hirschfeld, 1938). Shoes are more common than feet, and hands more than gloves, probably since shoe and hand are more often seen than feet and gloves. Hair and fur are less frequent fetishes than might be expected. Women's gloves and corsets, which used to be favorites, are losing popularity, and garter belts have replaced garters (Gebhard, 1969). With the exception of the foot, there appears to be a shift away from nonclothing objects and body parts toward sexy undergarments and material, especially leather, rubber, and vinyl (Greenacre, 1953; Gosselin and Wilson, 1984).

Preferences of forty-eight fetishists were obtained from psychiatric hospital files and are presented in Table 6.1.

Some unusual fetish objects have been reported, for example, slightly smoking automobile exhaust pipes (Bergman, 1947). For one person, pianos with new and shiny cases induced

TABLE 6.1
Fetish Preferences

Type	Percent (N = 48)
Clothes	58
Rubber	23
Parts of Body	15
Footwear	15
Leather	10
Soft Materials (silk)	6
Clothes of Soft Material	8
Other	18

Source: A. J. Chalkley & E. E. Powell (1983), The clinical description of forty-eight cases of sexual fetishism. *British Journal of Psychiatry*, 142:292–295.

sexual arousal and orgasm without masturbation (Glover, 1933). Another fetishist collects snails, ants, and cockroaches, placing them on his body while he masturbates (Dewaraja, 1988). Other rare fetishes are the raised umbilicus (Heilbrunn, 1975); sexual arousal through damaging women's handbags and baby carriages (Raymond, 1956); and looking at safety pins (Mitchell, Falconer, and Hill, 1954).

Classification

Fetish objects can be divided into those that are inherent (body parts and qualities as hair color and voice), and those that are adherent (articles of clothing, objects such as hairbrushes and materials) (Hirschfeld, 1938). Either the substance or form of adherent objects may be important to the fetishist. Substances of leather or rubber, regardless of shape, may be more important than their form as shoe or undergarment. If the fetish is indeed a substitute for women or parts of women, then whether the object is hard or soft may have diagnostic value. Hard substances like rubber and vinyl, usually in the form of constricting garments, are often associated with sadomasochism. Soft substances such as fur, satin, and women's underwear are used as pure fetishes (Gebhard, 1969).

A more meaningful system of evaluating fetishes is to class them according to the psychological distance from stimuli that are usually sexually arousing. Thus, genital, buttock, and breast partialism would be at the near end of the scale, while foot, hand, shoe, and especially material fetishes, would be at the distant end.

So far, we have grouped fetish objects and not their importance to the attracted person. Binet makes such a distinction in his discussion of minor and major fetishism. Minor fetishism pertains when the fetish is the center of attraction, but does not rule out the possessor; in fact, attraction generalizes from the fetish to the possessor. In major fetishism, there is a complete substitution of the object for the person and for the sexual act, the part takes the place of the whole.

Ellis (1906) has proposed a more detailed, four-step grading system. Those in the first category would not be considered fetishists:

1. A particularly fascinating aspect of a person who is loved in their own right.

2. A single attractive aspect of a person who must otherwise be attractive. For example: "So I am a shoe and boot fetishist only in the sense that this gear must be on the foot of the woman who is already sympathetic to me, in which case it will symbolize to me above all the idea of womanly energy and decision" (Hirschfeld, 1940, p. 41).

3. An aspect that is prized regardless of other characteristics of a person, who may actually be unattractive: "I was overcome and awe-stricken by the beauty of any girl with a mess of lustrous hair, regardless of color, as long as it had a beautiful sheen. Actually, the girls involved were far from beautiful" (London and Caprio, 1950, p. 463).

4. The aspect is supreme, and there is no association with a person. This level is like that described by Glover (1933), where the person is regarded as "one or more organs held together by an indifferent mass of connective tissue—the body" (p. 494). A hair collector explains: "It is indifferent to me whether the person to whom the hair belonged is young and beautiful, or old and ugly: my only interest is in the hair" (Bloch, 1908, p. 618).

This distance from a person is probably related to the degree to which the fetish is necessary for erotic arousal and orgasm; whether the fetish is major or minor.

Discrimination in Selection

Fetishists usually have one preferred object to the exclusion of other objects. Thus, the more interest expressed by leatherites in leather, the less they are attracted by rubber (Gosselin and Wilson, 1980). Other objects may attract them at different times or concurrently with the fetish of choice (Greenacre, 1955). The number of fetish objects has been determined from the files of a psychiatric hospital. About half (54%) used one or two objects, one-quarter were fond of three different objects, and a fifth had four or more fetishes (Chalkley and Powell, 1983).

It is not uncommon that the fetishist will progress from an almost indiscriminate attraction to his object of choice, say any feminine shoe, to a very discriminating attraction to a specific style and color of shoe.

Specific Fetishes

Pregnant and lactating women. Hirschfeld (1940), in what he calls "the most remarkable case of all," tells of a man who would walk the streets in search of pregnant women; the further along the pregnancy, the more aroused he became. This fetish for pregnant and lactating women is not quite as rare as Hirschfeld thought. Magazines featuring pregnant women constitute less than 1 percent of pornographic magazines, while 3 percent feature extremely large breasts (Dietz and Evans, 1982).

On the other hand, there are those with an antibreast fetish. A physician was partial to flat-chested women and had an even stronger antifetish for the female breast. The sight of the breast, even in pictures, made him nauseous. Even the words *breast* and *bosom* caused him discomfort, and he had great difficulty saying these words. Overtly, he was completely heterosexual, but his fetish for flat-chested women points to the possibility of a homosexual or pedophilic orientation. Indeed, pedophilia may be an expression of an antifetish for female breasts and pubic hair (Hirschfeld, 1940).

Nose. One of Freud's (1927) early cases was a man who was fascinated by a certain "shine on the nose" in German, "Glanze auf der Nase." This patient had been brought up in England where his fetish originated, but he had forgotten the English language. Originally, then, it was not a shine on the nose, but a glance at the nose. Nose is regarded as a phallic symbol in psychoanalytic literature. The following ode was composed by a nose fetishist:

> Oh sweet and pretty little nose, so charming unto me;
> Oh were I but the sweetest rose, I'd give my scent to thee,
> Oh, make it full with honey sweet, that I may suck it all;
> T'would be for me the greatest treat, a real festival.
> How sweet and how nutritious your darling nose does seem;
> It would be more delicious, than strawberries and cream.
> [Krafft-Ebing, 1902, p. 200].

Hair. Especially in the eighteenth century, it was common to preserve a sample of the loved one's hair as a remembrance (Bloch, 1908). The exciting qualities of hair are its arrangement, odor, texture, and above all, its length and color. Unfortunately for the hair fetishist, his object of adoration is not so easily acquired as shoes or undergarments. Sexual arousal and ejaculation may accompany the act of cutting the hair and it may be used later as a masturbation aid. Where the greatest pleasure occurs at the time of cutting, sadism would be suspected. "For me, the child does not exist. It is her beautiful, fine hair that attracts me. I could often take it at once, but I prefer to follow the little girl and take time; it is my satisfaction, my pleasure. Finally, I come to a decision, I cut the ends of the curly locks and I am happy" (Haire, 1934, p. 470).

A less severe case is that of a man who, to achieve a satisfactory orgasm, had to cut his wife's hair during foreplay. His earliest recollection was of his mother washing her hair (Romm, 1949).

A homosexual hair fetishist, known as "the barber," was especially aroused by a part in the hair. He would seat the person in front of him, apply hair dressing and comb the hair. As he parted the person's hair, he ejaculated (Hirschfeld, 1940).

Defect or negative fetishes. A thirty-year-old writer insisted that his wife walk on crutches and take them to bed, where he would have sexual intercourse with her. Since the age of five, the sight of crutches had aroused him sexually. His wife was becoming unhappy with this ritual, feeling that he was more responsive to crutches than he was to her (Hirschfeld, 1940). Another person would follow crippled men for hours, but never dared to approach them. He was fully potent with women by using a fantasy of forcing crippled men to undress and climb ladders (Peto, 1975). The most preferred female amputee is a single limb above the knee provided a stump remains (Ampix, 1978).

The defect, usually a missing limb, is most often desired in the partner, but sometimes the person wishes or imagines he has a missing limb (Money and Simcoe, 1986). One such person reports that "the image of myself as an amputee has as an erotic fantasy (each one different) accompanied every sexual experience of my life" (Money, Joboris, and Firth, 1977, p. 117). Almost three-fourths (71%) of a group of amputee fetishists had fantasied themselves as amputees and of these, three-fourths had enacted that role (Ampix, 1978).

Several cases of self-demand leg amputees have been reported, each having a persistent desire to have a leg amputated above the knee. All were preferential homosexuals, masturbated while viewing pictures of amputees, contemplated self-amputation, and had fantasies of overcoming their hoped for handicap. One had a minor clubbing of a foot and later a leg fracture. Another suffered an accident to his leg in childhood that made it impossible for him to walk for a year. They enjoyed seeing the asymmetry of the amputee (Money et al., 1977). In another man, who also had some homosexual inclinations, the amputation was not desired for itself, but so that he might use a wooden leg (Everaerd, 1983).

Feet, shoes, and boots. Foot and shoe are rich in symbolism. They may represent the profane, for the Lord said to Moses, "Draw not nigh hither; put off thy shoes from off thy feet" (Exodus 3:5). They also symbolize strength and power as seen in the word *impede,* whose Latin root is to entangle the feet. And, washing another's feet is an act of homage.

It is not simply any shoe or boot that is attractive to the fetishist, but certain qualities such as style, color, and even noise. A teacher reveals: "[I] am forced to follow women whose shoes creak when they are walking. The rhythmic sound of fine shoes excites me sexually to a great degree, and I delight in this sound until there is an ejaculation" (Hirschfeld, 1940, p. 41).

While foot and shoe worship are common aspects of sadomasochistic scenes, certainly not all foot and shoe fetishists are also sadomasochists. For the pure fetishist, foot and shoe are the most lovable part of the person, parts to adore and idealize (Ellis, 1906): "God Eros himself takes shape in these gloves and shoes . . . to me they are the sacral vessel of love. Only in them the delight of love's union, sensuousness, and ecstasy, my whole erotic existence can be realized" (Boss, 1949, p. 41).

Rubber. The current popularity of rubber, especially in

England, may be traced to events of World War II, when many of today's rubberites were children. First, it was an especially stressful time with father absent, overprotection by mother, deaths in the family, and for some, evacuation to the country. Second, there was an abundance of rubber items, such as groundsheets and gasmasks, a current fetish rage (Gosselin and Wilson, 1984). Urination and incest fantasies are more common in rubberites than in leather lovers (Gosselin and Wilson, 1980).

Words used to describe the attractive qualities of rubber involve all the senses. It feels cool, slippery, smooth, soft, and supple. When worn, it is skin tight, clings, and hugs the body. It is binding, warm, and gives a feeling of being secure and fully protected. It has a wet look, a satiny sheen, makes a rustling sound, and has a divine odor.

Olfactory factor. A macintosh (i.e., rubberized cotton rain-coat) fetishist describes the effects of odor: "The smell of a mac is so good it goes right down inside me, into my entrails" (Hunter, 1954, p. 304).

Abraham (1910) expands on a suggestion by Freud that the sense of smell may have a role in the development of some fetishes. He begins his analysis of a case of foot fetishism with the assumption that certain component sexual instincts, especially the desire to smell, to look, and the anal sadistic, are abnormally strong. These components, together with displacement, set the stage for fetishism. We have already noted that the fetish is idealized. In psychoanalytic literature, this overidealization is seen as the fetishist originally having sought something unaesthetic and disgusting—body odors, urine, and feces. The odor of the fetish symbolizes feces, mother's excreta (Balint, 1935).

At first, Abraham's patient was attracted to a schoolmate's shoes, but was later interested only in women's dainty and elegant shoes; ugly shoes repelled him. What especially intrigued him was the thought of the discomfort such shoes must cause the wearer, indicating a strong sadistic component. His high aesthetic idealization of shoes belied a reaction formation to some unaesthetic and disgusting attraction. This earlier attraction was pleasure in smelling feces and other bodily discharges.

He used to hug his mother in order to get a whiff of her armpits. This interest in smelling had undergone severe repression, whereas his interest in looking was displaced from mother's phallus to shoes, especially those with high heels.

Behavior Toward the Fetish

Acquisition of the fetish may pose some difficulty, especially since most prefer an object that has been used. Consequently, about a third resort to stealing their fetish (Chalkley and Powell, 1983). However, services are available, especially for panty collectors, that supply such articles.

Once acquired, the fetish is used for sexual arousal either alone or with a partner where either one or both may wear the fetish. Some are able to call up the fetish in imagination to achieve potency, like the nightcap fetishist who recalls his first erection at age five when he saw a relative put on a nightcap. He was impotent with his wife for several nights after marriage until, at the time of intercourse, he imagined his wife to be an old lady in a nightcap (Hirschfeld, 1940).

In major fetishism, a sexual partner is incidental and orgasm can be achieved only by employing the fetish in actuality or in fantasy (Romm, 1949). He either puts the object on or touches it to a part of his body (Balint, 1935). A hair collector reports, "After I have cut the lock, I go home and kiss the charming hair again and again, I press it to my nose and cheeks, and breathe in the precious fragrance of it" (Hirschfeld, 1940, pp. 79–80).

Orgasm is achieved through masturbation, although for some ejaculation occurs with the mere sight, touch, or thought of the fetish. To obtain these psychic orgasms there must be a low threshold of excitability and orgasm (Epstein, 1960). Nagler (1957) sees this reliance on autoerotic activity and restricted sexual contact with others as a product of the fetishist's low general activity.

A survey of psychiatric files reveals a wide range of behavior toward the love object (Chalkely and Powell, 1983). See Table 6.2.

Some fetishists collect objects of their desire and so acquire

TABLE 6.2
Behavior Toward Fetish

Behavior	Percent (N = 48)
Wearing	44
Stealing	38
Seeing Someone In	23
Gazing At	12
Placing in Rectum	13
Hoarding	12
Fondling	8
Sucking	4

Source: A. J. Chalkey & E. E. Powell (1983), The clinical description of forty-eight cases of sexual fetishism. *British Journal of Psychiatry*, 142:292–295.

a virtual harem. Over two-thirds (68%) of a group of amputee fetishists had collections of photographs of their desired women (Ampix, 1978). For the pubic hair collector, these items were not souvenirs of conquests, but desired for themselves. One collector amassed a pubic hair museum in which each little bunch was neatly tied with a string and labeled with the woman's name. These hairs give him, he says, "great gusto, colossal delight" (Stekel, 1930a). A young college student had a collection of young men's trousers. He stole some, others he purchased about once every three weeks, wore them once and then used them to rub against his penis (Marshall, 1974).

THE PERSON

Biological Basis

Early writers invoked vague constitutional predispositions to help explain fetishism. Freud (1905) spoke of an "executive weakness of the sexual apparatus" and others have assumed a psychopathic disposition.

Later writers in search of some constitutional basis have concentrated on the brain's temporal lobes. Epstein (1960) proposes that the fetishist is "organismically excitable," that he reacts excessively to stimuli both in degree and diffuseness. This excitability is manifested in low orgasmic threshold, sleep disturbances, emotional outbursts, and sometimes, epileptic states. Excitability is attributable to cerebral pathology, particularly in the temporal lobe. To oppose this excitability, there develops "organismic controls," defenses, including compulsions, obsessions, and a facade of emotional reserve.

The fetish serves as a compromise between excitability and controls. The excitatory aspect is seen when the fetish intrudes into consciousness in fantasy and dreams. Through the fetish, excitability is controlled or channeled when sexual and aggressive urges are focused on it, preventing them from spilling over onto other people. Epstein speculates that the temporal lobe is involved in sexual arousal, imitation, and identification—the three processes involved in fetishism.

In four of five cases of fetishism and/or transvestism, there was definite evidence of temporal lobe EEG abnormalities, and in the fifth, the evidence was highly suggestive (Epstein, 1961). One fetishist obtained "thought satisfaction" that was better than intercourse by looking at safety pins. This was followed by epileptic attacks. Not only the epilepsy, but also the fetish was relieved by excision of a portion of his temporal lobe. It is possible that the attacks were triggered by the intense emotion aroused by safety pins. He vividly recalls collecting and playing with "bright, shining safety pins" in early childhood (Mitchell et al., 1954).

Some slim evidence of a heredity factor is seen in a unique instance of rubber sheet fetishism in identical twins. In both, onset was in the fifth to sixth year; both received satisfaction by rubbing their bodies against a sheet. There was no evidence of collusion between them (Gorman, 1964).

Why is it that most fetishes come from a narrow range of potential objects? It may be that the human brain is programmed to respond sexually more readily to certain forms and substances than to others. Such an idea is similar to Seligman's concept of readiness for certain phobic stimuli (Marks, 1972). The slickness, shine, texture, and smell of fetishes may be phylogenetically determined to evoke the sexual response

(Epstein, 1975). Or, perhaps they are expressions of Jungian archetypal language (McCully, 1976).

Childhood Recollections and Origins

If there is an organic basis for fetishism, it functions as a predisposing condition, making the acquisition of fetishism more probable. The future fetishist must acquire a set of constructs referring to both people and a particular object. First, women are not to be counted on to satisfy his needs. Since they frustrate his needs, they become objects of his aggression. Yet, somehow, in spite of this, he still adores them. Second, he comes to look upon an object as a trustworthy facilitator of tension reduction. His chosen object takes the place of women, it stands for them, and is worshipped. No single event in early life fixes his fetishism, rather it is the product of many experiences covering a several years span.

Early Recollections

Many, but not all, fetishists can trace the beginning of their paraphilia to childhood impressions. For example, a towel fetishist, when eight years old, hiding behind a curtain, witnessed his mother having sexual intercourse with her lover. The man left and the boy could see his mother's genitals, which she was wiping with a towel. When she left the room, he grabbed the towel, smelled it, wrapped it around his penis, and masturbated. Soiled towels were his thing from then on (Lukianowicz, 1960b).

However, according to Freud (1905), these recollections of onset are screen memories, behind which the full significance lies hidden. The case of a six-year-old boy described by Freud (1916–1917) is a model for the psychoanalytic views of the origin of the fetish. This boy sits on a stool beside his governess. Her foot is troubling her, it is thin and slippered and she has propped it on a pillow. For some reason, the boy looks up her leg, past the calf, knee, thigh, then—horrors—no penis in sight. If she has no penis, then he could lose his as she has lost hers. He cannot even contemplate such a possibility. The shock is too great; the discovery must be denied. All he recalls as an adult is sitting on a stool beside his governess. All he knows is that there is some association between this recollection and the fact that he is completely indifferent to women's charms; that only a thin, slippered foot is capable of arousing him sexually. The governess's hoped for phallus was transferred to the slipper, so to him slippers represent a denial of castration (Freud, 1927). The fetish is an affirmation that castration does not occur and it serves as a screen behind which lies the remembrance of the castrated female.

This denial of female castration via fetish requires a split in the ego so that two mutually contradictory ideas are held to be true at once. Use of denial in childhood facilitates such an ego split (Fenichel, 1945). The six-year-old's traumatic discovery that he could lose his male member was not resolved by hallucinating a female penis (psychosis), or by accepting the reality that women do not have penises. Rather, there was a compromise achieved by ego splitting whereby he could both affirm the reality that "women do not have penises," and deny reality by maintaining "women do have penises." The denied side of the split is displaced to some other part of the woman's body or to an inanimate object, resulting in fetishism (Freud, 1940).

Because this account fails to explain why the boy looked up the woman's leg and also why the slipper became capable of arousing him sexually, a slightly revised scenario has been suggested. It was no accident that he looked up her leg, he was curious and excited about what he might find up there, perhaps he even had an erection. As in traumatic amnesia, his memory of these events stops prior to his horrifying discovery and his interest in the expected female penis is displaced to the slipper. When sexual excitement abates, it is safe for him to acknowledge that the woman indeed has no penis. But it is only with the aid of this fetish that he can reenact his sexual excitement prior to looking up her leg (Katan, 1964).

It is not difficult to imagine what Curious Harry was looking for when, at age four, he would stroke and kiss shoes of women he especially liked, lift their skirts, and peer underneath (Lorand, 1930).

A thirty-year-old's interest in rubber began when he was

four, at the birth of his sister. A rubber sheet was used for diaper changes. He recalls that the smell of rubber excited him and produced pleasurable sensations. Now he steals rubber aprons, draws one corner between his legs like a diaper, and orgasms. Stealing was interpreted to mean that man robs woman of her penis, which is then refuted by his ritual where he, as his sister, retains the penis (Kronengold and Sterba, 1936).

The traumatic discovery can be made in many contexts, such as mother and sister undressing, or in viewing the legs of a sitting female, itself an arousing sight. Therefore, there is a random factor in the choice of a particular fetish. Sometimes it is a standard phallic symbol, but often it is simply one of the last objects seen prior to viewing female genitals. In fur fetishism, fur represents the pubic hair which may, the fetishist hopes, conceal a penis. Women's underwear serves a similar function (Freud, 1927).

Children are fascinated by many objects, so why do only some become fetishes? Why is castration anxiety overcome in most, but leads to homosexuality and fetishism in others? What accounts for the rigid adherence to the precipitating experience, and why is it that such experiences are not well established in many cases? Freud (1927) set aside many of these questions, but later analysts have sought answers in preoedipal phases of development (Bak, 1953; Katan, 1964; Greenacre, 1979).

Childhood Experiences

Severe and/or continuous disturbances in mother–child relations during early childhood constitute "not good enough" mothering, and this is a contributing factor to disturbances in general. Mother is always close to the child, but he is handled impersonally as if he were contaminated. She does not provide him with comfort, yet he still wants to cling to and touch her (Bak, 1953). Mothers of amputee fetishists are described as not only lacking warmth, but also disciplining and expecting high standards of performance from their sons (Ampix, 1978). Increasing his need for comforting is bombardment with noxious stimuli in the form of intense parental quarreling, witnessing the primal scene, and unmanageable pain from injuries or surgical operations. With all of this, the child is learning that women frustrate rather than satisfy his need for security and comfort.

Additionally, there begins a disturbance in his body image caused by either actual changes from rapid weight gain or loss, sensations of body change resulting from fever, or from certain activities such as body massages, and being tossed in the air. Such experiences result in increased clinging and continuation of primary union with mother and fear of separation from her (Bak, 1953). This fear is heightened by losses through divorce and death (Greenacre, 1979). His infantile wish to be one with mother will augment his later castration anxiety.

During the second year of life, other situations occur that increase the probability of fetish development. Some of these are experiences that promote confusion over male and female bodies. In part, the individual forms his own body image, especially of difficult to view parts such as face and genitals, through viewing others. The future fetishist is in close visual contact with a female, usually near to his own size, whose genitals he can see. This produces a "bisexual splitting of the body image," that is, his own body image contains impressions not only of his penis, but also of the penisless female. Other events that can add to his body image confusion are accidents and surgical operations that he interprets as threats of loss of his own penis.

Mac, a child pantyhose fetishist, experienced a very painful circumcision at age one. His wound did not heal properly, so he was recircumcised three weeks later. The compassionate physician ordered Mac's mother to, "Hold him." She reports, "I held him. And he cut him. I didn't look. I was sobbing. And Mac was screaming." She was instructed to pull back the foreskin for three months, Mac "having a bloody fit every time" (Stoller, 1985b, pp. 97–98).

When he is about four years old, the future fetishist experiences an exaggeration of castration anxiety. This may come about through a continuation of the disturbed relation with his mother, in addition to real castration traumas, such as witnessing mutilations, births, or abortions—any scene where much blood is involved. The boy develops a strong body = phallus equation, where a part represents the whole.

In reaction to all of this, he latches on to an object that must be stable, visible, tangible, and often smelly, since in smell one can take in the object without diminishing it in size. This object, according to Greenacre, represents the penis (Greenacre, 1953, 1955, 1960, 1979). Unlike mother, whom he cannot control, he can control the object; it is there when he needs it.

As with the mighty Sampson, hair was a sign of masculinity for this fetishist. He remembers his mother cutting his long locks when he was about three years old and the excitement he experienced as he picked them up and put them in a box (Epstein, 1969).

Several incidences in the life of a thirty-one-year-old schoolmaster, a macintosh fetishist, probably induced separation and castration anxiety. He was weaned from the breast at eleven months with bitter aloes. He has vague and frightening memories of his circumcision at two years, and his mother controlled him by using threats of leaving him (Hunter, 1954).

The Question of Early Childhood Fetishism

Fetishism has been reported in preoedipal children, but it is debated whether early childhood fetishism is true fetishism. Those who accept Freud's view that fetishism is a symptom of castration anxiety deny that preoedipal children can be fetishists. But, others claim that a transitional object may be used as a fetish.

Heated controversy was generated by Wulff's 1946 paper on "Fetishism and Object Choice in Early Childhood" wherein he reports on five cases of purported early childhood fetishes. Wulff sees the fetish object not as a substitute for mother's penis, but for mother's body, particularly her breast, in which the senses of smell and touch are crucial. Early childhood fetishism is a pathological attempt to allay separation anxiety rather than castration anxiety. There is, he says, a probable connection between these early childhood fetishes and adult fetishism. Another analyst goes so far as to propose that the aim of the fetish in adults is to relieve fears of separation and that this function is independent of any genital aim (Weissman, 1957).

Orthodox psychoanalysts consider Wulff's conclusions in error. Thus, Gillespie (1952) declares that childhood fetishism is impossible until the oedipal situation has taken place. Rather, seemingly fetish objects are simply transitional objects. Calling a transitional object a fetish simply because both are inanimate neglects the fact that the use of a fetish is specific to the phallic phase. True, there are distorted transitional objects that originate in severe maternal deprivation and are usually connected with feeding and represent mother's breast. However, the true fetish's function is to defend against castration anxiety by invoking the phallic woman fantasy (Bak, 1974).

While fetish and transitional object are both inanimate objects and somewhat associated with mother's body, there are differences. Transitional objects are quite common. They are used equally by boys and girls, they appear in infancy, and are usually given up in childhood. Fetishes, however, are quite rare, used predominantly by males, onset is in childhood, and they are tied to sexual performance.

Fortunately, compromises are possible that link the transitional object to the fetish. Perhaps the fetish has the same significance as the transitional object since it not only represents preoedipal objects but also defends against castration anxiety (Parkin, 1963). The fetish may be a persistent transitional object that becomes linked to mother's phallus (Winnicott, 1953). And, it may be that castration anxiety brings about a partial regression to the stage of the transitional object (Gillespie, 1952).

Another compromise is offered by those who propose an early phallic phase, somewhere between sixteen and twenty-four months. They allow for early childhood fetishism if three criteria are met. First, sexual arousal must be established. Second, the child must have observed the anatomical differences between the sexes. And, third, there is instability in self and object relations through separations, illness, and lack of "good enough" mothering (Roiphe and Galenson, 1973).

Oedipal Period

The first fetish is usually taken from mother's or sister's possessions. For instance, a man was caught in a department store thrusting a bra into his pocket. To purchase a bra held no thrill for him; he had to steal it. He was shy with women and repelled by the sight of their genitals. At age nine, he used to spy on his sister and experienced a tingling excitement when she removed her bra. Her further disrobing had no special effect on him (Chesser, 1971).

Stekel (1930a) finds the nucleus of fetishism in incestuous wishes and the sense of sin that these wishes generate. These lustful desires for a close relative are soon repressed. Generalization takes place, so that all women become cues for sinful, incestuous thoughts. Coitus becomes the grossest depravity, not only because mother or sister and therefore all women are evil, but also because of his oedipal sexual attraction toward them.

Mother's Contribution

Little Kurt never employed a suitable transitional object; he threw his teddy bear out of his crib, and refused a pacifier. Kurt could not accept his total mother, but focused on her feet. They could not serve as a transitional object, however, since they went where she went. Kurt's fascination with mother's feet began when he was one year old, and by five, he was still removing her shoes, excitedly licking her feet, while fingering his erect penis. At six, his father threatened to "snip off" his penis if he continued to play with it, but his mother, while bathing him, would fondle it and call it "cute."

Although Kurt's mother claims she tried to discourage his manipulations of her feet, she did not wear stockings, making them readily available to him. At first, she encouraged his behavior, thinking it was cute. Later she actually paid him for a "foot massage" which included mouthing and licking (Bemporad, Dunton, and Spady, 1976).

Mother may actively participate in formation of her son's attachment to an object. She may exhalt its value, encourage him to seek relief in his transitional object, and use it as a substitute for dealing with his separation and other anxieties. This object brings temporary comfort and so replaces the breast and even mother herself. The object becomes the focus of the child's emotions as he projects them onto it: "Teddy is angry."

One mother used a transitional object in toilet training by allowing her child to keep the object as he sat on the toilet. She took it away if he failed to produce and returned it when he did. The lost feces was replaced by the transitional object. Thus, the child's sexuality, usually resolved by interaction with parents, becomes stunted, identification with parents is distorted, and aggressiveness is displaced from parent to object (Dickes, 1963, 1970).

In the early history of fetishists there is a strong attachment to mother. Mother resists her child's separation, but does not allow overt clinging behavior. When Mac, the child pantyhose fetishist, was eighteen months old "he would whine because he couldn't follow me around the kitchen or from room to room. It drove me up the wall. Maybe some mothers can take that but . . ." (Stoller, 1985b, p. 115).

So, mother continues the relation through the fetish, thus maintaining a facade of normality. Such mothers are exhibitionistic, seductive, narcissistic, frustrating, and they overstimulate the child's partial instincts (Sperling, 1963).

Mother's complicity is illustrated by the case of Harry. His mother used to lie with him as he nursed from the bottle. He would stroke her silk-stockinged legs and drift off to sleep. Mother decided to let him nurse alone and gave him her stocking along with his bottle. At age six, Harry carried strips of silk to school, and to bed, sometimes rubbing his scrotum with them (Sperling, 1963).

In addition to the female's missing penis, "every component of the infantile sexual instinct has some connection with the fetish object, so that this object is associated with all the repressed infantile sexual experiences" (Payne, 1939, p. 166). The fetish, like a magnet, attracts many elements. As development proceeds, more and more stimuli become linked to the fetish and sexual stimuli are excessively focused on it (Epstein, 1960). It grows and expands in the meanings condensed on it as the child acquires new experiences. For a macintosh fetishist the mac represented the anaesthetic mask of the surgeon who circumcised him at age two, mother's rubber apron, mother's sweaty odor, and her suffocating breast itself (Hunter, 1954). In another case, analysis revealed that macintoshes represented father's penis, mother's penis, her nipples, body odors, and anus, as well as both parents' feces.

Socarides (1960) found the origin of fetishism in males to be an active preoedipal feminine identification with the mother and a corresponding wish to have a child. The fetish was a substitute for the wished for baby. In other cases, the fetish is said to represent breast-skin, buttocks-feces, and father's penis (Balint, 1935; Bak, 1953; Garma, 1956).

The case of a woman with a nonobligatory baby-pillow fetish illustrates this development. During her first year, she used a doll as a transitional object, but the doll disintegrated. Then came the pillow, which not only appropriated the meaning of the doll, but also took on meanings of its own; first, mother's breast, buttocks, anus, and genitals, and later father's genitals and buttocks (Dickes, 1963).

Adolescence

Fetish-induced sexual excitement may start as early as four or five years, as with the five-year-old who was given to caressing feet and smelling stockings with great genital excitement (Garma, 1956). However, the sexually arousing quality of the fetish usually makes its appearance in adolescence, but may occur later under pressure of life stress (Gebhard, 1969). Mean age when rubber became an attractive material was eleven years, with half of a group of rubberites experiencing the material's attraction from ages five to seventeen (Gosselin, 1979). The average age at which amputee fetishists were first attracted to girls without limbs was twelve, with three-quarters realizing this before age fifteen (Ampix, 1978).

Usually fetishism is benign, but occasionally it signals the beginnings of serious offenses (Snow and Bluestone, 1969). By the time the notorious William Heirens was seventeen in the 1940s, he had committed twenty-five burglaries and three murders of females. He started as a panty fetishist at age nine, becoming interested in "the feeling and color" of women's underclothes. He began stealing them, first from clothes lines and then from houses. As his excitement over breaking into houses increased, his interest in underwear waned. As he entered the window, sexual excitement and erection occurred; going through the window produced emission (Kennedy, Hoffman, and Haines, 1947).

Adulthood

The fetish is such a peculiar and salient aspect of a person's life that it is given more attention than the fetishist himself. Just as one cannot understand a part in isolation from the whole, "A real comprehension of the causes of this sexual anomaly can only be obtained by considering the fetish in its relation to the individual's whole psychical development and by taking into account the other morbid symptoms which are invariably present" (Payne, 1939, p. 169).

Unfortunately, this prescription was not heeded. A review of early psychoanalytic literature on fetishism reveals that, except for "glimmerings here and there . . . no picture of the fetishistic patient—of his personality—emerged from the studies" (Nagler, 1957, p. 737) and no deeper insights have appeared (Parkin, 1963).

The fetish is only one manifestation of pathology which, in addition, includes acute depressive episodes, anxiety, paranoid fears and fantasies, and suicidal tendencies (Payne, 1939). A survey of psychiatric patients revealed that in only 1 percent was fetishism the admitting complaint, although some presenting complaints were conceivably related to the patients' fetishism; for example, marital discord and stealing. One fourth were socially anxious, and one third had never experienced coitus (Chalkely and Powell, 1983).

There may be some relation between fetishism and skin disorders. A rubber fetishist had occasional acute skin irritation on arms and legs. He reports that when dressed from head to foot in rubber, his whole skin is so stimulated that he ejaculates (Joseph, 1971). A homosexual foot fetishist suffered from allergic dermatitis of the scrotum and inner thighs as a child (Nagler, 1957).

Part-Whole Confusion

Cognitively, the fetishist confuses the part–whole relation. He chooses a part object, identifying it with the whole (Mittelmann,

1955). This confusion may be more general than his fetish behavior. Little Kurt, the child foot fetishist, populated his fantasy land with detached penises of people who had died. He also dichotomized the world into good–bad, strong–weak, assertion–retribution (Bemporad et al., 1976).

Fantasy

The fetishist is a daydreamer who lives largely in his fantasy world (Nagler, 1957), but his fantasies are repetitive and stereotyped (Epstein, 1960; Greenacre, 1979).

Shyness and Sense of Aloneness

It is only from the ruins of relations with humans that an attachment to an object can come about (Bergman, 1947). The child's first relation with another person, his mother, left his needs ungratified. So, when he craves intimate contact, he shuns humans; he acts alone. The fetishist, at least in his sex life, is a loner. Amputee fetishists remain unmarried longer than the general population (Ampix, 1978). Ellis (1906) speculates that he is a naturally shy, timid, nervous, and sensitive person, prone to formulate strong erotic symbols. Then, when he realizes that he is different from others, his natural secretiveness is further exaggerated. On a psychological questionnaire, rubberites scored more impersonal, prudish, showed a greater need for social acceptability than nonfetishists (Gosselin, 1979). However, rubberites were only slightly introverted and leatherites no more introverted than a comparison group (Gosselin and Wilson, 1980).

Concerns over Masculinity

While Freudian analysts interpret castration anxiety in literal terms, Nagler (1957) asserts that the basis of fetishism is not fear of actual penis loss, but the feeling that, in a way, the individual has already been castrated. He fears his ability to assume the masculine role because of his overwhelming sense of inadequacy and low self-worth. He lacks a firmly established sense of masculinity and the fetish serves somehow to enhance his uncertain masculinity (Storr, 1957; Greenacre, 1968). For instance, "Boots" (1957), a homosexual fetishist, reports that "men's rubber boots became a symbol of superior manhood" and that being in his buddy's boots "gave a feeling of being more virile, more masculine, more energetic, and more like the one I loved" (p. 746).

Both a father and his son were shoe fetishists with similar dynamics. Father's mother was dominant and given to belittling her husband. One day, he tried on one of his mother's shoes and felt a sense of power coupled with sexual excitement. His son, too, viewed his mother as strong, father as weak (Gilberg, 1981).

He may have hidden wishes to be a woman, as seen in the link between fetishism and transvestism. The shoe lover imagines how beautiful his foot would look in that shoe, and the panty lover, how lovely he would appear with the panty on (Stekel, 1930a). However, there was no indication of femininity in rubberites, as they scored the same as controls on a masculinity scale.

Subservience and Hostility

Feeling inadequate in his masculinity, he is outwardly a reserved, nonassertive, passive, dependent, and insecure individual (Epstein, 1960); he symbolizes and substitutes rather than executes his desires (Romm, 1949).

His feelings toward women are a compound of adoration and hate, which stems from his concept of mother as an all-powerful frustrator of his needs. In his fantasies he seeks to win women's favor by serving them adoringly. His foot and shoe worship are attempts to gain acceptance by paying homage to what represents women to him—their shoes. Likewise, the homosexual fetishist, whose fetish represents the power and authority of his father, serves a male master (Nagler, 1957).

Masochistic fantasy themes abound (Karpman, 1934; Epstein, 1960). "Boots" (1957) reveals that, "I secretly enjoyed any rough treatment from my beloved pals, and was content to be subdued by them" (p. 746). Masochistic fantasies of being fettered are an expression of the need to inhibit hyperexcitability (Epstein, 1960). In addition to his fantasy of having intercourse with a woman when both are dressed in rubber, a patient also fantasized that figures in rubber attack and beat him while he is dressed in rubber (Joseph, 1971).

At a descriptive level the fetishist does appear to be masochistic—suffering from his compulsion, denying himself the pleasures of heterosexual love. Stealing his fetish seems to be as active as he ever gets. But overt passivity and masochism may disguise elements of aggression and sadism (Storr, 1957). His overt masochistic stance may be an atonement for his basic sadism (Stekel, 1930a,b). His hate and sadism are seen in his objectifying women, his possessiveness and need for complete control over his fetishes (Romm, 1949), and frequent sadistic masturbation fantasies (Karpman, 1954).

Frankly sadistic behavior in childhood is reported. Before puberty, the exhaust pipe fetishist's favorite pastime was torturing animals—birds, rats, and cats. Their bodies were torn open and they were left to die, eyes were removed, and some were burned alive. He suppressed this sport shortly before puberty and the onset of his fetish (Bergman, 1947).

The man who cut his wife's hair during foreplay fantasized gouging pieces out of her scalp (Romm, 1949). A women's undergarment fetishist avoided sexual relations with his slender wife because he "thought she was going to break in two" (Snow and Bluestone, 1969). Another fantasized about adolescent girls wrapped in mackintoshes in humble stance as though controlled by a strict governess. When he was seven years old, he felt humiliated and helpless as his father helped him on with his mackintosh (Parkin, 1963). The fetish may protect the fetishist against the fear that an actual sexual partner will mutilate him and also against his fear that he will kill the partner (Payne, 1939; Snow and Bluestone, 1969).

His sadism is often displaced onto the fetish which is sometimes both revered and ill-treated. Psychoanalysts trace this double attitude to the ego split of both denying and affirming women's castration. When there is identification with and adoration of the female, the fetish is worshipped. When there is a strong father identification, the fetish is not only worshipped, but also symbolically castrated (Bak, 1953). Because the child assumes that father was the castrator of the women, in his father identification he himself becomes the castrator. This castrator role is seen in braid cutters, with hair symbolizing the penis: "So, the woman still has a phallus; I, the castrator, will remove it" (Freud, 1927; Fenichel, 1945).

Sexuality and Relations with Women

It is said that the fetishist is sexually hyperesthetic. In one sense, this refers to the diffuseness of objects and events capable of exciting his sexual feelings. Thus, a boy of fifteen was aroused to erection by watching the coupling of flies, horses, and other animals, seeing women's underclothes and statues of nude women, contact with a mature woman's body, and so on (Ellis, 1906).

Hyperesthesia also means strong sexual urges. Genital excitability has been noted in the early life of fetishists (Mittelmann, 1955), as has precocious and compulsive masturbation (Greenacre, 1953; Epstein, 1960). One possible consequence of a strong and precocious sex urge is that the child becomes attached not only to objects, but to members of his family earlier and more strongly than normal children. He considers this sexual attraction sinful, and so seeks the protective mechanism of the fetish (Stekel, 1930a). That he has a strong sex drive is supported by the finding that rubberites have a greater number of sex thoughts and more sexual excitement from them than a nonfetish group of men (Gosselin, 1979).

It is not only what stimulates the fetishist that is important, but what does not (Romm, 1949). Either women do not arouse him or, if they do, he is incapable of satisfactory intercourse with them. He is restricted in his sexual contact with others; there is a marked reduction of heterosexual activity (Abraham, 1910).

There is an association between fetishism and impotence, but the direction of the relation is disputed. Krafft-Ebing (1902) held that the fetish is the cause of impotence since the concentration on the fetish precludes potency without its presence. But, the relation between impotence and fetishism is more complex. It may well be that fear of sex produces the impotence, and this, in turn, gives rise to fetishism. Castration anxieties may be reactivated in the act of coitus when the man views the penisless woman and watches or feels his own member disappear into her.

Stekel (1930a) maintains that the root of fetishism is not so much fear of the sex partner, but of the sex act. In his fear of sexual relations, he is avoiding sin—the sin of incestuous relations. His fetish is a compromise between strong sexual urges and strict piety. He achieves asceticism in avoiding the sexual act, while finding sexual release in relations with his fetish. The idea of an antisexual attitude was confirmed in a group of rubberites who displayed greater prudishness than a group of nonfetishists (Gosselin, 1979).

According to Freud (1927), every fetishist has an aversion to the female genitals. His castration concerns give rise to two conflicting views of female genitals—dirty, degraded, and mutilated, or the illusion that there is a female penis (Greenacre, 1968). He attempts to escape from these fearsome women, but when this escape is blocked, he compromises by depreciating and objectifying them (Romm, 1949). In an experimental setting, males who had been twice rejected by a female rated pictures of women more negatively than did accepted and control males. Also, rejected males rated pieces of feminine clothing (panties) and body parts (feet) more favorably than pictures of women themselves. It was not that objects became highly valued after rejection, but that women became devalued (LaTorre, 1980).

The fetish may symbolize the fetishist's ideal woman, devoid of the negative traits of real women: "The difference between a macintosh and a woman is this—the mac has no power over me and can't hit back. Being inanimate, it can't withdraw its affection" (Hunter, 1954, p. 304). To realize this ideal object, several transformations are necessary. For instance, the child, deprived of love and comfort by mother, imagines his needs would be met if he were lame. At the same time, he imagines trading places with mother, so that she is lame and thus deprived of power and must be dependent on him. The situation reversed, in contrast to her behavior toward him, he feels compassion for her. As an adult, he seeks a woman who is lame or who has had a limb amputated. Behind his stated desire to take care of her is his wish to be taken care of by her (Ampix, 1978). This sequence of transformations is illustrated by the case of Z., who was raised by a tutor. In early childhood, he not only limped about using brooms as crutches, but also was very sympathetic toward the lame. Z. fantasized that he, "as a pretty lame child," would meet a pretty girl who would be sympathetic with his condition. He also imagined feeling sympathy for a lame girl. Later his limping girl fantasy became sexualized and used in masturbation. His hope was to find a lame girl, who, because of his love for her, would take pity on him (Krafft-Ebing, 1902).

The way in which the heels of shoes come to stand for different types of women is illustrated by a foot fetishist, whose mother abused alcohol when he was a child. Flat heels are refined, pale-faced, and puritanical and represent the idea of women who use no alcohol. Moderately high heels, flushed face, are respectable, and take a little wine. Sex is possible if he can transform them with wine into the next class. Extremely high heels flaunt their sexuality; they disgust him. He was ambivalent toward flat heels since he could not have sex with them out of respect, yet he suspects them of hypocrisy (Glover, 1927).

In his interactions with women, he displays little spontaneity or emotional warmth (Epstein, 1960). While he may feel tenderness toward them, the sex act is seen as too aggressive and his fear of castration too great for him to consummate (Greenacre, 1955). A fetishist, who described himself as passive, sought out women who were aggressive. When several of these women told him they were essentially homosexual, he felt relieved that he did not have to perform sexually (Romm, 1949). A macintosh fetishist clung to a relationship with an emotionally cold woman who would allow no caresses or tender words. This relation was important to him because it guarded against his feared desire for closeness (Gillespie, 1940). And a rubber fetishist who had poor relations with women ridded himself of his own sexual wishes and dependency needs by attributing them to women in his life, and then promptly lost interest in them (Joseph, 1971).

Attitude Toward Deviancy

While regarding themselves as different, fetishists do not consider their peculiarity a symptom of disease. In fact, they are content with their attachment to their fetish (Freud, 1927). It is, after all, an easy way to obtain sexual gratification: no dependence on women; no rivalry with men (Romm, 1949). Only a small percentage (14%) of amputee fetishists, whose desired female is not readily available, have visited a psychiatrist (Ampix, 1978).

7 PEDOPHILIA

INTRODUCTION

Sexual attraction to prepubescent children is not limited to pedophiles since "normal" heterosexual and homosexual males are aroused by pictures of nude children. Using penile volume changes to measure arousal, heterosexual and homosexual males responded maximally to their preferred partner. But also, both groups were aroused by pictures of prepubescent children of their preferred sex, though less so than to adults. There was even arousal to slides of younger children of the nonpreferred sex. Thus, the sexual arousal value of children may pertain to a much larger group of males than those who sexually misuse them (Freund, 1981). Indeed, it has been suggested that the pedophile's acts stem from a failure to inhibit an impulse that is prevalent, though weaker, in the average man (Langevin, 1985).

Child Pornography and Prostitution

Recent attention given to child pornography, "kiddie porn," and the increase in arrests of teenage prostitutes, demonstrates that sexual interest in children and adolescents is not confined to a few men. This attention also points up the abhorrence at

211

the victimization of minors. Federal laws have been tightened and penalties increased for producing, distributing, and receiving child pornography.

In the late 1970s, it was estimated that less than 10 percent of pornography in the United States dealt with children. Even so, it is a half- to two-billion dollar business (Geiser, 1979; Dworin, 1984). Boys' clubs, homes for neglected children, and even nursery schools have become production companies for movies and sources of child prostitutes (O'Brien, 1983). Of a large sample of pornographic magazine cover photos, about 3 percent depicted models posing as children (Gayford, 1978; Dietz and Evans, 1982). In addition to commercial sources, pedophiles often exchange photos of children with whom they have been involved (Henry, 1985).

To combat these evils, the Protection of Children against Sexual Exploitation Act, 1977, and the Child Protection Act, 1984, were enacted. These laws prescribe punishment for those who use children under sixteen years of age in sexually explicit films or photos and for the children's parents or guardians who participate. It also makes illegal the sending or receiving of such material (Lamborn, 1978).

Prevalence and Recidivism

Sexual misuse of children ranks with exhibitionism as one of the most common of all sex offenses. In the United States there are an estimated 50,000 men who actively seek sexual contacts with boys aged twelve to sixteen, and at least 1 million men over twenty-one who have had one or more sexual contacts with teenage boys (Rossman, 1976). In a survey using a subtle polling technique, the randomized response, one in twenty-five men admitted having sexually misused a child (Crewdson, 1988).

Estimates of reported cases of misuse per year vary from 75,000 to 150,000. Since unreported cases are at least four times as many as those reported, incidence is from 300,000 to 600,000 each year (Sarafino, 1979; Crewdson, 1988).

Another way to estimate the extent of sexual misuse of children is to find how many adults were sexually accosted when they were children. From 5 to 30 percent of adult males report that they had, as minors, sexual experiences with adults. Four-fifths of these encounters were with males. Ten to 30 percent of adult women report such experiences as minors, with 10 to 25 percent having been sexually molested when they were children (Landis, 1956; Gagnon, 1965; Finkelhor, 1979a; Herold, Mantle, and Zemitis, 1979; Fritz, Stall, and Wagner, 1981; Bagley, 1985; Crewdson, 1988; Sheldon, 1988). Overall, the ratio of girls to boys is two-and-a-half to one (Finkelhor and Baron, 1986). Most of the incidences involving females were not actual physical contact, but witnessing a man exposing himself (Landis, 1956; Gagnon, 1965).

From 20 to 60 percent of child sex abusers have offended more than once (Ellis and Brancale, 1956; Swanson, 1968) yet recidivism of both heterosexual and homosexual offenders has been judged low to moderate (Gebhard et al., 1965; *British Medical Journal,* 1966).

Attitudes Toward Pedophilia

Sexual use of children is the least acceptable deviation in Western civilization (Mohr, Turner, and Jerry, 1964). As media attention and public awareness of child sexual abuse has increased, accusations against alleged abusers has burgeoned. As a reaction to this increased sensitivity, there is rising concern over false accusations against adults, especially among teachers and child care workers. The organization Victims of Child Abuse Laws (VOCAL) has 120 chapters, whose members claim to have been falsely accused (Crewdson, 1988).

There are those who do not look upon pedophilia with horror. The biologically oriented Kinsey group suggests that this horror is lessened when the behavior of other mammals is examined, since it is common for adult animals to engage in sex with the immature (Gebhard et al., 1965).

While disavowing the right of any grown-up to manipulate children's genitals, Ullerstram (1966) makes a plea for a more humane attitude. He claims that, in general, the pedophile may do a service to the child who is neglected at home by satisfying that child's craving for physical contact. He laments the fact that there is no way to supply pedophiles with children, but believes that these men should be allowed to fulfill their desires. Righton (1981) goes a bit further when he argues that in a warm relation with a pedophile, the boy profits from the friendship and is probably not harmed by sexual activities.

Two self-help pedophile groups originated in England in the early 1970s—Paedophile Information Exchange and Paedophile Action for Liberation. In the United States, there are the Rene Guyon Society, whose motto is "Sex before eight or then it's too late," Childhood Sensuality Circle, Lewis Carroll Collectors Guild, and the North American Man Boy Love Association (Rush, 1980; O'Brien, 1983; Dworin, 1984). Interestingly, while most surveys indicate a predominance of heterosexual pedophiles, pedophile organizations espouse boy love (Righton, 1981). For example, at a pedophile working group convention in the Netherlands, 96 percent of those in attendance said they preferred boys, and 4 percent both boys and girls (Bernard, 1975).

These groups praise pedophilia as "Greek love," champion lowering the age of consent, act as support groups, aid pedophiles in "coming out," sponsor meetings and lectures, and attempt to create a favorable public image by adopting a code of pedophile ethics (Rossman, 1976; Plummer, 1981).

The Childhood Sensuality Circle, asserts that:

—a child's sexuality is a part of his whole person from birth, making his sexual rights inherent and inalienable,
—the child's sexual rights should be encompassed in the United Nations Declaration of Human Rights,
—a child not allowed to express all instinctive desires becomes unhappy, frustrated, antisocial and potentially criminal [cited by Rossman, 1976, p. 193].

Is adult sexual contact with children wrong, and if so, why? Frequently, those who condemn it point to studies indicating that children are psychologically harmed by such contact. But, this conclusion is not firmly established, since there are reports of children where no evidence of damage was found. Indeed, much of the harm may be presumed to come from the strong negative reaction of adults to the disclosure that the child has been sexually abused.

The most cogent reason for the wrongness of such contact is the ethical position of consent. Consent means that one knows what is being consented to, that is, it must be informed consent, and it means that one has the freedom to say "yes" or "no." Young children neither have this knowledge, nor are they free to say "no" because of the power imbalance between them and adults. While they may cooperate, children are incapable of giving informed consent (Finkelhor, 1979b; Groth, Hobson, and Gary, 1982).

Female Pedophiles

Reports of female pedophiles are rare. For one group that had been reported to the authorities, the modal age of the children was five and about two-thirds were girls. In two-thirds of the instances, the offender was baby-sitting at the time. One-half claimed to have been sexually abused themselves. Half of the acts involved oral, anal, or vaginal intercourse or penetration with an object or finger. The other acts were sexual fondling (Fehrenbach and Monastersky, 1988).

The discrepancy between the numbers of male to female offenders can be traced to differing masculine and feminine stereotypes. Masculine connotes sexual, whereas feminine carries with it strong maternal and nurturant significance. Consequently, when a female embraces and pets a child, she is demonstrating her nurturant feelings; when a man does the same, he must be a child molester (Plummer, 1981). Females have greater latitude in expression of feelings toward children. They may hug, kiss, and cuddle without observers assuming a sexual motivation (Righton, 1981).

Another explanation is that a majority of men who, as children, had sexual contact with a woman consider that contact "good" rather than "bad" and, therefore, were not apt to report it. Sixteen percent of college men and 46 percent of prisoners report having such contacts, half of which involved intercourse. The men's age at the time was about twelve and the women were in their early twenties (Condy, Templer, Brown, and Veaco, 1987).

DEFINITION

Differing Conceptions

Pedophilia means, literally, love of boys or children. Krafft-Ebing (1902) coined the term *pedophilia erotica* to refer to "the sexually needy subject [who] is drawn to children not in consequence of degenerated morality or physical impotence, but rather by a morbid disposition" (p. 457).

Most definitions specify that the child is prepubescent and the adult's intent sexual: "The expressed desire for immature sexual gratification with a prepubertal child" (Mohr et al., 1964, p. 20).

DSM-III-R specifies that the age of the child is thirteen or younger and that the perpetrator is sixteen or older and is at least five years older than the child; if he is an adolescent, no age different is prescribed. The definition includes sexual activities with prepubertal children who are related to him (incest).

A most precise definition is:

> Sustained erotic preference for children (within the age range up to and including 11 or 12) as compared to the subject's erotic inclination toward physically mature persons, and under the condition that there is a free choice of partner as to sex and other attributes which may co-determine erotic attractiveness [Freund, 1981, p. 161].

When the adult's sexual preference is for postpubertal females, he is called an "ephebophile," "hebephile," or "nubiphile." Pederasty, literally love of boys, refers to pedophilia involving early adolescent boys. A pederast is a "man over the age of eighteen who is erotically attracted to younger adolescent boys" (Rossman, 1976, p. 11).

Pedophilia and *pederasty* are primarily psychiatric terms. Corresponding legal categories are "lewd and indecent acts with children," "child molestation," "contributing to the delinquency of a minor," "impairing the morals of a minor," and "statutory rape." Most of these cover a wider territory than does pedophilia. For example, indecent liberties with minors may include obscene language, exposure, physical advances, and manipulation. Statutory rape must involve actual penetration of a person who is below the legal age of consent, even if the minor consents to the act (Lamborn, 1978).

Child molestation usually refers to sexual contact other than intercourse, such as fondling, digital penetration, and masturbation. A child molester is "a significantly older person whose conscious sexual interest and overt sexual behaviors are directed either partially or exclusively towards prepubertal children" (Groth et al., 1982, p. 132).

Sexual abuse of children is a popular label, but too diffuse in meaning since it covers a range of acts from having a child pose nude to sexual assault and murder. Other abusive activities include viewing sexual activities of adults, being exhibited to, use in pornographic productions, and sexual contacts with adults (Kempe, 1978; Conte, 1982). Child sexual abuse is not synonomous with pedophilia for only one-fifth of a group of child abusers had a long-standing and abiding interest in children as sexual partners (Swanson, 1968).

Because the child is not always a passive victim, the term *sexual misuse* has been proposed as "exposure of a child to sexual stimulation inappropriate for the child's age, level of psychosexual development, and role in the family" (Brant and Tisza, 1977, p. 81).

Relation to Other Paraphilias

Exhibitionism

A distinction is made between the exhibitionist who exposes to children and the pedophile. The exhibitionist usually exposes at a distance from the child, who is most often a stranger, with no intention of bodily contact. The pedophile, who may also expose himself to the child, does so in close proximity to the child, is often known to the child, and has the intention of further bodily contact (Mohr et al., 1964). A comparison of the two paraphilias yields many differences. For example, pedophiles tend to be older than exhibitionists, fewer of their fathers are alive, relationship with their parents is less positive, they have less schooling, perform less well academically, have poorer work records, are heavier consumers of alcohol, and fewer are having heterosexual relations with adults (Meyers and Berah, 1983).

Incest

Incest refers to sexual relations between family members other than husband and wife. Note that none of the definitions above exclude incest. Most incest offenders do not have sex with children outside their families (Conte, 1982). Many studies on child abuse and molestation include incest offenders in their samples, presumably because the child is prepubescent. These two groups have similar profiles on personality tests, with high scores on depression and asocial tendencies. A difference is that incest offenders score higher on social introversion than do pedophiles (Panton, 1979).

Pederasty and Homosexuality

In a series of one hundred homosexuals seen in private practice, seventeen were attracted to prepubescent boys, and of these, twelve were not also attracted to adult males (Curran and Parr, 1957). However, there is little other evidence of a stronger association of sexual use of children with homosexuality than with heterosexuality (Bell and Weinberg, 1978; Newton, 1978). Three-fourths of psychiatrists surveyed agreed that homosexuals are not more prone than heterosexuals to child molesting (Galdston, 1978).

Varieties and Types

Preference for Girls or Boys

The majority of pedophiles have a definite sex preference and the undifferentiated or bisexual group ranges from 5 to 25 percent (Cameron, 1985; Erickson, Walbek, and Seely, 1988). While some studies report an almost even split between abuse of boys and girls (Mohr et al., 1964; Rada, 1976), most report that from 60 to 90 percent of the instances involve girls (Revitch and Weiss, 1962; Swanson, 1968; Jaffe, Dynneson, and ten

Bensel, 1975; Groth, 1977; Swift, 1979; Ellerstein and Canavan, 1980; Conte and Berliner, 1981; Fritz et al., 1981; Rimza and Niggeman, 1982; Cameron, 1985; Spencer and Dunklee, 1986; Marshall, Puls, and Davidson, 1988; Bradford, Bloomberg, and Bourget, 1988). There probably is a relative underreporting of homosexual pedophilia, since boys are more reluctant to relate their experience than are girls (Landis, 1956; Swift, 1979; Fritz et al., 1981). It is estimated that around Times Square in New York City there are five times as many boy as girl prostitutes (Lloyd, 1976). Since there are relatively more homosexual pedophiles than heterosexual pedophiles (Cameron, 1985), it has been speculated that sex preference for children is basically different from preference for adults (Freund, Heasman, Racansky, and Glancy, 1984).

Few differences have been found between heterosexual and homosexual pedophiles except that the homosexuals had more siblings, fewer had been married or had a current sexual partner (Meyers and Berah, 1983). Their masculinity–femininity scores differ only slightly (Hall, Maiuro, Vitaliano, and Proctor, 1986), but heterosexuals report more aggressive behavior during childhood (Freund and Blanchard, 1987). Homosexuals tend to have had two or more boy partners, whereas most heterosexuals have misused only one girl (Freund, Watson, and Rienzo, 1987).

Types

There is a wide variety of men who use children sexually. About a third to a half can be considered pedophiles. In this group are those who have an abiding preference for children as sexual partners. There are others who, while attracted to children, adequately suppress their urges until some environmental stress weakens controls. Others would choose older partners, but also find children sexually desirable. A small group of heterosexual offenders are sociosexually underdeveloped, rather young (under thirty), and have nothing close to normal heterosexual experiences for their age. They suffer from feelings of inferiority, shyness around women, and sexual deprivation. Unable to make contact with adult females, they simply continue their prepubescent sex play patterns.

Amoral delinquents lack control over their behavior and, when sexually aroused, use whatever object is close at hand. They are younger than pedophiles proper, and are less apt to repeat child abuse (Virkkunen, 1976).

The situational type has no special interest in children as sex partners, but find themselves sexually involved as a matter of convenience or coincidence. The contact is usually brief and does not recur. Finally, there is the catch-all category that includes mentally retarded people, psychotics, chronic alcoholics, and senile deteriorates (Gebhard et al., 1965; Swanson, 1968, 1971).

From work with five hundred offenders (including incest), Groth (Groth et al., 1982) proposes two classes—fixated and regressed. Roughly half of the offenders are of each type. In the fixated, there is an arrest of psychosexual development. Since adolescence, they have had an obligatory attraction to and a fixation on children. Any sexual contact with age mates has been situational, like being seduced. Most have not been married. They are more childlike than adult and are more at ease with children. Their targets are primarily boys, and they relate to them as boy to boy. In many cases they are strangers to the child, perhaps a sign that their acts are premeditated (Groth and Birnbaum, 1978).

For the regressed type, involvement with children is a departure from their usual attraction to adults. However, demands of adult life, conflict or abandonment by an adult partner, precipitates a turning to children as surrogates for an age-mate relationship. These individuals prefer adult females, so they use girls as partners and relate to them as if they were adults. A summary of these two types is presented in Table 7.1.

Evaluation of Literature

Of all the literature on pedophilia, only a few studies reflect a systematic effort to investigate adult sexual interest in children (Freund and Langevin, 1976). Most of the three dozen reports of the use of behavior modification with pedophiles concentrate

TABLE 7.1
Characteristics of Fixated and Regressed Pedophiles

Characteristic	Fixated	Regressed
Primary Sexual Orientation	Children	Adults
Onset of Interest in Children	Adolescence	Adulthood
Precipitating Stress	None	Evident
Premeditation	Planned	Initially impulsive
Identification	With child	Child as adult
Sex of Child	Male	Female
Sexual Contacts with Age Mates	Little or none; usually single	Coexists with child contact; usually married
Alcohol, Drug Abuse	Not a factor	Often alcohol related
Character	Immature	Traditional life style
Dynamics	Developmental arrest	Attempt to cope with life stress

Source: N. Groth, W. F. Hobson, & T. S. Gary (1982), The child molester: Clinical observations. *Journal of Social Work and Human Sexuality*, 1:129–144.

on techniques employed and neglect describing the patient in any detail. Psychoanalysis has made little, if any, significant contribution to our understanding (Socarides, 1959, 1988).

Even some of the best studies that include incest offenders in their samples do not separately analyze homosexual and heterosexual pedophiles, and include children over twelve years old. Adults studied are child abusers and molesters, mostly obtained from court or prison samples, so that many are not, strictly speaking, pedophiles. This situation has led to the conclusion that "pedophilia research is, in general, characterized by some serious theoretical and methodological flaws" (Araji and Finkelhor, 1985).

To overcome some of these problems, researchers have attempted other means to gather samples of pedophiles. For instance, Rossman (1976) obtained his pederasts from those who ordered material from a pornographic mail order house. Over two hundred filled out a questionnaire and eight hundred submitted written material to him. Also, he interviewed three hundred male adolescents who had been involved with these men.

HETEROSEXUAL PEDOPHILIA

The Act

Precipitating Factors

As is typical of the regressed type of pedophile, prior to their contact with girls, over half experience some disturbance in relations with women, such as conflict, loss, or rejection (Hartman, 1965; Swanson, 1968; Peters and Sadoff, 1970). Another precipitating factor is concern over decreasing sexual potency (Karpman, 1954; *British Medical Journal,* 1966). Unable to cope with such situations, they react in a passive, immature manner, turning to children for companionship and affection. Sexual urges are not necessarily involved, since many pedophiles were having adequate sexual relations at the time of the offense (Gebhard et al., 1965). About a third claim that, at least occasionally, seeing explicit pornography instigated the offense (Marshall, 1988).

Alcohol is involved at the time of the offense in from 30 to 50 percent of the incidents, often with heavy consumption (Gebhard et al., 1965; Peters and Sadoff, 1970; Rada, 1976; Rada, Kellner, Laws, and Winslow, 1978). One study, however, reports low (14%) involvement of alcohol (Frosch and Bromberg, 1939).

Despite the prevalence of alcohol use, over two-thirds of the contacts are obviously premeditated (Gebhard et al., 1965). But sometimes, the urge comes as a surprise. " 'I took these kids on a field trip—having sex with any of them wasn't at all on my mind. Then one of the little girl students came in—real upset and she needed some affection. Well, I needed affection too—it was a horrible time in my life. Before I knew it, there we were' " (Sanford, 1980, p. 107).

The Girl

Reports of the average age of sexually used girls vary from about eight or nine (Mohr et al., 1964; Gebhard et al., 1965) to ten or eleven (Landis, 1956; Finkelhor, 1979a; Ellerstein and Canavan, 1980; Finkelhor and Baron, 1986), with a range of from about one to twelve years (Gebhard et al., 1965; Hobbs and Wynne, 1986). However, there may be a trend toward reporting cases in which younger children are sexually misused. In about a fourth to a half of reported cases, the child is younger than five or six years old (MacFarlane and Waterman, 1986; Erickson, Welbek, and Seely, 1988; Marshall et al., 1988). Adolescent child molesters, aged about fifteen, use girls of about seven years (Shoor, Speed, and Bartlet, 1966; Groth, 1977).

Relation to Offender

Information on the relation of the offender to the child taken from reported cases is heavily biased. Where the offender is known, identification and apprehension is easier than when he is a stranger, but also the girl's parents may be loathe to report the incident to the authorities; it is they who account for 75 percent of reports. Another source of bias is whether the sample includes exhibitionists, who would be strangers, and incest offenders, who are known to the child.

Anywhere from a fifth to over a half of child abuse incidents involve family members (Mohr et al., 1964; Resnik and Peters, 1967; Burgess and Holstrom, 1975; Peters, 1976; Ellerstein and Canavan, 1980; Conte and Berliner, 1981; Rimza and Niggeman, 1982; Kahn and Sexton, 1983; Spencer and Dunklee, 1986; Marshall et al., 1988). Even with incest excluded, most studies report that well over half the adults are well known to the child (Mohr et al., 1964; Gebhard et al., 1965; Resnik and Peters, 1967; Peters, 1976; Groth, 1977; James, Womack, and Stauss, 1978; Herold et al., 1979; Kahn and Sexton, 1983; Spencer and Dunklee, 1986). However, one study reports only 20 percent of offenders were known to the child (McGeorge, 1964). Baby-sitters account for about 5 percent of reported cases (Shoor et al., 1966; Ellerstein and Canavan, 1980), and almost half (47%) of adolescent males charged with indecent liberties with minors were baby-sitting at the time (Fehrenbach, Smith, Monastersky, and Deisher, 1986). In two reported cases, both were males, aged fifteen. One sexually fondled girls aged three to five; the other sexually molested a nineteen-month-old girl (Kourany, Martin, and Armstrong, 1979).

Resistance/Participation

A comparison of official records with offenders' statements on degree of girls' resistance or participation shows marked discrepancies as shown in Table 7.2. Resistance does not refer to any great struggle, but simply pulling away or attempting to avoid the man's actions (Gebhard et al., 1965).

These large differences may be due to the offender's attempt to lessen guilt by blaming the child's lack of resistance. Also, it cannot be assumed that the meaning of resistance, passivity, and encouragement are the same for adult and child. The girl's passivity may mean encouragement to the adult, and her slight resistance may be read as "no means yes."

Reports differ on the use of force from none to 20 percent; however, coercion and threats are not uncommon (Peters, 1976; Groth and Birnbaum, 1978). Force and/or threat occur in about a third to a half of the cases (Ellis and Brancale, 1956; Peters, 1976; Groth and Birnbaum, 1978; Conte and Berliner, 1981). But, what is coercion to the child may not seem so to the adult. Children are taught to obey adults, and even a softly spoken command may be interpreted by the child as a direct order, as a form of coercion.

Some investigators conclude that, quite often, the child is not only a willing participant, but actively instigates the sexual encounter (Weiss, Rogers, Darwin, and Dutton, 1955; Revitch and Weiss, 1962; Mohr et al., 1964; Burton, 1968). Just over

TABLE 7.2
Report of Child's Resistance from Record and Offender

Percent:	Resistance	Passivity	Encouragement
Record	75	8	16
Offender	15	37	48

From: P. H. Gebhard (1965), *Sexual Offenders.* New York: Harper and Row, p. 72.

half of psychiatrists surveyed agreed that sexually molested children contribute to the incident because of unmet needs (Galdston, 1978). One researcher states that, "what with twelve-year-olds wearing lipstick and high heels, artificial pneumatic accessories and sophisticated clothes one cannot help but wonder whether the age of consent should not be lowered" (McGeorge, 1964, p. 246). But, another asserts that regardless of the child's behavior, he or she bears no responsibility for a sexual assault (Elwell, 1979).

The Pedophilic Encounter

About a third of offenders use seduction and enticement (Groth and Birnbaum, 1978). Their method is to first establish a friendly relation with the girl, gradually initiate greater familiarity, and finally sexual activities. If she resists, he resorts to greater enticement and manipulation, but not actual force (Groth et al., 1982).

> I used all the normal techniques used by pedophiles. I bribed my victims; I pleaded with them, but I also showed them affection and attention. . . . Almost without exception, every child I molested was lonely and longing for attention. For example, I would take my victims to movies and to amusement parks. . . . I used these kinds of tricks on children all the time. Their desire to be loved, their trust of adults, their normal sexual playfulness and their inquisitive minds made them perfect victims [Henry, 1985, p. 8].

About a half of sexual contacts take place in the residence of the child or adult. Other locations are out of doors, such as in parks, autos, and theaters (Mohr et al., 1964; Gebhard et al., 1965; Peters, 1976; Ellerstein and Canavan, 1980). Since 90 percent of the encounters are not observed by others, it is up to the child to decide whether to report the contact (Gebhard et al., 1965). Girls are more likely to report less serious offenses, like exhibitionism, than the more serious, like attempted coitus (Landis, 1956).

Mondays and Fridays between early afternoon and early evening are at-risk times (Peters, 1976). In Minneapolis, half of the reported cases of indecent liberties with minors took place from May through September (Jaffe et al., 1975).

Pedophilic acts are classed into three categories—coitus, deviant, and immature (Mohr et al., 1964). Coitus is rare, partly because it is anatomically difficult and partly because it is not the pedophile's intent. Where intromission is accomplished, the girls are from eight to twelve years old (Gebhard et al., 1965). However, in another sample, 36 percent involved attempted or accomplished "carnal knowledge" (McGeorge, 1964). Attempted or accomplished anal penetration occurred in almost two-thirds of one group of children, and may be a common form of abuse that often escapes detection (Spencer and Dunklee, 1986).

Deviant acts, such as those with sadistic components, are rare (Groth, 1978). However, it is just such incidents that are given publicity, such as the child rapist and torturer who said: "Defile the innocent. Make them scared of sex. It is dirty. And I didn't have a happy childhood, either. Neither will they. Revenge" (Linebaugh, 1984, p. 18).

Most pedophilic acts resemble the immature sex play of children and orgasm is rarely the goal (Turner, 1964). Over half consist of touching and fondling, usually of the girl's vagina, legs, and buttocks (Mohr et al., 1964; Conte and Berliner, 1981; Mohr, 1981; Erickson et al., 1988). Sometimes, the man exposes his member and has her handle it (Gebhard et al., 1965). Other, less frequent sexual acts include penis–vaginal contact with and without penetration, oral stimulation, and attempted or accomplished anal penetration (Peters, 1976; Conte and Berliner, 1981; Rimza and Niggeman, 1982; Erickson et al., 1988).

The duration of the sexual act with a child is much shorter (69% took less than fifteen minutes) than with an adolescent (50% lasted one hour) (Peters, 1976).

Child Sex Rings

These rings involve one or more adults, often with legitimate authority figures (teacher, scout leader, school bus driver) and children who know one another and about their sexual participation. The adults involved, all males, range in age from thirty to eighty; the children are from six to fifteen years old. These rings vary from one man with several children to several adults with up to fifty children in a well-structured organization involved in recruitment, production of pornographic material, and in supplying sexual services. One child may be the leader and recruiter: "Mary was the ring leader and she put pressure on her friends to go over to his house" (Burgess, Groth, and McCousland, 1981, p. 113). A father, who had a five-year incestuous relationship with his daughter used her to recruit eight of her friends for his sexual misuse (Berliner and Stevens, 1982).

Initiation in sexual activities is usually indirect, such as showing the children kiddie porn, urging them to undress, or fondling them. All use pornography for instructional purposes. Or initiation may be more direct: "He put his mouth on my private" (Burgess et al., 1981, p. 113).

The group is held together by threats, bribery, loyalty, and peer pressure. Secrecy is essential to group maintenance and is achieved through threats of physical harm. Adults may take photos of the child engaged in sexual acts or lure the child into illegal activities like stealing, drinking liquor, or taking drugs, after which the child is threatened with exposure. The majority of the children are involved for more than a year and up to four years (Burgess et al., 1981; Burgess, Hartman, McCousland, and Powers, 1984; Wild and Wynne, 1986).

The Person

Current Status

Age and onset. Contrary to the stereotype of the pedophile as a dirty old man, less than 5 percent are over sixty years old (Revitch and Weiss, 1962; McGeorge, 1964). Reports of mean age at apprehension vary from twenty-eight (Jaffe et al., 1975) to thirty-seven (includes incest) (Fisher, 1969), with the great bulk between twenty and fifty years old (Apfelberg, Sugar, and Pfeffer, 1944; McGeorge, 1964) as shown in Table 7.3. Some 50 percent either attempted or committed their first sexual encounter with a child before they were sixteen years old (Groth et al., 1982).

Three peaks in the distribution of pedophiles' ages have been identified, suggesting that there may be different factors associated with each age group. The youngest, aged fifteen to twenty-four, engage primarily in delayed sexual exploration. For those men aged twenty-five to forty-four, mostly in their middle to late thirties, marital maladjustment and alcoholism are rather prevalent. Almost half are incest offenders. The forty-five and older group, mostly in their late fifties, are sounder socially than the others, but lonely, and socially and sexually isolated. A fifth are incest offenders (Mohr et al., 1964).

There is a relation between the ages of pedophiles and girls (Revitch and Weiss, 1962). With increase in men's ages, girls' ages at first increase and then decrease. For pedophiles between fifteen and twenty-four, the girls' mean age is six-and-a-half. Males between twenty-five and forty-four use girls whose mean age is eleven. And, for men over forty-five, girls' mean age drops to nine-and-a-half (Mohr et al., 1964). In one study, however, there was no relation between pedophile and victim ages (Bradford, Bloomberg, and Bourget, 1988).

Intelligence, occupation, and interests. In many outward respects, the pedophile is much like the average citizen. Both mean IQ and distribution of scores are essentially normal. Educational attainment is not appreciably different from the general population (Groth, 1978). Distribution of religious affiliation is close to that of the general population (Mohr et al., 1964).

All occupational groups are represented, although there

TABLE 7.3
Age of Convicted Pedophiles

Age	Percent (N = 190)
<20	10
20–30	30
30–40	30
40–50	20
50–60	10

From: J. McGeorge (1964), Sexual assaults on children. *Medicine, Science, and the Law,* 4:248.

is a trend toward trades and semiskilled occupations (Mohr et al., 1964). By and large, they are competent, law-abiding, and productive (Groth et al., 1982). Well over half have adequate or better work records (Swanson, 1968), with older pedophiles having better work records than the younger. These men give the impression that they try to just get along in an uneventful way (Mohr et al., 1964).

Social contact with adults is limited and any social participation consists mostly of activities with youth groups. They are primarily interested in solitary sports, such as cars, boats, and fishing (Mohr et al., 1964). Adolescent child molesters are loners, socially awkward, with no peer group activity (Shoor et al., 1966; Fehrenbach et al., 1986).

Marriage and partners. The pedophile may marry in the hope of curbing his abnormal desires. Estimates of the percentage of child abusers who are or have been married range from fifty to eighty, with most studies reporting about 60 percent (McGeorge, 1964; Gebhard et al., 1965; Fisher, 1969; Nedoma, Mellan, and Pondelickova, 1971; Rada, 1976). Of those over twenty years old, 90 percent were or had been married (Mohr et al., 1964). One study reports that 27 percent were married at the time of the offense (Rada et al., 1978).

While age at marriage is about the average twenty-four, they tended to rush into marriage, with a consequent high divorce and separation rate. Even so, they claimed their marriages were very happy (Gebhard et al., 1965).

Wives are described as controlling and sexually aloof (Resnik and Peters, 1967). They feel responsible for their husbands' difficulty, believing they had not met their sexual needs. They defend and excuse their husbands, showing little regard for the feelings of the children involved. Self-esteem is low, with pronounced needs for reassurance and approval. They claim to be orgasmic and to enjoy intercourse (Bastani and Kentsmith, 1980).

Psychopathology. Estimates of incidence of alcoholism or heavy consumption of alcohol vary from a low of less than 20 to over 50 percent (Frosch and Bromberg, 1939; Ellis and Brancale, 1956; Gebhard et al., 1965; Swanson, 1968; Rada, 1976;

Groth, 1978; Meyers and Berah, 1983). They drink more to lower inhibitions than to assert masculinity (Rada, 1976).

Few are psychotic, but from 10 to 40 percent are diagnosed as severely neurotic (Ellis and Brancale, 1956; Gebhard et al., 1965). Schizoid personality is a common diagnosis manifested by self-centeredness, emotional isolation and detachment, concrete rather than abstract thinking, and impaired use of fantasy. Because affectional and sexual needs are not satisfied in fantasy, there is a tendency to act them out in unconventional ways (Apfelberg et al., 1944; Hammer and Glueck, 1957; Swanson, 1968; Hall et al., 1986). In a group of adolescent outpatient sex offenders, about half were diagnosed as conduct disorders with poor impulse control and antisocial behaviors (Kavoussi, Kaplan, and Becker, 1988).

Biological Basis

Since the majority of pedophiles engage in childish sex play with children, and since there is a disproportionate number of homosexual pedophiles, it has been suggested that there is some as yet unknown physiological factor that interferes with development of sexual preference (Freund et al., 1984). However, age of onset of puberty does not differ from other groups of sex offenders (Gebhard et al., 1965).

While testosterone levels are not elevated (Rada, Laws, and Kellner, 1976), there is some evidence of specific familial transmission of pedophilia. About a fourth of all deviants have first-degree relations with some sexual deviancy. And, while family members of nonpedophile deviants are not pedophiles, deviant relatives of pedophiles are pedophiles (Gaffney, Lurie, and Berlin, 1984).

Endocrine testing has revealed some evidence that, in contrast to other paraphiliacs and controls, pedophiles have some hypothalamus–pituitary gonad dysfunction (Gaffney and Berlin, 1984). Several cases have been reported where onset of sexual activities with children occurred after the men suffered central nervous system impairment with consequent cognitive deficits (Regestein and Reich, 1978). And, there is evidence of structural or functional brain impairment, particularly in the left temporal–parietal area, in two-thirds of heterosexual, homosexual, and bisexual pedophiles (Hucker, Langevin, Wortzman, Bain, Handy, Chambers, and Wright, 1986).

Early Life

Family. There is nothing distinctive in birth order (Mohr et al., 1964), but they are one of the few sexual offender groups that has more sisters than brothers (Gebhard et al., 1965). There are fewer (67%) heterosexual pedophiles from large families (more than five children) than homosexual pedophiles (99%) (Meyers and Berah, 1983).

The proportion coming from broken homes is not unusual. Where there was a break in the family, it occurred when the child was about eight years old, a relatively late age (Gebhard et al., 1965). More experienced prolonged absence of father (25%) than mother absence (0%) (Mohr et al., 1964).

Fathers. These men provide a paucity of information concerning their fathers, often describing them in terms of work performance—"hard working" and "honest." When they do use personal terms, passivity and distance are mentioned; for example, "completely dominated by mother" and "had not much to say" (Mohr et al., 1964). About half claim positive relations with fathers (Meyers and Berah, 1983).

Mothers. Mothers of adolescent child abusers are dominant and overprotective, and fathers are passive (Shoor et al., 1966). Perception of mothers is in terms of meeting dependency needs, as "depended on her," "kind, but high strung," and "rather cold" (Mohr et al., 1964). There is some indication of maternal deprivation during infancy and childhood, with consequent fear of separation from mother (Kurland, 1960). Mother is preferred over father (Gebhard et al., 1965), with two-thirds reporting positive relations with her (Meyers and Berah, 1983). However, anger toward both parents and an ambivalent attachment to mother has been reported (Hartman, 1965). They were passive, quiet, "good" children, containing their anger and rage at mother (Kurland, 1960).

Sexuality

In their prepubertal years, pedophiles did not differ from other groups in incidence of masturbation, heterosexual and homosexual sex play, or in their sex play techniques (Gebhard et al., 1965), although a third were compulsive masturbators (Longo and Groth, 1983).

There is evidence of a history of sexual victimization (Groth and Birnbaum, 1978), with about a third having been assaulted, most often by an adult male, when they were between ages one and fifteen. And, one half of adolescent sex offenders report having been sexually abused (Kahn and Lafond, 1988). Half of these early contacts with women included coitus (Gebhard et al., 1965; Groth, 1979). These early seductions might be construed by the future pedophile to mean that adults are allowed to sexually use children.

In one case, a pedophile, when seven years old, was seduced by a very hairy woman. She ordered him to disrobe and placed him on top of her. He experienced an indescribable sense of horror on seeing her pubic hair: "It seemed to me I was going to be swallowed up within this mass of hideous hair . . . I was so frightened I was unable to talk or move" (Karpman, 1954, p. 87). As an adult he could not bear to see women's pubic hair and finally convinced his wife to shave her pubic hair so he could enjoy intercourse. He did not especially want young girls, but they did not have what he feared (Karpman, 1950, 1954).

Many were sexually precocious, with about half having engaged in some petting at age twelve, ranking them near the top of all sex offender groups in heterosexual activity. However, this initial spurt waned as they peaked out at this early age. Thereafter, petting incidence, unlike other offenders, leveled off (Gebhard et al., 1965). Some preoccupation with oral–genital contact has been noted (Kurland, 1960). While incidence of such contact is only moderate, compared to other groups relatively more pedophiles gave rather than received oral sex (Gebhard et al., 1965).

Pedophiles are not distinctive in incidence of premarital coitus. However, those who did not engage were severely inhibited, reporting that they were restrained by moral considerations, fear of pregnancy, and of sexually transmitted diseases. These inhibitions are strong in relation to other offender groups (Gebhard et al., 1965). Indeed, according to one report, two-thirds are sexually inhibited (Ellis and Brancale, 1956). They are moralistic, guilt-ridden, but also impulsive (Gebhard et al., 1965). And, their attitudes toward sex are more restrictive than those of other sex offenders and homosexuals (Goldstein and Kant, 1973).

Further support for their sexual inhibition is the observation that they had less exposure to erotica as adolescents and adults than nondeviants and few could recall a vivid exposure to erotica during their adolescence. Of those that could recall such an experience, four-fifths reported feelings of shame or disgust, while only half of controls experienced such feelings (Goldstein and Kant, 1973).

Not only are they sexuallly inhibited, but also their method of relieving sexual tension is diffuse. While other men desired heterosexual relations after a vivid erotic exposure, pedophiles wanted any type of sexual activity (Goldstein and Kant, 1973). Other evidence of early deviant sexuality is that 28 percent repeatedly exposed themselves and 20 percent repetitively peeped at women undressing or having coitus (Longo and Groth, 1983).

While incidence of sexual contacts with animals is not large (16%) compared to other males, the frequency of such contacts is exceptionally high. In early adolescence there were about five contacts a year, and in late adolescence, about nine contacts (Gebhard et al., 1965). In a group of offenders against very young children, 22 percent had had animal contacts and over half had engaged in postpubertal homosexual acts (Gebhard and Gagnon, 1964). As is the case with sexually immature boys, adult pedophiles lack discrimination in acceptable sexual objects, so that both adult women and girls are sexually arousing (Langevin, Huncker, Ben-Aron, Purins, and Hook, 1985).

Even though frequency of marital coitus and sexual contacts with adults does not differ from other men (Gebhard et al., 1965; Langevin, Huncker, Ben-Aron, et al., 1985), something is definitely amiss in their intimate relations with adult women. Many are hyposexual and experience erectile failure

(Frosch and Bromberg, 1939; Fisher, 1969) and three-fourths are rated as having inadequate sex lives (Swanson, 1968). While almost all nondeviant males' preferred sexual activity is vaginal intercourse, only three-fourths of pedophiles prefer that activity. They rely heavily on prostitutes as sexual partners both before and after marriage. And, in some age brackets, coitus with prostitutes exceeds that with companions. Even those who are married are strongly dependent on masturbation as a sexual outlet. Masturbation fantasies differ from those of other males in greater incidence of sex with animals and "unusual" sexual practices (Gebhard et al., 1965; Marshall, 1988).

Personality

The typical pedophile is described as shy, timid, childlike, passive–dependent, deferent, subservient, and insecure, with feelings of sexual inadequacy and low self-esteem (Frosch and Bromberg, 1939; Kopp, 1962; Fisher, 1969; Peters, 1976; Virkkunen, 1976; Groth, 1977). However, they do not differ from community controls on measures of assertiveness and shyness (Langevin, Huncker, Handy, Hook, Purins, and Russon, 1985). A third are regarded as basically hostile (Ellis and Brancale, 1956), but have difficulty in expressing their anger (Fisher, 1969). In fact, they have a history of more violent offenses than do the homosexual or bisexual pedophiles (Langevin, Huncker, Handy et al., 1985). A personality test profile reveals pedophiles to be hostile, irritable, impulsive, and avoiding of emotional involvement (Armentrout and Hauer, 1978).

"Ah, leave me alone in my pubescent park, in my mossy garden. Let them play around me forever. Never grow up" (Nabokov, 1970, p. 23). Immaturity is a common characteristic (Ellis and Brancale, 1956; Hammer and Glueck, 1957; Kurland, 1960; Revitch and Weiss, 1962; Stricker, 1967; Bell and Hall, 1971; Groth, 1977), meaning inability to cope with life's problems and difficulty in making decisions and in forming warm personal attachments. They fail in their attempts to attain heterosexual adjustment (Apfelberg et al., 1944) and retreat to childhood to escape the insurmountable challenges of adulthood (Revitch and Weiss, 1962). Thus, one of the reasons for

selecting a child as a partner is the emotional congruence between the two (Araji and Finkelhor, 1986).

Relations with Girls and Women

A man's sexual partner may not be his preferred partner; he
may settle for second or third best. This is especially true of
many pedophiles, as less than 1 percent report a preference for
girls under twelve years of age (Gebhard et al., 1965). However,
stated preferences by convicted offenders are probably biased.
A more accurate determination of preference is physiological
arousal. Using penile volume changes in response to pictures,
pedophiles are most aroused by female adolescents, next by
female children, and least by adult females. Lowest arousal is
to male children, adolescents, and adults (Freund, 1967). Those
with two or more charges against them are aroused more by
female children than by adult females, whereas those with only
one charge are more excited by adult females than by children.
For the one-time offender, the child serves as a surrogate for
an adult partner (Freund, McKnight, Langevin, and Cibiri,
1972), whereas for the multiple offender, adult women are used
as substitutes for the preferred girl–child. Humbert Humbert
says,

> Overtly, I had so-called normal relationships with a number of terres-
> trial women having pumpkins or pears for breasts; only, I was consumed
> by a hell furnace of localized lust for every passing nymphet whom as
> a law-abiding poltroon I never dared approach. The human females
> I was allowed to wield were but palliative agents [Nabokov, 1970, p. 20].

Pedophiles' feelings toward adult females may vary from
disinterest to aversion. Using pupillary dilation or contraction
as a measure of positive or negative affect, pupils of offenders
against girls contract to pictures of adult females whereas nondeviant prisoners' pupils dilate. When shown slides of little girls,
there is dilation in pedophiles, but constriction or no change
in controls (Atwood and Howell, 1971). It appears, then, that
there is some aversion to adult females and an attraction to
younger females, especially adolescents, but also children.
    Not only do these men have difficulty in establishing close

relations with women (Kurland, 1960), they may even fear women (Socarides, 1959), especially sexual contact with them. A commonly used explanation for avoidance of adult females as sex partners is fear of castration. However, heterosexual pedophiles rank low in castration anxiety (Hammer and Glueck, 1957).

If it is not because of castration anxiety, then why is he unsatisfied in relating to adult females? Perhaps he has homosexual urges that he cannot admit and settles for prepubescent girls, whose bodies are similar to those of boys (Kopp, 1962). However, no available evidence supports this lurking homosexuality, although there may be a blurring of gender distinctions (Johnston and Johnston, 1986). Pedophiles do not differ from offenders against boys in degree of childhood feminine behaviors (Freund and Blanchard, 1987). Similarly, the antipubic hair fetish hypothesis does not fare well, as pedophiles are more aroused at the sight of pubic hair in phallometric testing than are controls (Langevin, Huncker, Ben-Aron et al., 1985).

In any one case, castration anxiety, homosexual impulses and antipubic hair fetishism may be operative. But a more general reason for difficulty in relating to women is that they are seen as unobtainable, remote, and cold (Bell and Hall, 1971), which is associated with poor heterosexual skills and social anxiety (Segal and Marshall, 1985). Unmarried adolescent offenders are not likely to engage in sex with females of equal or older age as they perceive these women as being out of their reach (Mohr et al., 1964). For some, heterosexual intercourse is possible only if they assume a passive role and are seduced by a woman (Kurland, 1960). A thirty-five-year-old who had sexual contact with two girls aged ten and twelve explains: "I'm tongue-tied with girls—never took one out—I'm afraid they might hurt my feelings. One reason is I have a small penis and I'm ashamed" (Frosch and Bromberg, 1939, p. 767).

The pedophile views himself as a child, is happy in the company of children, and seeks out children as compensation for unfulfilling relations with women and for his inability to meet demands of adult life (Groth et al., 1982). Feeling lonely, inadequate, and deprived, he longs for intimacy and affiliation that he cannot fulfill with adult women. So, he turns to children, whom he finds easy to relate to, and who give him a sense of closeness and warmth (Hammer and Glueck, 1957; Revitch and Weiss, 1962). He may desire an ongoing relation with a child that includes, but is not limited to, sex. Children are used, not so much for sexual gratification, but sex is seen as a demonstration of the child's acceptance and caring. He is attracted to children by their innocence, because he feels less inferior to them, and they are less demanding than adults. He conceives of them as less forceful and dominant than adults (Howells, 1978). Since he is more in control, there is less risk of rejection. And, because of their lack of experience, his sexual prowess is not unfavorably compared with that of others' (Kopp, 1962). All this gives him a feeling of being powerful, respected, and wanted (Araji and Finkelhor, 1986), feelings he cannot attain in the adult world.

He may be attempting to relive an idyllic teenage romance, or he may be trying to reenact some childish sexual experience. For instance, a shy, withdrawn fifteen-year-old molested small girls who resembled his sister. The extent of his heterosexual experience was that he once saw his one-year-old sister in the nude. This scene came to mind as he masturbated, but he suppressed it as too dirty (Waggoner and Boyd, 1941).

Attitude Toward Deviancy

Several reactions to being apprehended have been reported. Some put on a sanctimonious air, boasting of being regular churchgoers and honest citizens. About a fourth of heterosexual offenders deny outright any offense (Gebhard et al., 1965): "It never happened. That kid is lying. I wasn't even around her when she says I did it" (Sanford, 1980, p. 87).

Many admit to the possibility of the offense, but deny remembering what they did, claiming they were under the influence of alcohol (Frosch and Bromberg, 1939). Blaming alcohol allows the man to admit the offense, but deny identity with other child molesters. "Drinking is the reason. I could always get a woman. I can't figure it out. A man's mind doesn't function right when he's got liquor on it" (McCaghy, 1968, p. 48).

After repeated denials, some admit the offense, often accusing the child of being the initiator. "They ought to have separate beaches for men and women. Wearing shorts for girls is like advertising. They (little girls) are worse to the public than any criminal. They are cunning, devilish and tricky. You can't help blushing when you are in their presence" (Frosch and Bromberg, 1939, p. 767).

The offender may attempt to minimize the event: "It was an accident, the kid came in while I was in the bathroom, and now she says I exposed myself and tried to do things to her . . . I forgot to close the door. So what?" (Sanford, 1980, p. 88).

HOMOSEXUAL PEDOPHILIA

The Act

Precipitating Events

A fourth to a third of offenders had been drinking at the time of the offense; nonetheless, premeditation was present in over four-fifths (84%) of offenses (Gebhard et al., 1965; Rada, 1976). About 40 percent reported that, at least occasionally, viewing explicit pornography precipitated the offense (Marshall, 1988).

The Boy

Mean age of the boy is between ten and twelve years of age, with a range from three to sixteen years (Mohr et al., 1964; Gebhard et al., 1965; Ellerstein and Canavan, 1980). The age of boys consistently increases from five to about twelve, and then levels off. Age twelve, about the onset of puberty, probably represents the cut-off between pederasty and adult homosexuality (Mohr et al., 1964). In Windham's (1965) novel, *Two People*, Forest, the adult, "could not fit the boy into any category he knew. The boy's figure, lean and rounded, evoked neither masculinity nor femininity, rather the undivided country of adolescence" (p. 41).

The boys seem to be motivated by needs for affection, adventure, sexual curiosity, and sometimes money (Rossman,

1976). Two types have been identified (Fraser, 1981): one is the boy whose sex with an adult is merely a part of his general delinquency. Probably a runaway from a dysfunctional home, his relation with an adult affords him security, status, affection, and money. A goodly number of these boys are male prostitutes. Thirteen percent of boys from thirteen to sixteen said that, if they really needed the money, they would have sex with a man who paid them for it (Sorensen, 1973). The other type is the timid, conforming lad who receives little warmth and affection at home. He may be in a boarding school or a member of a youth organization. This love-starved youth finds his needs met by a sympathetic teacher or leader.

By and large, boys who become sexually involved with adults come from families where the fathers are alcoholic, violent, or absent, and mothers rejecting. The majority of these boys were seeking affection, and some are sexually curious (Ingram, 1981).

In keeping with the low incidence of homosexual incest, very rarely are boys related to the offender. Of nonincestuous cases, over a half were close friends or known to the child (Mohr et al., 1964; Gebhard et al., 1965; Ellerstein and Canavan, 1980).

The Encounter

A large proportion of pederasts profess devotion to the boy, a close friendship, with loyalty, patience, and giving of help when needed (Righton, 1981). Sexual relations occur in a context of this close, loving relationship. These men tend to see the boy as sexually provocative (Ingram, 1981). One man claimed he waited a year before he made his move. "I'd worked with those kids for a full year on nothing but their batting and fielding before I ever molested them. It took me that long before they trusted me and stopped treating me like a tough adult coach" (Sanford, 1980, p. 103).

Others set out to entice boys. They initiate sex play, and their sexual acts are devoid of expressions of affection (Ingram, 1981). One such man describes his technique.

> If I set out to seduce a boy, I'd use the same method boys use on each other. I'd simply start telling dirty jokes, and I'd encourage the boys

to tell dirty jokes, until I could tell by the tone of their voice, their emotional reaction, their laughter, their lack of embarrassment, which boy was experienced and available [Rossman, 1976, p. 160].

Three-fourths of the men take the initiative and over two-thirds of the boys are either passive or encouraging. A majority of boys claim that they sought out the relationship and the rest say they had fantasized such a liaison to the point that they were ready to consent (Rossman, 1976). Threats and use of force are rare. Where the boy does resist, force is rated as mild to moderate (Gebhard et al., 1965).

Almost all boys who were contacted through their adult partners viewed their sexual contact as a predominantly positive experience. Some parents knew of their sons' relationship and the rest suspected the sexual nature of the relationship (Sandfort, 1984).

A third to a half of the sexual contacts take place in the residences of the adult or boy. The rest occur out of doors as in a park, in the adult's auto, movie theaters, and public toilets (Mohr et al., 1964; Gebhard et al., 1965; Ellerstein and Canavan, 1980).

Pederastic acts do not differ appreciably from those engaged in by adult homosexuals. Most frequent are fondling of the boy and masturbation. Manipulation of the boy is more common than the man being masturbated, and mutual masturbation is usually initiated by the boy. Other acts are anal or intercrural intercourse, mouth–genital contact, with orgasm sought in half of the instances (McGeorge, 1964; Mohr et al., 1964; Gebhard et al., 1965; Ingram, 1981; Langfeld, 1981; Erickson et al., 1988). In a study of boy partners of adults in the Netherlands, the adult most often was the fellator. Oral–anal contact occurred in a third of these relations, with the adult using his mouth on the boy. Where anal penetration was practiced, most often boys were the insertors (Sandfort, 1984).

Several types of man–boy relationships have been described (Rossman, 1976). Some occur in settings where women are unavailable, as in boarding schools, correctional institutions, or in cultures where unmarried women are strictly chaperoned.

The boy serves as a substitute for a woman. Man–boy relationships that occur in youth organizations are usually mutually affectionate. The adult sees himself as a tutor in sex and usually deliberately avoids intimate sexual contact, limiting himself to affectionate embraces only. Some adults are the highly masculine type—policeman, sportsman—who express their pederastic inclinations in rough-and-tumble play. They deny that these activities are homosexual and avoid oral or anal sex, engaging mostly in mutual masturbation.

For a few, sex is a game. They get as much excitement from "cruising" as from actual sexual contact. Others are jaded heterosexuals, looking for new erotic experiences. Fortunately, rare are those men who receive sadistic gratification in harming boys or in serving as a pimp for boy prostitutes. Finally, closet pederasts substitute fantasies and fetishes for actual sexual contact with boys, collecting boys' used underwear, or simply reading pederastic books.

The Person

Current Status

Onset and age. Three-fourths of the members of a pedophile working group report they first became aware of their sexual attraction to boys before they were twenty years old, and two-thirds had their first sexual contact with a boy before age twenty (Bernard, 1975).

Reported average age of apprehended pederasts is thirty to forty years (Gebhard et al., 1965; Bernard, 1975; Fisher, 1979), and two-thirds are less than forty years old (McGeorge, 1964), as presented in Table 7.4.

As with heterosexual pedophiles, the age distribution for pederasts shows several peaks. However, sample size is small (N = 23) and therefore not as reliable as for heterosexuals (Mohr et al., 1964). Whereas only a few in the youngest group (15–24) report previous homosexual acts, half the men over twenty-four years old have had homosexual contacts. Half of the twenty-five to forty-four age group are youth group leaders, and most display a parental attitude toward boys. Younger pe-

TABLE 7.4

Age Distribution of Homosexual Child Abusers

Age	Percent (N = 200)
<20	3
20–30	34
30–40	28
40–50	13
50–60	16
>60	6

From: J. McGeorge (1964), Sexual assaults on children. *Medicine, Science and the Law*, 4:248.

dophiles, from fifteen to twenty-four years, choose boys with a mean age of ten years, whereas pedophiles over twenty-five have boys whose mean age is thirteen years.

Intelligence, education and interests. In overt characteristics, pederasts are virtually indistinguishable from other men. Mean IQ is average and the distribution is approximately normal. Educational attainment is not appreciably different from that of the general population. All occupational groups are represented, with a tendency toward business and service. Distribution of religious affiliation is close to that of the general population. While some are interested in sports, many tend more toward the artistic, such as music and painting (Mohr et al., 1964).

Marital status. Most estimates of apprehended pederasts show close to 50 percent as never having married (Glueck, 1956; Mohr et al., 1964; Gebhard et al., 1965; Fisher, 1969; Rada, 1976; Rossman, 1976), which is higher than for other homosexuals (Curran and Parr, 1957; Gebhard et al., 1965). In a nonprison sample, 90 percent were unmarried (Bernard, 1975). For those who are married, there is a lack of closeness (Mohr et al., 1964).

Psychopathology. There is more blatant schizophrenia than is seen in heterosexual pedophiles, with three-fourths of convicted pederasts displaying some form of schizophrenic reaction. Among convicted pederasts estimates of alcoholism vary from a fifth to almost a half (Gebhard et al., 1965; Rada, 1976).

Early Life

Early family life was anything but stable. Nearly two-thirds come from broken homes, placing the homosexual offender second highest of all sex offenders in this category. Father was absent for prolonged periods in a third of the cases, and mother was absent in a fifth. And, for a fourth, adjustment between parents during the offender's teen years was poor (Mohr et al., 1964; Gebhard et al., 1965).

As is typical of homosexuals during their midteens, pederasts had poor relations with their fathers (Gebhard et al., 1965). While some describe their fathers as "kind" and "generous," they seem to perceive a lack of closeness as indicated by statements such as, "hated him, but wanted to be close," and "solid but little time for me" (Mohr et al., 1964, p. 61).

In a prison sample, pederasts, during their midteens, had the poorest relations with mothers of all sex offender groups, but still favored mothers to fathers (Gebhard et al., 1965). Feelings toward mother are admiring and somewhat idealized, reflected in descriptions of her as "energetic," "refined," "intellectual," and "artistic" (Mohr et al., 1964).

Sexuality

In common with other homosexuals, the pederast was quite active in prepubertal sex play. Of those who were active, heterosexual and homosexual experiences were about equal. A quarter had exclusive homosexual contacts, but unlike other homosexual groups, a fifth had heterosexual play exclusively, but these liaisons were of rather short duration. Many were masturbating prepubertally, and two-fifths learned to masturbate by being stimulated by another, compared to only one-eighth of a nonoffender group (Gebhard et al., 1965).

Their first heterosexual petting experience was at age fifteen, and thereafter the number engaging in this activity drops off drastically. The frequency with which petting led to orgasm is low and their techniques were less sophisticated than those of other offender groups (Gebhard et al., 1965).

Twice as many pederasts were sexually misused as children as were heterosexual pedophiles (Groth, 1979). Like other homosexuals, about a third report having been approached by adult males during their preadolescence, and a fifth of these approaches eventuated in sexual contacts (Gebhard et al., 1965; Gaffney et al., 1984). In adulthood, they play the role of their abuser, but negate the abuse aspect of their experience by romanticizing their relations with boys (Groth et al., 1982).

Almost a quarter had sexual contacts with animals in their postpubertal lives, and many dreamed and fantasized about such contacts (Gebhard et al., 1965).

While premarital heterosexual intercourse incidence is low, number of partners–companions, plus mostly prostitutes, is high. Frequency of marital coitus is low, but masturbation is an important sexual outlet. For instance, single pederasts, between twenty-one and twenty-five years, have over half of their orgasms in this fashion compared to about a third of nonoffender males. Incidence of homosexual masturbation fantasy is large (69%), but smaller than for homosexual offenders against teenagers (78%) and adults (91%) (Gebhard et al., 1965).

Despite their early sexual activity, they are sexually inhibited. They are uncomfortable in talking about sex and are opposed to premarital sex. During their childhoods, nudity was frowned upon and there was no discussion of sex at home. Compared with controls, pederasts had less exposure to erotica during adolescence, except they had the same exposure to homosexual material. Eighty percent recall feelings of shame or disgust over their most vivid experience with erotic material during adolescence. The type of sexual activity desired after this vivid experience was masturbation, with a few desiring some sadomasochistic activity. Whereas four-fifths of controls report that they thought about sex a good part of the time during their teen years, only one third of the pederasts did so. Their predominant sexual fantasy was of homosexual oral–genital contact (Goldstein and Kant, 1973). As adults, two-thirds usually or always use "deviant" masturbation fantasies (Marshall, 1988).

Personality

According to personality test profiles, pederasts are passive, dependent, lonely, depressed, and sexually and emotionally inadequate in relations with adult women (Glueck, 1956; Wilson and Cox, 1983).

Seventy-six percent of convicted pederasts describe themselves as being somewhat to markedly feminine in childhood and 12 percent as overcompensatedly masculine (Glueck, 1956). Their adult personality profiles resemble the feminine pattern (Fisher and Howell, 1970). In common with homosexuals who prefer adult partners, pederasts recall the same lack of aggressive behaviors during childhood (Freund and Blanchard, 1987). As adults, however, they score higher on a heterosexuality scale than do heterosexual abusers (Fisher, 1969), perhaps indicating further compensation for their basic femininity. They display more castration anxiety than do heterosexual pedophiles (Hammer and Glueck, 1957).

Relations with Adults and Boys

Heterosexual interest is low, and when such relations are attempted, functioning is chronically and severely impaired. Sexual self-concept is markedly inadequate (Glueck, 1956; Mohr et al., 1964).

Pederasts are like homosexuals in many respects, yet share quantitatively less of these characteristics. While more tolerant of male homosexuality than heterosexuals, they are less approving than other homosexuals (Gebhard et al., 1965; Goldstein and Kant, 1973), and are socially isolated from them (Curran and Parr, 1957). In turn, they are shunned by most homosexuals. Most are ill at ease with adult males. Some deny they are homosexual and may even express dislike for them:

> "I was never a homosexual. I was crazy about girls ever since I can remember. I knew it was wrong to have sex with little girls, for they were going to be wives and mothers and should be protected, not abused. It never occurred to me as a youngster that sex with a boy was wrong or against the law. . . . When I was in the Navy I took a violent dislike to gays" [Rossman, 1976, p. 199].

Others qualify their homosexuality: "Yes, I'm gay in that I simply don't like women. . . . However I'm not gay in that I'm not attracted to males over sixteen" (Rossman, 1976, p. 201).

Four-fifths report having had homosexual experiences with adults, a lower incidence than other homosexual offender groups. Yet, two-fifths report having had extensive experience with partners over twenty-one years old. A large majority of their adult partners were pickups where the pederasts took the initiative (Gebhard et al., 1965).

About a third state they prefer boys under twelve years, but the majority opted for partners in their teens, with an average optimal partner age of sixteen. They are anything but monogomous, with nearly half having had relations with twenty or more partners and some claiming up to fifty boy partners (Gebhard et al., 1965; Bernard, 1975).

A majority of pederasts (those who prefer boys between twelve to sixteen) in a nonprison sample claimed they were either bisexual or otherwise heterosexual (Rossman, 1976). This assertion is not confirmed by arousal patterns. Using penile tumescence as a measure of preference, rankings for pederasts were male child, adolescent; female child, adolescent; male adult, and female adult. While sex of the child is important, immature females are more arousing than adults. This contrasts with other homosexuals for whom sex of partner is the primary consideration—their first three ranks being male adult, adolescent, and then child, with female adult, adolescent, and child least arousing (Freund, 1967).

Pederasts are not attracted to homosexual or effeminate boys, but rather to masculine boys (Rossman, 1976). A prominent factor in their attraction to boys is that they feel superior and can pose as a mentor. Also, boys make fewer demands and do not make unfavorable comparisons as do adults. Some pederasts claim they are attracted by boys' smooth softness and their expressiveness and spontaneity (Gebhard et al., 1965).

One important element in pederasty may well be a sexual experience the pederast had as a boy, either with an adult or an age mate male. It is possible that his sex play with boys did not have negative consequences, whereas his sex play with girls met with punishment (Fox, 1941). As an adult, he remains an eternal adolescent, attempting to recapture this initial pleasure by selecting young boys as sex partners. His choice of a boy reflects his own ideal self-image (Socarides, 1959): "As soon as Marcello was gone . . . [Forest] felt as though a part of his own self had departed, leaving him only half able to breathe or to move" (Windham, 1965, p. 167).

Alternatively, the adult pederast may put this adolescent experience away, relive it occasionally in fantasy, and even marry and have children, only later to act it out. "I have a good marriage, but these inclinations continue to pop up once in a while, especially when I meet the kind of lovely well-bred younger kid I slept with when I was seventeen. My spine still tingles to remember the magic of that experience" (Rossman, 1976, p. 67).

Attitude Toward Deviancy

Even though over half of pedophile working group members had been sentenced for child abuse, only 8 percent said they would like to be rid of their pedophilia (Bernard, 1975). Consistent with their efforts to lower age of consent, they blame society's restrictive standards: " 'I'm just a victim of an uptight, Victorian society. If people . . . knew how beautiful sex with kids can be, I wouldn't have been busted for loving Jimmy' " (Sanford, 1980, p. 104).

8 FATHER–DAUGHTER INCEST

INTRODUCTION

Prevalence

Early estimates of the prevalence of incest ranged from less than one to five per million population (Weinberg, 1955). Incest was so rarely reported in the Kinsey survey that the authors conclude that, "heterosexual incest occurs more frequently in the thinking of clinicians and social workers than it does in actual performance" (Kinsey, Pomeroy and Martin, 1948, p. 558).

However, more recent surveys of adult women report that from around 1 percent (Hunt, 1974; Finkelhor, 1979a) to 3 percent (Wolfe, 1981) had experienced incestuous relations. Specific samples yield higher estimates. For example, of several hundred females in public institutions in Northern Ireland, 4 percent reported father–daughter incest (Lukianowicz, 1972). Mental health professionals estimate prevalence of incest involving females at from at least 5 to as high as 15 percent (Woodbury and Schwartz, 1971).

That actual prevalence is much higher than usually reported is seen in information from Santa Clara County, California (pop. 1,159,500), where in 1971 a Child Sexual Abuse

249

Treatment Program was established. In that year, twenty-six cases of father–daughter incest were processed. Just a few years later, after a media campaign, one hundred eighty cases were referred, and in 1978, six hundred families were serviced by that program—a dramatic increase in reported cases, but probably no increase in actual occurrence (Giarretto, 1981).

Attitudes Toward Incest

About four-fifths of adolescents consider sex between parent and child and between brother and sister abnormal or unnatural even if they both wanted it, with girls more negative than boys (Sorensen, 1973; Arndt and Ladd, 1981). Attitudes toward the incest offender are extremely negative. And some, more males than females, blame the daughter (Jackson and Ferguson, 1983).

A small minority do not view incest as an aberration. Guyon (1933), for example, says that incest is in conformity with nature and that its prohibition is merely a convention with no basis in biological reality. Other advocates for incest have been heard from more recently (DeMott, 1980).

Despite these negative attitudes, there appears to be a fascination with incest among some males. In an incidental sample of one thousand pornographic books, 26 percent were clearly identifiable as dealing with incest of all types, and 5 percent were of the father–daughter type.

Some are of the opinion that researchers in this area allow their attitudes to influence their studies. Herman and Hirschman (1981) claim that up until 1975, research on incest was so contaminated by sex bias that it is virtually useless. By sex bias they are presumably referring to reports of "the seductive daughter" and "the collusive mother." These authors consider father–daughter incest to be the "paradigm of female sexual victimization."

DEFINITION

Derivation and Use

The word *incest* is thought to come from the Latin cestus which refers to the girdle of Venus worn by the wife and loosened by her husband as a sign of marital happiness. Failure to use the cestus, incestus, meant that the relationship was unlawful and unchaste. Later, incestus came to mean immodesty with a blood relative or with a young girl, but it also referred to adultery. In the 1100s, the meaning was narrowed to blood relatives (Weinberg, 1955; Maisch, 1972).

Research on incestuous families is plagued by many problems with resultant confusing and sometimes contradictory data. One of these problems is the definition of incest. There are two key portions—the relationship between the participants and the specific acts engaged in. Some studies do not differentiate between natural fathers and stepfathers, even though the dynamics of the two may be different (Finkelhor, 1979a).

Another difficulty concerns the age of the daughter at onset and offset of the affair, since the dynamics involving a six-year-old child may differ from those of a twelve-year-old. In their quest for accuracy, Gebhard, Gagnon, Pomeroy, and Christenson (1965) group their cases according to the daughter's age at termination, not onset, thereby obscuring differences due to the initial age of daughter. Finally, even though several types of incest offenders have been proposed, few studies consider them separately.

It is expected that parents behave affectionately toward their children. And, at times, such behavior may seem to others as having sexual overtones. A mother, while bathing her son, may manipulate his penis out of curiosity; a father may cuddle his daughter in bed. If his daughter is postpubertal, he may even engage in some household peeping. Such behaviors need not be incestuous, harmful, or exploitive. And, children engage in seemingly sexual acts toward their parents. In a nonclinical sample, 30 percent of daughters up to ten years old had touched their fathers' genitals and 45 percent of boys from eight to ten had touched mothers' breasts or genitals (Rosenfeld, Bailey, Siegel, and Bailey, 1986). So, just where is the boundary between expected parental behaviors and incest?

Unfortunately, "the objective distinction between loving support and lustful intrusion are disquietly subtle" (Summit and Kryso, 1978, p. 237). The question is, when does the loving caress that enhances self-esteem become pleasurable overstimulation that floods the child with excitement and fear of loss of control (Brant and Tisza, 1977)?

The acts engaged in that qualify as sexual differ from study to study. Legal definitions and therefore studies based on samples from court referrals and prisons severely limit the nature of the act to sexual intercourse between blood relatives (Weinberg, 1955; Ellis, 1967; Ciba Foundation, 1984). Only five states use broader definitions of the act, and only twenty-four states include steprelatives in their definitions. Those cases not meeting the legal definitions of incest can be charged with "indecent liberties with children," "corrupting the morals of a minor," and so on. (Herman and Hirschman, 1981).

Those who choose to broaden the nature of the act face the problem of specifying what constitutes sexual contact. Meiselman (1978) includes "successful and unsuccessful attempts at exposure, genital fondling, oral–genital contact, and/or vaginal or anal intercourse, as perceived by the patient" (p. 59). She excludes "seductive behavior," while Finkelhor (1979a) includes sexual propositioning. Others avoid specifying the acts and focus on characteristics or consequences. For instance, "any physical contact that had to be kept a secret" (Herman and Hirschman, 1981, p. 70). Or, an act that is "perceived to be of a sexual nature and of sufficient intensity to cause disturbance in that younger person" (Renvoize, 1982, p. 31). The reference to incest causing disturbance is unfortunate, since if there is no disturbance manifest at the time, then the act is not incestuous.

In studies of incest, consideration should be given to degree of relationship, ages of the two participants, type and degree of sexual activity, amount of resistance of the younger person, and degree of prepubertal association between the adult and the child (Bixler, 1983).

Relation to Pedophilia

There is seldom any relation between incest and other types of sexually deviant behavior other than pedophilia. Unfortunately, some studies group incest offenders together with pedophiles on the basis that both take children as sexual partners. But, there are differences between the two. In incest, it is often signs of coming maturity that trigger a father's interest in his daughter, whereas for the pedophile these same signs are a turnoff (Maisch, 1972). Daughters' mean age (12.7) is higher than that of victims of pedophiles (10.9) (Langevin, Handy, Russon, and Day, 1985). Also, there is some evidence that the pedophile's orientation is bisexual, whereas the incest offender is primarily heterosexual. Incest offenders are more socially introverted and are more deficient in social skills than are pedophiles (Panton, 1979). Finally pedophilic tendencies in incest offenders are rare (Maisch, 1972; Alstrom, 1977; Meiselman, 1978).

Varieties of Incest Offenders

Weinberg (1955) has provided a useful threefold classification. One group is "endogamic." Concealment is the hallmark of the endogamic family, and all members fear separation (Rosenfeld, 1979). This type of offender avoids social and sexual contacts outside his family. He considers it sinful to go outside the family for sex, but views his daughter as one that already belongs to him. She is seen as a substitute for his wife; not his wife as she is in the present, but as she was when she was younger, more attractive, and more in love with him (Cormier et al., 1962). Often his daughter reminds him of an older relative, sometimes his own mother (Rosenfeld, 1979).

The next type, the indiscriminately promiscuous offender, uses his daughter because of unavailability of other females. Sexual contact with her is transient and purely physical. This man displays an inability to tolerate frustration, is hostile and sometimes physically abusive. He is variously labeled a psychopath, sociopath, and amoral delinquent.

The pedophiliac is the third type. He sometimes seeks sexual relations with young girls other than his daughter. He is not especially attracted to adult women. When he does have relations with adult females, he selects those who will not resist or ridicule him.

The Gebhard group's (1965) typology is specific to each of the daughter age groups, but they do overlap. The most common (75%) offenders against daughters under twelve years are the dependent type and are similar to Weinberg's endogamous type. These men are socially incompetent and dependent on their wives for social and financial support. They are depressed and irritable. Incest begins during a time of marital discord. At first they feel guilty, but then rationalize their behavior; for example, by claiming sex education as their excuse. Force is not used and coitus not attempted. These men are preoccupied with sex. They engage in much sexual fantasizing and talking about sex. They seem to be seeking relief from tension in their sexual relations.

Amoral delinquents, commonly called sociopaths, dominate their families, who fear them. They have more arrest records and are more aggressive than other incest offenders. Offenders against adults and minors are often of the subcultural variety, that is, they are members of a subculture in which any postpubertal female is considered a suitable sex object. These men are poor, uneducated, unintelligent, and are likely to live in rural areas.

Only a few are classed as drunkards, pedophiles, mental defectives, psychotics, or situational, that is to say, those whose offense is the result of a series of chance factors.

The various typologies are summarized in Table 8.1.

Origin and Function of the Taboo

Before proceeding to theories of the origin of the incest taboo, several points must be clarified. One involves the relation between exogamy and incest, since confusion has arisen over lack of separation between these two rules. Exogamy is the rule that sanctions marriages between individuals belonging to different groups and therefore forbids marriages within a group. Incest taboo refers to sexual relations between individuals belonging to the same group. These two rules are not completely congruent, since while exogamy may be enforced, incest may not be forbidden. Another issue concerns the extent of the ban on incest. While the incest taboo is not universal, all societies have some rules about sexual relations and marriage with related persons. The strength of the incest prohibition varies from sheer horror to simple derision (Fox, 1980).

TABLE 8.1
Classification of Incestuous Fathers

Endogamic	Heavily dependent on family for emotional needs. Unwilling or unable to satisfy sexual needs outside the family.
Personality Disorder	Shy and ineffectual in social relations. Intellectual defense structure and tendency to paranoid thinking. Intensely involved with daughter, overcontrolling of her. Sometimes preoccupied with sex. Often involved with prepubescent daughter.
Subcultural Variety	Lives in isolated rural area. Moralistic, periodically atoning for sins. Social milieu semi-tolerant of incest. Usually involved with postpubertal daughter.
Psychopathic	Criminal history. Sexually promiscuous, unrestrained by marital bonds. Little emotional attachment to daughter.
Psychotic	Severe ego disorganization of organic or functional origin.
Drunken	Incest occurs only when father is extremely intoxicated.
Pedophiliac	Generally attracted to young children as sex partners. May lose interest in daughter as she ages.
Mental Defective	Low intelligence a factor in reduced ego controls.
Situational	Incest occurring only during high-stress period for father.

From: C. Meiselman (1973), *Incest*. New York: Jossey Bass, p. 111.

During the 1800s, it was asserted that primitive people were aware of the deleterious effects of inbreeding and so placed a ban on them. This formulation was roundly criticized on two points. First, negative effects of inbreeding were exaggerated, and second, even if they exist, primitive people would not have been able to attribute them to inbreeding. So, these theories fell into disrepute. But, Lindzey (1967) presents evidence that inbreeding does cause a decrease in fitness for survival. He then proposes that, despite a natural sexual attraction for those who are similar and close to us, some societies instituted incest taboos and demanded exogamy and others did not make such rules. Those societies that allowed inbreeding produced offspring who, over generations, were less and less viable. Those that prohibited inbreeding increased their genetic diversity, producing behavioral variations that broadened their adaptability to changing environments. In this process there is no need to assume that primitive people were aware of the relation between inbreeding and physical status.

To succeed in the eternal struggle for survival, cooperation and mutual aid among peoples are necessary. Starting with this self-evident premise, White (1948) builds an economic theory of the taboo's origin. It is natural, he maintains, for the child to focus its sexual interest on those who are close at hand, namely the family. To some extent this sexual binding facilitates cooperation within the family. But, the family unit is too small to cope effectively with its threatening surroundings. If cooperation within the family is beneficial, why not cooperation among families? "Marry out or die out" became the rule of the day. Unions within the family (endogamy) were forbidden so that marriage outside the family (exogamy) became necessary. The marriage contract brought an alliance between families and between even larger groups. Royal incest was allowed since the family was already powerful, but required within-family solidarity.

The theory that humans acquire a natural absence or aversion to sexual relations with persons with whom they have lived during childhood was proposed by Westermarck and others. This is an elaboration of the "familiarity breeds contempt, not breeding" idea (Fox, 1980). If natural aversion does develop, detractors ask, then why do we need a taboo on behavior that we are already averse to?

Starting with an assumption quite opposite to the Westermarckian, Freud (1912) proposed that humans are sexually attracted to their family members. He presents his theory via the primal family ruled over by a father who forbade his sons access to his wives and daughters. The frustrated sons revolted and slew their father. But after ridding themselves of the tyrant, they felt remorse since not only did they hate him, they also loved, admired, and identified with him. Through the mechanism of "deferred obedience," the brothers denied themselves access to the women they had murdered for. This myth, Freud maintained, is replayed in the life of every male as the Oedipus complex.

Westermarckian and Freudian theories are irreconcilable only if each is held to be the sole explanation (Fox, 1980). There is evidence suggesting that both theories are valid under different conditions. Evidence for the Westermarck effect is presented in studies of Israeli kibbutz children who are raised in a nursery where sexual permissiveness prevails. The sexes sleep in the same room, shower together, regularly view one another in the nude, and engage in sexual play. What are the consequences of being raised so intimately together? By the sixth grade, the girls spontaneously develop a sense of sexual shame—not wanting to be seen in the nude. Also at this time there emerges a mutual hostility between the sexes. And, there was not a single teenage couple formed of these children who had grown up in this intimate climate. Among second-generation adolescents and adults, there was no evidence of heterosexual activity, and of over two thousand marriages, no pair was from the same peer group (Sepher, 1971; Spiro, 1975).

The work of Wolf (1966) on two types of marriage arrangements in Taiwan lends additional support to the "familiarity breeds contempt" contention. In both forms, the union is arranged by the parents. They differ in the time the bride enters the groom's father's home. In one form, she comes to live with her future husband's family when she is three years old or younger, while in the other form, she enters the home at a marriageable age. In the first form, the little girl is in contact with her future husband almost every hour of the day. The outcome of these two forms of marriage are consistent with the findings in kibbutz studies. The young people who have lived together during childhood are clearly unhappy with marriage. Many refuse to get married, and those who do marry, continue to be unhappy, describing their marriages as "embarrassing" and "shameful." Husbands visit prostitutes and take mistresses more often than in the case of couples not reared together. Wolf concludes that being raised with a person creates an aversion to sexual relations with them and, therefore, a reluctance to marry them.

Consistent with Wolf's conclusion is the finding that young males who have sisters have more negative attitudes toward incest than those without sisters (Arndt and Ladd, 1981).

But, what is it about being reared together that fosters an aversion toward sexual relations? An answer is suggested by Fox (1980) who puts forth the following hypothesis in an attempt to reconcile the Westermarckian and Freudian theories: "The intensity of heterosexual attraction between co-socialized children after puberty is inversely proportionate to the intensity of heterosexual activity between them before puberty" (p. 50).

This hypothesis fits well with the data from Israeli kibbutzim and the reared-together bride and groom of Taiwan. Intense heterosexual activity left unconsummated produces frustration and subsequent avoidance of the person who was associated with that frustration. But, what of the Freudian theory? Most likely, his patients had been reared in strictly moralistic homes where physical contact between the sexes was discouraged. Also, outside the family avenues for sexual release were forbidden by the moral code. In this case, the natural sexual attraction between family members would generate strong incestuous desires and consequent guilt over these desires. The Fox hypothesis has the advantage of accounting for the varying intensity of the incest taboo against the several types of incest. The greatest degree of physical contact in the family is between mother and child, second, between father and child, and finally, brother and sister. This order coincides with the varying strengths of the taboo in Western society with mother–son the strongest, father–daughter second, and brother–sister last.

Next we turn to some proposed functions of the taboo. Parsons (1954) views the family as a self-liquidating group whose function is to socialize its offspring, preparing the child to take its place in society. The family is self-liquidating in that the child must eventually leave the home.

One of the most powerful tools in socializing the child is the erotic urge. This urge binds child to parent and sensitizes it to the attitudes of the parent. However, there is danger in this erotic urge in that the tie must be gradually broken during the child's socialization. If this rope is not severed, the child remains fixated on or predisposed to regress to childlike attachment to the parent or sibling. The function of the incest taboo, then, is to prevent a clinging attachment to a family member and to aid the child in seeking an erotic choice outside the family.

A not unrelated view of the function of the taboo was proposed by Malinowski (1929). Sex within the family, except between the parents, would upset the family organization, disrupt age and generational distinctions, and confuse roles of family members, thereby interfering with the socialization process of the children.

THE ACT

The Family

Older Conceptions

Early studies, using court referrals and prison samples, found that incestuous families came from the lower economic strata, were large, and lived in overcrowded conditions. In Sweden, reported incest predominated among the lower occupational levels, especially farm laborers (Riemer, 1940), and in Northern Ireland, among working-class families in industrial towns (Lukianowicz, 1972). In a Boston study, the largest number of offenders were seaman and longshoremen (Kaufman, Peck, and Taguiri, 1954). In the Chicago area, none of the fathers had professional or managerial jobs (Weinberg, 1955).

Later studies, however, using nonprison samples, report

that fathers are occupationally stable and fairly successful (Mei-selman, 1978; Herman and Hirschman, 1981). Clients seen at Santa Clara County Child Sexual Abuse Treatment Program represent a cross section of the county, and occupational level tended toward professional, semiprofessional, and skilled labor (Giarretto, 1981).

Related to the purported low occupational level of incest offenders was the assertion that such families are large and live in overcrowded conditions. In 1899, it was claimed that, "in the slums of the large cities where families are herded together like swine there is a horrible indulgence in every kind of incest by adults as well as children" (Weinberg, 1955, p. 55, citing Fink). Incest was thought to be the consequence of "close domestic intimacy in small dwellings . . . not infrequently among the lower classes of the population" (Bloch, 1908, p. 639).

Again, this large family/overcrowding contention comes from studies of detected cases. Recent studies report that crowd-ing is not related to incidence of incest (Weiner, 1962; Meisel-man, 1978; Finkelhor, 1979a). Overcrowding, where it does exist, has a twofold effect: it facilitates consummation of the act where father desires it and the relative lack of privacy has a detrimental effect on the family's sexual attitudes. Rather than a contributory cause of incest, fathers often use sleeping ar-rangements as a pretext and an excuse for their behavior. Even where father and daughter slept together, other sleeping ar-rangements could have been made (Weinberg, 1955; Maisch, 1972). In one middle-class family everyone slept in a king-size waterbed, even though the children had their own bedrooms (Meiselman, 1978).

While overcrowding is not characteristic, large numbers of children are reported since 36 percent of incestuous families have more than four children compared to only 6 percent in the general population (Julian and Mohr, 1979). This has been interpreted as a sign of the dependency and powerlessness of the mothers (Herman and Hirschman, 1981).

Family Disorganization

If not poverty and overcrowding, then what does characterize the incest family? Family disorganization has been implicated as the common denominator (Lustig, Dresser, Spellman, and Murray, 1966). Almost 90 percent of incest families were disorganized as evidenced by expressed hostility, constant tension, or interpersonal indifference (Maisch, 1972). There is more family discord, alcohol dependency, and mental health problems in incestuous families (66%) than in families where physical abuse occurs (42%) (Julian and Mohr, 1979).

One form of disorganization is illustrated by families seen at one adolescent clinic, where a majority were asocial. There was physical abuse and neglect. Parents had been accused of murder, assault, and drug dependency. Children had engaged in arson, drug dealing, thievery, and sexual promiscuity (Nakashima and Zakus, 1977).

The dysfunctional family, unable to tolerate or cope with stress, develops a compulsive and repetitive pattern of interactions. These interactions are required to either avoid or to repeat traumatic events in the parents' lives. Also characteristic of such families are attempts to blame others as the source of stress on the family. Both mother and father have strong fears of separation (Gutheil and Avery, 1977). They hold the belief that close, intimate relations with other adults are risky, and at the same time, that separation signals abandonment and disintegration (Mrazek and Bentovim, 1981).

A relatively infrequent (10%) symptom of disorganization is polarization of relationships. Relations between husband and wife are strained, daughter is hostile toward mother, and emotionally dependent on her father. Father and daughter form an exclusive alliance against the rival mother (Maisch, 1972). Such polarization makes mother resentful and, in turn, daughter feels guilty (Herman and Hirschman, 1981). One such family consisted of father, mother, their own child, and mother's daughter by another man. Through his suspiciousness, father managed to split the family into two camps—their daughter and himself who shared a strong relation of trust, and the mother and her daughter who were put on the defensive. Since such patterns of disorganization obtain prior to onset of father–daughter sexual relations, incest is a symptom of a disturbed family and not the cause (Maisch, 1972).

In families where both father–daughter and brother–sister

incest occurs, disorganization is even more severe than in single incest families. These severely disorganized families minimize sexual restraint and accept promiscuity (Weinberg, 1955).

What is it about the disorganized family that makes it prone to incest? First, where there is parental strife, the child receives contradictory messages about appropriate values regarding sexual and other behaviors, and there is poor role modeling of coping techniques against abuse. Second, the child receives less supervision, making her more susceptible to incestuous advances. And third, parental conflict sensitizes the child to fear abandonment and, in turn, sexualizes the tie between father and daughter (Finkelhor, 1979a).

Family disorganization is the context in which incest takes place and does not, of itself, explain why incest occurs. Attention must also be given to the peculiar fears and needs of the parents.

The Parents

Father's Role

Often it is father who is the main disorganizing agent. In the indiscriminately promiscuous family, father is unable to restrain his gratification, is intolerant of frustration, and is irresponsible, hostile, and suspicious. He lacks emotional attachments to wife and children (Weinberg, 1955).

In the endogamous family, father is possessive, domineering, suspicious, and yet dependent on his family for emotional and social support. Sexuality is focused on his wife, and when she becomes unavailable for whatever reason, he turns to his daughter for emotional support.

The incestuous father is often described as an authoritarian head of the household—the complete patriarch who enforces the traditional division of labor. He supervises and controls the females' activities; for example, discouraging his wife from driving the car or visiting relatives, but grants freedom and privileges to his sons (Herman and Hirschman, 1981).

His dominance does not necessarily stem from his role as provider, since he may be unemployed and supported by other family members. He often assumes his dominant position by threats, intimidation, and sometimes by physical abuse (Weinberg, 1955). Incidence of violence was 50 percent for incestuous fathers and only 20 percent for fathers who were seductive toward their daughters, but not sexually involved with the child (Herman and Hirschman, 1981).

While tyrannical at home, the incestuous father often does not look or act that part outside the family, where he appears meek and ingratiating. He differentiates between safe and inappropriate places to exert power (Herman and Hirschman, 1981). Here is a description of a father who had molested and terrified his entire family: "And in walked this tiny person, not more than 5 feet 2 inches, shaking and nervous, a very slight man with no kind of presence whatsoever. Yet they were all scared stiff of him! He didn't even work" (Herman and Hirschman, 1981, p. 74).

Some fathers, however, are kind and considerate until some stressful event occurs, such as loss of job, sickness, or injury (Weinberg, 1955). Major problems here are father's lack of impulse control and confusion of family roles (Summit and Kryso, 1978).

It appears that the presence of a stepfather enhances the probability of incest (Maisch, 1972; James, Womack, and Stauss, 1978; Meiselman, 1978; Finkelhor, 1979a; Martin and Walters, 1982; Perlmutter, Engel, and Sager, 1982). Whether there are differences in the psychological consequences to the daughter between incestuous natural fathers or stepfathers is an open question (Kaufman et al., 1954; Finkelhor, 1979a). The relatively high incidence of incestuous stepfamilies fits with the idea of family polarization. It is likely that there is increased mother–daughter conflict with the daughter forming an alliance with her stepfather against mother. Even though there were steprelatives in these families, there was no increase in other types of incest (Finkelhor, 1979a). Divorce and multiple marriages are more common among mothers of incest victims than for the general population (Lustig et al., 1966; Maisch, 1972), which may account for the overrepresentation of stepfathers. Another possibility is that the natural father is more apt to be immunized against incest by his physical contact with his daughter during her early years, whereas the stepfather had no such contact. Lending support to the importance of early contact is the finding that incestuous fathers had been less frequently involved in giving care and nurturance to their daughters than were nonincestuous fathers (Parker and Parker, 1986). And, more stepfathers have prior sex offenses than do natural fathers (Erickson, Walbek, and Seely, 1987).

Mother's Role

Sometimes mother contributes to family disorganization (Maisch, 1972). Perhaps she has grown tired of her husband, of her marital and maternal roles. She may seek escape outside the family by getting a job or in sexual affairs. One mother, even shortly after her second marriage, was staying away from home, having affairs with strangers, and was drunk most of the time (Maisch, 1972). Maybe because of jealousy of her budding daughter, like Snow White's stepmother, she demeans her and attempts to retard her social development (Summit and Kryso, 1979).

Often mother plays a key role in the incestuous affair. Initially she overprotects the target daughter, then turns over to her more and more household and maternal duties. Daughter receives special privileges and responsibilities and is molded into helper, confidante, and advisor. Mother becomes dependent on her for communication with her husband and advice on topics ranging from groceries to sex. Then, when this daughter becomes independent or hostile, mother turns against her, and in a sense, abandons her (Kaufman et al., 1954; Lustig et al., 1966). In entering into a relationship with her father she might be seeking revenge against her frustrating, unloving mother (Gordon, 1955). Almost half (45%) of the daughters in one study had been molded into the little mother role before they were ten years old. Whatever their other household duties, a special assignment was to "keep Daddy happy" (Herman and Hirschman, 1981). A mother reports: " 'It got so Barbara was the lady of the house. By the time she was seven, she was literally running the house, telling me what to do, telling me what to fix for dinner, and what the whole family was going to do on the weekends. . . . Ever since she was a little girl, I didn't feel

Barbara was my daughter, I felt she was my rival' " (Woodbury and Schwartz, 1971, p. 208).

Situation Prior to Onset

Many fathers stay home because of unemployment, illness, or injury (Weinberg, 1955) and from a third to a half of the mothers are either absent or have a disabling illness (Maisch, 1972; Hall Williams, 1974; Herman and Hirschman, 1981). The home setting prior to incest is one of increasing tension and strained relations between husband and wife (Weinberg, 1955; Maisch, 1972). Almost invariably in the intact family shortly before incest, sexual distance increases between husband and wife (Weiner, 1964; Westermeyer, 1978), sometimes on the grounds of the husband's alcohol abuse (Virkkunen, 1974). Herman and Hirschman (1981) accuse those who emphasize the wife's withdrawal from sexual relations of implicitly blaming the mother.

Discord increases with quarrels, wife beating, and nagging (Riemer, 1940). Father reacts to this "deprivation" with quarrelsomeness, increased domination, suspiciousness, and possessiveness, yet remains dependent upon his family. He is restless and tension is intensified by stress, such as financial losses (Weinberg, 1955; Maisch, 1972). Alcohol abuse by the father is often mentioned (Frosch and Bromberg, 1939; Rada, Kellner, Laws, and Winslow, 1978), but it is more of a symptom than a primary factor.

Oftentimes incest is imminent when both father and daughter feel that mother has abandoned them (Kaufman et al., 1954). A father reports that his wife rejected him sexually and emotionally and that they no longer could communicate: " 'I began to turn to my stepdaughter. I wasn't looking for any special involvement, but she was the only one in the family who was close to me . . . I began to depend on Karen for this kind of nurturing, and I felt she had the same need herself because her mother was away such a lot of the time' " (Renvoize, 1982, p. 20).

A daughter describes a similar situation: " 'My father and I came to each other out of great neediness. I wanted emotional sustenance, an assurance of love, an obliteration of the fear of abandonment. He wanted sexual gratification, perhaps to ease the pain of his own emptiness' " (Brady, 1979, p. 41).

Whether father's advances are tolerated and/or not resisted or whether they are condemned and stopped depends on the presence or absence of a restraining agent—someone who can effectively thwart his designs. In the first case, mother either does not assume a protective role or is so subservient to her husband that she is ineffectual. Sometimes these families have a loose sex culture where there is little privacy and an open and permissive attitude toward sex. One such father woke up his daughter so that she could watch him and his wife have coitus.

In the second case, where father's impulses are checked, mother or some other person acts as restraining agent. In such families there is restraint in sexual matters and father tries to keep his advances secret. In one family, while mother was away, father forced his daughter to have relations with him, warning her not to tell anyone, especially mother. The next day, again when mother was gone, he attempted to have relations, but this time the daughter fended him off with a poker. Later when he overheard his daughter tell mother what had happened, he promised never to repeat the offense, but mother was so outraged she had him arrested (Weinberg, 1955).

An important difference between a group of fathers who were seductive toward their daughters but did not engage in sexual contact and fathers who did commit incest was the role of the mother, who in the seductive family exercised parental authority (Herman and Hirschman, 1981).

Initiation of Incest

Father's Approach

Father is almost always the initiator of incest (Riemer, 1940; Meiselman, 1978) and often approaches his daughter in an affectionate and seductive way (Yates, 1982). A common approach is caressing his daughter while she is asleep. A daughter describes her reaction: " 'Waking up and realizing that daddy was sitting on the edge of my bed, hands under my nightgown, leaning to kiss me. Mostly startled, then some panic that he would realize that I was awake. Mostly, I couldn't figure out what was going on' " (Armstrong, 1978, p. 141).

In whatever way he approaches his daughter, he acts not as an adult male courting an adult female, but as an inept adolescent in his first love affair or as a brother coaxing his sister into some mischief. Like the adolescent love affair, he at first feels love, loyalty, jealousy, and tenderness, but it ends with feelings of revenge, distrust, contempt, and hate (Cormier et al., 1962; Shelton, 1975). Fleeing from his current stressful, unfulfilling life, he attempts to assume the role appropriate to a more exciting time of his life—his teens. But, since he holds to the traditional conception of husband devoted to his family, and since he fears adult women, he acts out this regressed role with his daughter (Summit and Kryso, 1979).

The two extremes of popular opinion that suggest incest stem from the precocious, seductive actions of the girl to depicting the daughter as an innocent, struggling victim of rape, do not jibe with the evidence. Seldom (6%) do daughters display sexually provoking behavior (Maisch, 1972). Father's perception of his daughter's seductiveness usually results from his total misinterpretation of her behavior, mistaking her playful tenderness for the sexual overtures of a mature woman. He misconstrues the tenderness of the child as the passion of an adult (Ferenczi, 1932). Also rare are father's use of threats, violence, physical force, and bribes (Ellis and Brancale, 1956; Maisch, 1972; Meiselman, 1978; Boatman, Barkan, and Schetky, 1981). However, whether force or threats are employed is really irrelevant since the power relation between father and daughter is so clearly imbalanced with father possessing the authority (Meiselman, 1978; Herman and Hirschman, 1981).

While daughter might be interested in father's attentions at first, when she realizes what he actually wants, she is resistant. But she is too afraid to scream or report his actions (Riemer, 1940). Most react passively, pretending to be asleep, or with younger ones, put up with father's new "game"; a few do physically resist; and even fewer are sexually curious and actively cooperate (Maisch, 1972; Meiselman, 1978). The most common reactions are surprise, fear, disgust, shame, and bewilderment (Maisch, 1972; Herman and Hirschman, 1981).

An example of rare initial pleasure occurred when a sixteen-year-old daughter and her thirty-four-year-old stepfather were left home alone one night. They began talking about their difficult childhoods. The daughter reports that: " 'It was then that I realized I liked my stepfather and not just as a daughter. I didn't resist his caresses because I wanted him. I thought of my mother but then I also remembered that my parents had not been very happy together for some time. Then my thoughts got muddled' " (Maisch, 1972, pp. 179–180).

Some cases are reported where mother's actions play no small part in initiation of incest. One mother, saying that her husband's snoring disturbed her, slept in another room. Concerned that her husband might be lonely, she sent her daughter to sleep with him (Kaufman et al., 1974).

An often cited case involves Sergeant R., who came home one evening to find his wife dressed in her "sexiest outfit." She mixed him a cocktail even though they had argued over his drinking. She made sexual allusions and acted seductively during the early evening. Sergeant R., becoming aroused by her behavior, approached her. She countered that he had been drinking and anyway she had to go to a club meeting. Mrs. R. went to the bedroom to change her clothes. Sergeant R. was about to follow her in anger when she placed their ten-year-old daughter in his lap saying, "You two take care of each other while I'm gone" (Lustig et al., 1966, p. 35).

After initiation of incest, mother responds with one of two patterns. She may tolerate and even condone the affair. A particularly blatant example involves a daughter telling mother what father and sister are doing. Mother responds, " 'Let's just keep that our little secret. We have a nice home and money. We don't want anything to change, do we?' " (de Young, 1981, p. 565). Or, mother may be aware of or strongly suspect the affair, but render herself oblivious to what is going on (Riemer, 1940; Weiner, 1964).

Incestuous relations cannot last long without mother's knowledge (Molner and Cameron, 1975). Two-thirds of psychiatrists surveyed thought that mother was usually aware of the sexual activity (Galdston, 1978). Mother tolerates or denies the situation out of her fear of separation and disintegration of the family unit (Nakashima and Zakus, 1977). Incest releases her from the disliked maternal role and may even provide vicarious satisfaction of her own incestuous longings (Gutheil and Avery, 1977). Thus, the current intrafamilial equilibrium and distorted role relations are sustained and mother avoids responsibility (Machotka, Pittman, and Flomenhaft, 1967).

Age of Daughter

Most studies report age of daughter as eight or nine years when incest begins (Lukianowicz, 1972; Herman and Herschman, 1981; Silver, Boon, and Stones, 1983) and others report age of onset several years later from twelve to fifteen years old (Weinberg, 1955; Maisch, 1972; Kirkland and Bauer, 1982). Age range of daughters is from five to nineteen years (Kaufman et al., 1954; Lukianowicz, 1972; Maisch, 1972). Most frequently (64 to 80%) father chooses his eldest daughter (Weinberg, 1955; Herman and Hirschman, 1981; Kirkland and Bauer, 1982). When he does become involved with a younger one, it is because the eldest resists, is not living at home, or she had already been involved with him (Weinberg, 1955).

The incestuous approach of some fathers seems to be cued by early signs of puberty, especially breast development (Maisch, 1972). This finding is confirmed by both daughters and fathers. For instance, "things changed when I was something like fourteen and I began to develop round the breasts. He kept looking at me for long periods, wouldn't let me go anywhere" (Maisch, 1972, p. 177). A forty-three-year-old father states that, "my daughter who was then fourteen, had just previously had her first period and was already a young woman. The shape of her body excited me" (Maisch, 1972, p. 177).

Age of daughter may be related to type of offender. The indiscriminately promiscuous father may not approach his daughter until he views her as a sex object when she attains puberty. The pedophile father uses his daughter sexually until the first signs of puberty. The endogamous father's incest would not be related to daughter's age. Rather, it may be that daughter's ability to assume the maternal role is more crucial than her chronological age (Lustig et al., 1966).

The Incestuous Affair

Duration

Once initiated, the relation often lasts a considerable time. About a fourth of the cases are single occurrences, with the rest lasting from one to three or four years (Kaufman et al., 1954; Weinberg, 1955; Maisch, 1972; Molner and Cameron, 1975; Meiselman, 1978; Herman and Hirschman, 1981). One study reports that half of the affairs lasted five or more years (Silver et al., 1983). About twelve years is maximum (Lukianowicz, 1972; Molner and Cameron, 1975).

Sexual Activity

Sexual activity between father and daughter depends on daughter's age. Oral–genital acts are most often reported when the girl is under twelve years old (22 to 30%) (Gebhard et al., 1965; Meiselman, 1978). Genital manipulation is quite common (90%) (Silver et al., 1983), especially with girls under twelve (Gebhard et al., 1965). Attempted or simulated intercourse occurs more often with girls of about ten years, while actual penetration is accomplished in most all cases (70 to 90%) with those over twelve or thirteen years old (Gebhard et al., 1965; Maisch, 1972). In ongoing relations, frequency of incestuous contacts varies from every night to once a week (Lukianowicz, 1972; Silver et al., 1983).

Course of the Relation

After incest begins, a new family equilibrium is established and previous tension and quarreling may subside. The daughter may even feel that it is up to her to preserve the family unit. According to a twelve-year-old, "they were always fighting. I couldn't figure out why. It finally did stop when he started messing around with me" (Sanford, 1980, p. 157).

During the course of the relation, father engages in behaviors aimed at sustaining incest. Threats become more common as the relation progresses (Weinberg, 1955; Meiselman,

1978; Herman and Hirschman, 1981). Many fathers (77%) demand, exhort, and plead with their daughters to say nothing. Some authoritarian fathers threaten them with the possibility of being placed in a juvenile home and other dire consequences.

Gifts and favors are offered (34%) as inducements to continue (Maisch, 1972). Often there are attempts to isolate the daughter socially by jealous control of her social contacts, spying, and baseless accusations of sexual conduct outside the home. Other scare tactics include warnings of possible infection from boys and that they will take advantage of her (Weinberg, 1955). In those cases where there is mutual involvement (18%), father assumes a caring and protective attitude (Maisch, 1972).

By the time she realizes that the relation with her father is wrong, she may be receiving gratification, if not sexual, then favored child status, attention, and nurturance (Weiner, 1962; Yates, 1982).

There are two situations in which affection is present (Weinberg, 1955). In incest attachment, father is emotionally attracted to his daughter either because of genuine affection or possessive lust. The father in this relation attempts to restrict his daughter socially, forbidding her to attend parties or to have dates.

In the other variety, incest love, there is mutual attraction between father and daughter, they are companions and share common interests. Such relations are rather rare (Meiselman, 1978).

Two types of daughter reactions may emerge and sustain the incest: passive–tolerating (57%) and encouraging–provoking (23%). Motives for continuing of the passive–tolerating daughter include fear of father, lack of knowledge of her rights, succumbing to threats of possible punishment, feeling that somehow she shares the guilt, fear of family breakup, and deference to father's authority. Sexual motives are excluded from this constellation. Motives of the encouraging–provoking daughter include sexual satisfaction, material advantages, the experience of a caring, protective father, and fear of losing her father if their secret were to be revealed. Relations that began with passive–tolerant attitudes may develop into the encouraging–provoking type (Maisch, 1972).

Role Confusion

One of the consequences of long-term incest is increasing confusion of roles for daughter, father, and mother. Daughter may replace the wife in father's eyes and he attributes to his wife qualities of the threatening, punishing mother (Cormier et al., 1962), and may view his daughter as the nurturing mother (Heims and Kaufman, 1963). Especially if mother is absent, daughter may take over household duties and assume the mother–wife role. She may even consider herself her father's equal and thus lose respect for him. "And I'd say, 'Cool it, daddy, it ain't getting you anywhere.' That's how I actually talked to him, you know. I was on the same level with him. He was no longer a father to be respected, so I didn't treat him with any respect, except in front of my mother and my brothers and sister" (Woodbury and Schwartz, 1971, p. 82).

She may assume the role of mistress, while her father becomes her husband or seducer. She becomes mother's unwilling rival, feeling that she is "stealing mother's man" and thus placing a distance between herself and mother (Weinberg, 1955). In such a situation there is a power shift from father to daughter (Boatman et al., 1981). She now has special leverage where her father is concerned, as with this daughter: " 'It doesn't bother me to say it. Like using my parents—blackmailing my father to get what I wanted I really did that. If he didn't do what I wanted, I wouldn't participate—I wouldn't let him do something' " (Woodbury and Schwartz, 1971, p. 26).

Where mother is aware of what is going on, but does not directly interfere, she may attempt to compete with her daughter by using such attention-getting devices as flirting and being forward sexually. If father sides with his daughter in family disputes, mother and daughter are further alienated. Thus, generational role distinctions are destroyed. Daughter is put into service of her parents' needs, rather than parents gratifying the needs of their child. Parents act like children and children act like adults (Eist and Mandel, 1968). This role confusion adds to daughter's disturbance and disorientation (Furness, 1985). Often the daughter rebels when role conflict becomes sufficiently intense.

Effect on Siblings

Other children in the family are affected by the incestuous relation. They probably already lack affection, and then when one child is singled out for special attention, they become resentful and envious (Weinberg, 1955; Cormier et al., 1962; de Young, 1981). The manner in which they express their jealousy can put additional strain on an already tenuous family structure (de Young, 1981).

Focused on his daughter, father often ignores or is hostile toward his sons (Cormier et al., 1962). If the relation is incest attachment or love, sisters might develop incest envy (Meiselman, 1978). One sister noticed that father brought her older sister presents and often took her places. She hated her sister for this and thought, "What has she got that I haven't got?" (Sanford, 1980, p. 183).

Termination

It is usually daughter who terminates the relationship, not father giving it up voluntarily (only 6%). Her attitude toward the relation changes as she becomes interested in dating, becomes aware of her rights, develops increased feelings of guilt and shame, and increasingly resists father's advances. Her withdrawal produces an increase in tension to which father often reacts with increased jealousy, surveillance of her activities (40%), threats, and abuse (Maisch, 1972; Herman and Hirschman, 1981). She may be denounced as a "whore" or "boy crazy" and given an inferior position in the family (Weinberg, 1965).

Age of daughter at the end of the affair is fifteen to sixteen (Maisch, 1972; Silver et al., 1983), which coincides with the increased importance of extrafamily activities such as job seeking, training for a vocation, and male companionship.

About a fourth of incestuous relationships end either by father or daughter moving to separate dwellings (Meiselman, 1978). A few (14%) terminate because of discovery by mother or some other person, and from 10 to 20 percent of the affairs end because of pregnancy (Riemer, 1940; Maisch, 1972; Hall Williams, 1974). In incestuous pregnancies, incidence of mortality, prematurity, and congenital abnormalities is higher than in the nonincestuous (Alstrom, 1977).

The majority of daughters told no one as long as they were living at home (Herman and Hirschman, 1981). Daughters' disclosure of incest increases with her age and length of the relationship (Farrell, 1988). When they do tell someone most (42%) report it to their mothers, and others tell another relative (23%) or an unrelated person (26%) (Maisch, 1972). However, these revelations rarely result in directly ending the affair. When they do seek mother's help, she either disbelieves them or is unlikely to take action even if she is already aware of the incest (Kaufman et al., 1954; Gebhard et al., 1965; Lukianowicz, 1972; Herman and Herschman, 1981). She is more likely to take action if she is dissatisfied with the marriage (Meiselman, 1978).

The desire to disbelieve is illustrated by this mother, whose daughter reported that her stepfather was making sexual advances:

> "I'm a nurse and I used to work nights. When she was fourteen she told me that my husband had come into her room one night when I was working and tried to have sex with her. Well, I wouldn't believe it. As you can imagine at the time I'd only been married a couple of years. I wasn't going to believe any such thing about my husband. I think it was sort of a self-protective mechanism. But, I've learned a lot since then" [Finkelhor, 1979a, p. 68].

Child protection workers are of the opinion that incest is often accompanied by father's physical abuse of mother and daughter. Where such abuse obtains, mother's collusion and failure to report may stem from her fear of her husband's retaliation (Dietz and Craft, 1980).

Father's Reaction

Despite the assertion that the recidivism rate is relatively low (Maisch, 1972), about one-fourth of fathers, after termination of affairs with one daughter, move on to another daughter (Weinberg, 1955; Molnar and Cameron, 1975; Meiselman, 1978; Herman and Hirschman, 1981; Ciba, 1984).

Amount of guilt experienced depends on the type of offender. Little guilt would be expected from the indiscriminately promiscuous. Endogamous fathers' guilt is obviously present, but in some cases denied or repressed. Guilt over having harmed his wife may be expressed in his seeking her forgiveness so he can return home (Cormier et al., 1962). Some fathers show great concern over having hurt their daughters and fear retaliation for this (Cavallin, 1966). There were no suicide attempts by fathers in 201 families studied (Goodwin, 1981).

Fathers are reluctant to admit the offense, many denying it altogether with incidence of denials to the authorities increasing with daughters' age. Their denials have a paranoid, moralistic tinge to them. They claim that false charges were brought against them to secure a divorce, to gain control of their property, or because they had opposed their daughters in some way (Gebhard et al., 1965). It must be noted that not all accusations of incest are valid. The incest hoax may be used by a daughter who hates her father, by a mother who is delusional, or one who is seeking custody of the child (Goodwin, Shad, and Rada, 1978). Where child custody and visitation rights are involved in the divorce, one-half of the allegations of incest are unsubstantiated (Green, 1986; Awad, 1987). Overall, however, the prevalence of such hoaxes is under 5 percent (Bross, 1984).

Incest offenders are adept at explaining away their behavior, minimizing their responsibility, thus avoiding guilty and shameful feelings. Rationalizations include refusal of sexual relations by his wife "forced" him to turn to a daughter (Renvoize, 1982). A common reason offered is that the daughter needed to be taught the facts of life (Weiner, 1962). He may claim that he wanted to keep his daughter off the streets since what he did was better than "frivolous relations with outsiders" (Riemer, 1940).

Impact on Family

Incest is a pathological attempt to establish equilibrium in an already severely dysfunctional family. Therefore, some family members may fear collapse of the family unit if father is removed (Cavallin, 1966; Lustig et al., 1966). The negative impact on the family brought on by legal authorities and punishment of father may be more serious than that of incest itself (Alstrom, 1977). Exposure of father to the authorities brings on economic hardship (42%), breakup of the family unit (42%), and sending the daughter to a juvenile home (36%) (Maisch, 1972). Ostracism of family members, especially the daughter, must have a frightful impact on many families.

The agency to which the offense is reported can make a difference on the family structure. Mental health agencies attempt to keep the family together, while reporting to legal authorities tends to divide family loyalty between mother, father, or daughter (Burgess, Holmstrom, and McCausland, 1977). Changes in family structure after detection also depend on mother. If she has tolerated the affair, her position is compromised. She may blame her daughter and scold her for not reporting it to her. Where she opposed the affair, her hostility is directed at her husband and she assumes the dominant role as protector of her children. Rather than distancing herself from the daughter participant, she becomes friendly with her. Tension subsides, especially if father was not the sole means of support (Weinberg, 1955).

THE PERSONS

Father

Current Status

Age of father offenders is usually early forties (Riemer, 1940; Weinberg, 1955; Maisch, 1972; Hall Williams, 1974), with some yet in their thirties (Kirkland and Bauer, 1982; Lukianowicz, 1972). Age range is from twenty to midsixties. They are somewhat older than fathers who physically abuse their children (Julian and Mohr, 1979). All are or have been married and their marriages are rather stable (Gebhard et al., 1965; Cavallin, 1966).

Information on education and intelligence is clearly influenced by the population from which the sample was taken. In a court referral sample, average formal education was five years with two-thirds in the dull normal range of intelligence or below

(Weinberg, 1955). In contrast, other studies report little difference from normal intellectual functioning and education (Weiner, 1962; Cavallin, 1966; Maisch, 1972; Meiselman, 1978; Kirkland and Bauer, 1982).

In one study of native born Americans, blacks had a higher proportion of incest than whites, and of the foreign born, Poles tolerated incest more than other groups (Weinberg, 1955). In a more recent study there is little evidence of disproportionate ethnic group representation. Protestants and Jews were underrepresented, while Catholics and "none" were slightly overrepresented (Meiselman, 1978).

Contrary to the popular belief that anyone who commits incest must be crazy, very few fathers were diagnosed as psychotic before incest (Weinberg, 1955; Ellis and Brancale, 1956; Weiner, 1962; Cavallin, 1966; Maisch, 1972; Meiselman, 1978). In fact, fathers display perceptual accuracy, adequate reality testing, and sufficient behavioral controls. They tend to intellectualize rather than inhibit affect, and are impersonal and objective (Weiner, 1962). Psychosis, when it obtains, becomes manifest after disclosure of incest (Weinberg, 1955; Weiner, 1962; Cavallin, 1966; Lukianowicz, 1972).

Criminality is not characteristic of incestuous fathers (Cavallin, 1966; Maisch, 1972; Alstrom, 1977), except for the amoral delinquents or sociopathic type. When there is a criminal record, it is for crimes against property and order rather than persons—petty thievery, vagrancy, family disturbances, and drunkenness (Gebhard et al., 1965; Lukianowicz, 1972; Maisch, 1972; Alstrom, 1977). On the basis of Minnesota Multiphasic Personality Inventory (MMPI) profiles, two-fifths were diagnosed as being "sociopathic" (Groff, 1987).

Alcohol abuse is often mentioned (Frosch and Bromberg, 1939; Kaufman et al., 1954; Cavallin, 1966; Maisch, 1972; Herman and Hirschman, 1981; Martin and Walters, 1982) with an increase in reported alcohol dependency as age of daughter decreases (Gebhard et al., 1965). The offender who is alcoholic compared to the nonalcoholic offender has more prior criminal offenses, is more aggressive at home, and was more often under the influence at the instigation of incest (Virkunnen, 1974). While intoxication is a facilitator of incest, it is certainly not a cause (Gebhard et al., 1965; Maisch, 1972). It is likely that the emphasis on alcohol as reported by the father or daughter is an attempt to excuse his behavior by attributing it to the bottle (Meiselman, 1978).

There is a group of offenders, the amoral and indiscriminately promiscuous, who fit the stereotype of highly sexed men with violent and irrascible temperaments, especially when they have been drinking. They have poor work records and histories of minor criminal offenses. In essence, they lack both normal self-control and an ordered way of life (Maisch, 1972).

Family Background

There is nothing unusual in the birth order of father offenders or in the sex of their siblings other than a preponderance of brothers for the offenders against children, and the presence of two or more older sisters in many (40%) of the offenders against adult daughters (Gebhard et al., 1965). Their families were relatively large with an average of slightly over five children (Cavallin, 1966).

Future offenders had disturbed relations with their fathers, sometimes through separation and loss. Their fathers are described as strict, abusive, and harsh disciplinarians. They were feared and hated and their sons assumed a passive–dependent relation with them (Weiner, 1962). These fathers served as incest models, even though they may not have actually engaged in incest.

Absence of at least one parent, usually mother, was common, and if not absent, mothers are described as "indifferent," "critical," "narrow minded," "strict," or "very religious" (Cavallin, 1966). Fathers who engage in incest with a child daughter have the poorest parental relations and preferred their mothers, while offenders against adult daughters got along with both parents equally well (Gebhard et al., 1965).

Their families were disorganized in varying degrees with the crucial outcome that they did not learn appropriate family member roles (Kahn, 1965). It is not uncommon that some form of incest was practiced in these families (Cooper and Cormier, 1982).

In addition to not learning appropriate roles, these men experienced mistreatment and rather severe emotional deprivation, receiving little warmth or understanding (Kaufman et al., 1954; Weinberg, 1955; Parker and Parker, 1986). Prominent in their histories are separations and losses resulting in anxiety over being deserted (Kaufman et al., 1954). Little wonder that many of these boys left home early (Riemer, 1940; Kaufman et al., 1954). A relatively high percentage of offenders come from broken homes (44 to 59%) or had parents who got along poorly. Few lived fifteen or more years with both parents (Gebhard et al., 1965).

Personality

While the vast majority of fathers are not psychotic, strong paranoid trends have been noted (Weiner, 1962; Cavallin, 1966; Raphling, Carpenter, and Davis, 1967; Meiselman, 1978). Paranoid features consist of distrust of the obvious, attention to minute details, suspiciousness, and a tendency to project hostility onto the environment. Depreciation of others is used as an expression of hostility and also to decrease the power attributed to others (Weiner, 1962). For example, some accused their wives and daughters of carrying on secret affairs when they saw them talking to men; those wives who were sexually unresponsive were accused of infidelity (Weinberg, 1955).

The dominant attitude displayed by some fathers runs from the sociopath who looks upon others, including his family, as subjects of his desires, to the endogamic father who attempts to control all aspects of family life (Meiselman, 1978). About a third (29%) of fathers are described as "family despots" who brook no opposition from family members, have quick tempers, and occasionally beat their wives and children. These behaviors are confined to the family circle (Maisch, 1972). This encapsulated behavior is called restricted pathology; that is, signs of pathology that are expressed in only one area of life; in the case of incest offenders, the family. In other areas, fathers function at a relatively mature level, often as seemingly well-adjusted members of society (Wells, 1981). It should be noted that the incidence of father domination depends on who is reporting

—father, family members, or others (Lustig et al., 1966; Meiselman, 1978).

Many fathers are passive–dependent, immature, with regressive longings. They are subject to chronic insecurity, social alienation, with exaggerated needs for affection. They are inadequate in social skills, are shy, and have difficulty in making decisions (Vander Mey and Neff, 1982). There is some evidence that fathers who misuse older daughters are concerned with power and dominance, while fathers of preschoolers are more passive and dependent, and suffer from low self-esteem (MacFarlane and Waterman, 1986).

Sexuality and Masculinity

While the general impression from some studies is that incest offenders do not differ from other groups in terms of total sexual outlet (Gebhard et al., 1965; Maisch, 1972), others report unusually strong sex drives coupled with weak or absent inhibitions (Riemer, 1940; Lukianowicz, 1972). In general, incest offenders have a low incidence and frequency of premarital masturbation. Incidence of premarital heterosexual petting is low with only a few partners. Frequency of marital coitus is also low (Gebhard et al., 1965). Only a few were exposed to hard core pornography during their pubertal years. As adults, unlike pedophiles, deviant masturbation fantasies are rare (Marshall, 1988).

We have already noted that one of the precursors of incest is denial by the wife of sexual access. This may appear to give credence to hypersexuality, but more probably father's craving for sexual relations functions to shore up his self-esteem and confirm his sense of masculinity (Weiner, 1964). They are unable to differentiate sex from affection (Weinberg, 1955).

Adult masculine identity is stunted and some display feminine identification. They react to their unmasculine trends by asserting independence and by assuming an empty masculine, patriarchal persona (Weiner, 1962; Kirkland and Bauer, 1982). Another explanation offered for patriarchal dominance and heightened heterosexual activity is that they are defenses against homosexual longings (Weiner, 1964; Raphling et al.,

1967). The fact is that incest offenders are strongly heterosexual in their orientation, have minimal homosexual contacts, and strongly disapprove of homosexuality (Gebhard et al., 1965). This data does not contradict the homosexual hypothesis if it is assumed that these men's homophobia is a defense against their own homosexuality.

Religiosity, moralistic attitudes, and sexual inhibitions are prevalent characteristics (Gebhard et al., 1965). For instance, one father was prudish, insisting that his family maintain high moral standards. Several years prior to the onset of incest, he sought moral principles to live by from "God and the church" (Raphling et al., 1967). Another, who experienced a psychotic episode, was preoccupied with morality and religion and attempted to save the souls of his wardmates (Weiner, 1962). A prison official relates that when guards see a new prisoner enter prison carrying a bible, they assume he is an incest offender (Weinberg, 1955).

Conception of Women

Often, the incest offender is strongly hostile toward his mother and views his wife as rejecting and threatening (Cavallin, 1966). Relations with women depend on incest type. The endogamous shies away from meeting people and has few social contacts with women. He does not respect them, viewing them as untrustworthy (Weinberg, 1955).

A multiply incestuous father viewed all women with hostility as images of his own seductive mother. He was jealous and suspicious of his wife, accusing her of having affairs, yet curiously, he urged her to have sexual relations with his close friend. He even urged his pubertal son to have sexual relations with her (Raphling et al., 1967).

The promiscuous type is hostile, insulting, and abusive toward women, considering them as sex objects. The sole purpose in relating to women is to seduce them. The pedophile type turns to children, including his own, usually after being refused sexual access by his wife or other adult women (Weinberg, 1955).

Mother

Descriptions of mother vary widely, depending on the type of incest families studied. Characterizations range from intelligent and artistic to dull, promiscuous, and alcoholic (Maisch, 1972). Two-fifths were diagnosed as "sociopathic" on the basis of MMPI profiles (Groff, 1987).

In samples that are biased toward lower socioeconomic groups, mothers come from backgrounds similar to those of their husbands—poverty, alcoholism, poor education, and little warmth and understanding. Father likely had deserted, leaving his wife to care for their children. About a fourth came from families where there was physical abuse or incest. Prior incest incidence is not different for incest and physical abuse families.

Their mother was masculine, stern, demanding, controlling, and hostile, rejecting the daughter and pampering her sons. The daughter became the object of mother's resentment against her lot in life. Often this daughter was teased about her tomboyishness and denied feminine things (Kaufman et al., 1954). Despite this ill-treatment at her mother's hands, the target mother is dependent on her, seeking to extract affection from her (Machotka et al., 1967). An example is Mrs. T. whose mother told her she would be paying a visit, but gave no information about arrival time or means of transportation. For several days, Mrs. T. met all planes and buses arriving from her mother's departure point. When mother did finally arrive, she informed Mrs. T. of her decision to travel on rather than stay (Eist and Mandel, 1968).

The man she marries is dependent, and sometimes abusive, a man similar to her father (Kaufman et al., 1954), yet she is extremely dependent on this husband (Lukianowicz, 1972). Those mothers who set up the incestuous relation between husband and daughter may be vicariously having a sexual relation with their own father (Rhinehart, 1961).

In her struggle to satisfy her needs for affection and support and to deny a sense of worthlessness, she may assume a "much-suffering, masochistic" stance (Kaufman et al., 1954; Lukianowicz, 1972). Commonly, she is passive–dependent, submissive, weak, and powerless (Cormier et al., 1962; Meiselman,

1978; Herman and Hirschman, 1981). Her dependency, desire to be mothered, lack of sexual responsiveness, hostility, and unloving nature may stem from feelings of having been deprived and deserted as a child (Cormier et al., 1962; Lustig et al., 1966). Consequently, she is distant toward and does not provide emotional support to her daughter (Furness, 1985).

Chronic depression has been assigned a central role in mother's behavior. Her depression is often directly responsible for withdrawal from her husband and her assigning maternal and household duties to her daughter (Browning and Boatman, 1977).

Loose sexual behavior has been noted in the history of many mothers—eloping with lovers, bringing men home when their husbands were away (Lukianowicz, 1972), and a large number of pre- and extramarital children (51%) (Maisch, 1972). However, this finding of mother's loose sexual behavior comes from studies where incest had been reported to social agencies or legal authorities. In more representative samples, few mothers were promiscuous and some extremely averse to sex. One daughter reports that, "Mother always made it pefectly clear that sex was a drag" (Meiselman, 1978, p. 125). Signs of strong unconscious homosexual urges have been reported (Lustig et al., 1966).

9 EXHIBITIONISM

INTRODUCTION

Prevalence

Indecent exposure constitutes about a third of reported sex offenses (East, 1924; Arieff and Rotman, 1942; Apfelberg, Sugar, and Pfeffer, 1944; Hirning, 1945; Taylor, 1947; Ellis and Brancale, 1956; Mohr, Turner, and Jerry, 1964; Rooth, 1970; Jaffe, Dynneson, and ten Bensel, 1975; Rosen, 1979). Each year for twenty years there were never less than two thousand convictions for indecent exposure in England and Wales (Rooth, 1970).

Another indication of the prevalence of this offense is that about half of adult women have witnessed indecent exposure sometime in their lives (Landis, 1956; Gittleson, Eacott, and Mehta, 1978; Herold, Mantle, and Zemitis, 1979).

Besides being an open and frequent offense, many exhibitionists do not take special precautions to avoid apprehension. However, only a small proportion of incidences are reported to the police (Bejke, 1953; Herold et al., 1979). But, since exhibitionists tend to repeat the offense, a fair proportion are caught sometime in their careers (Jones and Frei, 1979). The rate at which exhibitionists repeat their offense varies according to the time span of the follow-up study. And arrests give a higher rate than prison sentences since the vast majority (81%) of those arrested are never imprisoned (Berah and Myers, 1983).

From 20 to 40 percent have more than one arrest or conviction (East, 1924; Hirning, 1945; Taylor, 1947; Mohr et al., 1964). Over a seven-year period, the average number of convictions was three, with a range of from one to eighteen. Almost half had only one conviction and a quarter had four or more (Berah and Meyers, 1983). These estimates are much too low. While officially, only a third of exhibitionists seen at a diagnostic center had previous arrests for sex offenses, two-thirds admitted to having committed such offenses (Ellis and Brancale, 1956). In all, the recidivism rate is relatively high (Rooth, 1973).

The exposure of the sex parts, as such, is not a deviation. Actually, few if any behaviors are strictly forbidden by society. Rather, society imposes certain time, place, mode, and object restrictions on behaviors (Murray, 1938). Thus, skinny dipping may be tolerated at night, but not in daylight. Nudity at sanctioned beaches and nudist camps is allowed, but not on downtown streets. Exposure in the mode of tight-fitting pants that accentuate the sex parts can be fashionable, but not exposure of the parts themselves. If the witness is one's spouse, no untoward consequences ensue, but if it is the neighbor's nubile daughter, then a complaint may be lodged. In fact, "the avoidance of nudity during coitus is a perversion of what is, in a biological sense, normal sexuality" (Kinsey, Pomeroy, Martin, and Gebhard, 1953, p. 365).

Exposure becomes abnormal when the urge cannot be controlled and confined to appropriate times and places and when it becomes an end in itself, rather than a preliminary to further sexual contact (Rickles, 1950).

A not unusual reaction on the part of the general public toward exhibitionists is pity and ridicule. Ullerstram (1966) claims that society practices violent discrimination against those who exhibit and advises against reporting them to the police. A humanitarian society, he says, would provide these people with an outlet for their deviation by arranging for groups of persons who did not object to such behavior to act as their audiences.

Exhibitionism in Women

A thirty-three-year-old housewife would raise her skirt, spread her thighs and rub her lower abdomen during what appeared to be an epileptic attack. However, her EEG was normal and her condition did not respond to anticonvulsives (Guttman, 1953).

A forty-three-year-old professional woman was unable to form close ties with others. Her feelings of worth increased upon receiving respect and admiration for her job performance. But when she lost this position, she experienced feelings of emptiness and despair. Exposing her breasts and genitals from her car to passing truckers made her feel "alive again" (Grob, 1985). Another woman, suffering from severe penis envy, would expose her genitals to truckers when driving in her father's auto (Zavitzianos, 1971).

Women are seldom charged with indecent exposure. When some do expose, it takes the form of a vulgar display, as a woman in a bar dunking her bare breast in someone's beer (Scott, 1977). For those who expose within socially acceptable limits, the motivation is seductiveness and affirmation of their lovableness.

In psychoanalytic literature, exhibitionism on the part of women is attributed to their feeling that they have been castrated, in other words, having suffered a narcissistic wound. Women try to conceal this deficiency and displace the urge to exhibit onto other body parts, usually breasts and buttocks. The male, however, fears the loss of his member and displays it to reassure himself that he still has one (Fenichel, 1945).

Other explanations for the sex difference in exhibitionism have been offered. One is based on the different degrees of intimacy between boys and girls and their mothers. Girls are allowed more physical closeness and often engage in mutual grooming that promotes displaced exhibitionism. Boys, however, are suddenly shut off from such intimate contact with mother, being told to leave the room while she is dressing, and being forbidden to accompany her to the bathroom. Such maternal behavior instills in the boy's mind that there is something forbidden and mysterious about the sex parts (Allen, 1980). A much simpler explanation of why women do not expose their genitals is that they feel they have nothing to show (Rickles, 1950).

An often told story points to part of the reason for the sex difference in exposing. If a man stops by a window to watch a woman undress, the man is arrested for peeping. If a woman stops by a window to watch a man undress, the man is arrested for exposing.

DEFINITION

Origin and Meanings

A man had been periodically exposing his genitals to women in a church as they knelt in prayer. He always did so after dark and would disappear into the shadows after exposure. One night he exposed himself in front of an elderly nun whose screams brought the guard who apprehended him. Since he was from a respectable family, well educated, and held high public office, the court sought medical evaluation from Charles Lasegue.

In 1877 Lasegue published an article in which he described this and other such men he had examined. Since there was no established medical term for such behavior, he coined the word *exhibitionism*. At first he thought that these men must be uncouth, debauched, and impotent, but examination showed they were respectable people who had access to normal forms of sexual expression. Other than their exhibitionism, their lives were beyond reproach and they recognized the absurdity of their behavior. Lasegue found it difficult to establish rapport with these men because they were ashamed of their behavior, trying to excuse themselves by claiming that they acted impulsively and unconsciously. He noted that there was no effort to become intimate with the viewer and that the act was repeated, often at the same place and time (Rickles, 1950). Some years later, Garnier, consultant to the Paris Police, defined exhibitionism as:

> A sexual aberration, obsessive and impulsive, characterized by the irresistible need to display in public, generally under certain conditions of time and place, the genital organ in a state of flaccidity quite apart from any voluptuous or provocative manipulation. The act is induced by sexual desire, and its performance puts an end to an agonizing struggle and terminates the attack [cited by Haire, 1934, p. 411].

From these early descriptions and definitions, it can be seen that exhibitionism is not the same as simple exposure. To qualify as exhibitionism, the act must be deliberate and inappropriate, have a particular purpose, and must take place before a particular person or persons (Gebhard et al., 1965). There is disagreement concerning its purpose; some specify sexual gratification (Mohr et al., 1964; Bastani, 1976), and others only sexual arousal (DSM-III-R), or sexual or nonsexual rewards (Evans, 1970). All agree that there is no desire for further sexual contact. The witness is not just any person, but must be "an unsuspecting female" (Mohr et al., 1964; Bastani, 1976) who is a stranger (DSM-III-R).

Indecent exposure is a legal term and is defined as the "willful exhibiting of one's genital organs usually in public places" (Arieff and Rotman, 1942, p. 523). A majority of those arrested for indecent exposure are true exhibitionists (Rooth, 1970; Jones and Frei, 1979).

Varieties

Some writers, instead of defining types of exhibitionists, describe groups of indecent exposers. Among those who expose, but are not exhibitionists, are those with poor judgment regarding acceptable public behavior, such as the mentally handicapped, people suffering from senile dementia, alcoholics, and epileptics (Krafft-Ebing, 1902; Ellis, 1906; East, 1924; Hirschfeld, 1938; Rickels, 1950; Gebhard et al., 1965). Another group expose as a preliminary to sexual contact with a child or to attract women. Finally, there are true exhibitionists whose exposure is obligatory and periodic.

Two types of exhibitionists have been defined. In simple exhibitionism, the act follows some trauma, such as disappointment or loss, or is attributable to old age or alcoholism. These men are usually shy and reserved, but otherwise of stable personality. The phobic–impulsive type is given to habitual exhibiting stemming from infantile fixations. Where impulsivity predominates, they display other deviations such as transvestism and peeping (Rosen, 1979).

Relation to Other Paraphilias

Courtship Disorders

Exhibitionism is one of a group of paraphilias called "courtship disorders" or "allurement" paraphilias, that include peepers, obscene phone callers, and frotteurs (those who rub up against a female) (Freund, Scher, and Huncker, 1983; Money, 1984b; Freund and Blanchard, 1986). Both self-report and phallometric testing reveal a substantial association among these paraphilias. They all involve an exaggeration, intensification, and distortion of one of the first phases of sexual interaction, and the omission or attenuation of the other phases: peeping involves the location of partner phase; both exhibitionists and obscene phone callers emphasize the pretactile phase; and frotteurs engage in preliminary tactile behavior.

Homosexual Exhibitionists

While there are homosexual exhibitionists who derive satisfaction from exhibiting to males, usually such exposure is for the purpose of solicitation for sexual activity. It commonly occurs in public toilets, baths, and other places where, in a sense, it is socially appropriate (Gebhard et al., 1965).

Pedophilia

The pedophile is often given to exposing himself to a child, but there are several points of difference between this and exhibitionism proper. In exhibitionism the viewer is usually a stranger, while in pedophilia the child is usually known to the exposer. The exhibitionist maintains a distance between himself and the viewer and the act takes place in public, whereas the pedophile exposes in close proximity to the child and does so in private (Mohr et al., 1964).

There is a group of exhibitionists who prefer to expose to children. They have a higher repeat rate and are less responsive to treatment than those who expose to adult females (Mohr et al., 1964).

Peeping

There is a frequently mentioned relation between exhibitionism and peeping. This supposed connection is based on the Freudian assumption that partial impulses occur in contrasting pairs, one active, the other passive; one is a conscious impulse, the other, unconscious (Freud, 1905). Using this assumption as fact, it has been asserted that every exhibitionist is also a voyeur (Christoffel, 1936; Allen, 1980).

These psychoanalytic theorists maintain that narcissistic pleasure in looking at one's self is the precursor of showing to others. Several transformations take place between narcissism and exhibiting. It all starts with the viewing of one's own body. This original object, one's self, is exchanged for another, an external person, leading to the pleasure in viewing another. Next, the active aim of looking is given up and replaced by the passive aim of being seen (Freud, 1915).

Estimates on peeping behavior of exhibitionists vary from only 3 to 30 percent (Hackett, 1971; Rooth, 1973; Freund and Blanchard, 1986). These data, however, do not refute the psychoanalytic contention, since they assert that one of the pair of partial impulses is unconscious (Rosen, 1979). The reason given for peeping being unconscious is that the exhibitionist is afraid to look at female genitals since there is no penis. Therefore, the opposite pole, to show, predominates (Allen, 1980).

If, indeed, they are afraid to look at vulvas, it is interesting that they are not adverse to performing cunnilingus. A fifth engaged in this act with a premarital partner, placing them in the upper half of all imprisoned sex offenders (Gebhard et al., 1965).

Another interpretation of the relation between exhibition-ism and peeping is that, as a child, the exhibitionist found pleas-ure in looking at his mother or sister and therefore naively assumed that women also would derive pleasure in seeing his genitals (Caprio, 1955).

Evaluation of the Literature

Since indecent exposure is a sexual offense, much of our in-formation on exhibitionism comes from samples drawn from court referrals and prison inmates. Such data is clearly biased since not all of those charged with this offense are exhibitionists, and not all exhibitionists are apprehended and/or charged, or are charged with some other offense.

A much used method in studying sexual offenders is the survey, where information is obtained from large numbers of people using a standard set of questions. The most valuable of the sex surveys are the Kinsey reports, especially the 1965 vol-ume, *Sex Offenders.* The Kinsey Institute staff inteviewed over 1300 convicted offenders including exhibitionists and offenders against children. In this volume are found answers to questions about family background, prepubescent sex life, incidence and frequency of masturbation, premarital petting, and homosexual activity. The focus is on the facts of incidence and frequency—the proportion of the sample who had ever engaged in a particular behavior and how often it was done. It is straightforward, fac-tual information. In a eulogy to these studies, we also find a description of their shortcomings. "We are heirs to a fine tra-dition initiated by the Kinsey researchers. It is a behavioristic tradition, numerate rather than literate, scientific rather than imaginative" (Laws, 1984, p. 197).

THE ACT

Precipitating Events

" 'I have a tight, frightening feeling in my chest and pit of my stomach, my head is pounding, and I feel like I am bound to exhibit myself' " (Ritchie, 1968, p. 43). Most often, the best description the exhibitionist can give of his state just prior to exposing is, "something comes over me" (Jones and Frei, 1979), or "I got extremely tense and keyed up" (Daitzman and Cox, 1980). The act may be preceded by negative feelings, such as an increase in tension, restlessness, fearfulness, and apprehension (Karpman, 1954); exhilaration, nervousness, heart palpitations (Silverman, 1941); and even boredom (Evans, 1980). In such cases, the act is a premeditated effort to be rid of these feelings. In one sample there was evidence of definite premeditation in 86 percent of cases (Gebhard et al., 1965).

The precipitating situation may be an increase in sexual arousal and tension arising from threats to masculinity and self-esteem. Increase in the sex urge may be spontaneous or brought on by pornography or the sight of an attractive woman (MacDonald, 1973). Examples of threats are loss of a job, argument with wife (Rosen, 1979), failure on an examination, death of mother or her remarriage, a broken engagement (Karpman, 1954), an impending marriage (Hirning, 1947), and birth of a child (Turner, 1964). Sometimes, there is simply a sudden and irresistible impulse to expose (Mohr et al., 1964; Karpman, 1948).

That the act of exhibiting is not related to sexual deprivation is seen by the fact that 60 percent were having sexual relations at the time of their offense (Meyers and Berah, 1983).

Alcohol is a contributing factor in from a fourth to a half of cases studied (Arieff and Rotman, 1942; Hirning, 1945; Ellis and Brancale, 1956; Gebhard et al., 1965; Rada et al., 1978). For some of these men, alcohol serves to ease the tension to exhibit (Christoffel, 1936), while in others it dissolves the inhibition to exhibit.

The Exposure

Few use special clothing for the act other than overcoats that can be opened and closed quickly. Some develop strategies, such as pretending to be urinating behind bushes or adjusting trousers so exposure appears accidental (Jones and Frei, 1979). Very few attempt to disguise themselves (MacDonald, 1973).

Usually only the penis and surrounding area is exposed, with total nudity occurring in less than 10 percent of the cases (MacDonald, 1973). In the majority of instances, the penis is erect, but may be flaccid (Hirschfeld, 1938; Gebhard et al., 1965; Jones and Frei, 1979). Most handle their penises to achieve sexual arousal or release (Witzig, 1968; Jones and Frei, 1979). Feelings during the act are sexual excitement, anxiety, and depersonalization (Jones and Frei, 1977). These characteristics vary from time to time in the same individual (Mohr et al., 1964).

It is rare that the exhibitionist attempts to touch his viewer or even to come close to her. Touching or grabbing occurs in only about 2 percent of exposures (MacDonald, 1973; Rooth, 1973). The average comfortable distance from the viewer is about twelve feet. If the viewer moves closer than this, the exhibitionist feels like fleeing (Jones and Frei, 1977), demonstrating that sexual contact is not his aim, that the meaning of exposing is nonsexual (Zechnich, 1971).

Those who remain at a considerable distance attract attention by a cough or by making lewd remarks such as, "That's my magic flower" and "I have the biggest peter you ever saw" (MacDonald, 1973, p. 53).

The site and circumstance of exposure preclude sexual union (Witzig, 1968). The favored place is out of doors (60–70%) often from an automobile (20–40%), and a few (15%) from their residences (Arieff and Rotman, 1942; Mohr et al., 1964; Gebhard et al., 1965; MacDonald, 1973).

Peak time of exposure is between eight and nine in the morning and again from three to five in the afternoon. Very little seasonal variation in incidence was found in Denver (MacDonald, 1973), but in Westchester County, New York, April through October were peak months, with no such variation in other sex crimes (Hirning, 1945).

Viewer Characteristics and Reactions

Description of the viewer is complicated since in half the incidences exposure is in front of more than one person (MacDonald, 1973), and often the act is determined more by location and impulse than type of viewer (Mohr et al., 1964). Ninety percent of the exposures take place in view of women and children who are strangers, with the rest being neighbors (Gebhard et al., 1965; MacDonald, 1973; Herold et al., 1979).

The majority expose themselves before young adults (Gittleson et al., 1978), but 20 to 30 percent of viewers are children (Arieff and Rotman, 1942; Taylor, 1947; Mohr et al., 1964; Rooth, 1973). Perhaps the reason children are selected is that they are more likely to be impressed by the exposure (Hirning, 1947). The number of children exposed to may be inflated because they are usually in groups at the time and since exposure to children is considered to be a more serious offense than to adults, it is more likely to be reported (Mohr et al., 1964).

Other than their choice of children or adults, and the virtual exclusion of wives, men, and little boys (Hirning, 1947), few show any selective bias (Mohr et al., 1964). For some, any adult or child will do. Where there is a preference for a particular sort of woman, it is idiosyncratic. In some instances, his ideal target may resemble his wife or mother (MacDonald, 1973). One, whose wife did not want children, exposed himself to a pregnant woman and to a woman pushing a baby carriage. Others may unconsciously seek out the masculine type (Christoffel, 1936). It is fairly well agreed that the viewer's reaction provides the source of enjoyment.

"I think there are really two things involved. While I expose myself I have an erection and a sexual desire. But I do not want the woman to whom I expose myself. . . . Scaring her gives me an exhilarating effect. I have frequently exposed myself after satisfactory intercourse with my wife—the two have nothing to do with one another. . . . It is when I am depressed or extremely tired when the desire for exposure occurs" [Tuteur, 1963, p. 523].

This man is an exception, for most exhibitionists either cannot or will not give a description of their feelings during the act, making it difficult to study their intentions. From what is known, the sought after viewer reactions are pleasure, approval, surprise, excitement, awe, indignation, and even amusement; if he meets with indifference or scorn, he is devastated (Smith,

Rhoades, and Llewllyn, 1961; Jones and Frei, 1977). Even though the act is well calculated to shock the viewer, many claim they do not want this reaction (Jones and Frei, 1979).

Frequently he misreads his viewer's reaction to conform to his own hopes. For example, giggling children are perceived as spellbound and sexually excited. For those who hope to please their viewer, any powerful emotion will be interpreted as a sign of pleasure. Those whose exposure is an expression of an aggressive–defiant attitude will perceive their viewers' reaction as shock and fear (Mohr et al., 1964). The ones who flee from the scene without waiting for a reaction probably supply the viewer's reaction using their own fantasies.

Ellis (1906) sees this act as symbolic courtship, where exposure takes the place of solicitation and the exhibitionist becomes excited by the thought that he is sexually arousing the female. It is a mimicry of the early phase of sexual encounter, although at a distance and with no thought of consummation. Maybe at some level of consciousness, he hopes the female will reciprocate by exposing herself to him (Freud, 1905; Romm, 1942; Karpman, 1954), reminiscent of the childhood "I'll show you mine, if you'll show me yours." For instance, a man, exposing from his car, carefully watched his viewer's facial expression. If favorable, he became excited and imagined she was exposing herself to him (Silverman, 1941). His hope is that the woman will show him her penis, as in this exhibitionist's dream: "As she approached me I noticed that her breasts were abnormally high and not quite full. She also had a penis and scrotal sacs. She put her arms around my head and I could feel her soft warm flesh" (Sperling, 1947, p. 34).

Psychoanalysts explain exhibitionism as a technique for warding off castration anxiety by overemphasizing the component impulse of showing. It is a magical gesture with an infantile aim. The exhibitionist is unconsciously and symbolically making three statements to his victim: first, "I am convinced I have a penis because of your reaction at seeing it"; second, "Your shocked reaction assures me that you fear me and that I need not fear you"; and third, "I wish you would show me that you, too, have a penis" (Fenichel, 1945). From a deeper, preoedipal level he is declaring that he no longer needs his mother's breast, since he has his own breast (penis = breast). As mother deprived him of her breast, he will not give his to her, but will only show it (Socarides, 1988).

A phallometric study was designed to answer "What responses from the female arouse the exhibitionist?" and "What does he seek from the female?" Slides of a female expressing pleasure, anger, admiration, and fear were not arousing to the exhibitionists. For controls, pointing to her genitals was arousing only if preceded by a slide indicating her sexual interest by coy looks. For exhibitionists, exposing and pointing were arousing only if not preceded by the "coy, courtship" slides. It seems, then, that what exhibitionists are seeking is not a strong emotional reaction, but an invitation for sex in a sexually unaroused female. What exhibitionists are avoiding is not the act of coitus, for they have intercourse with their partners, but rather they are attempting to avoid those intimate behaviors that precede coitus like petting, embracing, and kissing (Kolarsky and Madlafousek, 1983).

Inhibitionism

Exhibitionists dislike other exhibitionists. The thought of having their wives, girl friends, or daughters exposed to arouses ideas of violence (Rooth, 1973). A frequent activity of the exhibitionist is inhibitionism, that is, watching for and scaring off other exhibitionists, sometimes by posing as a detective or reporting the other to the police. Inhibitionism alternates with exhibitionism and is thought to be an expression of the individual's hostile voyeuristic attitude toward the same sex (Christoffel, 1956).

Risk Taking

While consciously denying any desire to get caught, the exhibitionist takes untold risks (Jones and Frei, 1977). When exposing from his automobile, his identity is displayed on his license plate; if he uses his residence, he is asking for trouble (Arieff and Rotman, 1942). One man, stark naked, knocked on doors of houses in broad daylight (MacDonald, 1973). As his exposures continue, he seems to be less cautious, acts with greater abandon, and takes more risks (Smith et al., 1961). Reasons for this risk taking are unknown. Perhaps it adds spice and excitement (Bowman, 1951), the courting of danger making him feel more manly (Romm, 1942). At some level, he may want to get caught. Maybe he is reenacting the oedipal situation, where exposure elicits the woman's (mother's) disgust and the police's (father's) punishment (Russell, 1972).

After the Act

The immediate feeling after exposure is reduction of tension. But soon, remorse, guilt, shame, humiliation, or relief at being caught set in (Hirning, 1947; Karpman, 1954; Smith et al., 1961; Evans, 1970; Jones and Frei, 1977). When apprehended, only a few resist arrest (MacDonald, 1973). Estimates of those who admit to the offense vary widely, from a few (Hirning, 1947; MacDonald, 1973), a half (East, 1924; Taylor, 1947), to about two-thirds (Arieff and Rotman, 1942; Gebhard et al., 1965).

When shame and humiliation predominate, the exhibitionist goes to great lengths to disavow his actions and is ingenious in explaining away what actually happened. For example, a man walking about a nightclub with his hand on his exposed penis explained, "I had to go in a hurry, I just had my zipper undone, but I didn't get it out" (MacDonald, 1973, p. 58). Another, who had his pants down to his knees for ten minutes, remarked, "I was taking a leak, it was an extreme necessity" (pp. 58–59). Often he claims that he was in a stupefied state. However, in many cases, this is merely an attempt to disown responsibility (Rickles, 1950).

Obscene Phone Callers

Sixty-one percent of women surveyed had received obscene phone calls and three-quarters of these had from two to more than five such calls (Herold et al., 1979). While DSM-III-R classifies telephone scatologia (lewdness) as a paraphilia not otherwise specified, there are important similarities between this condition and exhibitionism.

A sixteen-year-old threatened mothers over the phone with harm to their daughters, claiming to hold these daughters captive. He said he would damage their breasts or genitals unless mother mutilated herself by burning her own breasts or genitals. His urge to call increased when he became concerned about his adequacy in numerous areas. The mothers' reactions gave him a sense of power and importance by frightening them (Nadler, 1968).

In another case, a twenty-five-year-old married man was arrested for multiple obscene calls to males. In his teen years he had fantasized being hugged by "very macho gym teachers," but does not consider himself a homosexual. His selection of males was traced to his anger and competitiveness toward his father and his identification and conflict with his mother (Goldberg and Wise, 1985).

Exhibiting by phone allows more free play of the imagination; and, since there is lower risk, the caller is usually more aggressive than the genital exhibitionist (Nadler, 1968). Obscene phone callers suffer from low self-esteem and dependency on others for assurance of worthiness, coupled with both rage toward and fear of women (Goldberg and Wise, 1985).

That obscene phone calls can substitute for genital exhibitionism is seen in the case of a twenty-two-year-old, who began his calling when he was in therapy for genital exhibitionism. After he began calling, he had no desire to expose. His feelings when placing these calls were similar to those when he exposed. The process began with a compelling urge, imagining the shocked reaction of the victim, and then masturbation (Kentsmith and Bastini, 1974).

The difference between the exhibitionist and phone caller is explained in the psychoanalytic literature as regressions to different parts of the body. During the early narcissistic stage of development, a loss or lessening of love is reacted to by withdrawal of libido from the love-giving object and this libido is invested in the child's own body. The part of the body chosen is determined by previous fixations—oral, anal, phallic. The exhibitionist, fixated at the phallic level, hostilely exposes his penis, while the obscene phone caller, fixated at the oral stage, displays his anger verbally (Rosen, 1979).

Frotteurism

Frotteurism is a seldom reported courtship disorder and has some aspects in common with exhibitionism. The frotteur achieves arousal and orgasm by rubbing his exposed or covered penis against another person, usually a woman. His favorite haunts are crowded stores, elevators, escalators, and public conveyances. In these places he can easily claim that his touching was accidental. He uses the other person's buttocks or thighs, not because he is partial to these areas, but because they are convenient (Bloch, 1908; Karpman, 1954; Caprio, 1955; de River, 1958). DSM-III-R classifies frotteurism as an independent paraphilia.

THE PERSON

Current Status

Age and Onset

Less than 10 percent of exhibitionists are over fifty years old (Arieff and Rotman, 1942; MacDonald, 1973). The highest incidence of arrest is in the twenties and early thirties (Arieff and Rotman, 1942; Apfelberg et al., 1944; Hirning, 1945; Mohr et al., 1964; MacDonald, 1973), and from then on there is a sharp decline in incidence. Viewers' reports overestimate exposer's age, with half retrospectively estimating the age as over forty (Gittleson et al., 1978). Age at time of arrest is presented in Table 9.1.

Average age at first arrest is the midtwenties, with a range from fifteen to the late twenties (Mohr et al., 1964; Gebhard et al., 1965; Berah and Myers, 1983). Age of first arrest or conviction does not coincide with first exposure, since many men have been exhibiting for five or more years before they are apprehended. Almost all exhibitionists began exposing be-

TABLE 9.1
Age of Exhibitionists at Arrest

Age	Percent (N = 100)
17–20	27
21–30	35
31–40	22
41–50	7
51–60	3
61–90	6

Source: A. J. Arieff & D. B. Rotman (1942), One hundred cases of indecent exposure. *Journal of Nervous and Mental Disease*, 96:523.

fore they were twenty-five years old and some were younger than fifteen (Gebhard et al., 1965; Rooth, 1973; Smukler and Schiebel, 1975).

There are two age peaks in the records of repeating offenders, with a cluster of charges in the midteens, few in the late teens, and then another cluster in the twenties (Mohr et al., 1964).

What happens in the midteens and in the twenties that might induce a man to expose himself? It could be his first encounter with menstruation (Christoffel, 1936). More likely, these are the ages where he is expected to assume adult sexuality, when he initially becomes involved with dating in the midteens and marriage in the early twenties (Mohr et al., 1964; Smukler and Schiebel, 1975; Jones and Frei, 1979). Being ill-prepared for such relations, he retreats to earlier, more impersonal modes of relating (Karpman, 1948, 1954).

The impact of life stresses is illustrated in the case of a man who began exposing at age sixteen, five months after his mother's sudden blindness. Exposure stopped for five years, but started again at the time of his wife's pregnancy and his promotion at work (Levitan, 1963).

Many recall trigger episodes, such as mutual genital showing, exposing playfully as a prank, hearing a report of exhibition, or masturbating while secretly watching girls (Jones and

Frei, 1979). These episodes strike a consonant note, and precipitate their first exposure.

Ethnic and Religious Background

Reported incidence of black exhibitionists is low compared to whites (Arieff and Rotman, 1942; Hirning, 1945; Karpman, 1954; MacDonald, 1973; McCreary, 1975; Forgac, Cassel, and Michaels, 1984). Mexican-Americans are overrepresented in Denver (MacDonald, 1973), but underrepresented in Los Angeles data (McCreary, 1975).

Religious affiliation of a Toronto sample did not differ from the census distribution (Mohr et al., 1964). But in Westchester County, New York, which was not predominately Roman Catholic at the time, Catholic exhibitionists outnumbered Protestants by two to one (Hirning, 1945).

Intelligence and Education

Mean IQ is around 100, with a roughly normal distribution (Bejke, 1952; Mohr et al., 1964). Some years ago there was a discrepancy between their IQ scores and educational attainment. Over half of court referrals had an eighth grade education or less (Arieff and Rotman, 1942), and only 15 percent had progressed beyond the tenth grade (Mohr et al., 1964). This midteen exodus from school corresponds with one peak period of onset of exhibition. Ambitions are high, but they remain unfulfilled (Christoffel, 1936).

Occupation and Interests

Occupationally, they tend to be laborers (Arieff and Rotman, 1942) and skilled craftsmen (Mohr et al., 1964). Of those in business, the favored position is sales. Attempts to work on their own are unsuccessful; when working for others, they have difficulty with their superiors. In general, they are hard working and conscientious, but sensitive to criticism. When asked their occupational preference, they name those they considered manly, for instance, an insurance salesman was envious of skilled workers (Mohr et al., 1964).

Social interests are typically masculine, with major interest in sports, especially swimming, boxing, martial arts, and weight-lifting. Team sports are least favored (Mohr et al., 1964).

Psychopathology

About three-quarters of exhibitionists in one study were diagnosed as mild to severe neurotics (Ellis and Brancale, 1956). Incidence of obsessive–compulsive disorders ranges from a high 80 percent (Rickles, 1950) to a low 35 percent (Arieff and Rotman, 1942) or next to none (Mohr et al., 1964). The description of the act of exhibiting does bear the stamp of obsessive–compulsive behavior, with rising tension, increasing pressure to expose, struggle against the impulse, and a feeling of relief after exposing. However, to consider exhibitionism a symptom of obsessive–compulsive neurosis is probably erroneous, since the compulsion to act in deviant ways is present in all paraphilias. Therefore, all deviants would then be classed as obsessive–compulsives. Unlike the neurotic, whose symptom is the consequence of repression, the exhibitionist acts out directly an element of his infantile sexuality (Allen, 1980).

Incidence of other problems, such as psychosis, epilepsy, and mental retardation, is rather low (East, 1924; Arieff and Rotman, 1942; Ellis and Brancale, 1956; Rader, 1977). Signs of personality disturbance are impulsivity, irritability, distrust-fulness, estrangement, and tension-reducing acting out behaviors (Forgac et al., 1984).

Alcohol use is "rarely a factor" (Mohr et al., 1964). Only a very few (3%) have a history of "intemperance" (East, 1924) and three-fourths are low consumers of alcohol (Meyers and Berah, 1983); organic factors play only a minor role (Karpman, 1954). Patients with temporal lobe seizures may engage in automatic behaviors that simulate exhibitionism, such as removing their pants by the side of a highway, but they do not qualify as exhibitionists (Hooshmand and Brawley, 1969).

Other paraphilias are relatively rare (Hirning, 1945; Mohr et al., 1964). The most common is peeping, from incidental to repeated (Rooth, 1973; Smukler and Schiebel, 1975). A few have engaged in pedophilic acts in adolescence or adulthood and some in frottage (Rooth, 1973).

First timers give an essentially normal personality test (MMPI) profile, but as number of arrests for indecent exposure increases, so does degree of psychopathology (McCreary, 1975). However, this relation holds only for those with arrests for other than indecent exposure. For the 36 percent who had arrests for indecent exposure only, there was no such relation (Forgac et al., 1984).

Estimates of those who commit nonsexual criminal offenses ranges from about 20 percent (Ellis and Brancale, 1956; Mohr et al., 1964) to 66 percent (Forgac et al., 1984). These other offenses include crimes against property, and assault. Sex-related offenses are indecent assault and offensive behavior (Berah and Meyers, 1983).

Information on the relation between incidence of exhibiting and other criminal behaviors is contradictory. In one study it was found that the more convictions for exhibitionism, the more likely are convictions for other offenses (Berah and Myers, 1983). In another, those who had criminal records had less incidence of exposing than those without such records (Forgac et al., 1984). It is, therefore, premature to conclude, as Hirning (1945) did many years ago, that "they appear to be a relatively harmless group of sex offenders" (p. 144).

Marital Status and Partners

Estimates of those married range from about 40 to 65 percent (East, 1924; Arieff and Rotman, 1942; Hirning, 1945; Taylor, 1947; Gebhard et al., 1965; McCreary, 1976; Forgac et al., 1984). Of those over twenty-one, from a half to about three-fourths were married (Arieff and Rotman, 1942; Mohr et al., 1964). Good marital adjustment has been reported (Smith et al., 1961), but marriages tend to be infertile (Mohr et al., 1964; Gebhard et al., 1965).

Wives are usually cooperative, but also rather ineffectual. Often they resemble the exhibitionist's weak, passive father (Rickles, 1950). Descriptions of wives fall into several categories.

Most prominent is the dependency–dominance theme; for example, employing crying and helplessness to control. Other categories are nervous and shy, jealous and restrictive, like mother, afraid of sex and childbirth, and promiscuous (Mohr et al., 1964).

Early Life

Siblings

Birth order does not appear to be a factor (Mohr et al., 1964; Gebhard et al., 1965). In one sample there were significantly more brothers than sisters. Exhibitionists' relations with their sisters during childhood were good and rivalry with brothers was not prominent. Older brothers were sometimes viewed as father substitutes, and often they were resented (Mohr et al., 1964).

Father

About a third of the fathers were absent from home for extended periods of time during exhibitionists' childhoods (Mohr et al., 1964). For the most part, they were sufficiently present to encourage masculinity, but failed to provide guidance and nurturance (Allen, 1980).

No consistent picture emerges of the son's relations with father. Those having positive relations vary from a fourth (Mohr et al., 1964) to over two-thirds (Meyers and Berah, 1983). Many fathers are described as distant or erratic, swinging from affectionate to threatening (Mohr et al., 1964), and some as cruel (Apfelberg et al., 1944). Of those who express positive feelings, the quality of the relation is more like a peer than a father–son relation. Typical statements are "real pal," "liked kids," and "just like me," rather than statements reflecting protection and guidance (Mohr et al., 1964).

Mother

Mother is definitely favored over father (Gebhard et al., 1965), with from almost 50 to 90 percent reporting positive relations with her (Meyers and Berah, 1983) and only a very few feeling distant from her (Mohr et al., 1964). The mother–son relation is described as tender (Christoffel, 1936) with excessive attachment (Hirning, 1947). Whatever the feelings expressed, love, resentment, or both, they are strong (Mohr et al., 1964).

Some statements about mother reflect respect for her competence, such as, "irreplaceable," "good manager"; others indicate some pampering: "soft-hearted," and "favored me." Some ambivalent statements describe strong dominance and control themes as "good mother, but treated me like a baby," and "close to her but resented her domineering" (Mohr et al., 1964, pp. 140–141). Her son is afraid of her, but also afraid of losing her. This ambivalent feeling toward mother interferes with his assumption of his own independent existence (Allen, 1980).

Mother has been described as frustrating, controlling, and seductive. After one man in group therapy told of his embarrassment as a child when his mother gave him an enema with his female cousin present, all the others remembered similar experiences. They had been confused and enraged by their mothers' enema administrations. They thought that mothers were trying to use the nozzle as a penis on them, which perhaps made them feel their own penises were inadequate (Freese, 1972).

Rickles (1950) places special emphasis on mother's efforts to encourage a dependent attachment. She uses her son as a replacement for the departed or ignored husband. If the husband is present, the child senses the tension and hostility between his parents. If he is absent, he is likely to be disparaged by mother. Exhibitionists in group therapy recalled their mothers' uncomplimentary remarks about their fathers (Freese, 1972).

Mother pets and admires her son, not expecting him to reciprocate. Thus, the future exhibitionist learns at an early age that his body, particularly his penis, is to be admired for its own sake, while he remains the passive recipient of affection and admiration. For instance, "during bathing Mother would look at me with fascinated, devouring eyes, voluptuously stroking and caressing my body" (Karpman, 1948, p. 220, citing Sadger, 1926). His motto becomes, "Not to love, but to be loved" (Karpman, 1948).

Mother molds her son in this fashion because of her own envy of the masculine role and her narcissism. She reacts to her envy of masculinity in one of two ways. She may rebel against the feminine by assuming the masculine role as she sees it, and by hostilely seeking revenge on males. She is masculine in appearance and manner, strong willed, and aggressive. The other alternative reaction is to become the clinging vine, the passive martyr who dominates by seeking sympathy, giving the impression of a pathetic person in need of support. Some mothers display a mixture of these two reactions.

She is so identified with her son that he becomes an extension of herself so that she now possesses the envied penis. Since he is a part of her, her self-love is lavished on him, and displaying him satisfies her own narcissism. Her envy and hatred of males is expressed in her attempts to dominate and control her son. She virtually lives his life for him, leading to his abject dependence on her.

The son is subjected to both sexual inhibitions and sexual arousal, resulting in a conflict between incestuous wishes and strict taboos on them. The home environment is strict (Apfelberg et al., 1944) and family attitudes toward sex are puritanical (Hirning, 1945), with special emphasis on modesty. At the same time, mother allows much physical closeness. The child is so stimulated by her displays of affection that his incestuous desires are aroused, producing a strong attachment to her. Many had shared a bed with their mothers or sisters, arousing sexual feelings which had to be suppressed (Freese, 1972). In one extreme case, a seminary student slept with his mother during childhood. When he was fifteen, she started masturbating him and continued this when he returned from the service at twenty-one. Even after his marriage, she masturbated and fellated him (Guttmann, 1953). Another engaged in mutual exposure with sister and later simulated intercourse by rubbing against her, and an aunt rubbed his penis when bathing him (Karpman, 1948).

Childhood

It has been suggested that there was a lack of privacy in the exhibitionist's childhood home, so that others would walk into his bedroom while he was dressing or into the bathroom when he was showering. These conditions led him to assume that, "It doesn't make any difference, for I have nothing that requires covering." As an adult, when he exposes, if viewer response is indifference, his assumption is confirmed. If the response is shock, it is disconfirmed: "I do have something impressive" (Zechnich, 1971, p. 71).

As children, exhibitionists were shy and retiring (Smith et al., 1961). They recall having felt odd, unloved, isolated, and different from their peers. They tried to please their mothers by helping with household chores and behaving differently from their fathers (Freese, 1972).

Schooldays, too, are remembered as times of isolation and loneliness. Exhibitionists had few friends (Mohr et al., 1964), with only a handful having numerous companions (Gebhard et al., 1965). They were either fearful of being bullied or engaged in fights. All this points to poor social adjustment and difficulty in coping with aggression during these years (Mohr et al., 1964).

There is often a history of stammering and bed-wetting (Fenichel, 1945; Alexander, 1956; Smith et al., 1961). Both of these problems draw attention to the child who becomes a nuisance. In stammering, communication is interfered with, just as exhibiting inhibits sexual communication (Christoffel, 1936).

Their social isolation did not result in any deficit in prepubertal sex play (Gebhard et al., 1965). In fact, future exhibitionists were rather uninhibited in sex play with other children (Christoffel, 1936, 1956). Between ages five to nine, they had a high incidence (72%) and frequency of sex play with girls, in which mutual inspection of the genitals was the predominant activity (Maletzky, 1980).

During preadolescent years, few were sexually approached by adult males, but 12 percent did receive such attention by adult females. There was some petting, but this did not lead to coitus—a model of his adult behavior with approach but no intimate contact (Gebhard et al., 1965).

While less than half masturbated prior to puberty, later in life they are strongly dependent on this outlet (Gebhard et al.,

1965). Often the boy is troubled with conflict over masturbation stemming from some traumatic episode, as this father reports, "I was very severe. I looked for evidences. I told him he would injure himself if he did it and that I would punish him if I found out. I told him that it was easy to see if a boy was masturbating," threatening the boy with circumcision. Later in life the son recalls, "It happened about five times in my life. . . . I thank God it hasn't been more" (Hirning, 1947, p. 561).

Father's punishment for his son's masturbation is harsh, and so the boy becomes guilty and secretive about his self-pleasuring. Mother's reaction, however, is mild and forgiving and he may even find some pleasure in being caught in the act by her. In his adult exhibiting, he relives scenes of being discovered masturbating by his mother (Bejke, 1953).

Sexuality

With this sort of childhood training, it is not surprising that exhibitionists are puritanical, prudish, and exceedingly modest (Hirschfeld, 1938; Hirning, 1947). They are often modest even with their wives, never viewing them nude or being viewed nude by them, and having intercourse in a conventional manner (Rosen, 1979). This modesty stands in sharp contrast to their exhibitionism.

While they are not averse to intercourse (Freund, Scher, and Hunker, 1984), they are plagued with immature and disordered sexuality (Silverman, 1941; Apfelberg et al., 1944). Specific problems are abstinence, excessive masturbation, frequent nocturnal emissions, erectile failure, premature ejaculation, ejaculation at the sight of a woman, and inhibition in normal sexual relations (Fenichel, 1945; Karpman, 1954; Caprio, 1955; Fookes, 1969).

Sexual contact on an intimate basis is avoided. From a third to a half of court referral cases were heterosexually inexperienced (Arieff and Rotman, 1942; Mohr et al., 1964). For example, premarital petting to orgasm was a low 17 percent during their early twenties (control = 36%) (Gebhard et al.,

1965). They want to have sexual relations and their masturbatory fantasies are about sex with women, but they complain of shyness and difficulty in establishing relations with women (Mohr et al., 1964).

Their first sexual partners were twenty-one or older (Gebhard et al., 1965) and they tend to enter into "mother marriages." The more mature the woman, the less inclined is the exhibitionist to engage in sexual intercourse (Christoffel, 1956).

Exhibitionists tend to have a strong sex drive, but satisfy it in nonintimate ways. It is because he places the mask of his mother on other women that he has trouble establishing sexual relations with companions. Instead, he relies heavily on masturbation and prostitutes as sources of sexual outlet (Taylor, 1947; Rickles, 1950; Karpman, 1954; Gebhard et al., 1965). About a half masturbate even though they have adequate sexual relations (Arieff and Rotman, 1942). Dependence on masturbation is most clearly seen in married exhibitionists. Whereas incidence and frequency of masturbation decreases when the normal male has ready access to a female, for married exhibitionists masturbation accounts for 26 percent of total sexual outlet for ages thirty-six to forty (control = 2%). But masturbation is not especially pleasurable unless related to exhibiting (Hirning, 1947) and it causes marked concern and anxiety (Gebhard et al., 1965).

Use of prostitutes is seen especially in the age group thirty-one to thirty-five, where a fourth of their total outlet is with prostitutes (control = 14%), and premarital coitus with companions is a low 19 percent during this same age (control = 33%) (Gebhard et al., 1965).

Exhibition is not related to frequency of sexual intercourse (Smukler and Schiebel, 1975). While some may blame their exposure on lack of sexual relations, dissatisfaction and anxiety over sexual relations are more prominent complaints (Mohr et al., 1964).

The exhibitionist's sexual gratification from his exposing "results largely from phantasy indulgence, which the exposure stimulates and reinforces, and so to some extent seems to serve as a bridge connecting phantasy and reality" (East, 1924, p. 373). In two cases, boys were discovered urinating by attractive women. Later, when alone, they were sexually stimulated by recalling that scene, and masturbated. After many pairings of the fantasy of being seen with their penises exposed with masturbation, they both commenced to exhibit (McGuire, Carlisle, and Young, 1965). Young exhibitionists report sexual fantasies interfering with their schoolwork (Mohr et al., 1964). Fantasies are usually of preliminary sexual activities (Karpman, 1948). Having fantasies of exposing is related to outcome of aversion therapy. Although they did not differ in frequency of masturbation or sexual intercourse, more men in the failure than in the success group had exhibitionistic masturbation fantasies (Evans, 1970).

Masculinity and Anger

The exhibitionist is unable to rise to the challenge of the adult world. He cannot compete, assume responsibility, function independently, or actively bring happiness to others. In the face of this unfulfilling world, he regresses to childish self-love (Rickles, 1950), demanding attention in an infantile way. In addition, he is dependent on his mother, has problems with sexual relations, is timid, and lacks assertiveness (Silverman, 1941; Rickles, 1950; Hirning, 1945). It is little wonder, then, that he has doubts about his masculinity (Levitan, 1963). Because of this frail sense of manliness, he focuses on his penis as his personal symbol of masculinity (Allen, 1980) and equates masculinity with genital power (Hadden, 1973). This importance of the penis led early writers to suggest that exhibitionists have excessively large or very small penises (Ellis, 1906). However, exhibitionists' estimates of their penis size are not unusual (Gebhard et al., 1965).

Many events in his life are construed as threats to his already fragile sense of masculinity. These insults must be countered by a demonstration of manliness (Hadden, 1973), yet he is afraid to display what he considers masculine behavior. This fear is most obviously fear of retribution from authority figures. But, underlying this is fear of being seized by his infantile rage and destructiveness (Mathis and Collins, 1970; Mathis, 1980). Common to all exhibitionists is some abnormality in handling aggression and hostility (Jones and Frei, 1979). Therefore, he must keep his anger under tight rein even in such provocative situations as his wife flirting with another man, or belittling him in front of their children (Smukler and Schiebel, 1975). However, he may act the tyrant with his own family where he is safe from retaliation (Rooth, 1973).

Feeling unjustly treated by others and by life in general (Karpman, 1948; Smukler and Schiebel, 1975), he has a childish urge to strike back, to demonstrate that he is a man. His excessive hostility is directed outward, not inward (Jones and Frei, 1979). His exhibitionism serves as a demonstration of his manliness and convinces him that he is more aggressive than is in fact the case (McCawley, 1965; Witzig, 1968), and the attendant risk taking is construed as proof of his courage (Mathis and Collins, 1970; Allen, 1980; Mathis, 1980).

Exhibitionists display moderately nonconforming attitudes on personality tests (McCreary, 1975; Rader, 1977; Jones and Frei, 1979). His act of exposing is a magical, defiant gesture against all inhibitions, against moral authority in general, and specifically against his mother (Karpman, 1948). Its purpose is to intimidate and frighten, to show that he is a man of power and not a weak, dependent, fearful child (Guttmann, 1953). Exhibitionism is the functional equivalent of aggression (Rosen, 1979). It also signifies independence from mother, it is a compensation for impotence, and a substitute for incestuous strivings (Rickles, 1950; Karpman, 1954).

Some early writers saw genital exposure as an expression of animals' strutting and displaying for females. Others speculated that the exhibitionist reverts to a primitive adoration and reverence of his phallus which he conceives of as representing strength, power, and other mystical qualities (Ellis, 1906; Rickles, 1950; Bowman, 1951). More recently, on the basis of animal and anthropological evidence, it has been proposed that exposure is an archaic mechanism for displaying aggression, as in the meaning of the obscene gesture of giving the finger. Therefore, there may be an innate, biological predisposition to exhibit that is disinhibited by some cortical dysfunction, interacting with different types of personalities, and triggered by some particular experience (Jones and Frei, 1979; Fedora, Reddon, and Yeudall, 1986).

There is a fairly sizable group of exhibitionists who have elevated femininity scores (Freese, 1973; Jones and Frei, 1979). It is probable they are the passive type who express their aggression indirectly. Others, with high masculinity scores, more than likely act out their aggressiveness without regard for the consequences (Jones and Frei, 1979). They may allay the tension to exhibit by putting their masculinity to the test by achieving in some sport or in petty burglary (Christoffel, 1936).

Some have proposed that exhibiting serves as a defense against latent homosexuality (Karpman, 1954; Rosen, 1979). More than likely, however, they are pseudohomosexuals, that is, men who conclude that because of their masculine inadequacy they must be homosexual (Ovesey, 1969).

Interpersonal Relations

There are some exhibitionists who are loud, brash, and attention seeking, who use obscenity for shock value. However, the majority, as noted by Lasegue, are modest, self-conscious persons, who shrink from social contacts (Rickles, 1950; Kopp, 1962). In social relations they are described as lonely, withdrawn, submissive, and nonassertive (Hirschfeld, 1938; Hirning, 1947; Karpman, 1954; Hadden, 1973; Bastani, 1976). In group psychotherapy they are quiet, constantly embarrassed, and blush frequently (Kopp, 1962).

Blushing may substitute for exhibitionism. The three-layered sequence of events leading to excessive blushing starts in infancy with the child wanting to look at mother's breasts. This wish is denied and replaced by its opposite, buttocks display, where buttocks equal breasts. This urge, too, is denied expression, and the hind cheeks are displaced to facial cheeks. When attention is directed toward this person, he feels ashamed to have people look at his cheeks, and blushes. His blushing draws even more attention to himself, which is also the function of genital exhibitionism (Bergler, 1944). It is said that skin disease, especially hives, may also substitute for exhibitionism (Karpman, 1954).

Conception of Women

His conception of women and relations with them are cast in the mold of his mother. Mother monopolized his attention and limited his social contacts, and so he expects his relation with her to be duplicated by other women; that is, to be a source of pleasure to them without his having to put forth any effort. He seeks from them reaffirmation of the significance, beauty, and power of his body (Rickles, 1950). As his mother was a dominant, controlling person before whom he was helpless, so he conceives of other women as the same. He may even have an unconscious fear of being devoured by them (Christoffel, 1936). In their presence, he feels inferior, inadequate, insecure, and fearful (Apfelberg et al., 1944; Freese, 1972).

> I do not feel comfortable in the presence of women. I am just terribly ashamed before them. . . . I believe I would die of shame, if I would stand naked close to a woman, or if she would touch me. However, when a woman is away from me, when she cannot reach me and touch me, when she just looks at me . . . yes, that's it: even when I am sexually most excited I dare not be close to a woman. . . . When I show my penis to a woman, I imagine that her eyes play with it, caress it. Then it is heavenly [Boss, 1949, p. 74].

Both the timid and the brash exhibitionist feel dominated by women and resent it. Exposure serves to turn the tables on women, to dominate instead of being dominated, to make them his helpless victims, rather than being helpless before them (Kopp, 1962).

Alex's mother ruled his father with an "iron hand." His own wife was a head taller than he and one-and-a-half times his weight. She took every opportunity to point out his weaknesses. Soon after learning that she was pregnant, he exposed to a group of young girls. He realized that his exposure was an attempt to end domination by his wife, using the little girls as her surrogates (Schmideberg, 1956).

The exhibitionist conceives of his mother as having offered affection and then withheld it. Now, as an adult he is doing to women what he feels she did to him. Since to him breast equals penis, as mother did not give him her breast, he will not give women his penis. He teases women by showing his penis, but not giving it to them. This is illustrated by a patient in psychoanalysis who spent the weekend with his girl friend and another couple. His girl friend was willing to have sexual relations with him, but he gave his condom to the other man. He rubbed up against his girl friend, exciting her; then he ejaculated (Sperling, 1947).

Attitude Toward Deviancy

Some claim that exhibitionism is ego syntonic, that is, accompanied by little anxiety (Mathis, 1980; Rhodes, 1980). Negative aftereffects, they say, are experienced only when the exhibitionist is apprehended and resulting consequences such as loss of job and freedom, and shame before others. The act of exposing is both positively and negatively reinforcing. It is positive, in that it satisfies erotic and hostile needs; and negative in that it dissipates the unpleasant buildup of tension prior to the act.

Others maintain that the reason exhibitionists do not experience anxiety over their deviancy is because they have massive denial systems, allowing them to deny feelings and avoid expression of emotion (Bastini, 1976; Mathias, 1980). Denial is not limited to their exhibitionistic acts, but is their generalized method of coping (Mathis and Collins, 1970). During and after their first exposure, they may feel shame and remorse, but soon their denial takes over and even the abnormality of their act is denied. After each subsequent exposure, they are convinced that they will never do it again (Mathis and Collins, 1970). As an example of their denial and the elaborate systems of rationalization that they wrap around their deviancy, one patient replied to a question concerning the effect on his victim of his exposing: " 'The human body is beautiful, and our society is wrong in covering it up. There are many cultures where the body is freely displayed. We wouldn't have sexual hang-ups if we weren't so afraid of the body' " (Brownell, 1980, p. 176). If blame is involved, it does not fall on him. A well-educated professional man attributed his exhibitionism to three factors: his parents were first cousins, so heredity was involved; his middle name was the unmasculine Percy; and his penis was too small (Sperling, 1947).

10 SADISM

INTRODUCTION

The traditional conception of sexual relations pictures the male as hunter and penetrator, and the female as chased and recipient. There is nothing cruel or sadistic here, but simply the use of these terms as if they were the only way to describe sexual relations. Another aspect of the commonplace conception of sex is the belief that the female should resist the male's advances, since overcoming her resistance heightens his pleasure.

These predator and prey roles were enacted in certain courtship rituals. The female played the hunted animal, and the male, using energy and skill, captured her. This play heightened excitement in both. The custom of carrying the bride across the threshold symbolizes her abduction to the place where she will sacrifice her virginity (Ellis, 1913; Henriques, 1960).

Pornographers are fond of exaggerating male attack and female resistence, likening it to a battle scene. "He lunges forward, carries everything before him, and enters the fort by storm, reeking with the blood of his fair enemy, who with a scream of agony yields up her maidenhead to the conqueror, who, having put his victim hors de combat, proceeds to reap the reward of his hard fought and bloody battle" (Pearl, 1879–1880, p. 404).

It is not coincidental that this excerpt describes male assaults on virgins. During the late 1800s, when this material was published, a preoccupation with virgins, a "defloration mania" was rampant. It was difficult for brothels to stock a sufficient supply, so they resorted to various devices to simulate virginity (Henriques, 1960; Rush, 1980). This widespread longing to deflower a virgin is likely of sadistic origin. It is not simply a matter of the pain and blood involved, but also the thought of subjugation and conquest (Hirschfeld, 1938). Rather than being an act of mutual pleasure, the attack is seen as frightening, humiliating, and degrading for the female, while the male is able to display his superiority and contempt for her. The virgin is both feared and desired; feared because of being in the power of uncontrollable forces, and desired in order to master those forces (de Beauvoir, 1952).

An example of the mingling of an aggressive act with sexual arousal is the love bite. About 50 percent of men and women are aroused by being bitten (Gebhard, 1969). There is nothing abnormal or perverse in this practice. The tendency to bite at the height of sexual ecstasy is more common in the female than the male (Ellis, 1913; Van de Velde, 1926).

When, then, do we leave everyday expressions of lust and enter the territory of deviance? The boundary is crossed when sadistic acts are substitutes for normal connection, or when they constitute a necessary precondition for it.

Prevalence

From 10 to 20 percent of pornographic magazines feature bondage and discipline (Gayford, 1978; Dietz and Evans, 1982). About 5 percent of males and 2 percent of females say they have obtained sexual pleasure from inflicting pain (Hunt, 1974). This is probably an overestimate, since it includes such acts as the love bite and scratching. While 3 to 12 percent of females are aroused by sadomasochistic stories, 10 to 20 percent of males are so aroused (Kinsey, Pomeroy, and Gebhard. 1953;

Gebhard, 1969). And, one-third of females and almost a half of males have sexual fantasies where they tie up their partner (Arndt, Foehl, and Good, 1985).

There may be some cultural variation in the sex ratio of sadists to masochists. In England and Germany, where father is responsible for discipline, male dominant/female submissive is the preferred pattern. In the United States, mother is the disciplinarian and the prominent pattern is female dominant/male submissive (Green and Green, 1974).

The Female Sadist

The question of whether sadism is more prevalent among men or women must be left to speculation and anecdotal accounts, since there are no reliable surveys to call upon. Ellis (1913) observes that, within normal limits, the male is the victim of the female, but in more extreme cases it is the female who is the victim of the male. Krafft-Ebing (1902) claims that sadistic acts are much more frequent in men than in women. He supports this view by noting that the subjugation of another is a constituent of the male personality and that external and internal obstacles, such as modesty and reserve, inhibit sadistic acts in the female.

In advertisements in sadomasochistic (S&M) magazines, female dominants outnumber males by more than two to one (Weinberg, 1978). This same predominance of female sadists is seen in S&M pornography. But this literature is written for male masochists, and male authors have attributed sadistic characteristics to the female because this is what their readers want to believe (Eulenberg, 1911; Marcus, 1966). Among heterosexual members of an S&M club, the Eulenspiegel Society, named after a comic character who found discomfort in pleasure and pleasure in pain, there are more dominant males than submissive females, and more submissive males than dominant females (Herron, Herron, and Schultz, 1983).

It is estimated, using advertisements for the services of female dominants, that there are about 2500 dominants available at any one time (Scott, 1983). Many of these women are

probably not genuine dominants, but prostitutes who have cap-
italized on the demand for this rather lucrative speciality. In
one sample, over a fourth of the women were "professionals"
(Breslow, Evans, and Langley, 1985).

DEFINITION

Various Conceptions

The term *sadism*, first used in English in 1888, derives from the
French "sadisme" which refers to the writings of the Marquis
de Sade. His stories are filled with descriptions of brutality,
cruelty, maiming, torture, and murder, all for the purpose of
bringing his heroes and heroines to a high state of sexual ecstasy. The term was popularized by Krafft-Ebing who saw it as
an association of lust and cruelty ranging from humiliation to
destruction of another for sexual pleasure.

Some investigators focus on the infliction of pain as the
essence of sadism. Schrenk-Notzing (1895) introduced *algolagnia* (pain craving) with sadism as active, and masochism as passive algolagnia. This is the first time sadism and masochism
were clearly viewed as two poles of the same process. This term,
with its emphasis on pain, has rightly been criticized as too
narrow to encompass the wide variety of sadomasochistic fantasies and acts. The concept of pain was broadened to include
not only physical but also psychic pain in the form of degradation and humiliation (Eulenberg, 1911). Some contemporary
writers still emphasize pain, as in these definitions of sadism:
"the derivation of sexual pleasure from infliction of pain on
others" (Power, 1976, p. 111) and, "the desire to inflict pain or
suffering on the sexual object" (de River, 1958, p. 37).

Others see the crux of sadism as sexual arousal gained
through cruelty and the suffering of another. The official DSM-
III-R criterion is the infliction of "psychological or physical
suffering (including humiliation)" on the partner.

While it appears that cruelty is always present in sadism,
not all cruelty stems from sadism (Braun, 1967). Certainly, it

is an error to equate all cruelty with sadism, "to call every horror sadism, every submission masochism, every inclination eroti-cism is a generalization which will not help to bring clearness in the sexual field, but rather obscurity" (Hirschfeld, 1940, p. 224).

Other authors further temper the relation of sadism and cruelty by emphasizing the reactions of the partner to sadistic acts. Pain, cruelty, and humiliation are the means used to arouse emotions in the partner, and the sadist revels "in the fear, anger or humiliation of the victim" (Karpman, 1954, p. 11). For Ellis (1913), the sadist is not interested in pure cruelty and not in-terested in inflicting pain outside of the sexual area. Further-more, the sadist does not believe that he is administering pure pain, for he assumes and desires that the pain will bring his victim pleasure and be perceived as an indication of love. If this is a correct interpretation, then the sadist is projecting his con-ception of the relation of pleasure and pain onto his partner.

This interpretation can be only partially valid at best. It may well be a rationalization from the mouths of sadists, ex-cusing themselves for gaining pleasure at the expense of an-other's unpleasure. It sounds very similar to the perceptual distortion of preferential rapists who claim that their victims really wanted to have sex with them and actually enjoyed it regardless of their behavior (Abel, Becker, and Skinner, 1980).

It is difficult to imagine how the lust murderer or the necrophile believes that his actions are interpreted by the victim as an act of love. Also, it is extremely difficult to discern in the writings of de Sade any interest in the pleasure of the numerous victims. Perhaps, this equation of pain and love applies to cases of mild or minor sadism, but certainly not to major sadistic acts.

Most contemporary authors stress the importance of dom-ination, power, and control. Sadism is the will to power, a sex-ually accentuated desire to dominate, and a sense of triumph in overcoming the resistance of another (Karpman, 1954). Pain is important, not for itself, but because it symbolizes power and control (Weinberg, 1987).

A definition that places control, not pain or cruelty, at the heart of sadism is, "the repeated practice of behavior and fantasy which is characterized by a wish to control another person by domination, denigration or inflicting pain, for the purpose of producing mental pleasure and sexual arousal (whether or not accompanied by orgasm) in the sadist" (MacCulloch et al., 1983, p. 20).

Varieties of Sadism

A distinction is made between minor and major sadism. Minor sadism includes sadistic fantasies that are not put into action and actual humiliation of a consenting partner in the form of bondage, mild flagellation, and having the person commit degrading acts. Major sadism is reserved for more brutal acts performed on a nonconsenting person, as stabbing and lust murder, and also sexual relations with corpses (Hirschfeld, 1938). Minor sadism is referred to as bondage and discipline (B&D) or dominance and submission (D&S) while sadism is often reserved for more severe activities. In addition to this quantitative distinction, there may be a qualitative difference between the minor and major sadist. It may be an error to assume that the motivations of individuals who enjoy verbally humiliating others are the same as those operating in those who sexually assault and mutilate their victims (Siomopoulos and Goldsmith, 1976).

Several types of sadism have been proposed. One is sadism proper where sexual pleasure is attained by mistreating others because sex and aggression have been fused. In neurotic sadism, the ritual is performed to allay and defend against castration fears. Other sadistic acts are associated with altered states such as trances and religious ecstacies where there is loss of control, a surge of primitive emotions, and changes in body image. It is likely that the brain's limbic system is involved. The individual in an altered state is confused about the aim of his behavior "as if somebody had injected liquified lust" (Siomopoulos and Goldsmith, 1976, p. 636). Psychotics may engage in sadistic acts, but their psychosis channels their behavior rather than causing it. Finally, there is characterological sadism where humiliation of others is nonsexual and probably associated with paranoid personality (Siomopoulos and Goldsmith, 1976).

THE ACTS

Minor Sadism

Fantasies and Scenes

First to be considered is minor sadism, bondage, and discipline (B&D), or dominance and submission (D&S) where the participants are consenting. In the minor sadistic scene, the dominant places the submissive in a situation where he is helpless and then administers some form of discipline. This scene is staged and thus has a not-for-real quality about it. It is enhanced by costumes and toys. The dominatrix's standard outfit is black leather or rubber, hose, and spiked heels. She carries a whip, dog collar, or bonds. A dominant remarks on the effect of such clothing: " 'Suppose a woman comes to a party. She's wearing straight clothes and has her costume in her bag. Then she goes into the bathroom and changes. When she comes out, she has become someone new. She can feel it. She's a new being, and others can feel it, too' " (Scott, 1983, p. 173).

Certain features of the sadomasochistic scene have been identified from several years of field observations and interviews (Weinberg et al., 1984). These are: dominance–submission; role-playing; consent; sexual context; and a mutual definition of the scene's sadomasochistic nature.

Domination is most commonly expressed through administration of pain, humiliation, or bondage. Pain is usually associated with whipping, and less often by piercing and fisting (inserting a fist in anus or vagina). Humiliation is accomplished through roles of master–slave, teacher–pupil, guardian–child, and kidnapper–victim. Other means of humiliating include dressing the male submissive in feminine clothing, treating him like an animal (kennel discipline), fettering him, and sometimes urinating or defecating on him. Enemas can be used to deprive the submissive of control over one of his most intimate functions.

Both parties consent to enact a scene. The agreement may be made either in fine detail or in general outline. The more trust and intimacy there is between the partners, the looser the script can be (Weinberg, 1987). Dominant and submissive may participate in generating a scenario so that both can achieve arousal. Also, both define the scene as sexual, yet there may be no sexual act as part of the scene.

The dominant usually attends to the submissive's reactions. An experienced dominatrix describes the attention that should be paid to the reaction of the submissive: " 'Find that edge where your partner feels he can't take it anymore. Then get him to cross just beyond that edge—that's exciting. . . . Be aware of your partner. Though I may appear uncaring or mean as part of my role, part of me is always asking: "How is my partner? Can he take it?" ' " (Scott, 1983, p. 95).

According to one sociological viewpoint, unless both parties label the scene as sadomaschistic, then it is not sadomasochistic even though all other features are present. For example, the homosexual "leather" scene involves dominance, role-playing, consent, and sexuality, but few who participate view it as sadomasochistic. A recipient of fisting may define himself as tough enough to take it, or "as a gift to the master." He emphasizes the masculinity of what, to the outside observer, is submission. One who was defecated upon denied sadomasochism, and reported "I'm proud that I can do it and the other guys can't" (Weinberg et al., 1984, p. 387.).

Flagellation

The most common activity is flogging. A most valuable source of information on flagellation is the vast amount of fictional literature on this topic, much of it written during the Victorian era in England. Gibson (1978) points up several features in this flagellant literature. The female is portrayed as reveling in the administration of the whip. There are numerous stories of school mistresses eagerly applying the rod to their pupils' posteriors. This depiction of the female as flagellant is interesting in that female sadists are rare, and the frequency of whipping in girls' schools in England during the late 1800s was insignificant compared to what went on in schools for boys.

Ths mistress is often endowed with full breasts and with a harsh, severe demeanor. She is rarely the mother, but often a mother surrogate such as teacher, who is addressed with titles of authority. Sex of the victim is variable—sometimes school-boys, sometimes schoolgirls. Also found are stories where a male is the tormentor of a female. But, very rarely does a male inflict beatings on another male, despite the fact that homosexual relations were not uncommon in boys' schools and that in those schools birchings were administered by the headmaster. A notable exception is the poet Swinburne, who accepted whippings from male and female alike (Johnson, 1979).

In fiction and in actual scenes, the buttocks are selected to the virtual exclusion of other parts. Describing the sexual preferences of the four debauchees in his *The 120 Days of Sodom*, de Sade (1785) remarks that "the four of them had themselves buggered regularly, and that they all four worshipped behinds" (p. 210). The buttocks can be chastized with the least harm and it is an area that we are most modest about. Thus, when bared, as it must be, shame is induced in the victim (Green and Green, 1974).

The flagellator is aroused by the sight of naked buttocks, the view of the flesh quivering under the lash, the writhings of the victim that simulate coitus, the sight of the buttocks reddening and perhaps bleeding, and the cries and pleadings of the victim (Bloch, 1908). The reddening and bleeding of the buttocks play an important part in the flagellant's experience. Red is not only an exciting color, it is sexually exciting as well. In some, the sexual significance of red generalizes to the sight of blood. This association is strengthened in the sadist by the relation of blood to injury and infliction of pain. The word *cruelty* is from the Latin cruor, meaning blood.

Not only is there a fascination with buttocks, but also an aversion, even a loathing, for the front of the victim. Child victims in de Sade's (1785) *The 120 Days of Sodom* are advised, "by and large, offer your fronts very little to our sight; remember that this loathesome part, which only the alienation of her wits could have permitted Nature to create, is always the one we find most repugnant" (p. 251). Sight of the female front is so disgusting to these sadists that it induces impotence— "I may not be able to discharge this evening, thanks to that exhibition . . . unless I can succeed in getting the accursed image of that cunt out of my head" (p. 298).

Many of the features of flagellant literature are depicted in a poem attributed to Swinburne.

> How he blushes! I told you the Master would flog Charlie Collingwood well.
> There are long red ridges and furrows across his great, broad nether cheeks,
> And on both his plump, rosy, round buttocks, the blood stands in drops and in streaks.
> Well hit, Sir! Well caught! how he drew in his bottom, and flinched from the cut!
> At each touch of the birch on his bum, how the smart makes it open and shut [Pearl, 1879–1880, p. 89].

Bondage

Bondage may be heavy or light. Heavy bondage means total restraint including the use of gags and blindfolds. The dominant partner may fasten the submissive in spreadeagle fashion to a bed or to a specially constructed table. The submissive may be placed in a harness and hoisted up, feet off the floor. Using these methods, the dominant experiences the power of totally depriving the submissive of control. To heighten these feelings, the dominant may apply gags, blindfolds, and discipline helmets. In light bondage scarves are used to tie hands and feet. In either case, the partner is rendered helpless and immobile, akin to clinging to a person in an effort to ward off the fear of separation (Bak, 1968).

Water Sports

Water sports involve use of liquid on or in the submissive. He may be urinated upon or required to drink the dominant's urine. Perhaps he is made to substitute for toilet paper after the dominant has relieved himself. Another aspect of water sports is the use of enemas administered by the dominant who may require the submissive to retain the liquid for a long time.

Nipple and Penis Torture

The female breast incites disgust and often becomes the object of torture. "One may be certain indeed that a tit is a very infamous object. I never catch sight of one without being plunged straightway into a rage" (de Sade, 1785, p. 440). In more recent S&M literature, where a female is the submissive, breast torture is often depicted, using ropes to bind them tightly and clothes pins or mouse traps to pinch nipples. Where a male is the submissive, torture may be applied to his nipples and penis.

Other Techniques

Other methods of humiliating the submissive include dressing him in female clothing, often a maid's uniform and perhaps penetrating his rectum with the dominant's dildo. Treating him like an infant is degrading, with the use of diapers, a bottle, and a spanking for soiling himself. Foot worship seems rather popular—the dominant requiring that her boots or toes be licked clean by her submissive. Verbal degradation is an accompaniment to all these methods of control and degradation of another.

Leathersex

The first steps leading to being a homosexual sadomasochist are acknowledging to himself and others that he is homosexual and entering into that subculture. The future leatherman becomes disenchanted with the shallowness and possessiveness of the homosexual world. He withdraws, depressed and confused about his homosexual identity and how he fits into society. He, no doubt, has heard of leathersex and now becomes curious as to what is involved. He reads about it, and, if he lives in a large city, visits such homosexual S&M territories as a leather bar, bathhouse, or club. Something about this aspect of homosexual life strikes a concordant note and he seeks someone who will be his guide, his teacher. Finding a master or top man, he initially assumes the slave or bottom role. Gradually he develops a new identity and new sets of sexual–social relations (Kamel, 1983a).

There is a specialized culture for the homosexual involved in sadomasochism. In the leathersex territories, men meet to arrange scenes. This is a risky undertaking, since often the potential partners are strangers. However, both are known to others in the network and have established reputations that can be checked. Partners are screened to determine erotic preferences and, most importantly, dependability. Screening is facilitated by costumes and their embellishments. Position of a bunch of keys on a belt indicates preference for dominant or submissive role and color of handkerchief worn signifies favorite activities as oral, anal, or watersports.

After this initial screening and usually on the way to the place where the scene is to be enacted, the two negotiate the script: cowboy–bandit; policeman–crook; guard–prisoner; master–dog.

At the site, they commence their play, whose ingredients are restraint, masculinity, humiliation, and fear. Restraint is usually accomplished by physical bonds that immediately establishes who is top and who is bottom. Masculinity is exaggerated, especially in the master, by costumes of highly masculine roles—cowboy, policeman, motocyclist, and by the use of leather and steel. Humiliation is achieved by verbal abuse, but unlike heterosexual scenes, there is no attempt to treat the submissive as a female, for to do so would destroy the homosexual theme that they are two men. Instillation of fear in the submissive is accomplishsed by threats of impending pain through whipping or fisting. There is potential danger here if the master becomes too engulfed by his role and forgets that he is simply portraying a character in the scene (Kamel, 1983b; Lee, 1983).

Major Sadism

Stabbers

Piqueurs, the French word for stabbers, are almost always men. Since the 1700s there have been outbreaks where men roamed the streets stabbing girls. Later, around 1820 in Paris there was an epidemic of women being stabbed in the buttocks and thighs (Ellis, 1913). The piqueur obtains his excitement from inserting sharp knives or ice picks, usually in the buttocks or breast. After inflicting the wound, he makes a hasty escape (Eulenberg, 1911; de River, 1958).

Vampirism

Vampirism is sexual arousal derived from drawing blood, usually by cutting or biting. Often the blood is drunk, but this is not essential. Reports of vampirism are rare (Prins, 1985), but vampiristic wishes and fantasies are not as uncommon as thought.

Some men practice self-vampirism. One remembers being excited at the sight of blood dripping from his nose. His vampirism commenced at puberty when he would masturbate while watching blood drip from a nick he made in his arm. His fantasies were of puncturing prominent vessels in the neck of a long-necked, smooth-skinned adolescent youth. Later he learned to make the puncture in his own neck and catch the spurting blood in his mouth. This act increased in frequency under stress of accidentally wounding a friend, a car accident, and college examinations (Vanden Bergh and Kelly, 1964).

Another young man's earliest recollections were of a dog hit by a car lying in a pool of blood and of sitting on the toilet when his brother squirted water on him. His first masturbation at eleven was associated with drawing his own blood. Later he would puncture a vein or artery in his neck and watch the bleeding in a mirror or catch sprays of blood in his mouth. He performed this masturbatory ritual once every three weeks or so, sometimes experiencing the peace of being loved by someone or being subdued by an attacker. Most often, he masturbated with his fantasy of taking blood from a hairless boy, with no thought of the boy's body or any sexual contact (McCully, 1964).

Vampirism is often associated with other psychiatric disorders in people of very primitive mental and emotional status (Prins, 1985). Fenichel (1945) attributes vampirism to oral sadism. When oral gratification is frustrated in infancy, the person becomes fixated at this level and later demands redress for his earlier deprivation, not infrequently expressed in vampire fantasies.

What is important is the symbolic meaning of blood, as one man described his feeling of being "powerful, like I had taken something powerful from them" (Vanden Bergh and Kelly, 1964, p. 547).

Necrophilia

" 'If they were dead they could not object to my company and my behavior. . . . If you were dead, I could kiss and hug you as much as I liked, and you could not refuse' " (Brill, 1932, p. 23).

Necrophilia involves sexual relations with a human body without a will, a human form with no power to resist, and therefore capable of being absolutely subjugated. The "destruction of the dams of shame, disgust and morality, which must take place in the erection of necrophilia, requires more psychic labor than in the construction of any other perversion" (Brill, 1941, p. 443). In DSM-III-R it is classed as a paraphilia not otherwise specified.

Necrophilia was known to the ancient Egyptians. When female relatives of prominent persons or beautiful women died, their remains were not sent to the embalmers for several days to deter violation of the corpses (Herodotus, 424 B.C.).

Perhaps the most famous of all necrophiles is Sergeant Bertrand, a soldier in the French army in the mid-1800s. As a youth, he was of a delicate constitution and inclined to solitude. He began masturbating at age nine with the fantasy of having intercourse with a room full of women, then he imagined that they were corpses and he was defiling them. He progressed from copulating with already dead animals, to mutilating animals, to violating and mutilating human female corpses. Once, by chance, in a graveyard by a newly dug grave, he impulsively disinterred the corpse and hacked it with a shovel. From then on, the sight or thought of a new grave provoked heart palpitations, tremors, and severe headaches. His urge was so intense that one time he scaled a high wall and swam an ice cold ditch to reach his goal—a fresh grave. When there was no shovel handy, he dug with his bare hands, bloodying them (Krafft-Ebing, 1902; Stekel, 1929b).

While actual necrophilia is comparatively rare, attenuated forms are not infrequent (Klaf and Brown, 1958). Equivalents are fantasies or situations in which the other person is drugged, asleep, or is asked to assume a passive, inert role in sexual intercourse (Calef and Weinshel, 1972), sometimes in a coffin (Karpman, 1954).

Fantasies involving sexual contact with corpses are more common than is generally thought (Klaf and Brown, 1958). For example, a twenty-three-year-old student's masturbation fantasies were breast fondling, oral–genital and vaginal penetration of beautiful women who had been murdered by someone else. Having learned that women regard men's sexual excitement with scorn, contempt, and disgust, he was terrified at the idea of sexual contact with "a real live woman" (Lazarus, 1968).

A forty-year-old schizophrenic's interest in dead bodies began at age nine when he assisted in a funeral parlor. There he found contentment and peace by hugging corpses. His masturbation fantasies were of corpses but he imagined they were alive. During intercourse he would think of his wife as a corpse. While some men such as this one lead normal sexual lives, usually they have a low frequency of sexual activity (Klaf and Brown, 1958).

During hypnosis, a forty-three-year-old revealed he had dug up graves and had sex with female corpses. One contributing early event was that he had been put in a coffin by a cruel uncle. Another was that he had been sexually used by a neighbor lady. The most significant event was his relation, at about age fourteen, with Eunice, a girl in her late teens. She was a breath of fresh air in an otherwise dismal existence. They had intercourse once, but she soon died. He felt both angry at Eunice for leaving him and guilty that he might have caused her death. Later, when he dug up corpses, he hallucinated Eunice calling to him. These necrophilic acts served to deny her death and put life back into her by copulation (Ehrenreich, 1960).

By age twenty-three, another necrophile had partially strangled a score of women. A sickly and fearful child, he watched his drunken father attempt to strangle his stepmother. His own boyish aggressive acts included attacking his stepmother with heavy pots and knives, and cutting his sister's finger off. At fifteen, his stepmother slapped his penis because it was erect. His numerous offenses ranged from passing a bad check, indecent assault, and finally murder. His multiple perversions included voyeurism, self-hanging, and homosexual prostitution. As an attendant in a morgue, he had intercourse with corpses. During the marital act, his wife was required to "play dead"; if she refused, he would strangle her into unconsciousness. His search for a passive partner culminated with his multiple copulations with a woman he had strangled (Smith and Braun, 1978).

In necrophilia, destructive wishes toward the sexual partner and fear of retaliation for those wishes are controlled since the person, being or playing dead, is already destroyed and cannot make reprisals. The partner who is inert during sex gives the necrophile a feeling of power since, as in bondage, the helpless woman cannot attack or abandon him (Calef and Weinshel, 1972). Perhaps his urge to revenge himself against his mother is displaced onto the cadaver, which gives him relief from his feelings of inadequacy and heightens his sense of controlling women (Smith and Braun, 1978).

Sadistic Assault and Lust Murder

Lust murder refers to those cases in which the perpetrator derives sexual arousal or satisfaction in killing another person. In extreme cases, killing completely replaces the sexual act, so that there may be no sexual connection with the victim at all (Hirschfeld, 1938). The lust murderer seeks out or creates situations in which he can totally control a woman, situations which have been rehearsed in fantasy prior to his offense.

There are others who commit sexual assault and murder, but they do not rehearse their crime and their fantasies are of intercourse with willing females. Their assaults are clearly precipitated by environmental factors such as failure in sexual advances, unfaithfulness, or taunts of the partner, or an effort to silence the victim. In a group of sixteen nonpsychotic sexual assaulters, thirteen were of the sadistic type (MacCulloch et al., 1983).

Several types of sex murderers have been identified. In the compulsive type, the strong urge to murder is arousing in itself and may or may not be accompanied by erection and ejaculation. The catathymic crisis type is subject to a highly emotionally charged complex of ideas and the resulting accumulation of tension is released through the attack. The impulsive type is not a true lust murderer, for he does not require aggression for sexual arousal, but kills out of fear, anger, or because of his victim's resistance (Revitch, 1965).

Preceding the urge to murder may be some threat to self-esteem, such as a challenge to masculinity, or reversal in employment situation. Most often, though, there are no identifiable precipitating events. Murders are usually carefully planned with victims preselected or the choice left to chance. In one sample, a majority did not know their victim (Revitch, 1965).

Asphyxiation is more common than gross violence, with mutilation usually taking place after death. In asphyxiating his victim he has control in administering death which affords him a feeling of power. It is the sight of suffering that excites him, and this reaches its peak during the process of killing. Intercourse and orgasm do not always take place, although he may jam objects into the vagina and/or rectum, and may masturbate near the victim. When he does have sex, it is while she is unconscious or dead, suggesting a connection with necrophilia.

When the victim's body is mutilated, the most common parts attacked are breasts, genitilia, and rectum. Biting the breast and neck is common. He may save a piece of clothing or part of the body as a souvenir. After the deed, he feels relaxed and relieved of tension. Remorse and pity are absent and thus he is able to keep calm during interrogation. While regrets may be expressed, they are ungenuine and directed solely toward gaining leniency.

Usually the lust murderer is unmarried and under thirty-five years old, often between seventeen and twenty-five (Revitch, 1965; Brittain, 1970; Stack, 1983). Work record is usually poor. Often he chooses vocations where his urge to dominate can be expressed in nonaggressive ways, although butchering or slaughterhouse work arc not rare (Brittain, 1970).

There is little interest in sports, especially active team sports. Rather, his hobby may be collecting weapons, which he lovingly cleans, fondles, even giving them names. He may be a student of satanism, vampires, and werewolves. His spare time is spent alone, reading, listening to music, or at the movies (often horror films). Frequently he has some private place as a closet, workshop, or shed where he keeps paraphernalia appropriate to his several interests. There may be found feminine clothing, Nazi memorabilia, satan worship objects, and books by de Sade and other sadomasochistic writers (Brittain, 1970).

Any prior criminal offenses are mostly nonaggressive sex crimes, such as stealing women's clothes, peeping, exhibitionism, and obscene phone calls (Brittain, 1970). Thirty of forty-three had prior arrests, the majority being for breaking and entering, usually in search of women's intimate apparel (Revitch, 1965). These early offenses are not obviously connected with the later ones, but are mediated by sadistic fantasies (MacCulloch et al., 1983).

The most common psychiatric diagnosis is schizophrenia or schizoid personality (Revitch, 1965). In two cases of schizophrenic sadistic assaulters, the fantasy pattern was similar to those of nonpsychotics. The sadistic trend seems to exist in parallel with the psychotic process (MacCulloch et al., 1983).

There is some evidence of a link between lust murder and sexual asphyxia. Two men who practiced sexual asphyxia also committed lust murders, and another fantasized about murder (Brittain, 1968).

Sexual urges are weak and he is concerned about his lack of potency. He experiences difficulty in relating to women, and has little interest in dating them (Brittain, 1970). In his great contempt for women he sees the sex act as piercing, destroying, and degrading (Reik, 1941). His driving need is to completely possess a woman. He is preoccupied with thoughts of incest and the impurity of sex (Revitch, 1965).

While his father was authoritarian and punishing, his hostility is reserved for mother, for whom he has strongly ambivalent feelings of love and hate. He may be overtly devoted to her, often seen as a mother's boy. Or he may hate her while still trying to win her approval. This deep hostility stems from her overprotection, seductiveness, treating him as an infant, or outright attempts to feminize him. It is not unlikely that he had seen her naked. Related to hatred of mother may be dislike of, even to the point of torturing, cats, a feminine symbol (Revitch,

1965; Brittain, 1970). This hostility toward mother generalizes to most other women.

From an early age there is notable difficulty in social relations. At puberty this difficulty results in failures of social and sexual contact with partners. This lack of control over events in life is compensated for in fantasies (MacCulloch et al., 1983).

Sometime during puberty there begins an evolution of sadistic fantasies that are associated with presadistic acts. There is a correspondance between fantasy and offense, as illustrated in the development of fantasies in a twenty-five-year-old lust murderer presented in Table 10.1.

Almost all had regular heterosexual fantasies after puberty, but then began deviant fantasies featuring transvestism, fetishism, and exhibitionism. All shifted to sadistic content one to seven years after beginning masturbation. Mean age of shift was sixteen, with a range of from thirteen to twenty. After the shift there was an increase in frequency of masturbation.

Often, as in the case above, fantasized degree of control over the female increased and they began to try out nonassaultive portions of their fantasies, such as stealing purses or following girls. These tryouts were needed to maintain potency of fantasies and usually began within a year of onset of sadistic fantasy. Most engaged in tryouts once or twice a week.

Since in a majority there was a low level of sexual experiences and social contacts with girls, fantasies and tryouts were their only source of sexual arousal. A minority did have sexual experiences, but still used their fantasies in masturbation and to arouse themselves with their partners.

Outwardly prudish, the lust murderer condemns profanity, sexual jokes, and references. He neither drinks nor smokes. Religion is not alien to him, and he may be a regular, scripture quoting churchgoer (Brittain, 1970). An eighteen-year-old lust murderer was described as "a nice quiet kid . . . too deeply religious to go out with girls" (Revitch, 1965, p. 647).

He is a quiet person, lacking self-confidence, withdrawn from others whom he views as dangerous. In appearance he is studious, intelligent, neat, and clean. Fantasy life is rich, consisting of sadistic scenes and atrocities. Perhaps his excessive indulgence in sadistic fantasy has made him cold, cynical, and

TABLE 10.1
Evolution of Sadistic Fantasies and Behaviors
in a Twenty-Five-Year-Old Man

Age	Fantasy	Behavior
14	Does not have to approach girls as they take initiative	
15	Stealing girl's purse so he could offer to pay her way	Erections accompany fantasy
16	Kidnapping girls (using hypnosis, anesthesia, or blow on head). Takes them to hideaway for torture.	Snatching girls' purses
	"The climax of the fantasy would be when I caused the maximum amount of fear and disgust and I told her I would kill her or describe what I was going to do, or stabbing them" (p. 23).	Following the girls and observing their anxiety
25	"E," a girl well known to him is the victim in his fantasy; "I sat at home debating with myself should I or shouldn't I act out my fantasy" (p. 23).	Goes to "E" 's house. As she makes coffee he bashes her head with hammer and poker, then stabs her.

Source: M. J. MacCulloch, P. R. Snowdon, P. J. W. Wood, & H. E. Mills (1983), On the genesis of sadistic behavior: The sadistic fantasy syndrome. *British Journal of Psychiatry*, 143:20–29.

indifferent to the cruelty he inflicts on others. Concern is for himself alone, with others existing only to gratify or frustrate his wishes (Brittain, 1970).

His overrefinement, politeness, and excessive modesty are often interpreted as effeminacy by his fellows, who may suspect him of homosexuality (Brittain, 1970). In Reich's (1949) characterology he is phallic–aggressive, warding off passive–homosexual urges through the opposite, aggression.

Knowing that he is different from others, he feels isolated

and inferior, except in relation to his murders where he is superior and his victim is made to feel inferior. Beneath his mask of retiring timidity is heavy hostility that cannot be expressed except through lustful murders (Brittain, 1970; Stack, 1983).

THE PERSON

Current Status

From over a half to three-fourths of males became aware of their sadomasochistic tendencies before they were nineteen years old. Females and homosexual males took longer to recognize their tendencies (Spengler, 1977; Breslow, Evans, and Langley, 1985).

For two-thirds of the males, first exposure to sadomasochism came naturally, that is, without any external promptings from pornography or another person (Breslow et al., 1985). Sometimes the male can recall a childhood incident that provoked an association between punishment and undefinable excitement.

Most females do not report early sadistic fantasies and do not discover the pleasures of domination on their own. Rather, they were drawn into the scene by men who wanted to be sexually dominated and only then did they find the role exciting (Scott, 1983).

For S&M club members, median age of males is in middle to late thirties. Females tend to be in their late twenties to early thirties. About half of the males and a third of the females are college graduates. About a half of males and females are married (Spengler, 1977; Herron et al., 1983; Breslow et al., 1985).

Biological Basis

The only indication of an organic factor in sadism is some evidence of right temporal lobe abnormalities in a group of adistic rapists (Langevin, Bain, Ben-Aron, Coulthard, Day, Handy, Heasman, Huncker, Purins, Roper, Russon, Webster, and Wartzman, 1985).

Early Life

The infant's survival is dependent on being loved. He, in turn, loves those who bring satisfaction and hates those who cause frustration. Gratifier and frustrater are usually the same person—mother. Where hate is stronger than love, there is a tendency for sadism (Sadger, 1926).

The future sadomasochist is reared in a climate of parental hostility, rejection, and often some narcissism. Parental hostility takes the form of humiliating the child for his attempts at separation and autonomy. Mother's hostile and rejecting attitude does not usually result in physical abuse, but in psychological mistreatment conveyed by hateful looks and other signs of displeasure. She cannot abandon her child; rather she clings to him for she needs him as an object for her anger. She may even overprotect him to keep him bound to her.

If mother is also narcissistic, she sees him as an extension of herself and as an instrument for the satisfaction of her needs. Because her needs are paramount, she may reverse roles with her child, expecting him to fulfill her need to be loved. This role reversal is found also in child-abusing mothers. She conveys to the child the message, "I attend to you only when you force me to."

Thus is erected the sadomasochistic substratum where sadism and masochism are at opposite poles. In the face of the threatening parent, the child may either identify with her power or assume a submissive role. Which of these options is taken depends to a great extent on the nature of the child, perhaps the biological force. At the sadistic pole, the child's efforts to buy love are frustrated, so he gives up hope of being loved for his own sake. His concept of being loved becomes degraded into being paid attention to, being recognized. He is angered by his mistreatment and attempts to punish mother for not being loving, and gains attention from her through his angry behavior. His motto becomes "Love through Power." Later in life he attempts to repair his shame and humiliation by role-reversal where he plays the part of mother (dominant) and his partner (submissive) is assigned the part of the child he once was (Schad-Somers, 1982).

This hate for mother, which generalizes to other women, is expressed by one of de Sade's characters: " 'I abhorred her. As soon as I was in a position to do so, I dispatched her into the next world; may she roast there' " (de Sade, 1785, p. 293).

Sexuality

Male respondents to a questionnaire in an S&M publication were predominantly heterosexual, whereas females were bisexual (Breslow et al., 1985). Some female dominants view sexual intercourse as a penetration–recipient situation and therefore refuse to allow intercourse feeling it undermines their superiority. Such women prefer to find release in cunnilingus (Scott, 1983). They have, in common with female homosexuals, a distaste for men and an aversion for coitus, but they assume this attitude, not out of homosexuality, but because they equate dominance and power with masculinity (Hirschfeld, 1938).

Krafft-Ebing (1902) found that sexual hyperesthesia, easily aroused sexual excitement, was always present in sadism. Karpman (1954), however, found that the sadist is undersexed. Actually, there may be two types: one has weak potency and requires the venting of his aggression to stimulate him; the other type possesses strong sexuality, and when sexually aroused is overwhelmed by aggressivity (Chesser, 1971).

The sadist has negative feelings toward his own sexual impulses, is disgusted and repelled by them. When he does become sexually excited, he feels threatened. Rather than owning these feelings, he blames the other person for his excitement: "She made me feel this way." He hates and seeks to punish the woman for what she has done to him, thereby convincing himself that sexuality is bad, and that he is different from the sexually stimulating person (Eulenberg, 1911; Kelly, 1955; Bieber, 1966).

There is a fusion of sexual desire and anger, and the sadist substitutes expressions of anger for the usual expression of love and sex. The experience of anger merges with sexual excitement and augments it. There are several steps leading to this fusion of sex and anger. First, sex is identified as something foul and forbidden. Second, there is the belief that when engaging in sexual activities, the dominant is committing an offense against his partner. Finally, there is the equation of sex and violence (Partridge, 1960).

Several experimental studies have verified this fusion of anger and sexuality. In one, males were aroused to anger and then asked to make up a story to picture stimuli. When compared to nonaroused groups, angry participants produced more aggressive and sexual imagery (Barclay and Haber, 1965). In other studies, angered males who were also sexually aroused increased their expressions of aggression (Sapolsky, 1984). Other emotions confused with sexual stimulation and gratification are rage, anxiety, relief, vengence, ecstasy, and a sense of triumph (Bieber, 1966).

Related to this fusion of sex with anger is the principle of pleasure through comparison. The principle states that the degree of one's pleasure is not measured in relation to oneself, but in contrast to the situation of others. One of de Sade's libertines explains:

> There is one essential thing lacking to our happiness. It is the pleasure of comparison, a pleasure which can only be born of the sight of wreched persons, and here one sees none at all. It is from the sight of him who does not in the least enjoy what I enjoy, and who suffers, that comes the charm of being able to say to myself "I am therefore happier than he" [de Sade, 1785, p. 362].

Personality

Sense of Isolation

His years with a mother who subjected him to clinging rejection leaves the sadist with a sense of distrust of others and feelings of isolation.

> "The entire world is really my enemy. I am completely alone. I have to be on the alert all the time, because everybody tries to attack me. Even as a child I was terribly lonely and I built myself a real armored retreat. There is an isolating sheath around me. I cannot penetrate into anything. . . . I want to break down the walls, because they divide and isolate" [Boss, 1949, p. 86].

Yet, still he wants to reach out, to communicate with others, to have others respond to him, and his feelings of isolation only increase these desires to relate (Braun, 1967). He will extract this recognition by whatever means necessary. The will of others must be broken, so that they will surely become aware of his existence. When the submissive is under his control, he feels:

"Erotic pleasure which arises when I have opened up a woman and rendered her gentle and non-resistant. Then the melting water of her tears indicates that the ice is broken and that the time has come when my maleness can communicate with her innermost female being. We can fuse together and a common current of electricity unites our bodies" [Boss, 1949, p. 95].

Disappointment in his parents and loss of loved ones generalizes to distrust and hatred of mankind. Others are seen as enemies, as inferiors. This is a defensive paranoid mechanism whereby his partner represents a variety of threats and must, therefore, be dominated or destroyed (Bieber, 1966). This attitude toward others prevents his relating to them through affection. As he sees it, to seek affection from others would signify weakness and dependence, leaving himself open to exploitation (Avery, 1977).

Interpersonal Relations

For most male sadists, everyday behavior is at variance with their sexual predilections. The libertines in de Sade's stories have been called cowards and weaklings (de Beauvoir, 1966; Braun, 1967; Carter, 1979). In describing one of his debauchees, de Sade (1785) says that, "as soon as Blangis discovered he could no longer use his treachery or his deceit to make away with his enemy, he would become timid and cowardly, and the mere thought of even the mildest combat . . . would have sent him fleeing to the ends of the earth" (p. 202).

Such timid behavior depicts the nonsexual side of the sadist's nature. In his everyday dealings with others, he is not a cruel, brutal individual. Instead, he is a good-natured, solid, pious weakling (Hirschfeld, 1940; Alexander, 1956); a weakling who overcompensates through sadistic fantasies (Karpman, 1934). Invoking the "Law of the Balance of Opposites," Bloch

(1908) asserts that the sadist seeks to exert power and control over others in order to overcome his own feelings of inferiority, weakness, and powerlessness.

In the male, sadism is usually confined to the sexual sphere, but female sadism is often totalitarian, the dominant theme in all areas of her life, permeating her entire existence. Cold, calculated cruelty is said to be more common in females than in male sadists (Eulenberg, 1911; Hirschfeld, 1938; Braun, 1967).

Feeling that she has been deprived of power by men, she seeks revenge against the tyrants by dominating them. Her sadism stems from feeling stifled in her attempts at self-expression. She wants to be independent of men and is sexually frustrated by and embittered toward them. These feelings not only fuel her sadism, but also her bisexual preference. De Sade's (1797) female sadist, Clairwil, declares, "only men rouse me to serious cruelties; I adore revenging my sex for the horrors men subject us to when those brutes have the upper hand" (pp. 294–295).

However, some sexually dominant females are "balancers" in that they are soft, feminine, passive, and unassertive in nonsexual relations. Their dominant role in sexual relations affords them compensation in a sense of power, authority, and control over males (Scott, 1983).

In their relations with others, both male and female sadists view themselves and others as either being dominant and powerful or submissive and suffering. Basically, they see themselves as sufferers. According to their primitive either/or logic, one side is avoided only if the other side is expressed. The mask of domination worn in sexual encounters hides their inner submissiveness.

Controlling and humiliating others in fantasy and actual scenes serves a dual purpose. First, by dominating others, self-as-sufferer is disowned (Avery, 1977). Second, by identifying with his submissive, he can experience the emotions of the other. In minor sadism, the dominant finds satisfaction only if the submissive experiences pleasure. This is possible because he assumes, by naive projection, that his submissive must be experiencing pleasure from his abuse, because he himself would feel pleasure were he to be abused (Ellis, 1913). One of Ellis's female correspondents reports, "I believe that when a person takes pleasure in inflicting pain, he or she imagines himself or herself in the victim's place" (p. 160).

Essentially, therefore, sadists are also masochists. But their masochism is submerged because of fear of losing self-control and self-respect. A man who enjoys lashing and torturing women, occasionally allows women to beat, chain, and choke him:

> "Then the pleasure was almost greater than when I lashed them myself. But it is rather dangerous to let myself be beaten. It turns into something fathomless; I might give myself away and get lost. My deportment leaves me, I am like a small boy who has no responsibilities. However, when I do the beating, I retain control over everything. When the women beat me, I am afraid that they won't let me go any more and I won't have the strength to go away by myself. I shudder when I think of this. As far as thrashing is concerned, a woman is like a sorceress who I can only keep in check by being the active partner" [Boss, 1949, p. 86].

The sadist craves contact with others. His overriding interpersonal construct is that to be loved requires that either he submit to the power of another or that he extract a degraded form of love from another through power. He may switch from one pole of this construct to another. About two-thirds of male and female sadomasochists are always or usually either dominant or submissive, while a third are versatile (Breslow et al., 1985).

Many dominant women initially assumed the submissive role but found this oppressive and switched to the dominant role (Scott, 1983). The man, too, often begins at the submission end and graduates to domination. As a child, Daniel fantasized that he was cornered by a group of girls who urinated on him. His fantasy life evolved into women whipping him and forcing him to perform oral sex. So far, the prediction would be that Daniel is to become a masochist.

Seeking to put his fantasies into action, he began an extramarital affair with a woman who seemed dominant and somewhat masculine. However, she could not play the sadistic role, so Daniel set about teaching her by sexual domination. To their surprise, they both enjoyed their respective roles. Daniel had switched from submissive to dominant. Breaking off this affair, he introduced his wife to the submissive role and he played the dominant (Kamel and Weinberg, 1983).

Femininity

Because of this supposed connection of passivity and weakness with femininity, sadists have been described as feminine. Ellis (1913) has found that sadism in males is associated with feminine personality traits such as modesty and timidity. He cites Montaigne as having observed that cruelty is often found in individuals who also display a feminine softness. One of Ellis's female correspondents wrote that "the men I have known most given to inflicting pain are all particularly tender hearted when their passions are not in question" (p. 160). The man who is most scornful, arrogant, and aggressive toward women is the man who is uncertain of his masculinity (de Beauvoir, 1952). As a protest against his own femininity and passivity, he displays all kinds of aggressiveness (Schilder, 1936).

Male dominants, as well as submissives, scored high on a femininity scale, but dominants scored more masculine than did submissives (Herron et al., 1983). De Sade's male characters not only display a feminine but also a homosexual component. Scenes of sodomy abound and disgust over women's fronts is expressed. There is some evidence to support an unmasculine, though not necessarily a homosexual, role in sadism. Sadistic rapists are those who torture their victims and are aroused by their terror. Their masculinity and femininity scores were more similar to each other than were those of nonviolent sex offenders (Langevin, Bain, et al., 1985). It appears that femininity in heterosexual males is associated with violence and sexual aggression.

Conception of Women

Insight into the Sadean conception of women can be gained from a study of de Sade's portrayal of two of his characters in the companion novels *Justine* (1791) and *Juliette* (1797) (Carter, 1979). The two are sisters, but lead vastly different lives. Justine, the madonna, is given to virtue and suffers, while Juliette, the harlot, practices vice and triumphs. The two represent opposite poles of submission and dominance.

Justine is mistreated at every turn. There is no virtue in her suffering, for it brings even greater misfortune to herself and to those she aids. After she is raped, she thinks herself virtuous because she felt no pleasure. It is not rape that she fears, but seduction. She sees her life as dominated by chance events. When confronted by difficulty, she assumes the role of the prey and flees. Emotionally she is childlike in her candor and trust. While she feels that her virtue and beauty demand respect, she is ignorant of her own seductiveness.

Her sister Juliette's ruling tenet is that comfort and pleasure for one person demands misery from another. Faced with this choice, she opts for tyranny rather than slavery. She is rational and in control of herself, but is incapable of introspection. Sexual pleasure is not shared with a partner; the only reciprocity is role exchange.

11 MASOCHISM

INTRODUCTION

Early writers saw the root of the masochistic relationship in the female playing the hunted animal and the male playing the pursuer, even as both were seeking the same goal of sexual union. Ovid's contention that "a little force is pleasing to a woman" was cited to support the idea that there is a tendency in women to enjoy experiencing pain and in men of displaying force (Ellis, 1913).

Krafft-Ebing (1902) identified two sources of masochism that are in the normal range of sexual relations. The first is entirely physiological. When one is in a state of sexual excitement, any stimulus proceeding from the sexual partner is experienced as pleasing. So, scratches, light blows, and bites are perceived as caresses. In the words of Cleopatra, "the stroke of death is as a lover's pinch, which hurts, and is desired."

The second source of masochism begins as a dependence on the sexual partner. Sacher-Masoch (1870) explains: "Woman's power lies in man's passion. He has only one choice: to be the tyrant over or the slave of woman. As soon as he gives in, his neck is under the yoke, and the lash will soon fall upon him" (p. 22).

This dependence is called "sexual thralldom." Early writers

347

on masochism thought that an immoderate sex drive and a weak character allow the man to be dominated by his partner. The submissive role generalizes to other aspects of the relationship as in "henpecked" and "pussy whipped" men. Masochism may arise from sexual thralldom in that he who is tyrannized may in turn love to be tyrannized. This is based on a simple association of ideas. When lustful thoughts are continually associated with being dominated, lustful thoughts become attached to being dominated (Eulenberg, 1911).

The boundary from normal to pathological is crossed when masochistic acts either become a necessary precondition for sexual connection or when they become an end in themselves. The transition area ranges from being capable of normal relations to total dependence on masochistic thoughts, from the use of masochistic thoughts or acts as preliminary to sexual intercourse to gratification from these acts themselves.

Attitudes Toward Masochism

Some contemporary writers condone mild sadomasochistic (S&M) practices between consenting adults. These apologists ask, what if there is some dominance–submission and pleasure–pain in a relationship between consenting adults? We may feel that such behaviors are repugnant, but should we not respect the individual's right to engage in them? (Chesser, 1971).

While disavowing the argument that sadomasochism is a simplistic cure-all for the world's ills, Green and Green (1974) claim many benefits of such play. Basically, such games allow hidden, destructive motives to be drained off harmlessly. Further, masochism helps women to find new political freedoms; teaches people to empathize with the pain and suffering of the universe; and it may even cure impotency. A light S&M scene has been described as "joyful, fulfilling experience for both partners" (Scott, 1983, p. 201).

The Subculture

Many with masochistic longings find fulfillment in their own private fantasy worlds. Others seek to establish contacts in the

S&M subculture, where players have roles and role relations as they enact their scenes. Contact magazines are the most frequently used means of entry (Spengler, 1977; Breslow, Evans, and Langley, 1985).

For the heterosexual male, professional dominatrixes are available, either working on their own or in commercial houses. Typical is Mistress Heather who, "with spikes and leather will bring you to your knees with bodyworship, showers, bondage! Slaves, TV's and naughty boys call me."

Outcall services for men who like to play submissive are not new. An advertisement circulated in the late 1800s reads: "Single gentlemen, who are fond of representing school-boys, waited on by mistress and maid at any hour, at their own houses, there the delightful divertissement of being taken out of bed, horsed and whipt, for not going to school, will be played to admiration" (Fraxi, 1877, p. 259).

Also available are noncommercial clubs in major United States cities. One boasts of over 500 members. Some are specialized, such as a lesbian oriented S&M support group, dominant female/submissive male, dominant male/submissive female, and a homosexual men's S&M social and educational group. The first such club opened in 1971 in New York City and was called the Masochist Liberation Front, renamed Eulenspiegel Society, with several hundred members. In San Francisco, there is the Society of Janus and the Service of Mankind Church. These groups sponsor parties, workshops in piercing, bondage, and displays of S&M equipment (Scott, 1983).

Personal, noncommercial contacts for homosexuals are easier than for heterosexuals. In some areas there are "Leathersex" bars and bath houses. Contacts are made in bars, while bathhouses provide both contacts and small rooms where participants can engage in an S&M performance (Kamel, 1983b).

It is said that while sadism is prevalent in the U.S.S.R., masochism is very rare (Stern, 1979). In other Western countries, there appears to be a preponderance of masochists over sadists. At dominant–submissive club meetings men outnumber women by three to one (Scott, 1983). Submissive male heterosexual members of the Eulenspiegel Society outnumber dominant females, and there are fewer submissive females than dominant males (Herron, Herron, and Schultz, 1983). Of advertisers in contact magazines, 65 percent of the males are submissive, whereas only 17 percent of the females are submissive and these women seek other women or couples as partners (Weinberg, 1978). Male devotees of golden showers outnumber women by twenty to one (Janus, Bess, and Saltus, 1977). A possible explanation of the prevalence of men is our cultural taboo on causing harm to another, especially a female (Gebhard, 1969).

Prevalence

From the number of advertisements placed by female dominants, it is estimated that each year as many as 150,000 men visit such women. This figure does not include those who engage in noncommercial dominant–submissive sessions (Scott, 1983). For those who are active, the median number of S&M experiences is five with about five partners per year. Homosexuals have more contacts and fewer partners than heterosexuals (Spengler, 1977).

Masochistic fantasies are rather prevalent. Forty-six percent of males report having sexual fantasies of being kidnapped and raped by a woman. And 30 percent of females have fantasies of being a man's slave (Crepoult and Couture, 1980; Arndt, Foehl, and Good, 1985).

About 3 percent of men and almost 5 percent of women claim they have obtained sexual pleasure from receiving pain (Hunt, 1974). Twenty-six percent of both sexes report definite and/or frequent erotic response to being bitten during heavy petting or coitus (Kinsey, Pomeroy, Martin, and Gebhard, 1953). Almost 20 percent of pornographic magazines covers feature bondage, discipline, and spanking scenes (Dietz and Evans, 1982).

Sexual Masochism in Women

According to early writers it is within the normal range of behavior for women to subordinate themselves to men. This stems from their passive role in procreation and from long-standing social conditions. Thus, the foundation of female masochism was regarded as resting on a natural, biological base—a distortion of the "submissive impulse" (Hirschfeld, 1938). While pathological desires to be subjugated by men are not uncommon, these impulses are inhibited by women's modesty and by custom. Another reason given for the rarity of sexual masochism in women is that they have more command over their sexual impulses (Bloch, 1908). Krafft-Ebing (1902) knew of only two established cases of pathological masochism in women. It is said that in the woman, masochism permeates more of her personality, but is low key, lacking the distinctiveness, lustful intensity, and bizarre elements seen in the man (Ellis, 1913; Reik, 1941)—usually, she only dreams of surrendering herself, being kidnapped, or raped. However, this early view of female masochism may be a "chauvinistic masculine distortion." In fact, masochism in women may be as prevalent and as intense as it is in men (Asch, 1988).

For females as well as males, the seeds of masochistic fantasy are sown in the preoedipal period when mother is the most significant figure in the child's life. This may explain why so many female submissives seek other females as partners. Female heterosexual submissives must have given up mother and taken father as their love object. For male heterosexuals, females play the dominant role as did their mothers.

There may be cultural differences in the ratio of male to female masochists. While in the United States the female dominant/male submissive pattern is preferred, in Great Britain it is the male dominant/female submissive pattern that predominates. In paternal Britain it is the male who chastises the young, while in maternal America, it is the mother who wields the rod over her children (Green and Green, 1974).

DEFINITION

Differing Conceptions

The word *masochism* was coined by Krafft-Ebing after the novelist Leopold von Sacher-Masoch, whose stories depict males dominated by strong-willed females who use insults, bondage, and whips to humiliate them.

Krafft-Ebing's (1902) definition, offered many years ago, still captures the essence of masochism.

> By masochism I understand a peculiar perversion of the psychical vita sexualis in which the individual affected, in sexual feeling and thought, is controlled by the idea of being completely and unconditionally subject to the will of a person of the opposite sex; of being treated by this person as by a master, humiliated and abused. This idea is colored by lustful feeling; the masochist lives in fancies, in which he creates situations of this kind and often attempts to realize them [p. 127].

Note that this definition emphasizes the ideas of submission and humiliation, not pain, and that fantasy is given a prominent role, whether or not it is acted out. The definition rules out homosexual masochism, an assertion not born out by more recent studies.

There are three cardinal points in Krafft-Ebing's conception of masochism. First, the desire to be subjugated is a response to dependency on women and an effort to maintain a relationship with them. Second, this idea of being tyrannized becomes sexualized by repeated association with the loved one. And, third, masochism occurs in those with intensified lust. This hypersexuality is now seen as a combination of sexual inhibition and attempts to overcome it in esoteric ways (Bieber, 1966).

According to Berliner (1942) it is unfortunate that, disregarding Krafft-Ebing's observations, psychoanalytic definitions often stress the importance of pain and cruelty. For instance, "the seeking of unpleasure, by which is meant physical or mental pain, discomfort or wretchedness for the sake of sexual pleasure" (Brenner, 1959, p. 197); and a "tendency to seek physical or mental suffering in order to achieve . . . sexual gratification in the widest sense" (Loewenstein, 1957).

Freud's initial attempts to explain masochism were in terms of misdirected instincts. His first theory was that masochism was sadism turned inward against the person himself (1905). Later (1919) he incorporated elements of early homosexuality, oedipal feelings, and guilt. In his paper "Beyond the Pleasure

Principle" (1920), in which he discussed his ideas regarding the death instinct, he suggests that masochism, rather than sadism, is primary and that sadism is derived from it as masochism turned outward. Destructive impulses that cannot be expended on the environment are redirected inward as secondary masochism augmenting the primary.

Some psychoanalysts, while not denying the role of instincts, oedipal conflicts, castration anxiety, and guilt, prefer to view masochism as a defense, an adaptive maneuver. They see it as a disturbance in relationships with others, that is, being sexually stimulated and loving a person who ill-treats them (Berliner, 1958).

To meet DSM-III-R standards for a diagnosis of masochism, the individual must have "intense sexual urges and sexually arousing fantasies involving the act (real, not simulated) of being humiliated, beaten, or otherwise made to suffer" (American Psychiatric Association, 1987, p. 287). According to this definition, masochistic fantasies alone that do not cause discomfort do not qualify the person as masochistic. Kahn (1969) agrees that fantasies, when not put into practice, do not constitute perversion.

Varieties

Freud (1924) identified three forms of masochism: erotogenic, feminine (refers not to the female, but the male who assumes feminine passivity), and moral. Erotogenic masochism is the foundation of the other two; it is the biological basis of the merging of pain and pleasure; that is, sexual arousal through pain.

Erotogenic masochism passes through the several psychosexual stages and is modified thereby. In the oral stage it becomes the fear of being beaten by the father; in the anal, it becomes the desire to be beaten by the father, which accounts for the prevalence of the use of the buttocks in masochistic fantasies; during the oedipal period, castration anxiety enters the picture; and in the phallic stage, it takes the form of feminine masochism—assumption of the passive role.

Males with sexual or feminine masochism engage in sexually

arousing fantasies of being whipped, bound, mistreated, de-graded, and forced to obey a dominant female. These fantasies reflect the desire to be treated as a helpless, naughty child whose guilt over some unspecified transgression must be expiated.

The moral or social masochist walks through life pulling a black cloud over his head. He seems bent on achieving mis-fortune and complains loudly against his back luck. It is soon obvious to others that he makes the wrong decisions, marries the wrong woman, brings on one failure after another, seem-ingly deliberately choosing those courses that lead to suffering. Freud explains that the connection of the death instinct with libido is loosened and desexualized suffering in and of itself is sought. The moral masochist is constantly trying to assuage guilt heaped upon him by his sadistic conscience.

Some hold that all sexual masochists are also moral ma-sochists (Berliner, 1958). However, there seems to be an inverse relationship between moral and sexual masochism, one exclud-ing the other, so that the sexual masochist is free to live an apparently normal life. It is as if his self-punitive tendencies are limited to sexual expression (Alexander, 1956; Asch, 1988).

Over the years, the sexual connotations of masochism have been deemphasized and the term is used in a loose and variable way to refer to any self-inflicted suffering or submission; some-times the term is used synonymously with passivity (Berliner, 1958; Maleson, 1984; Grossman, 1986). For instance, eight-year-old Kathy was labeled masochistic because she pulled out her hair, deprived herself of TV as punishment for aggressive wishes toward her mother, and provoked her parents to punish her (Bernstein, 1976). According to Arlow (Panel, 1956), some authors use this broad definition without informing the reader, while others limit its use to paraphilia. Such confusion clouds the entire topic of masochism.

One of the few research studies concerning masochism addresses the question of types, none of which are obviously sexual masochists. Psychiatrists answered questions regarding suffering and mistreatment for patients they considered to be masochistic. Three patterns of masochism were identified. Vic-tims maintained a close relation to someone who was mistreating them. They were engaging and personable people who were demonstrative about their suffering and concerned about their own aggressive impulses. Doers were active, self-sacrificing, suspicious, denying any enjoyment, but felt that suffering is rewarded. Somatizers were a small group who voiced physical complaints (Shore, Clifton, Zelin, and Myerson, 1971).

Relation to Sadism

Masochism and sadism are seen as complementary by many authors. This relation is supported by findings that those who entertain masochistic fantasies also engage in sadistic fantasies (Arndt et al., 1985). Those who see sadism and masochism as a blending of aggressive and erotic drives explain masochism as a mix in which the erotic predominates (Panel, 1956). However, Panken (1973) does not find the two occurring in the same persons and claims that the dynamics of the two are different.

In a West German sample of sadomasochists, 32 percent were exclusively or mainly dominant; 38 percent were exclusively or mainly submissive; and 29 percent were versatile in that they alternated between dominant and submissive roles (Spengler, 1977). Considering the difficulty in finding partners, much of this versatility may be born of necessity (Gebhard, 1969).

THE ACT

Fantasy

Sacher-Masoch (1870) declared that, "with me everything has its roots in the imagination, and thence it receives its nourishment" (p. 75). While fantasy has a role in other deviations, it is essential in masochism. It seems that when the mode is passive, as in masochism and exhibitionism (to be looked at), fantasy is necessary. In sadism and voyeurism, fantasy may or may not be present. Like a ritual, the masochistic fantasy remains stable over many years, although details may be altered to keep it exciting. Thus, "the birthplace of masochism is phantasy" (Reik, 1941, p. 186).

Pain and Fear

For Freud (1905) the "main root" of masochism lies in the fact that muted painful feelings, including physical pain and fear, promote sexual excitement. It is not pain itself that is enjoyed, but the increase in sexual arousal (Freud, 1915). This is the erotogenic masochism that was Monsieur M.'s primary source of pleasure—"On the whole it is the pain which releases the ejaculation" (M'Uzan, 1973, p. 459). Monsieur M. was a sixty-five-year-old successful electronics engineer. Medical examination revealed that his body was covered with tattoos, such as, "My body loves to be hit, hit me hard." His right breast had been burned with a red hot iron. Molten lead had turned his navel into a crater. Skin had been peeled from his back and he had been suspended by hooks while being penetrated by a man. He had sawed off his little toe and smoothed the projecting bone with a rasp. Needles had been inserted into his chest and testicles; his penis had been injected with blue ink, a steel ring permanently placed in the head, and a magnetized needle introduced into the penile shaft, which could attract a compass needle (M'Uzan, 1973).

Hunger for stimulation is strong (Stekel, 1929a). If the strokes begin lightly and build in force as sexual arousal increases, the recipient may not experience great pain, but only augmented sexual stimulation. At the height of sexual arousal, the sense of pain is greatly diminished so that blows, bites, and scratches may not be sensed as painful (Kinsey et al., 1953).

While pain in an erotic context may be arousing, masochists do not enjoy pain and suffering for their own sake (Gebhard, 1969; Smirnoff, 1969). A stubbed toe is as painful and nonsexual to them as to anyone else. So, he is not seeking pain, but something connected with it (Reik, 1941). In fact, he fears pain and it is this fear that excites him (Stekel, 1929a). Pain not only produces emotional arousal, it is also provides atonement for guilt at desiring mother and bettering father (Janus et al., 1977).

Although fear is said to inhibit sexual excitation, there are reports of fear resulting in voluptuous feelings and ejaculation. Men sexually molested by women report levels of fright and panic, yet all had erections and a majority ejaculated (Sarrel and Masters, 1982).

The physiological component of any emotion such as fright, anxiety, and anger are arousing and can augment sexual arousal (Ellis, 1913; Kinsey, Pomeroy, and Martin, 1948; Bieber, 1966). An experienced female dominant explains that fear administered by a trusted person is erotic, since the physiological responses of fear and erotic arousal are similar—increase in respiration and heart rate. But, she notes, that without trust in the dominant, fear is fear and is definitely unpleasant (Scott, 1983). Monsieur M. explains:

> At the beginning, it hurt in the places where the torture was being applied: but then the erection comes. It continues, goes further, the pleasure begins to emerge. . . . The ejaculation follows at the moment when the pain is the strongest. . . . After ejaculation I suffered just like anyone else would have [M'Uzan, 1973, p. 459].

As the continually sated individual does not enjoy his meal, so perhaps pleasure must be alternated with pain to truly appreciate pleasure. The poet Heine expresses this idea.

> Madame Venus, beautiful lady,
> Of sweet wine and kisses
> I am sick unto death—
> I yearn for a taste of bitterness.

Solomon and Corbit (1974) have proposed an opponent-process theory to account for the temporal dynamics of emotion. The basic assumption is that an emotional state A is opposed in the central nervous system by state B which reduces the intensity of state A and promotes an opposite emotional state. This sequence, A then B, is automatic, which denies the necessity of any learned association between pain and consequent pleasure. The sequence is self-reinforcing and self-perpetuating.

Let us apply this theory to the first experience of the painful stimulation of being whipped. As aversive stimulation is applied, state A increases, but only to a point where state B, the opposite of A, is triggered and attenuates state A. On the first experience, B is only strong enough to lessen A, but not strong enough to be felt as pleasant stimulation. This may explain why the first masochistic experience is often said to be a disappointment.

Dynamics change after repeated sequences of A and B. With repeated induction of A, B is strengthened, that is, it will set in earlier, rise to a higher peak, and last longer. By setting in earlier, B mutes the painful experience of A; the pleasantness of B increases, and lasts longer. Thus, after several whippings, A becomes not one of pain, but tense, eager expectation of B, experienced as sexual arousal. It may be that state B is produced by endorphins, opiatelike substances produced in the brain in response to pain. These substances relieve pain and produce euphoria.

There is evidence that the magnitude of B is related to the strength of A. If this is so, then the masochist needs to increase the aversive nature of A to gain an even more pleasurable state B. Monsieur M. required ever increasing and prolonged sessions of pain (M'Uzan, 1973). Prolonged exercise of the opponent-process system eventually results in pronounced physiological stress with consequent exhaustion and debilitation.

In addition to a cerebral opponent process, there is a mechanical connection between gluteal stimulation and ejaculation because contraction of the anus occurs both in orgasm and as a result of spanking. Perhaps anal and gluteal muscle contractions produce orgasm by stimulating the perineal area and increasing blood flow to the genital structures (Kinsey et al., 1953; Masters and Johnson, 1966; Gibson, 1978).

The mechanical explanations so far considered are adequate in accounting for only a segment of masochistic phenomena. They focus primarily on physical pain and its admixture with sexual arousal. We have seen, however, that pain is not the crucial factor in masochism; it is rather humiliation and abasement. Many children have been spanked while across their mothers' knees without becoming adult heterosexual masochists, and many a British schoolboy has repeatedly felt the sting of the birch rod at the hands of the schoolmaster without resorting to homosexual masochistic practices as an adult. Mechanical theories fail to define the kind of person who is likely to develop into a masochist, and they do not account for the exciting role of masochistic fantasies where no actual pain is induced.

Domination and Humiliation

The essential characteristic of masochism is the desire to be submissive to another, to be humiliated and abased. Humiliation is a type of punishment where the person is made to feel ridiculous and demeaned both to himself and others (Eidelberg, 1959). The importance of submission and the role of fantasy is illustrated by the words of Rousseau (1778). "To fall at the feet of an imperious mistress, obey her mandates, or implore pardon, were for me the most exquisite enjoyments, and the more my blood was inflamed by the efforts of a lively imagination the more I acquired the appearance of a whining lover" (p. 13).

The desire to be dominated and degraded is strong and primary, with the manner in which this desire is fulfilled of secondary concern. There are several commonly used ways to achieve feelings of abasement. First is a lowering of status called "servilism" or "pageism" where a man desires to be treated as a female maid. The second manner in which abasement takes place is to be treated as a naughty child or even a baby—infantilism. Even more abasing is being treated as an animal, to be ridden as a horse or leashed like a dog in "kennel discipline" (Hirschfeld, 1938). The last form of abasement is to be used as a thing, as an ottoman or a toilet.

Masochistic behavior is not a violation of Freud's pleasure principle for it is not pleasure in pain, suffering, or humiliation. These feelings are prerequisites for pleasure. A clue to this behavior is found in the important feature of suspense, the temporary cessation, the repeated postponements of progress toward sexual gratification (Reik, 1941).

These suspensions are the result of a desire for the ultimate pleasure and a fear of that pleasure. Masochistic scenes have all the features of an approach–avoidance conflict, wherein the goal of sexual gratification is both sought and arouses anxiety. Conflict is maximal when the intensity of anxiety equals that of sexual arousal. At this point approach is halted, the action is suspended. The masochist must wait until either his anxiety is reduced and/or excitement is increased.

As in the origin of any approach–avoidance conflict, anxiety was associated with the goal. Two questions arise: what is the source of anxiety and how does further tormenting increase the individual's arousal and/or lessen anxiety? In psychoanalytic literature, the response to the first question is that sexual feelings are inhibited by oedipal guilt and the threat of castration. Guilt and fear of sexual relations account for the impotence of the masochist in normal coitus. Punishment dissolves this guilt and allows him to experience gratification. Pain and humiliation are tolerated so that sexual pleasure can be experienced, since punishment provides a license for the acts that follow (Fenichel, 1945). He has to pay in advance (Symons, 1927).

Since the process of generating sexual tension involves ever increasing anxiety, ultimate gratification must be postponed by suspension to allow time for mastery of small increments of anxiety. Once neutralized, anxiety becomes fused with sexual arousal and augments it.

The masochist masters his own discomfort by controlling its increase. By acting out his scenario in a playful manner, he protects himself from the unexpected. And, in attributing his discomfort to his dominant, he disowns his anxiety. He exchanges a future awesome threat for a partial, playful, manageable discomfort. Rather than suffering anxiety, he exposes himself to suffering (Reik, 1941). Thus, masochism is not instinctual, but is an adaptational device, a defense that protects him from greater harm (Bieber, 1953). And, his assumption of a passive, helpless role removes responsibility for his subsequent sexual excitement (Loewenstein, 1957).

Masochistic Scenes

Fantasy scripts vary from silly, as in a naughty schoolboy scene, to quite frequent castration themes (Loewenstein, 1957). A slightly disguised castration fantasy is reported by a man who, after placing a bug on a woman's shoulder, calls her attention to it. If she brushes if off and crushes it under her foot, he experiences intense sexual excitement [bug = himself and his penis] (Stolorow and Grand, 1973). Another man imagines that he places his penis in the mouth of a toothed worm and his penis is cut when he tries to take it out (Panel, 1981). For some male submissives, outright castration is the ultimate fantasy, the extreme symbolic relinquishment of masculinity. In one such scenario, the mistress lays the man down, shows him surgical instruments, blindfolds him, shaves his pubic area, and teases him about the pain of such a procedure. In conclusion, she decides he is not ready for the operation (Scott, 1983). His toying with the fantasy of castration serves to weaken his anxiety over losing his symbol of masculinity (Keiser, 1949). Some masochists may break out of the "as if" quality of their scenes and engage in truly dangerous exploits. For example, a middle-class woman could achieve orgasm only by prostituting herself in unsafe neighborhoods (Kernberg, 1988).

Many masochists, more heterosexual (20%) than homosexual (4%), had no partner at all, and the median number of experiences was only five per year. Thus, they must rely on fantasy and automasochism (28%), such as tying themselves up, self-flagellating, or applying nipple torture during masturbation (Spengler, 1977). A not uncommon problem for the submissive contemplating acting out his fantasy is that his scenario may be so specific and detailed that he finds it impossible to achieve a comparable real life situation (Scott, 1983).

Phone sex is available for those who do not wish to act out their fantasies with another person and yet are not fully satisfied with fantasizing alone. "Submit Slave! Kneel and be prepared to serve a true Mistress. Spanking, discipline and all other aspects of domination handled expertly over the phone."

Control

A common misconception is that the masochist turns over control to another, that he desires unconditional domination. In fact, the masochist's being dominated and controlled is more apparent than real. The scene is scripted in advance and fictitious power is granted to the dominant who is the real submissive in the scene. His defiance is expressed in his seeming passivity, but he is in control; he is the writer, producer, director as well as actor in his own play, staged for his own pleasure. He does not seek a genuine sadist for then he would not be in charge (Smirnoff, 1969).

There is a relation between masochism and humor as both are attempts to avoid a painful situation by rendering it controllable or absurd. There are two parts to the personality active in both: actor and observer, suffering child and liberated child (Dooley, 1941).

One example of the submissive's control is setting of limits. For a session to be satisfying and erotic, the dominant must respect two types of limits—categorical and quantitative. Categories of activities, such as piercing, water sports, or spanking are enjoyable for some and totally disagreeable to others. Qualitative limits involve how much humiliation, whipping, or bondage the submissive finds arousing. Being bound too long or whipped too hard ruins the erotic effect. The more the submissive trusts his dominant, the fewer limits he insists on (Weinberg, 1987).

The masochistic experience seems to reach its peak at this limit or sometimes just beyond the boundary between the erotic and the unbearable. The dominant may "push the limits" to heighten the pleasure. A "safe word" is agreed upon so that the dominant can distinguish between the usual pleadings for mercy prior to the limit and those sincere cries to stop past the limit (Scott, 1983).

Related to control is another characteristic, often seen, but not necessary—the provocative factor. This refers to the masochist's aggressive and forceful use of any means possible to provoke another into giving him the discomfort that is necessary for his pleasure (Reik, 1941). Provocation is a technique resorted to in actual behavior to obtain his ends and is not necessary in this fantasy where he is in total control of events. For example, one man would engage in scuffles with his drinking companions in the hopes of being bitten (Lihn, 1971). At D&S parties a submissive rudely touched dominant females on breasts or buttocks. When slapped for this behavior, he would orgasm (Scott, 1983). He insists, in a strong-willed fashion, that his wishes be carried out in the manner he prescribes. In this he is despotic, giving a hint of the underlying sadism.

Ritualism

A noteworthy feature of masochistic scenes, acted out or fantasized, is their ritualistic character. The scene is much like a theatrical production where the script is partly improvised or completely spelled out (Gebhard, 1969). Events, and sometimes their sequence, are prescribed. The slightest deviation from the script may result in failure to achieve the desired result.

This ritualistic quality of the ceremony guards the submissive against the unexpected and assures him that he is in control. While minor alterations may take place from time to time, the main theme must be maintained. After many repetitions, the fantasy may lose its potency and an entirely new script introduced, but the nuclear theme is retained (Reik, 1941). This ritualistic character has been incorporated in an updated definition of sadomasochism. "A relationship giving rise to the sexual interaction of two or more people via a ritual whose outward appearance involves coercion, pain, restriction or suffering of some kind but which has been agreed upon, tacitly or overtly, between the parties concerned and may in reality involve none of these constraints" (Gosselin and Wilson, 1984, p. 93).

Activities and Paraphernalia

The masochist usually has his own particular mode of arousal that is not interchangeable (Bieber, 1966). Preferred practices were determined from responses to questionnaires sent to male advertisers in S&M contact magazines and club members in Germany. The favorite activities are flagellation (66%) and bondage (60%), followed by anal manipulation (26%), women's clothing (14%), urine (10%), and nipple torture (9%) (Spengler, 1977).

There are sex differences in preferred activities. Males, more than females, desire to be treated as animals, receive severe pain, be orally humiliated (e.g., kissing the partner's buttocks), and have their partner engage in sexual activities with another person. Females, on the other hand, prefer being displayed in front of others in an embarrassing fashion (Baumeister, 1988b).

Flagellation Fantasy

> Let the birch be your love, St. Bridget your saint,
> Never flinch from the rod, nor think of a faint;
> Swish—swish—let it fall, till the glow of desire,
> Will run thro' your senses, and set them on fire.

Whippings, floggings, and canings are common in the fantasies of masochists and in pornography written for masochists, since four-fifths are interested in this activity (Breslow et al., 1985). Several factors converge to make whipping or its idea sexually stimulating. Whipping arouses emotions of fear, anger, shame, and excitement and these powerful emotions augment sexual arousal. Being treated as a naughty child in complete subjugation plays a part in the adult fascination for flagellation.

Flagellation is often referred to as the "English Vice" and this predilection seems to have reached a peak in the Victorian era. Pisanus Fraxi (1877), bibliographer of pornography during this period, declares that, "books innumerable in the English language are devoted to this subject alone; no English bawdy book is free from descriptions of flagellation" (p. xl).

From a review of such literature produced during the Victorian era, Gibson (1978) summarizes the common elements of this genre. He notes that the story line first describes the uncovering of the buttocks in a ritualistic manner. The victim is required to bend over; attention is directed almost exclusively to the buttocks. Conspicuous by its absence is any mention of the genitals which would be clearly visible, considering the bent-over position assumed. Singled out for detailed description are the twistings and writhings of the victim.

The floggings depicted are carried out in a strict ritualistic manner, similar to religious rites. Special costumes are sometimes donned. The severe mistress is dressed as a nurse, an elegant woman in furs, teacher's garb, or a riding habit. At times there is an audience viewing the ceremony—another point of contact with religious rites.

The dialogue between mistress and victim is tightly prescribed. Hesitation by the victim produces a second, sterner order which is not disobeyed. Pleas for mercy are disregarded and the beating begins. Often, either before or after the treatment, the victim is required to kiss the rod and to thank the mistress.

Flagellation scenes depicted in pornography could be a distorted view of reality (Marcus, 1966). Fortunately, we have an eye-witness description of such a scene by the anonymous author of *My Secret Life* (1882). Here can be seen a definite confusion of sexual identity where the victim dons a woman's dress and cap, but wears his socks and boots. His impotence is evident by lack of erection during preparation for the scene; achieving erection only after many strokes of the rod and manipulations by a female attendant. The ritualistic enactment of some childish incident is indicated by the diaglogue between the two—"Be a good boy or [she] will whip you hard." "Oh—no—no—pray don't." "Now she shall whip you, you naughty boy" (p. 666).

Bondage

Bondage and restraint are of interest to two-thirds of male and over four-fifths of female sadomasochists (Breslow et al., 1985). Being bound symbolizes that the submissive has surrendered control to a trusted dominant and allows him to feel helpless, vulnerable, degraded, and humiliated (Scott, 1983). Somehow, constriction and arrest of movement increases excitement (Weinberg, Williams, and Moser, 1984). When blindfold, hood, and gag are used in conjunction with bondage, the experience of being in the control of another is intensified as they deprive the submissive of sensory input and means of expression. Also, such devices force the submissive to focus attention on the ministrations of his mistress. A rebound effect is reported in that the submissive is overcome by a wave of thankfulness at being released (Scott, 1983). While in some cases it is easy to trace a predilection for whipping back to some childhood experience, this is not the case with bondage. The idea of being bound precedes the experience.

Mysophilia

The most common interests in mysophilia (attraction to filth) are coprophilia (feces) and urophilia (urine). When these substances are ingested, the suffix "philia" is replaced by "phagia." "Water sports" refers to urination and enemas which are of interest to about a third of sadomasochists (Breslow et al., 1985). For some, being urinated on is experienced as the height of humiliation and, consequently, "delicious shame" (Green and Green, 1974). A male submissive reports a merging experience—"One pleasure is to hold it in my mouth as long as possible and imagine that part of my mistress is in me" (Scott, 1983, p. 172). A dominatrix reports, "Sucking my dirty panties is humiliating. Yesterday, a client asked me to smear shit in my panties and make him lick it, and I did" (Weinberg et al., 1984, p. 383).

THE PERSON

Onset

About one-fourth of masochists discovered the joys of submission only as adults, sometimes seemingly by accident. Men who discover their submissive side as adults seem less threatened than do the early fantasizers since the former's concept of masculinity is more firmly set. Although for some, the emergence of this submissive side can force a basic reorganization of the self-concept (Scott, 1983).

Biological Basis

There has been some speculation that the masochist has heightened skin eroticism, that is, stimulation of the skin is more arousing for him than for others. Because of this, he has an increased need for physical contact in infancy, and later he experiences intense stimulation as pleasureable (Reik, 1941).

Early Life

Mother

Mother was the dominant figure in the home, excluding and contemptuous of her ineffective husband (Keiser, 1949). Father was either loud and punishing or weak and childish. The boy felt distant and estranged from his father, which severely interfered with his assumption of the masculine role and heterosexual partner choice (Panken, 1967, 1973).

The budding masochist's mother was depressed and unavailable to her son much of the time (Coen, 1988), and her feelings toward him were ambivalent (Bieber, 1966). More so than other mothers, she presented two faces to him. While taking no pleasure in mothering, she still sought to exercise control over him, smothering him with overprotection. During his early years, her dual nature unpredictably fluctuated between being depriving, frustrating, remote, and hostile to being devoted, oversolicitous, controlling, and infantilizing. The child was not overly abused, rather mother's ill-treatment was done under cover of caring martyrdom (Bromberg, 1959; Panken, 1973).

In his training, severe punishment was not the rule. If anything, training was overly indulgent, so that when he was reprimanded, the shock was more severe than if punishment were routinely administered. Punishment may have been eroticized, as when the battle over toilet training was won by mother using the enema as her weapon (Panken, 1967).

Mother was excessively prudish about sex and severely disapproved and inhibited any sexual expression by her son. Yet, she was seductive and sexually stimulated the boy (Bromberg, 1959; Coen, 1988). For instance, one mother allowed her son to come to her bed until he was eleven years old, and would embrace him while wearing only a nightgown (Keiser, 1949).

The child experienced rejection, a sense of being neglected and abandoned in the form of sudden weaning, harsh toilet training, severe measures to stop his masturbation, mother's absence, and sibling favoritism. Only sporadically did he experience facsimiles of love. Masochism arises out of resolution of a conflict between the wish to be loved and the experience of suffering meted out by the loved one (Berliner, 1947, 1958; Panel, 1956). As he did not receive genuine love, he created the illusion of being loved by disavowing mother's rejection and construing her ill-treatment as a sign of affection (Berliner, 1947; Schad-Sommers, 1982). He learned that he was not accepted for his own sake, but was granted attention for what he could do for mother, as if she were saying, "I tend to you when I want to, not when you need it." Her noble, self-sacrificing facade protected her from blame (Keiser, 1949).

Thus, he learned that he was relatively helpless in the sense of having little control over events in his life. In addition to mother's unpredictability, asthma, headaches, and accidents reinforced his sense of helplessness. He used these events to get mother's attention and her hoped-for comfort (Karpman, 1934; Panken, 1973). Her attention was purchased with weakness and surrender (Bychowski, 1959). To some extent, the masochist hopes to gain love by demonstrating his weakness and suffering as illustrated by this observation: "The more humble I was, the more I knelt before her, small and miserable, the more she loved me. She hated strength and manliness in me; to win her love I had to pretend to be wretched, so that she could pose as the stronger, play 'little mother' and console me" (Strindberg, 1913, p. 133). Continuing his distortion of the situation, he viewed mother as "good," blaming himself, the naughty boy, for her "badness" (Schad-Sommers, 1982).

Rather than admitting to himself his inability to evoke mother's love, he preserved his sense of mastery by imagining that he forced her to be cruel (Panel, 1984). He learns that what he considers love comes only through suffering and compliance (Schad-Sommers, 1982). By this compliance and suffering he attempted to extract caring from an unloving mother. He was made to feel guilty for these efforts, and in turn, tried to assuage guilt by more suffering. Not only did he feel guilt over approaching mother, but assumed guilt for other behaviors. For instance, a three-year-old had a terrifying tonsillectomy and

imagined this was punishment for previous sex play with a baby-
sitter (Glenn, 1984).

In healthy development, the child separates from mother,
becomes increasingly independent, and achieves a sense of
mastery. In the masochistic course, an excessively strong attachment to mother persists, his adoration of her continues.
For his continued efforts to be close to her, he is rejected and
shamed (Braun, 1967). Thus, oedipal guilt and castration anxiety set in after his masochistic course has been set and are
secondary contributions (Berliner, 1958).

The oedipal scene may supply the theme for his later masochistic fantasy. All of Sacher-Masoch's dominant female characters' names rhyme with "mama," as Wanda. Wanda's consort,
Alexis Papadopolis, is father. And, Severin, the masochist, is
the son. No genital sexuality takes place between Wanda and
Severin, but he does adore her furs, as a fetish substitute for
her genitals. If the masochist does witness the primal scene
between his parents, he interprets it as a brutal and aggressive
attack, placing himself in the victim role (Bonaparte, 1952).
Before going off together, Wanda has Alexis whip Severin, as
the oedipal father is supposed to punish his son (Lenzer, 1975).
And, in real life, Sacher-Masoch insisted that his women be
adulterous so that he could spy upon the couple. All this points
to the possibility that the masochist's fantasy is a reenactment,
under his direction, of his primal scene and oedipal experiences
(Kernberg, 1988).

In later childhood, mother is seen as all-powerful and all-
knowing, and in comparison, he is dependent and helpless. He
continues to be attached to, and dominated by, this unfeminine,
seductive women. But now he begins to harbor some disgust
and hatred toward her (Panken, 1967).

It is from this family climate that the future masochist
emerges. He is now prepared to acquire specific techniques to
cope with his situation and is sensitized for other, specifically
masochistic trigger experiences.

Seduction of Aggressor

In play with grown-ups, a child may learn the technique of
seducing the aggressor. For instance, a woman was playfully

scolding her year-old granddaughter for putting her thumb in her mouth. Baby was frightened, but when she saw a smile on grandmother's face, she put her finger back in her mouth with a taunting, naughty expression. She was learning protomasochistic behavior, a nonerotic precurser to masochism. Children exposed to this sort of treatment may, as adults, place themselves in threatening situations where they are able to remove threat by erotic complicity with the threatener (Loewenstein, 1957).

Comfort as Reinforcement

An older brother, apeing his father's hatred toward the boy, would routinely beat on his younger brother, sometimes with father looking on. After his beating, mother would comfort him. The sequence, repeated throughout his childhood, was naughtiness, being beaten, and comfort by mother or maid (Lihn, 1971).

Crucial to development of masochism is ambivalent treatment of the child with alternating punishing and comforting behaviors. This sequence of loving and comforting alternating with punishment and humiliation is seen repeatedly in the relation between Severin and Wanda in Sacher-Masoch's (1870) *Venus in Furs*. First, he is punished for being tender. In response to pressing his lips to her neck, Wanda tells him, "Now go!—you bore me—don't you hear?", boxing him on the ears. Second, his pain is followed by her tenderness, "did I hurt you?" she asked, softly touching him (pp. 136–137).

Learning Self-Punishment

The child finds that by punishing himself, parental hostility can be controlled, and so this behavior has adaptive value. A three-year-old was able to ward off her mother's threatened punishment by banging or burning herself (Bieber, 1966).

Specific Experiences and Fantasies

It is often possible to trace a masochistic fantasy to childhood experiences other than the child being himself punished. However, there is usually no one-to-one correspondence between these original events and the fantasy. Several transformations must be untangled. For instance, Monsieur M., who ate feces daily for many years, recalls that when he was four years old he saw a small girl eat her own excrement: "I was disgusted, and afterwards I had second thoughts" (M'Uzan, 1973, p. 458). In the original event a girl ate feces, while later it was Monsieur M. who ate them. And, disgust was transformed into desire.

A more complicated series of transformations is seen in a case reported by Reik (1941). For years, this patient had enacted this scene with satisfactory results: while wearing black trousers and bending forward, a tall, beautiful woman stood unseen behind him, ready to strike a blow to his buttocks. Excitement began during preparation for the scene and increased to the blow, when climax occurred.

During analysis, childhood experiences related to this scene were uncovered. Once, wanting to join his mother who was taking a mud bath, he entered the bathroom and saw her bending over, back to him, covered with mud. A sudden urge to spank her on the rump seized him. Originally, mother's backside was black with mud and he actively wanted to slap her; in his scene, he takes her place wearing black trousers and receives the blow.

Whence the urge to smack her? It came to light that his father was wont to playfully smack females on the rear, to which they reacted with giggles and feigned annoyance. The boy would imitate his father's behavior, and probably experienced some pleasure in this. It is reasonable to assume that when he did ape his father he was reprimanded. Originally it was father who spanked; in his scene it was a woman who delivered blows. Originally, he was punished when he sought pleasure in slapping; later he required punishment to achieve pleasure.

One more bit of information completes this analysis. One time the unexpected happened. He was prepared as usual, wearing black trousers and bending over, awaiting the releasing blow. For some unknown reason, he looked back and saw the woman's face and her fur boa. All of a sudden, his sexual excitement drained and was replaced by anxiety akin to horror. Something had struck him as familiar. Later, it was revealed that the woman's fur had reminded him of his father's beard. From this we can assume a repressed fantasy to be beaten by his father, a fantasy of "I am a woman and being sexually used by my father." Originally he desired love in the form of a spanking from his father. In his scene, the woman is a composite of the child's dreaded father and his adored mother—his original, incestuous love object. In his conscious fantasy he assumes passive femininity and the woman doing the beating is endowed with active masculinity.

Beating fantasies are not uncommon in psychoanalytic practice, especially in conversion reactions. Freud (1919) found that the original, deeply repressed, childhood incestuous fantasy was: "I am loved by my father." Guilt, castration fear, repression, and regression to the anal sadistic stage set in, and the child escapes from these homosexual urges.

This root wish is transformed into the unconscious masochistic fantasy of "I am being beaten by my father." This transformation from being loved to being beaten serves several functions. There is atonement through punishment for incestuous wishes toward his mother, where the beating symbolizes a mild form of castration, where a cut to the butt is substituted for a cut to the penis. In the adult masochist, watching and reading about flagellation can reassure him that although penises are uncovered, they are unharmed (Gibson, 1978). Beating by father is interpreted by the child as love, since he conceives of the primal scene as aggressive (Rubenfine, 1965). If this fantasy is not further transformed, it constitutes a masochistic homosexual fantasy such as one reported by a masochistic male transsexual. "My father and I are going down into the cellar. I know that he is going to beat me. We emerge from the cellar holding hands—like lovers—the peace and affection I feel is overwhelming, though I am in pain" (Meyer, 1974a, p. 539).

In the heterosexual masochist, the homosexual component is repressed. Now, the final transformation occurs, one which is conscious and sexually arousing: "I am being beaten by a woman (mother)." This represents a double role reversal where the male takes the passive role of the female and the dominant woman in the scene represents a male—the father, as occurred in the man in the black trousers.

These recalled childhood experiences are not the cause of masochism; rather they are trigger episodes used by the masochist as elements in his fantasies. Sometimes, ordinary childhood events stimulated submissive interests and erotic feelings, as when blindfolded in a game of hide-and-seek or being bound while playing cowboys and Indians. Others were cross-dressed by their mothers or punished by being babied, like having to wear diapers as punishment for bed-wetting. For instance, when Alex was eleven, his mother dressed him as a girl for a church costume party, thinking he would look cute. He enjoyed this experience and began dressing in his mother's clothes; she discovered him several times and he gave up cross-dressing. In his teens, the urge returned. Feeling guilty about this, Alex imagined a woman forced him to cross-dress by tying him up. Soon, he was binding himself while cross-dressed (Scott, 1983).

Most adult masochists entertained submissive fantasies when they were children. They spent many years engaging in these fantasies which troubled them as being unmanly. They would masturbate to their own fantasies or to S&M pornography. Some of these men acted out their fantasies with themselves, as in cross-dressing, tying themselves, and in self-flagellation. Attempts to share their fantasy with a companion often failed and many had their first experience with a professional dominant. Often they attempted to put these desires aside, but to no avail (Scott, 1983).

Reik (1941) proposes several stages in the development of masochism. First, the infant's aggressive and sadistic impulses are directed outward onto others—particularly mother. Since these attacks are met with withdrawal and punishment, he curtails attacks on external objects because of the anxiety aroused. Hostile urges and anticipation of punishment now blend and are enacted in fantasy. The aggression that cannot reach the external takes the self as object. Now the child must be both aggressor and victim as if the scene were enacted before a mirror with one actor playing both parts. For example, a patient revealed his fantasies of torturing women in which breasts were stabbed and thick objects were thrust into their anuses. He carried out these tortures on himself (Bergler, 1938). In the final phase, he finds another person, in fantasy and/or in fact, as the aggressor.

Sexuality and Partner Preference

One twenty-eight-year-old therapy patient had never had sexual intercourse nor had he orgasmed through masturbation. His only source of gratification was being bitten or dreaming of being bitten (Lihn, 1971). While sexual thoughts and urges are easily aroused (Krafft-Ebing, 1902), the masochist suffers from constant or periodic erectile failure (Karpman, 1934; Reik, 1941). Even when he is potent, sexual satisfaction is diminished. To experience orgasm, one must be passive in relation to mounting tension and orgasmic release. But, the masochist's fear of passivity prevents him from experiencing such gratification (Keiser, 1949). It is not at all uncommon that a session does not include sexual intercourse, even in a noncommercial relationship. In commercial B&D houses, the client may be allowed to masturbate at the conclusion of the session. He may not desire sexual connection, as a male submissive explains: "In a session, I see the dominant woman as far superior to me and place her on a pedestal. But, if we had intercourse, that would equalize the relationship" (Scott, 1983, p. 176).

Sadger (1926) noted the common combination of homosexuality and masochism. This connection receives some confirmation in the sexual orientation of sadomasochists, where exclusive homosexuals are greatly overrepresented (38%) (Spengler, 1977).

Heterosexual masochists may engage in homosexual relations. Monsieur M. had numerous homosexual experiences, with his partner assuming the sadistic role. He chose homosexual relations as a means of heightening his humiliation. "I gave the impression of being an invert, but I wasn't one for pleasure, but for humiliation. I get no physical satisfaction from it; it was moral satisfaction" (M'Uzan, 1973, p. 460). He recalls that in sexual games at boarding school, "I was, in no uncertain terms, the 'public woman' and that satisfied me" (p. 458).

In contrast to almost all heterosexual masochists who seek

dominant, seemingly cruel women, Monsieur M.'s wife, whom he deeply loved, was, like himself, a masochist to the extent that she was once penetrated by a male while suspended by meat hooks through her breasts.

Interpersonal Relations

Because of his heightened need for interpersonal intimacy and its early frustration, the masochist's desire to merge with another is strong. "I can no longer live without you, oh, wonderful woman. . . . I feel deep down in my innermost soul that my life belongs inseparable with yours. If you leave me, I shall weaken, break up into pieces" (Sacher-Masoch, 1870, p. 58).

However, his desire to lose himself in another evokes annihilation anxiety, a fear of loss of self. His dilemma is between closeness and intimacy or separateness and isolation (Glasser, 1979).

Being unable to discriminate between love and abuse, he uses a "pathological way of loving" (Berliner, 1947). He seeks erotic relationships in which there is a seeming power imbalance, expressed in terms of dominant and submissive. He appears to relinquish control to the other, finding this erotic. This transfer of power and loss of control is seen most clearly in the submissive who wants to be fettered.

Dominance–submission, exaltation–worthlessness are constructs used to view interpersonal relations in a polarized, either-or fashion. In the male, the woman is assigned the dominant, exhalted role, as Sacher-Masoch's (1870) Severin explains. "You cannot deny, that men and woman are mortal enemies; . . . which ever of the two fails to subjugate will soon feel the feet of the other on his neck" (p. 12).

Sacher-Masoch (1870) reasoned that, because of his insatiable need to relate, his mortal enemy, woman, gains power over him, becomes his mistress and thereby reduces him to slave status. Once he accepts this slave role, he knows what to expect. She will be cruel, faithless, pityless, despotic. The essential meaning of woman is a wrathful queen. The more she exaggerates her cruelty, the worse she treats him, and the more unhappy he becomes, his desire, love, and worship of her increases. However, in the end, she will betray him, and he will realize the cost of his lust. The woman, too, has a choice. For a permanent relationship, she seeks a whole man, a man who subjugates her, a man before whom she has to kneel. But, if she shows devotion to the man, he will become indifferent and domineering.

Goethe's "you must be hammer or anvil" is the overriding concept governing the relation between the sexes. There are no other alternatives. True, man has a choice whether to pursue either master or slave role, but because of his passion, he chooses to elaborate the slave role. Only if he understands himself, realizes the dangers of passion, will he choose to be the tyrant, and make the woman his slave. "All of a sudden I saw with horrible clarity whither blind passion and lust have led me—into a blind alley, into the net of woman's treachery, into misery, slavery and death" (Sacher-Masoch, 1870, p. 235).

In their everyday, nonerotic relations with others, a minority of submissives are "natural passives," that is, men who are socially inept, shy, withdrawn, and who experience special difficulty in relating to women. Most, however, are drawn from the ranks of men who wield power in their daily lives, who are of imposing appearance, energetic, strong, assertive, outgoing, determined, and thoroughly masculine (Bloch, 1908; Ellis, 1913; Scott, 1983). This is illustrated by Hitler's need to be kicked and humiliated by women. It was as if there were two sides to his personality: one, the soft, effeminate, passive person who wanted to be taken care of, the one who wept at the death of a canary; the other, a reaction formation to the first, hard, cruel, active, driving. It was the latter who said, "There will be no peace in the land until a body hangs from every lamppost" (Langer, 1972).

Von Cleef (n.d.), operator of a "house of pain," reports that some of her clients held positions of authority, were mean and domineering in relations with their employees. However, after one of her treatments, they were able to work well with others and were better liked by them. She illustrates this "cure" in the case of a judge who, when he was to preside over a murder trial, would come to her for a session. Otherwise, he said, he would be unable to give the accused a fair trial, being restive and irritable. After his treatment he was relaxed and unprejudiced. The treatment consisted of his being tied to a chair, washcloth stuffed in his mouth, and severely caned.

Hollander (1972) reports similar experiences, describing some of her masochistic clients as domineering and manipulating those who work for them as if they were puppets. This daily behavior, she suggests, leads to feelings of insecurity and a consequent craving to balance this dominant attitude with submissive scenes.

Bloch (1908) invokes this same mechanism of balance, suggesting that these powerful men are overcompensating in their masochistic behaviors by relieving themselves of the pressures of their masculine mask of authority. He refers to this mechanism as the law of the balance of opposites, also called compensatory reaction formation (Berliner, 1958). Their submissive sessions allow them to escape from a burdensome, high level of self-awareness as a person who takes responsibility, makes decisions, controls, and maximizes self-esteem. Pain, bondage, and humiliation promote a low level of self-awareness, narrowing attention to their body and the immediate present (Baumeister, 1988a). They are released from responsibility for their own behavior, punished for their aggressiveness, and humiliated as they have humiliated others. They find pleasure and excitement in turning power over to another, behaving submissively, and perhaps reliving fantasies of being mothered, and expressing worshipful feelings toward women. Natural passives are balancing, too, for in their weakness they turn to a strong, dominant woman (Scott, 1983). For the masochist it seems that success in one sphere of life is connected with failure and misfortune in other spheres. So, the satisfied sexual masochist is able to function well in other areas of life. But, if masochistic sexuality is blocked as in therapy, negative consequences appear in vocational and social spheres (Reik, 1941). It is as if there are two selves, the masculine attempting to preserve itself by imposing suffering and humiliation on the feminine, even to the point of annihilation (Wittels, 1937).

Rousseau (1778) relates that he felt as though opposite character traits were united in him. He describes himself as haughty, yet tender; weak, yet courageous; effeminate, yet invincible; timid; loathing of constraint, with a fondness for the imaginary. His passions were lively and impetuous, yet his ideas were produced only slowly.

Men in politics are more sexually active than men of comparable age in other occupations, and a large proportion use the services of prostitutes for deviant sex. The favored deviant practices are flagellation, bondage, discipline, and humiliation. The ratio of passive to active is eight to one (Janus et al., 1977).

For many politicians a fusion of sex and power motives fuels the pursuit of their political careers. But these men suffer a conflict between assertion and submission and this leads to swings in behavior between ruthlessness and dependency. After orgasm, they are transformed into dependent, infantile beings, wanting to be held, cuddled, and assured that they are "good little boys" (Janus et al., 1977).

There is some consistency in the descriptions of female masochists. Restif de la Bretome writes that women of strong temperament enjoy brutality in sexual intercourse. This conjecture has been verified by Maslow (1942) in a study of dominance feelings and sexuality in women. He found that high dominant females fantasize about being raped, while middle dominant women dream of being seduced. Heterosexual submissive females have about the same femininity score as submissive males, but a higher feminine score than dominant females (Herron et al., 1983).

Self Conception

Another reason for the masochist seeking to affiliate with a strong, dominant person is his deficient self representation. He suffers from a feeling of lack of cohesion of self, a feeling that major portions of his conception of himself are not related. This fragile self representation stems from traumas suffered during the preoedipal period (narcissistic mortification).

His masochistic scenes are attempts to ward off disintegration of his diffuse self representation and increase cohesion by merging with a powerful person and/or assuring himself of the existence of his body to counter his feeling of deadness. He seeks sensations, high tension levels, even pain so that he can

feel alive and experience his own identity (defense against depersonalization) (Panken, 1973; Stolorow, 1975; Panel, 1981).

To explain masochism some writers, notably Krafft-Ebing
and Freud, have invoked the bisexuality hypothesis that there
are two aspects to each personality: masculine—strong, active,
and aggressive; and feminine—weak, passive, and submissive.
Male masochism, then, results from a pathological exaggeration
of the feminine qualities of passivity and the desire to be subjugated to the power of another. It is a partial feminization, a
rudimentary homosexuality. Explanations of masochism on the
basis of femininity rest on the questionable equation of femininity with passivity.

Actually, he fears passivity and suffering, so he sets up
situations where he can control these feelings (Keiser, 1949).
His fear of passivity can be traced to a concern over loss of self,
of not being his own person. But this fear is in conflict with
another, the desire to merge (Glasser, 1979).

Others, who do not invoke the bisexuality hypothesis, also
describe the masochist as feminine, labeling him a
passive–feminine character (Reik, 1941; Reich, 1949), who is
defending against a deep hatred of others because of early
disappointments in being loved (Karpman, 1934). If he does
enact a feminine role, the masochist is modeling his conception
of the female as he would like to see her. He is not feminine,
but a caricature of femininity (Reik, 1941). While male masochism contradicts the masculine role, female masochism is an
exaggeration of the feminine role (Baumeister, 1988b).

While he may act in a passive, feminine manner, in his
ideal conception of himself he is tough and invulnerable. In his
scenes he is trying to prove he is courageous, and to make good
a distant failure (Lewinsky, 1944), assuming that women respect
and admire strong men and that strong means the ability to
withstand punishment and humiliation. While playing the submissive to his dominant, the masochist really has a destructive
attitude toward her. He expects that she will be punished, her
exertion will exhaust her, and that her sexual excitement will
harm her. He has defeated her because he was able "to take it"
(Keiser, 1949).

Hirschfeld (1938) sees the masochist as protesting against

the masculine role as he conceives it—one of activity, aggressiveness, and superiority. He flees from his conception of the masculine to its opposite the feminine, again as he construes it as dependence and degradation. He thus seeks to portray himself as unmanly, degraded as a servant girl, animal, or thing. Homosexuality is not involved here; this is not flight from the dreaded female, but from the masculine role. Submissive heterosexual male members of the Eulenspiegel Society have lower masculinity scores but the same femininity scores as dominant males (Herron et al., 1983).

Conception of Women

As the male masochist enacts a passive role, subservient to his female partner, he endows her with masculine qualities (Krafft-Ebing, 1902; Karpman, 1934). While debasing himself, he elevates by comparison his image of the all-powerful female (Berliner, 1947; Loewenstein, 1957). He assumes that to administer punishment is sexually arousing to her. He seeks the masculine aspect in women: "I am enraptured by masculinity in woman and I love to see the mistress' figure in tight silk breeches, such as are worn by men" (Hirschfeld, 1938, p. 422).

He has not one, but two conceptions of women—the madonna and the harlot. Sacher-Masoch's women are double-faced—both superior to men and subservient to them, both caring and dangerous (Lenzer, 1975). The madonna, his mother and wife, is pure, asexual, respected, and honored. The harlot is dirty, debased, sexual; used for acting out conflicts in the sexual arena. His "bad me" is punished by mother, but this leads to sexual arousal, which is evil, and therefore mother must be replaced by the harlot (Janus et al., 1977).

The two conceptions are often projected onto the same woman. This double nature is depicted in one of Severin's dreams.

> [Wanda] inclosed me in her arms, and began to kiss me. Suddenly I felt my blood running warm down my side.
> "What are you doing?" I asked horror-stricken.   .
> She laughed, and as I looked at her now, it was no longer Wanda,

but a huge, white she-bear, who was digging her paws into my body [Sacher-Masoch, 1870, pp. 139–140].

Woman is evil and rejecting, warm and giving, and the masochist believes he must love a cruel woman to be loved by her warm and giving aspect (Smirnoff, 1969).

Attitude Toward Deviation

By and large, sadomasochist respondents to a questionnaire were positive toward their S&M practices. Of those men active in the subculture, only 10 percent had ever visited a mental health professional because of their deviancy. The positive attitude of "I want to do it again" of 85 percent outweighed the negative "I've got to quit this" of only 6 percent (Spengler, 1977). Three-fourths of male and female respondents to a questionnaire in an S&M tabloid said that they never or rarely felt that they were perverted (Breslow et al., 1985).

12 ADJUNCTIVE PARAPHILIAS

The deviations in this group are often associated with other paraphilias, but are not an essential part of them. Sometimes they are practiced in pure form without any elements of other deviations. The conditions include voyeurism, sexual asphysia, piercing, klismaphilia (erotic use of enemas), and infantilism.

A characteristic shared by all is the paucity of information about them. This lack of interest by professionals cannot always be explained by the rarity of these practices since peeping and erotic enema use are rather common activities.

Another feature of these deviations is that those who practice them do not constitute a homogeneous group in terms of personality or early childhood experiences.

PEEPING

The terms *voyeurism* from the French word to see and *scopophilia* (pleasure in looking) are used to refer to the fairly common desire to view nudity and acts of coition (Ullerstram, 1966); others reserve the word *peeping* for the paraphilia (Gebhard, Pomeroy, and Christenson, 1965). Peeping is "an exaggerated desire to see, by stealth, a member of the opposite sex in some stage of undress, in the sexual act, or in the act of excretion, which is so intense that it suppresses in importance the normal sexual act" (Yalom, 1960, p. 305). Mixoscopia refers to the desire to watch a couple having intercourse. *The Diagnostic and Statistical Manual of Mental Disorders* (DSM-III-R) requires that the person or people viewed be unsuspecting, usually strangers. This rules out normal erotic looking and viewing pornography. Thus, King David does not qualify as a peeper because his watching Bathsheba while she was bathing was a single occurrence and his preference was to lie with her (2 Samuel 11:2–4).

Since looking at erotic scenes is so pervasive among males, it is difficult to determine when these acts are pathological. The act of peeping, even in the narrow sense of secretly looking at a disrobing female, is very common. In fact, few men would avert their eyes at such a scene (Kinsey, Pomeroy, Martin, and Gebhard, 1953). It is the forbidden nature of the looking that is the mark of the peeper (Karpman, 1954; Yalom, 1960; Hamilton, 1972). This violation of a proscription and the accompanying risk is exciting. Therefore, the peeper is not satisfied by viewing strip shows (Yalom, 1960). However, no difference was found in attending and enjoying strip shows between peepers and controls (Langevin, Paitich, and Russon, 1985). And, as explicit sexual material became accessible in Denmark, reports to the police of peeping decreased dramatically (Kutchinsky, 1976).

Clear-cut cases of male homosexual or female peeping are extremely rare (Yalom, 1960). And, because there are so few cases of preferential peeping, it has been questioned whether male heterosexual peeping is an independent anomaly (Paitich, Langevin, Freeman, Mann, and Handy, 1977). Rarely is it practiced by itself, rather it is associated with other more preferred paraphilias such as exhibitionism, heterosexual pedophilia, cross-dressing, and obscene phone calls (Yalom, 1960; Langevin, 1983; Langevin, Paitich, and Russon, 1985). There are similarities between peeping and exhibitionism. Both acts are courtship disorders in that they are preliminaries to sexual contact where the male is at a distance from the female (Allen, 1967). Psychoanalysts see the two as active and passive expressions of the same urge. However, despite these similarities the two are seldom seen together (Yalom, 1960; Langevin, 1983).

The act is not an accident, rather the peeper goes on an expedition. He does not simply stay on the sidewalk, but prowls alleys, driveways, and yards. Unlike teenage voyeurs who go out in groups, he is a loner. A few use peepholes drilled in public toilet or hotel room walls. Some houses of prostitution have allowed voyeuristic clients to watch sexual scenes secretly.

Peepers do not seek just any female in a stage of undress, but look for a target that meets their standard of attractiveness. However, it is difficult for them to describe just what ideal scene they hope to find. Desired scenes differ—female genitals, lesbian scene, heterosexual intercourse, or simply a partially nude female (Yalom, 1960). Fondling his penis while watching assures him he is an intact male in comparison to the castrated female he is viewing (Allen, 1967). He may masturbate to orgasm while viewing or return home to do so with the memory of what he saw.

While he is certainly taking risks, he is not as incautious as the exhibitionist. When apprehended in the act, it is usually because some third party, not the woman, notified the police. He may be charged with indecent behavior, attempted robbery, or attempted sexual assault. About two-thirds of peepers fully admit guilt (Gebhard et al., 1965).

While the onset of serious peeping is in the teens (Yalom, 1960), age at first conviction is about twenty-four years. Almost half (45%) of a prison sample were married. There is little evidence of neurotic or psychotic symptoms or of drug abuse (Gebhard et al., 1965).

Often the youngest child, the peeper had good relations with both parents. His early sex play was limited and he had few female companions in childhood and in his teen years. He is somewhat more prone than other sex offenders to homosexual experiences. His sexual fantasies are "peculiar," including sadomasochistic, animal contact, and "bizarre" themes. The content of fantasies during peeping may yield an accurate diagnosis of his preferred paraphilia (Langevin, Paitich, and Russon, 1985). He is said to be sexually impotent and to worry about his masturbation (Gebhard et al., 1965). Interestingly, the more sexual experiences peepers have, the greater the frequency of their peeping (Langevin, Paitich, and Russon, 1985).

So peeping does not appear to be a substitute for sexual contact with women.

A relation between peeping and sadism has been proposed. The eye, like the penis, is rich in symbolism as dangerous, powerful, and harmful; for example, the "evil eye" and being turned to stone by Medusa's glance. Thus, looking becomes the destructive act of devouring (Fenichel, 1935). His fear of loss of control and resultant harming of the female leads him to peep (Hamilton, 1972) as a defensive substitute for aggression (Yalom, 1960), using the mechanism of, "I did not harm her, but simply looked at her" (Fenichel, 1945). Peeping affords "the possibility of exclusive possession of the woman and of penetrating her secrets. . . . I want warmth and intimacy, but feel as if I am stealing it. I steal it because I can't afford it" (Hamilton, 1972, p. 284). However peepers were no more aggressive than a comparison group (Langevin, Paitich, and Russon, 1985).

The origins of peeping, according to some psychoanalysts, is similar to that of fetishism. Out of childish curiosity, the child spied on his mother and discovered she lacked a penis. This discovery augmented his castration anxiety and was repressed. His current peeping stems from his hunger for the screen experience and his search for the phallic woman (Fenichel, 1945; Yalom, 1960; Hamilton, 1972; Peto, 1975). Not only was the original sight of the penisless woman repressed, but also his desire to discover new things. So, it is claimed that, as an adult, he lacks curiosity (Alexander, 1956; Yalom, 1960). However, on a test of curiosity, peepers did not differ from a comparison group (Langevin, Paitich, and Russon, 1985). Another element in peeping is an increased need to maintain visual contact due to early object loss (Almansi, 1979).

SEXUAL ASPHYXIA

In his 1791 novel, *Justine,* de Sade describes a man who has himself hanged so that he might experience sexual ecstasy. In that same year the death of the musician Kotzwarra created quite a sensation. Susannah Hill was with him at his demise and was tried for his murder. Kotzwarra, whom she had never seen before, came to her house. After drinking and eating, they went into a back room where he asked her to cut his penis in half. This she refused to do. Then he said he would like to be hanged for a short time. She cut him down after a few minutes. He fell to the floor dead. Susannah was acquitted (Fraxi, 1885, citing *Bon Ton Magazine*).

Sexual asphyxia, also called hypoxyphilia and Katzwarrism, is in DSM-III-R considered a form of sexual masochism. It is not the hanging itself that is central, but the resulting asphyxia produced by compression of the neck's blood vessels or by a plastic bag (Johnstone, Hunt, and Ward, 1960; Burgess, Dietz, and Hazelwood, 1983). This results in blurring of consciousness due to a decrease in the supply of oxygen to the brain (cerebral hypoxia) (Dietz, 1983). If the carotid sinus reflex is triggered, unconsciousness is induced, and death may ensue. It is reported that judicially hanged men have an orgasm just prior to death (Janus, Bess, and Saltus, 1977). If true, orgasm is produced by a spinal reflex and not from asphyxia.

Because of the presumption of suicide and problems in reporting, estimates of fatalities from sexual asphyxia vary widely. From two to twenty or thirty deaths each year are estimated for Los Angeles (Litman and Swearingen, 1972; Noguchi, 1983). In one jurisdiction, almost a third of the deaths by hanging of males under twenty-one years old were attributed to autoerotic asphyxia (Sheehan and Garfinkel, 1988). For the United States, estimates range from five hundred to one thousand per year (Burgess et al., 1983), or one to two per million population (American Psychiatric Association, 1987).

Eighty-nine percent of autoerotic fatalities are by hanging, others by strangulation, plastic bags over the head, and by inhaling anesthetic agents (Burgess et al., 1983). The common features are that a person, usually male, is found hanged, often with self-applied bonds. He may be partially or fully undressed or partially or fully clothed in feminine attire. Ordinary indications of suicide are absent, but sexual elements are present in photographs, pornographic books, and sexual words scrawled on a bathroom mirror or wall. Sometimes the neck is protected from abrasions by a scarf or towel, and a mirror is placed so that he can observe himself. Self-rescue mechanisms are commonly found. There may be signs of self-inflicted pain induced as clamps or clothespins applied to the nipples and injured genitalia. Orgasm may be induced by asphyxia itself or by masturbation (Ford, 1957; Johnstone et al., 1960; Litman and Swearingen, 1972; Sass, 1975; Rosenbaum and Faber, 1979; Burgess and Hazelwood, 1983; Hazelwood, Dietz, and Burgess, 1983).

The discovery of the arousing experience of asphyxiation may come with a feeble suicide attempt, as in a seventeen-year-old who began hanging himself at about age ten: "I wasn't really trying to kill myself, but was thinking about it, and wondered what hanging would be like, so I tried it out" (Shankel and Carr, 1956, p. 486). Another man, when he attempted to strangle himself, noticed a feeling of pleasure, "it was a voluptuous sense of giddiness, like the feeling that overcomes one on a height . . . I need that sense of giddiness; I must have it!" His most pleasurable moment is just prior to ending his hanging, when he experiences "orgastic excitement" (Stekel, 1929b, p. 358).

Other means of discovery are noticing sexual arousal during an act that affects respiration, as breath holding or hyperventilation, either from others or from literature or news stories of fatalities (Hazelwood et al., 1983).

The bound body of a twenty-five-year-old baker's assistant was found in his locked room. He was dressed as a woman and was tied to the bed. A silk stocking was wound tightly around his neck. Police ruled out foul play (Allen, 1940). It has been hypothesized that some individuals, such as the baker, have an unfused, dual gender identity similar to that seen in transvestites. The male finds his female lover within himself with the aid of feminine attire and partial blurring of consciousness induced by asphyxia. He becomes both lover and loved. A related interpretation is that the immobilization and blurring of consciousness produce fantasies of remerging with mother (Resnik, 1972). This blurring of consciousness may be related to the distortion of body image while falling asleep where there is a regression in body image with some body parts correctly perceived, while other parts become distorted (Federn, 1952).

Some self-hangings are akin to lust murder with one person

playing both killer and victim roles (Shankel and Carr, 1956). For instance, a thirty-three-year-old man was found hanged wearing shorts, brassiere, men's socks, and his glasses. In front of him was an illustration of the strangulation of a woman wearing only a brassiere (Dietz et al., 1983). A very active fantasy life is indicated (Brittain, 1968).

Another hypothesis is based on the case of a fourteen-year-old boy whose mother found him blue in the face, masturbating on his bed with a rope around his neck. This act was explained as an effort to cloud consciousness to prevent awareness of his masturbation. Hanging stemmed from his desire to punish himself for masturbating, rather than an attempt to heighten sexual pleasure (Edmondson, 1972).

In a series of 132 deaths by sexual asphyxia, there were 127 males and five females. The practice is more common in Anglo-Saxon and German peoples than in blacks or Latins. Victims are predominately middle class and often rather intelligent, achievement oriented, and otherwise well adjusted (Litman and Swearingen, 1972; Rosenbaum and Faber, 1979; Burgess et al., 1983).

While onset may be in early teens or before (Shankel and Carr, 1956), median age at death is 26.5 with a range from preteens to seventies, with the years twelve to seventeen most common. Two-thirds (68%) are single, but their young age may reduce the incidence of marriage (Burgess et al., 1983).

No consistent picture emerges from adjectives describing these individuals: cheerful, happily married, poor mixers, happy-go-lucky (Johnstone et al., 1960), sensitive, weak-willed, rather feminine, and depressed (Stekel, 1929b). There is no evidence of psychotic disorders, although nonpsychotic depression is reported (Litman and Swearingen, 1972).

In females, there is no evidence of other paraphilias. The majority of males were into bondage (51%) and masochism other than simple bondage (12%), and in those who survive, masochistic fantasies were common (Litman and Swearingen, 1972). Twenty-two percent were cross-dressed when discovered. Five percent were into sadism, from 9 to 16 percent were fetishists, and 6 percent were homosexual (Dietz et al., 1983).

Some autoerotic fatalities are not due to asphyxia. For example, a man was found dead, with semen on his thighs. In front of him was a picture of a horse anally penetrating a man strapped to his underside. The man had been listening to a recording of a horse snorting. Cause of death was "misadventure" by inhaling aerosol spray propellant (Cordner, 1983).

Another potentially dangerous autoerotic practice is the use of electricity. In one case, a man was found with ankles and wrists bound, underclothes stuffed in his mouth. Electric wires were taped to his nipples and another wire placed in his anus. He was wearing a condom. In another case, the man was found naked with feminine clothes nearby. Wires were tapped to his nipples with another inserted in his anus (Cairns and Rainer, 1981).

For those who do not want to plug into house current there is the "Shocker." It is a battery operated device, complete with four electrodes—one for anal insertion, one for penis or vagina, and one for each nipple.

PIERCING

Nipple rings were worn in ancient Egypt and were mentioned in old Italian romances. In Spain they were implanted as instruments of torture. During the 1890s in London they were the vogue among sophisticates. It is said that the wearer experiences a tickling sensation as the rings move about in their holes (Bloch, 1901). Piercing is classed under sexual masochism in DSM-III-R. A magazine devoted to piercing, published by Gauntlet since 1977, has some one thousand subscribers. In an analysis of want ads, the male to female ratio was 154 to 6. Mean age was forty with a range of twenty-three to fifty-five. Besides expressing interest in piercing, some also indicated their more general sexual interests. Forty-nine percent were bi- or homosexual, 44 percent were sadomasochists, and 41 percent were interested in tattooing (Buhrich, 1983).

KLISMAPHILIA

Klismaphilia, the erotic use of enemas, is an understudied paraphilia. Clyster comes from the Greek to wash out and enema from the Greek to send in. DSM-III-R classifies klismaphilia as a paraphilia not otherwise specified. In 1973, Denko was "puzzled by lack of reports of this entity" (p. 246) and this dearth of reports has continued. While there are only a handful of journal articles on the topic, it is well represented in the sex tabloid literature. A nationally distributed publication is devoted exclusively to enemas, enema salons operate in major cities, and there are several specialized mail order houses. These houses trade in enema apparatus, videotapes, and magazines. One percent of pornographic magazine covers feature enema scenes (Dietz and Evans, 1982).

Enemas were used in ancient Egypt, Greece, and Rome. Prior to the 1500s equipment was a large syringe or funnel. Then Ambrose Pare devised equipment for self-administration. The Dutch anatomist, de Graaf, in the late 1600s, designed the prototype of modern enema apparatus (Barton-Jay, 1984). From the 1500s to 1700s it was a standard procedure for exorcizing devils (Shapiro, 1974).

The erotic use of enemas is linked with cross-dressing, as in the case of a recently divorced twenty-five-year-old who had his first peak orgasm through masturbation while giving himself an enema. Soon he discovered he could augment his excitement by wearing women's underclothes. Within a year he was cross-dressing whenever possible. Enema frequency increased when he was "lonely, bored or depressed." Over the years enemas themselves without masturbation induced orgasm, but cross-dressing by itself did not. When his wife discovered his feminine wardrobe and enema equipment, she divorced him (Carr, 1974).

A case has been reported where there was evidence of gender confusion and masochistic practices. A twenty-seven-year-old married Army officer found enemas more satisfying than coitus with his wife. His pleasure stemmed from watching himself in a mirror, from spanking himself, and pleasure from insertion. As the water was flowing into him, he thought of himself as a woman, visualizing the female buttocks. He had an "excessive loathing" for homosexuals. When three years old he enjoyed his enemas and at six he was self-administering (Denko, 1973).

Sexual impotence, gender confusion, and pedophilia can be involved as with a thirty-year-old whose mother gave him enemas until he was fourteen. The only way he could achieve orgasm was to have a small boy give him enemas. He had identified his wife with his mother and his impotency allowed him to distance himself from this mother image. He found this maternal image again, but disguised in the form of a small boy (Nacht, Diatkine, and Favreau, 1956).

All six members of a therapy group for exhibitionists and voyeurs recalled being given enemas by their mothers (Freese, 1972). One exhibitionist was so identified with women that he gave himself enemas with his wife's douche equipment. Orgasm would occur or be induced with masturbation (Christoffel, 1936).

From responses to an ad in a sex tabloid, Denko (1976) has identified three groups of erotic enema users based on their acceptance of their "habit" and its pervasiveness in their lives. The first group considers their use of enemas as shameful. Enemas started in childhood, originally administered by mother. They imagine themselves as women when giving themselves enemas. This practice seems to have little influence on other aspects of their lives. There may be some mild paraphilias in addition such as self-administered spankings, fetishism, and fecal smearing. The second group accepts their use of enemas and they either have a normal sex life with a partner or resort to masturbation. Those in the third group are accepting of their habit and also engage in a wide variety of other paraphilias such as masochism and transvestism.

The enema ritual consists of three phases—insertion, filling, and expulsion—each of which has its own unique sensations. The insertion of the enema nozzle is experienced as pleasurable since the anus is rich in nerve endings and the wall of the rectum is next to the prostate and seminal vesicles. Also, anus and rectum are the most forbidden, intimate areas of the body (Bieber, 1970; Feigen, 1972; Agnew, 1982; Barton-Jay, 1984). With the first enema from mother, "I felt the nozzle start to enter and it felt good!" The entering fluid produces feelings of being filled—"I enjoy the full, heavy feeling of large volumes," and "the wonderous joy of being filled." The expulsion of the water in the bowel is also accompanied by pleasurable sensations (Feigen, 1972)—"Feels good coming out."

Twenty-two letters were received in response to ads placed in sex tabloids by the present author inquiring about practices of erotic enema users. All respondents were male except one bisexual female. The median age was thirty-nine, with a range from twenty-five to fifty-four. Almost 60 percent were or had been married. Eighty percent reported being heterosexual and the rest bisexual. Median years of enema use was twenty, with a range from one to forty-three. Median number of enemas was twice a week, ranging from once a day to once a month.

About half self-administered only and the rest reported receving and/or giving with partners. Many of those without partners expressed desires to find an enema mate: "I'd like to find a good looking woman who shares all my enema desires and who will be most compatible in participating in the fulfillment of the ecstasy derived"; and "I hope to find a woman sometime who will bind me and give me an enema like I remember them."

Forty percent reported accompanying paraphilias that included mild spankings and other punishments. For instance, "I love a scene where I get spanked real strongly and then invited to at least 2 2 quart enemas like a good little boy."

About half were first administered an enema by their mothers. Mothers who give frequent enemas are probably acting out their own sexual feelings (Bieber, 1970). The child may conceive of the enema mother as invading and attacking him, forcing his submission. Along with the sexual feelings aroused, the child experiences hostility and humiliation. These early experiences serve to sexualize the anal area. While they do not directly cause later sexual pathology, they do serve as trigger episodes (Freytag, 1971; Kestenberg, 1976).

Another fifth first received an enema in a hospital when they were young; most of the remainder made the discovery on their own, either as children or adults, and one was introduced by an adult partner as part of golden and brown showers.

Self-discovery in childhood often stems from curiosity about enema apparatus: "I was always curious about seeing the old red bag hanging in back of the bathroom door and found it a turn on." Some who were given enemas as children were initially frightened and experienced pain, but later found it pleasurable. One man reports that he received his first enema when he was five years old from his mother and "although I felt fear and discomfort during the procedure, I eventually began to have fantasies of the enema ritual." Others have enjoyed the experience from beginning: "I never disliked enemas and only feigned protest. Often times I even lied about being constipated just to provoke an enema," and "Mommy always gave warm, soapy ones and gave them gently and lovingly. Mommy stopped but I didn't. . . . It began to turn me on and I was soon jerking off before, during or after."

Klismaphilia has been explained by erotic conditioning. When, during toilet training, parents react to bowel activity as they do to the sexual parts proper, an association with sexuality is established between the anal area and enemas. The connection between enemas and masochism is nicely explained by psychoanalysis since it is during the anal stage that sadomasochistic urges emerge.

INFANTILISM

Infantilism is the achieving of erotic feelings by being treated as an infant. Infantilists are not to be confused with those pedophiles who are sexually aroused by infants. This paraphilia combines features of fetishism, transvestism, and masochism; it is mentioned as a form of sexual masochism in DSM-III-R.

The only sources of information on this paraphilia are a few case reports and publications written for infantilists, such as *True Baby Experiences*, and *The Play Pen*. There are infantilist clubs, newsletters, correspondence networks, and mail-order houses that sell adult baby items. Magazines catering to this group include *Bladder Chatter*, and *Crib Sheet*.

The median age of a sample of infantilists was thirty-nine. Many had partners who babied them; half were bisexual or homosexual. Their favorite baby things were diapers, rubber or plastic pants, baby oil and powder, nursing bottle, pacifier, and rubber sheets. Although about a third had sought professional help, most of these did not want to be treated for their paraphilia, but for related symptoms such as depression (Speaker, 1986).

The infantilist may be attempting to reclaim affection from mother; dependency and sexuality become fused. A young college student would break into houses where he knew a baby lived, don diapers and defecate in them; having an orgasm with or without masturbation. He fantasized that an older woman who resembled his mother was in the background "smiling approval" at him. He started putting on diapers and defecating in them at age seven when his sister was born, beginning again when he was about thirteen. He was popular with his friends, athletic, sociable, and well mannered. He claimed he petted and had intercourse regularly (Malitz, 1966).

Wearing diapers has been preceded by cross-dressing and associated with gender identity confusion and temporal lobe involvement. A twenty-four-year-old male began cross-dressing at age ten, and at fifteen he started putting on diapers and sucking from a bottle. This gave him a feeling of well-being and confidence. He thought he would turn into a woman. Since eighteen months of age, he had had grand mal temporal lobe epilepsy (Pettit and Burr, 1980).

A physically retarded young man began receiving hormone injections when he was about fifteen years old. Three months later he started wearing diapers under his clothing and using a baby bottle. Each time he would have an erection, and frequently an orgasm. After five months of therapy he gave up diapers but began wearing feminine clothes for about one year (Dinello, 1967).

A twenty-year-old, who suffered brain damage at age five, began his infantilist behavior when he was thirteen. Every three to four months he puts on diapers, sometimes a female wig, and sucks a feeding bottle. Erection and ejaculation result (Bethell, 1974).

A desire to remerge with mother was suspected in one case. A young married man had worn diapers during early adolescence and wore them again along with rubber pants at age twenty-three. Wearing them all day kept him in a state of continuous erection. Sometimes he deliberately urinated in them, keeping the wet diapers on. He had had incestuous relations with his younger sister when he was fifteen (Tuchman and Lachman, 1964).

In one case, infantilism was coupled with obscene calls to mothers of small children. Posing as a school physician, a twenty-one-year-old called mothers of schoolchildren. He told them that their child had soiled themselves in school, and instructed them to keep the child in diapers. After his calls, he would annoint himself with baby oil and powder, put on diapers and rubber pants, recall his phone conversation, and masturbate. Occasionally he would defecate in the diapers. His favorite fantasy was that he was eight years old and had soiled himself. As punishment his mother made him put on diapers and treated him like an infant. He enjoyed the feeling of dependency (Fensterheim, 1974).

A survey of letters from infantilists published in speciality magazines (*True Baby Letters and Experiences*, 1985a) indicates that many were bed-wetters as children—"Like most adult babies I've heard of, I began to wet the bed at night" (p. 9). Dressing and acting like a baby provides an escape from the adult world to the helplessness and dependency of infancy. "Diapers are so important to the whole infantilism experience, that I can't see someone who's trying to recapture that feeling of helplessness and dependency settle for anything than a thick, absorbent cotton diaper!" (*True Baby Letters and Experiences*, 1985b, p. 15).

13 EPILOGUE

Previous chapters have presented separately the acts and personal characteristics of individuals whose gender conceptions are distorted and confused and individuals who are sexually aroused by less than ideal stimuli. It is now appropriate to attempt the derivation of some statements that are applicable to all these disorders. Also, it is now possible to present sketches of the pathways toward ideal sexuality and the byways to gender disordered and paraphilic adult sexuality.

1. With the possible exception of transsexualism, more cases of males than females with gender disorders and paraphilias have been reported. This discrepancy can be partially accounted for by the fact that females have greater leeway than males in expressing deviant impulses in socially acceptable ways. More basically, it is here proposed that females' self-esteem is less centered on their femininity than males' sense of worth is anchored to their masculinity. And, if anything, while females crave intimacy many males are either disinterested or fearful of it. Therefore, for females, sexuality is an aspect of an intimate relationship, whereas for males sexuality can easily be an autonomous activity. One reason for this difference can be found in separation–individuation. The female's femininity is founded on her early relationship with mother, whereas the male's mas-

culinity is formed by separating from mother, sometimes with a fear of remerging.

2. All males have a feminine aspect, and attenuated forms of paraphilias exist in all men, but they are low on the sexual preference hierarchy. This assertion is similar to Freud's polymorphous perversion of childhood. Desires to cross the gender line are seen in occasional envy of women, and in desires to be the passive recipient of sexual arousal from an active female. It is common for men to cherish some object which symbolizes their partner, to be mildly attracted toward young girls, to expose the genitals, and to consider intimate relations a power game. Whether these tendencies become exaggerated or not depends on a host of influences.

3. Many more men have strong gender disordered and deviant inclinations and fantasies than those who act them out. These tendencies are not acted out because of inhibitions such as guilt, shame, shyness, commitments to social norms, and religious scruples. For those who do act out, there are disinhibitory factors, both internal and external. Some internal disinhibitors are temporal lobe abnormalities and a general lack of regard for society's proscriptions. External disinhibitors include alcohol, induced asphyxia that alters consciousness, and neutralization of traditional norms through contact with deviant subgroups.

4. There is a biological force, although direct evidence for this is not well established. The most probable biological influence on sexuality is the effect of prenatal hormones that tend to demasculinize the baby boy both in body conformation and in the hypothalamic–pituitary–neuroendocrine function and hemispheric lateralization. More elusive biological contributions include skin eroticism that increases the need for close bodily contact, and a hereditary preparedness for sexual arousal. These biological forces, by themselves, are not decisive, but interact with early experiences as in Freud's complimental series. Even slight innate characteristics can be augmented by early parental feedback.

5. Many paths lead to the same consequence. For example, prenatal androgen deficiency may stem from excessive maternal stress, ingestion of certain drugs and estrogens, tissue in-

sensitivity to androgens, and problems in enzyme and protein synthesis.

6. The role of early experiences is highly influential, with mother being the most decisive agent. Her behavior, interacting with the child's temperament, results in disturbances in symbiotic attachment and, some months later, in complications in separation–individuation that create fears of intimacy and abandonment along with desires to reexperience the original blissful state of unity.

Whether mother is angry and punishing, warm and close binding, or ambivalent she needs her son and keeps him closely attached to her. Later, when father's influence should become more important, he fails to interfere with the mother–son relationship and does not aid the boy in forming his masculine gender representation. He accomplishes this by either being passive and remote or abusive. The common outcome is that the son does not perceive him as affectionate, nurturant, or a strong parent.

Which bypath the individual ultimately takes is influenced by the timing and maximum impact of these disturbances and how they are coped with by mother and child. For example, blatant gender disorders set in early as core gender identity is highly involved; paraphilia routes set in later when gender representations are emerging. Distortions of these representations include idealization of the masculine, and envy and partial identification with the feminine due to inability to live up to the man's conception of the masculine role. Manifestations of split masculinity and femininity are most clearly seen in the gender disorders, but are also found in the paraphilias. Representations are exaggerated, dissociated, rigid, they are impermeable and remain concrete. This concreteness is evidenced later by an objectification of women. The feminine representation is split: one is represented as being admired, loved, helpless, and shy. The other is lustful, deceitful, powerful, controlling, threatening, fearsome, castrating, and frustrating. Associated feelings are worship, adoration, fear, and hate. These distorted representations interfere with perceptions of women and relations with them. Often, some chance trigger episode occurs that organizes and gives concrete form to these representations.

7. In his sexual fantasies, which are often based on a specific organizing experience, he rehearses these distorted conceptions. As these fantasies evolve, they undergo transformations through reversals, displacements, and symbolic substitutions. There are exchanges of objects from self to other and shifts from active to passive participant. The fantasy script may be patterned after the oedipal struggle or some other significant childhood experience.

8. Paraphilias are not deviations of the sex drive. Rather they are expressions of distortions of gender representations which interfere with the experience of the intimacy that is necessary for a satisfying sexual union. Support for this assertion is found in those events that precipitate the deviant act such as separation from a loved one, loss of jobs and other threats to self-esteem, and demands for masculine assertion. That the deviant act is not simply an expression of frustrated sexual outlet is seen in the fact that many deviants have adequate sexual outlets concurrent with their deviation. And, it is often noted that the onset is recalled as having taken place in early childhood, before the actions were sexually arousing.

The aim of the sex drive is not solely the pleasure of orgasm. If this were so, then solitary masturbation devoid of fantasy accompaniment would be the predominant sexual outlet. The urge to sexual activity also demands a partner. Sexual desire is a heterogeneous complex of many emotions, all of which require interaction with another person.

What the paraphiliac seeks to avoid is not sexual connection, but what this implies; namely, close intimate relations with another that activate his conflict between independence and masculinity on the one hand, and engulfment and loss of control on the other. It is not that these individuals lack desires for intimacy, but that intimacy is feared. Gender disorders and paraphilias offer a compromise; they allow a sexualized relationship with both closeness, albeit degraded, and distance at the same time. Dehumanization of the female aids in keeping her at a distance.

If anything, more individuals with paraphilias are basically antisexual than are sexually uninhibited. Sexual impulses are feared because they were punished during childhood, and in the male paraphiliac's mind they require intimacy with a fear-some female. These impulses are often disowned and attributed to others.

Itinerary Leading Toward Ideal Sexuality

The departure point is in those first weeks after conception when androgen production begins to masculinize the embryo. Body build and, most importantly, brain structures are switched toward masculine settings. As a newborn, the male is somewhat irritable, active, and exploratory.

At first merged with mother, he gradually disengages from this symbiotic attachment. His separation is not traumatic since he is fascinated with the world and mother does not cling to him for her own fulfillment. His union with mother is gratifying and his desire to merge with another in a warm, intimate relationship persists. But, this urge becomes functionally independent of remerging with mother and is transferred to others.

He begins to form an image of his body out of the reflected appraisals of others, principally his mother. Because she handles him with caring and tenderness, he comes to value his body positively. Especially important is his evaluation of his genital area. Since mother does not react negatively toward his early genital toying or when she is cleaning him, he looks upon that site as the source of pleasurable sensations without also being anxiety arousing.

During his second and third year of life, he knows for sure he is a boy and will always be so. Around this nucleus of identity, gender role is formed. As this becomes established, he starts dropping more and more feminine behaviors. Since mother is less gender conscious than father, it is up to him to aid the boy in defeminizing. His father is affectionate, warm, and nurturant, and becomes an important part of the boy's life. Mother, while not passive, is not seen by the boy as the dominant, powerful parent. Even if mother is somewhat possessive, his nurturant father encourages the loosening of maternal ties. The boy's behavior moves from the protofeminine toward the masculine.

His gender role concepts are organized into gender representations, both masculine and feminine. He clearly identifies himself with the masculine and values himself positively without denigrating his complementary feminine representation. For a while these representations are rigid and concrete, but in several years they become more flexible and abstract.

In childhood and early adolescence he practices his masculine representation and its complement in his play with other children. This play involves some sexual shadings that are not punished. Privately in fantasy, he rehearses these relationships. In his fantasies that accompany masturbation, he tests for compatibility and arousal value. Those that are congruent with his gender representations and have strong arousal value increase in frequency, while the others become less preferred. He labels correctly his sexual urges and owns them as his.

Itinerary Leading Toward Deviant Sexuality

Prior to birth, something is amiss in his hormonal environment. The consequence is that his body and also his brain were not fully masculinized, so that as a baby he is somewhat timid, docile, underactive, and more needful of physical contact than other male babies. This biological predisposition, however slight, is subjected to deviation amplifying feedback from others.

His mother has problems with her own gender role conceptions. She resents the fact that she is female and both envies and dislikes males, especially intimate sexual connection with them. She uses her son as an extension of herself to ease her gender confusion and to assuage her feelings of worthlessness, emptiness, and incompleteness. She either identifies him as her longed for phallus or employs him as an object for her hatred of men. Depending on whether she is warm and close-binding or rejecting and punishing, he experiences too much or too little contact comfort. This intensifies his need to relate, to affiliate, to communicate, even in a degraded fashion. This need is heightened by scenes of parental quarreling, losses, illness, and separations. He comes to define intimacy as something dangerous; not as a relation between equals, but as dominance, submission, simply as being responded to, or something unobtainable with another adult human being.

Because of her pathological need for him, coupled with his contact hunger and docile temperament, his separation–individuation is fraught with difficulties that interfere with his core gender identity, and thwart his separation, independence, and masculinity. His attainment of masculinity is further complicated because mother does not encourage its development and may even reward his femininity. Father does not mitigate her influence because he is either weak and passive or threatening and abusive.

These early developmental complications distort his masculine and feminine gender representations through rigidity, concreteness, idealization, dissociation, and incomplete identification. Because such a high price is paid for his tenuous male identity and masculine identification, the masculine representation is idealized in terms of power, control, and aggressiveness, an ideal he can neither identify with nor realize. Consequently, he either wishes to be rid of it or fears losing it. The main threat resides in an intimate relationship with a woman.

His feminine representation, with which he partially identifies, is split into at least two extreme components: the dangerous harlot and the benign madonna. Because his gender conceptions remain concrete, his penis and testicles become salient symbols of his masculinity, evoking feelings such as fear of loss, extreme pride, and loathing. Women are concretized as clothing, breasts, and vaginas. Also exaggerated are his feelings toward his representations as hatred, loathing, adoration, and worship. In his primitive either-or thinking, opposites can never be resolved, so that masculine and feminine forever remain at odds, even at war. His longing that the two may be magically united is expressed in such concrete manifestations as dreams of the ubiquitious phallic woman.

Early genital toying and sexual curiosity are interfered with, even punished, with mother communicating her disgust and anxiety. His sex urge is an amalgam of interpersonally disruptive emotions and feelings. Sexual arousal becomes mysterious and intriguing but also anxiety provoking, unpleasurable, even foul. Later, due to his basic prudishness and guilt, the source of these urges is disowned and attributed to external sources. Since sexual arousal stimulates anxiety and fears of remerging, he fears loss of control.

Despite mother's negative attitudes toward sexuality, she sexually arouses her son and, at the same time, imbues him with the idea that sex is wrong. Incestuous longings are both provoked and punished. This frustrating sexual stimulation further complicates his acceptance of an adult female as an intimate sexual partner. The sexual arousal value of women after puberty is inversely proportional to intensity of unfulfilled arousal by women before puberty. Thus, he is pushed further away from perceiving women as appropriate sexual partners.

He is slower than his peers to defeminize and has difficulty in assuming the masculine role. He experiences himself as different and this difference is intensified by deviation amplifying feedback from his peers which, in turn, increases his sense of isolation and alienation. He may react by compensatory masculine behaviors, or he may either withdraw to fantasy, seek the company of girls and/or aggress against other boys. He feels wronged by others, and fails to incorporate peer-group norms.

Relationships between his gender representations are played out in his fantasy life. Peculiar masturbation fantasies are at first vague and have uncertain endings, but persist and become elaborated through transformations of early experiences. Gradually, he creates his preferred sexual fantasy which he uses in masturbation. Later, deviant sex play is rewarded and/or not punished.

Sometime in childhood or early adolescence, some trigger episode strikes a consonant chord and he finds his own peculiar pathway to safe sexual arousal. At first he reins in these impulses. Disinhibition then sets in and he gradually assumes a deviant label that eventually becomes the controlling one. This shift requires that he neutralize his shame and rationalize and disown responsibility for his being different. He may blame his heredity or hormones, attribute his actions to alcohol or clouded consciousness, rail and retaliate against unrealistic demands of a sexually uptight society. He wears a breastplate of righteousness to compensate for his deviancy. He comes in contact with his speciality pornography and perhaps joins a club or fraternity of like-minded individuals and assumes new deviant norms of behavior.

REFERENCES

Abel, G., Becker, J., & Skinner, L. (1980), Aggressive behavior and sex. *Psychiat. Clin. N. Amer.*, 3:133–151.

Abraham, K. (1910), Remarks on the psychoanalysis of a case of foot and corset fetishism. In: *Selected Papers of Karl Abraham*. New York: Basic Books, 1953.

Ackroyd, P. (1979), *Dressing Up*. New York: Simon & Schuster.

Acton, W. (1867), *The Functions and Disorders of the Reproductive Organs*. Philadelphia: Lindsay & Blakiston.

Agnew, J. (1982), Klismaphilia—A physiological perspective. *Amer. J. Psychother.*, 36:554–566.

Aiman, J., & Boyar, R. M. (1982), Testicular function in transsexual men. *Arch. Sex. Behav.*, 11:171–179.

Akesson, H. O., & Walinder, J. (1969), Transsexualism: Effect on rate and density-pattern of change of residence. *Brit. J. Psychiat.*, 115:593–594.

Alexander, F. (1956), A note on the theory of perversions. In: *Perversions Psychodynamics and Therapy*, ed. S. Lorand. New York: Gramercy Books.

Allen, D. W. (1967), Exhibitionistic and voyeuristic conflicts in learning and functioning. *Psychoanal. Quart.*, 36:546–570.

——— (1980), A psychoanalytic view. In: *Exhibitionism: Description, Assessment and Treatment*, ed. D. J. Cox & R. J. Daitzman. New York: Garland STPM Press.

Allen, E. (1940), *The Sexual Perversions and Abnormalities*. London: Oxford University Press.

Almansi, R. J. (1979), Scopophilia and object loss. *Psychoanal. Quart.*, 48:601–619.

Alstrom, C. (1977), A study of incest with special regard to the Swedish penal code. *Acta Psychiat. Scand.*, 56:357–372.

American Psychiatric Association (1980), *Diagnostic and Statistical Manual of Mental Disorders*, 2nd. ed. (DSM-III). Washington, DC: American Psychiatric Press.

407

———— (1987), *Diagnostic and Statistical Manual of Mental Disorders*, 3rd ed. rev. (DSM-III-R). Washington, DC: American Psychiatric Press.

Ampix (1978), *The Ameloatist: A Statistical Profile*. Lawndale, CA: Ampix.

Anchersen, P. (1956), Problems of transvestism. *Acta Psychiat. Scand. Supplem.*, 106:249–256.

Anon. (1882), *My Secret Life*. New York: Grove Press, 1966.

———— (1939), Obituary—Havelock Ellis. *Brit. Med. J.*, 2:203–204.

Apfelberg, B., Sugar, C., & Pfeffer, A. Z. (1944), A psychiatric study of 250 sex offenders. *Amer. J. Psychiat.*, 100:762–770.

Araji, S., & Finkelhor, D. (1985), Explanations of pedophilia: A review of empirical research. *Bull. Acad. Psychiat. & Law*, 13:17–37.

———— ———— (1986), Abusers: A review of the research. In: *A Sourcebook on Child Sexual Abuse*, ed. D. Finkelhor. Beverly Hills, CA: Sage Publications.

Arieff, A. J., & Rotman, D. B. (1942), One hundred cases of indecent exposure. *J. Nerv. & Ment. Dis.*, 96:523–528.

Armentrout, J. A., & Hauer, A. L. (1978), MMPIs of rapists of adults, rapists of children and non-rapist sex offenders. *J. Clin. Psychol.*, 34:330–332.

Armstrong, L. (1978), *Kiss Daddy Goodnight*. New York: Hawthorn Books.

Arndt, W. B., Foehl, J. C., & Good, F. E. (1985), Specific sexual fantasy themes. A multidimensional study. *J. Pers. & Soc. Psychol.*, 48:472–480.

———— Ladd, B. (1981), Sibling incest aversion as an index of oedipal conflict. *J. Personal. Assess.*, 45:52–58.

Asch, S. S. (1988), The analytic concepts of masochism: A reevaluation. In: *Masochism: Current Psychoanalytic Perspectives*, ed. R. A. Glick & D. I. Meyers. Hillsdale, NJ: Analytic Press.

Atwood, R. W., & Howell, R. J. (1971), Pupillometric and personality test score differences of female aggressing pedophiliacs and normals. *Psychonom. Sci.*, 22:115–116.

Avery, N. C. (1977), Sadomasochism: A defense against object love. *Psychoanal. Rev.*, 64:101–109.

Awad, G. A. (1987), The assessment of custody and access disputes in cases of sexual abuse allegations. *Can. J. Psychiat.*, 32:539–544.

Bagley, C. (1985), Child sexual abuse and juvenile prostitution. *Can. J. Publ. Health*, 76:65–66.

Bahl, J. D. (1979), Compensatory masculine responding as a function of sex-role. *J. Consult. & Clin. Psychol.*, 47:252–257.

Bak, R. C. (1953), Fetishism. *J. Amer. Psychoanal. Assn.*, 1:285–298.

———— (1968), The phallic woman. The ubiquitous fantasy in perversions. *The Psychoanalytic Study of the Child*, 23:15–36. New York: International Universities Press.

———— (1974), Distortion of the concept fetishism. *The Psychoanalytic Study of the Child*, 29:191–214. New Haven, CT: Yale University Press.

Baker, H. J. (1969), Transsexualism—Problems in treatment. *Amer. J. Psychiat.*, 125:1412–1418.

———— Green, R. (1970), Treatment of transsexualism. *Curr. Psychiat. Ther.*, 10:88–99.

Baker, R. (1968), *Drag*. London: Triton Books.

Bakwin, H. (1960), Transvestism in children. *J. Pediat.*, 56:294–298.

———— (1968), Deviant gender-role behavior in children: Relation to homosexuality. *Pediat.*, 41:620–629.

Balint, M. (1935), A contribution on fetishism. *Internat. J. Psycho-Anal.*, 16:481–483.

——— (1956), Perversions and genitality. In: *Perversions Psychodynamics and Therapy*, ed. S. Lorand. New York: Gramercy Books.

Barahal, H. (1953), Female transvestism and homosexuality. *Psychiat. Quart.*, 27:390–438.

Barclay, A. M., & Haber, R. N. (1965), The relation of aggressive to sexual motivation. *J. Pers.*, 33:462–475.

Barker, J. C. (1966), Transsexualism and transvestism. *J. Amer. Med. Assn.*, 198:448.

Barlow, D. H., Abel, G. G., & Blanchard, E. B. (1977), Gender identity change in a transsexual: An exorcism. *Arch. Sex. Behav.*, 6:387–395.

——— ——— ——— (1979), Gender identity change in transsexuals: Follow-up and replication. *Arch. Gen. Psychiat.*, 36:1001–1007.

——— Mills, J. R., Agras, W. S., & Steinman, D. L. (1980), Comparison of sex-typed motor behavior in male-to-female transsexuals and women. *Arch. Sex. Behav.*, 9:245–253.

——— Reynolds, E. J., & Agras, W. S. (1973), Gender identity change in a transsexual. *Arch. Gen. Psychiat.*, 28:569–576.

Barr, R. F. (1973), Responses to erotic stimuli of transsexual and homosexual males. *Brit. J. Psychiat.*, 123:579–585.

——— Blaszczynski, A. (1976), Autonomic responses of transsexual and homosexual males to erotic film sequences. *Arch. Sex. Behav.*, 5:211–222.

——— Raphael, B., & Hennessey, N. (1974), Apparent heterosexuality in two male patients requesting change-of-sex operation. *Arch. Sex. Behav.*, 3:325–330.

Barton, D., & Ware, P. D. (1966), Incongruities in the development of the sexual system. *Arch. Gen. Psychiat.*, 14:614–623.

Barton-Jay, D. (1984), *The Enema as an Erotic Art and its History*. New York: The David Barton-Jay Projects.

Bastani, J. B. (1976), Treatment of male genital exhibitionism. *Comprehen. Psychiat.*, 17:769–774.

——— Kentsmith, D. K. (1980), Psychotherapy with wives of sexual deviants. *Amer. J. Psychother.*, 34:22–25.

Bates, J. E., & Bentler, P. M. (1973), Play activities of normal and effeminate boys. *Develop. Psychol.*, 9:20–27.

——— ——— Thompson, S. (1973), Measurement of deviant gender development in boys. *Child Develop.*, 44:591–598.

——— ——— ——— (1979), Gender-deviant boys compared with normal and clinical control boys. *J. Abnorm. Child Psychol.*, 7:243–259.

——— Skilbeck, W. M., Smith, K. V. R., & Bentler, P. M. (1974), Gender role abnormalities in boys: An analysis of clinical ratings. *J. Abnorm. Child Psychol.*, 2:1–16.

——— ——— ——— ——— (1975), Intervention with families of gender-disturbed boys. *Amer. J. Orthopsychiat.*, 45:150–157.

Baumeister, R. F. (1988a), Masochism as escape from self. *J. Sex Res.*, 25:28–59.

——— (1988b), Gender differences in masochistic scripts. *J. Sex Res.*, 25:478–499.

Beatrice, J. (1985), A psychological comparison of heterosexuals, transvestites, preoperative and postoperative transsexuals. *J. Nerv. & Ment. Dis.*, 173:358–365.

Becker, H. (1963), *The Outsiders: Studies in the Sociology of Deviance*. New York: The Free Press.

Beigel, H. G. (1969), A weekend in Alice's wonderland. *J. Sex Res.*, 5:108–122.

———— Feldman, R. (1963), The male transvestite's motivation in fiction, research, and reality. In: *Advances in Sex Research*, ed. H. G. Beigel. New York: Hoeber.

Bejke, R. (1953), A contribution to the theory of exhibitionism. *Acta Psychiat. & Neurol. Scand. Suppl.*, 88:233–243.

Bell, A. P., & Hall, C. S. (1971), *The Personality of a Child Molester*. Chicago: Aldine Atherton.

———— Weinberg, M. S. (1978), *Homosexualities: A Study of Diversity Among Men and Women*. New York: Simon & Schuster.

Bell, R. A. (1968), A reinterpretation of the direction of effect in studies of socialization. *Psychol. Rev.*, 75:81–95.

Bemporad, J., Dunton, D., & Spady, F. H. (1976), Treatment of a child foot fetishist. *Amer. J. Psychother.*, 30:303–316.

Bender, L., & Pester, S. (1941), Homosexual trends in children. *Amer. J. Orthopsychiat.*, 11:730–744.

Benjamin, H. (1954), Transsexualism and transvestism as psycho-somatic and somata-psychic syndromes. *Amer. J. Psychother.*, 8:219–230.

———— (1964), Clinical aspects of transsexualism in the male and female. *Amer. J. Psychother.*, 18:458–469.

———— (1966), *The Transsexual Phenomenon*. New York: Julian Press.

———— (1967), Transvestism and transsexualism in the male and female. *J. Sex Res.*, 3:107–127.

———— (1971), Should surgery be performed on transsexuals? *Amer. J. Psychother.*, 25:74–82.

———— Ihlenfeld, C. L. (1973), Transsexualism. *Amer. J. Nurs.*, 73:457–461.

Bentler, P. M. (1976), A typology of transsexualism: Gender identity therapy and data. *Arch. Sex. Behav.*, 5:567–584.

———— Prince, C. (1969), Personality characteristics of male transvestites III. *J. Abnorm. Psychol.*, 74:140–143.

———— Prince, C. (1970), Psychiatric symptomatology in transvestites. *J. Clin. Psychol.*, 26:434–435.

———— Rekers, G. A., & Rosen, A. C. (1979), Congruence of childhood sex-role identity and behavior disturbances. *Child Care, Health, & Develop.*, 5:267–283.

———— Sherman, R. W., & Prince, C. (1970), Personality characteristics of male transvestites. *J. Clin. Psychol.*, 26:287–291.

Berah, E. F., & Meyers, R. G. (1983), The offense records of a sample of convicted exhibitionists. *Bull. Amer. Acad. Psychiat. & Law*, 11:365–367.

Berg, I., Nixon, H. H., & MacMahon, R. (1963), Change of assigned sex at puberty. *Lancet*, 2:1216–1217.

Bergler, E. (1938), Preliminary phases of the masculine beating fantasy. *Psychoanal. Quart.*, 7:514–536.

———— (1944), A new approach to the therapy of erythrophobia. *Psychoanal. Quart.*, 13:43–59.

Bergman, P. (1947), Analysis of an unusual case of fetishism. *Bull. Menn. Clin.*, 11:67–75.

Berliner, B. (1942), The concept of masochism. *Psychoanal. Rev.*, 29:386–400.

———— (1947), On some psychodynamics of masochism. *Psychoanal. Quart.*, 16:459–471.

———— (1958), The role of object relations in moral masochism. *Psychoanal. Quart.*, 27:38–56.

Berliner, L., & Stevens, D. (1982), Clinical issues in child sexual abuse. *J. Soc. Work & Hum. Sexual.*, 1:93–108.

Berman, L. H. (1953), Perception and object relation in a patient with transvestite tendencies. *Internat. J. Psycho-Anal.*, 34:25–39.

Bernard, F. (1975), An enquiry among a group of pedophiles. *J. Sex Res.*, 11:242–255.

Bernstein, I. (1976), Masochistic reactions in a latency-age girl. *J. Amer. Psychoanal. Assn.*, 24:589–607.

Bernstein, S., Steiner, B., Glaister, J., & Muir, C. (1981), Changes in patients with gender-identity problems after parental death. *Amer. J. Psychiat.*, 138:41–45.

Bethell, M. F. (1974), A rare manifestation of fetishism. *Arch. Sex. Behav.*, 3:301–302.

Bieber, I. (1953), The meaning of masochism. *Amer. J. Psychother.*, 7:433–448.

———— (1966), Sadism and masochism. In: *American Handbook of Psychiatry*, ed. S. Arieti. New York: Basic Books.

———— (1970), Answers to questions: Enemas and sex. *Med. Asp. of Hum. Sexual.*, 4:89.

———— (1976), A discussion of "Homosexuality: The ethical challenge." *J. Consult. & Clin. Psychol.*, 44:163–166.

Billings, D. W., & Urban, T. (1982), The socio-medical construction of transsexualism: An interpretation and critique. *Social Probl.*, 29:266–282.

Bixler, R. H. (1983), The multiple meaning of incest. *J. Sex Res.*, 19:197–201.

Blacker, K. H., & Wong, N. (1963), Four cases of autocastration. *Arch. Gen. Psychiat.*, 8:169–176.

Blanchard, R. (1985a), Typology of male-to-female transsexualism. *Arch. Sex. Behav.*, 14:247–261.

———— (1985b), Gender dysphoria and gender reorientation. In: *Gender Dysphoria*, ed. B. W. Steiner. New York: Plenum.

———— Clemmensen, L. H. (1985), Gender dysphoria, gender reorientation, and the clinical management of transsexualism. *J. Consult. & Clin. Psychol.*, 53:295–304.

———— ———— (1988), A test of the DSM-III-R's implicit assumption that fetishistic arousal and gender dysphoria are mutually exclusive. *J. Sex Res.*, 25:426–432.

———— ———— Steiner, B. W. (1983), Gender reorientation and psychosocial adjustment in male-to-female transsexuals. *Arch. Sex. Behav.*, 12:503–509.

———— ———— ———— (1987), Heterosexual and homosexual gender dysphoria. *Arch. Sex. Behav.*, 16:139–152.

———— McConkey, J. G., Roper, V., & Steiner, B. W. (1983), Measuring physical aggressiveness in heterosexual, homosexual and transsexual males. *Arch. Sex. Behav.*, 12:541–547.

———— Steiner, B. W. (1983), Gender reorientation, psychological adjustment, and involvement with female partners in female-male-transsexuals. *Arch. Sex. Behav.*, 12:149–157.

Bloch, I. (1901), *The Sexual Extremities of the World.* New York: Award Books, 1964.

——— (1908), *The Sexual Life of Our Time.* New York: Allied Books.

Blos, P. (1967), The second individuation process of adolescence. *The Psychoanalytic Study of the Child*, 22:162–186. New York: International Universities Press.

Boatman, E., Barkan, E., & Schetky, D. (1981), Treatment of child victims of incest. *Amer. J. Fam. Ther.*, 9:43–51.

Bonaparte, M. (1952), Some biophysical aspects of sado-masochism. *Internat. J. Psycho-Anal.*, 33:373–384.

Bonime, W. R. (1969), Masturbatory fantasies and personality. *Sci. & Psychoanal.*, 15:32–47.

"Boots" (pseud.) (1957), The feelings of a fetishist. *Psychiat. Quart.*, 31:742–758.

Boss, M. (1949), *Meaning and Content of Sexual Perversions.* New York: Grune & Stratton.

Bowman, K. M. (1951), The problem of the sex offender. *Amer. J. Psychiat.*, 108:250–257.

——— Engle, B. (1957), Medicolegal aspects of transvestism. *Amer. J. Psychiat.*, 113:583–588.

Boyar, R. M., & Aiman, J. (1982), The 24-hour secretory pattern of LH and the response to LHRH in transsexual men. *Arch. Sex. Behav.*, 11:157–169.

Bradford, J. M. W., Bloomberg, D., & Bourget, D. (1988), The heterogeneity/homogeneity of pedophiles. *Psychiat. J. Univ. Ottawa*, 13:217–226.

Bradley, S. J. (1985), Gender disorders in childhood: A formulation. In: *Gender Dysphoria*, ed. B. W. Steiner. New York: Plenum Press.

Brady, K. (1979), *Father's Days.* New York: Dell.

Brant, R. S., & Tisza, V. B. (1977), The sexually misused child. *Amer. J. Orthopsychiat.*, 47:80–90.

Braun, W. (1967), *The Cruel and the Meek.* New York: Lyle Stuart.

Brecher, E. M. (1969), *The Sex Researchers.* Boston: Little, Brown.

Brenner, C. (1959), The masochistic character: Genesis and treatment. *J. Amer. Psychoanal. Assn.*, 7:197–226.

Breslow, N., Evans, L., & Langley, J. (1985), On the prevalence and roles of females in the sadomasochistic subculture: Report of an empirical study. *Arch. Sex. Behav.*, 14:303–317.

Brierly, H. (1979), *Transvestism.* New York: Pergamon Press.

Brill, A. A. (1932), The sense of smell in the neuroses and psychoses. *Psychoanal. Quart.*, 1:7–42.

——— (1941), Necrophilia. Part I. *J. Crim. Psychopathol.*, 2:433–443.

British Medical Journal (1966), Editorial. Sexual offences against children. 5488:626–627.

Brittain, R. P. (1968), The sexual asphysias. In: *Gradwohl's Legal Medicine*, 2nd ed., ed. F. D. Camps. Baltimore: Williams & Wilkins.

——— (1970), The sadistic murderer. *Med., Sci. & Law.*, 10:198–207.

Brogdan, R. (1974), *Being Different: The Autobiography of Jane Fry.* New York: John Wiley.

Bromberg, W. (1959), Stimulus-response cycles and ego development. *J. Amer. Psychoanal. Assn.*, 7:227–247.

Bross, D. C. (1984), In: *Protecting our Children: The Fight Against Molestation. A National Symposium.* Washington, DC: U.S. Government Printing Office.

Brown, D. G. (1957), Masculinity–femininity development in children. *J. Consult. Psychol.*, 21:197–202.

——— (1960), Psychosexual disturbances: Transvestism and sex-role inversion. *Marr. & Fam. Living*, 22:218–227.

Brown, G. R. (1988), Transsexuals in the military: Flight into hypermasculinity. *Arch. Sex. Behav.*, 17:527–537.

Brown, J. C. (1983), Paraphilias: Sadomasochism, fetishism, transvestism and transsexuality. *Brit. J. Psychiat.*, 143:227–231.

Brownell, K. D. (1980), Multifacted behavior therapy. In: *Exhibitionism: Description, Assessment, and Treatment*, ed. D. J. Cox & R. J. Daitzman. New York: Garland STPM Press.

Browning, D. H., & Boatman, B. (1977), Incest: Children at risk. *Amer. J. Psychiat.*, 134:69–72.

Buchner, H. T. (1970), The transvestic career pattern. *Psychiat.*, 33:381–389.

Buhrich, N. (1977), A case of familial heterosexual transvestism. *Acta Psychiat. Scand.*, 55:199–201.

——— (1978), Motivation for cross-dressing in heterosexual transvestism. *Acta Psychiat. Scand.*, 57:145–152.

——— (1983), The association of piercing with homosexuality, sadomasochism, bondage, fetishism, and tattoos. *Arch. Sex. Behav.*, 12:167–171.

——— Beaumont, T. (1981), Comparison of transvestism in Australia and America. *Arch. Sex. Behav.*, 10:269–279.

——— McConaghy, N. (1976), Transvestite fiction. *J. Nerv. & Ment. Dis.*, 163:420–427.

——— ——— (1977a), The clinical syndromes of femmiphilic transvestism. *Arch. Sex. Behav.*, 6:397–412.

——— ——— (1977b), The discrete syndrome of transvestism and transsexualism. *Arch. Sex. Behav.*, 6:483–495.

——— ——— (1977c), Can fetishism occur in transsexuals? *Arch. Sex. Behav.*, 6:223–235.

——— ——— (1979), Three clinically discrete categories of fetishistic transvestism. *Arch. Sex. Behav.*, 8:151–157.

Bullough, V. L., & Bullough, B. (1977), *Sin, Sickness, and Sanity.* New York: Meridian.

——— ——— Smith, R. (1983), A comparative study of male transvestites, male to female transsexuals, and male homosexuals. *J. Sex Res.*, 19:238–257.

Burgess, A. W., Dietz, P. E., & Hazelwood, R. R. (1983), Study design and sample characteristics. In: *Autoerotic Fatalities*, ed. R. R. Hazelwood, P. E. Dietz, & A. W. Burgess. Lexington, MA: Lexington Books.

——— Groth, A. N., & McCausland, M. P. (1981), Child sex initiation rings. *Amer. J. Orthopsychiat.*, 51:110–119.

——— Hartman, C. R., McCausland, M. P., & Powers, P. (1984), Response patterns in children and adolescents exploited through sex rings and pornography. *Amer. J. Psychiat.*, 141:656–662.

——— Hazelwood, R. R. (1983), Autoerotic asphyxial deaths and social network response. *Amer. J. Orthopsychiat.*, 53:166–170.

——— Holmstrom, L. L. (1975), Sexual trauma of children and adolescents: Pressure, sex, and secrecy. *Nursing Clin. N. Amer.*, 10:551–563.

———— ———— McCausland, M. P. (1977), Child sexual assault by a family member: Decisions following disclosure. *Victimology*, 2:236–250.

Burton, L. (1968), *Vulnerable Children*. London: Routledge & Kegan Paul.

Bychowski, G. (1959), Some aspects of masochistic involvement. *J. Amer. Psychoanal. Assn.*, 7:248–273.

Cairns, F. J., & Rainer, S. P. (1981), Death from electrocution during autoerotic procedures. *N.Z. Med. J.*, 94:259–260.

Calef, V., & Weinshel, E. M. (1972), On certain neurotic equivalents of necrophilia. *Internat. J. Psycho-Anal.*, 53:67–75.

Calogera, R. C. (1987), The transvestite and his wife. *Psychoanal. Rev.*, 74:517–535.

Cameron, P. (1985), Homosexual molestation of children/sexual interaction of teacher and pupil. *Psychol. Rep.*, 57:1227–1236.

Cappon, D. (1970), Intersexuality and transsexuality. Part 2. *Postgrad. Med.*, 48:287–288.

Caprio, F. S. (1955), *Variations in Sexual Behavior*. New York: Citadel Press.

Carpenter, E. (1908), *The Intermediate Sex*. London: George Allen & Unwin.

Carr, J. E. (1974), Behavior therapy in a case of multiple sexual disorders. *J. Behav. Ther. & Experiment. Psychiat.*, 5:171–174.

Carter, A. (1979), *The Sadeian Woman*. London: Virago.

Carter, D. B., & McCloskey, L. A. (1984), Peers and the maintenance of sex-typed behavior: Children's conceptions of cross-gender behavior in their peers. *Soc. Cognit.*, 2:294–314.

Cavallin, H. (1966), Incestuous fathers: A clinical report. *Amer. J. Psychiat.*, 122:1132–1138.

Chalkley, A. J., & Powell, G. E. (1983), The clinical description of forty-eight cases of sexual fetishism. *Brit. J. Psychiat.*, 142:292–295.

Chesser, E. (1971), *Strange Loves*. New York: William Morrow.

Childs, A. (1977), Acute symbiotic psychosis in a postoperative transsexual. *Arch. Sex. Behav.*, 6:37–44.

Christoffel, H. (1936), Exhibitionism and exhibitionists. *Internat. J. Psycho-Anal.*, 17:321–345.

———— (1956), Male genital exhibitionism. In: *Perversions Psychodynamics and Therapy*, ed. S. Lorand. New York: Gramercy Books.

Ciba Foundation (1984), *Child Sexual Abuse Within the Family*. London: Tavistock Publications.

Cleef, M. von (n.d.), *The House of Pain*. Secaucus, NJ: Lyle Stuart.

Cleveland, S. E. (1956), Three cases of auto-castration. *J. Nerv. & Ment. Dis.*, 123:386–391.

Coen, S. J. (1981), Sexualization as a predominant mode of defense. *J. Amer. Psychoanal. Assn.*, 29:893–920.

———— (1988), Sadomasochistic excitement: Character disorder and perversion. In: *Masochism: Current Psychoanalytic Perspectives*, ed. R. A. Glick & D. I. Meyers. Hillsdale, NJ: Analytic Press.

Cohen, B. (1980), *Deviant Street Networks*. Lexington, MA: Lexington Books.

Coleman, R. O. (1983), Acoustic correlates of speaker sex identification: Implications for the transsexual voice. *J. Sex Res.*, 19:293–295.

Condy, S. R., Templer, D. I., Brown, R., & Veaco, L. (1987), Parameters of sexual contact of boys with women. *Arch. Sex. Behav.*, 16:379–394.

Conn, C. (1974), *Canary: The Story of a Transsexual*. Los Angeles: Nash.

Conte, J. R. (1982), Sexual abuse of children: Enduring issues for social work. *J. Soc. Work & Hum. Sexual.*, 1:1–19.

—— Berliner, L. (1981), Sexual abuse of children: Implications for practice. *Soc. Casework*, 62:601–606.

Cooper, A. J. (1963), A case of fetishism and impotence treated by behaviour therapy. *Brit. J. Psychiat.*, 109:649–652.

Cooper, I., & Cormier, B. M. (1982), Inter-generational transmission of incest. *Can. J. Psychiat.*, 27:231–235.

Cordner, S. M. (1983), An unusual case of sudden death associated with masturbation. *Med., Sci. & Law*, 23:54–56.

Cormier, B. M., Kennedy, M., & Sangowicz, J. (1962), Psychodynamics father-daughter incest. *Can. Psychiat. Assn. J.*, 7:203–217.

Crepault, E., & Couture, M. (1980), Men's erotic fantasies. *Arch. Sex. Behav.*, 9:565–581.

Crewdson, J. (1988), *By Silence Betrayed: Sexual Abuse of Children in America.* Boston: Little, Brown.

Croughan, J. L., Sagher, M., Cohen, R., & Robins, E. (1981), A comparison of treated and untreated male cross-dressers. *Arch. Sex. Behav.*, 10:515–528.

Culp, R. E., Cook, A. S., & Housley, P. C. (1983), A comparison of observed and reported adult-infant interactions: Effects of perceived sex. *Sex Roles*, 9:475–479.

Curran, D., & Parr, D. (1957), Homosexuality: An analysis of 100 male patients seen in private practice. *Brit. Med. J.*, 1:797.

Daitzman, R. J. & Cox, D. J. (1980), An extended case report. In: *Exhibitionism: Description, Assessment, and Treatment*, ed. D. J. Cox & R. J. Daitzman. New York: Garland STPM Press.

Dallaert, R., & Kunke, T. (1969), Investigations on a case of male transsexualism. *Psychother. & Psychosom.*, 17:89–107.

Davenport, C. W. (1986), A follow-up study of 10 feminine boys. *Arch. Sex. Behav.*, 15:511–517.

—— Harrison, S. I. (1977), Gender identity change in a female adolescent transsexual. *Arch. Sex. Behav.*, 6:327–340.

Davies, B. M., & Morgenstern, F. S. (1960), A case of cysticerosis temporal lobe epilepsy and transvestism. *J. Neurolog. & Neurosurg. Psychiat.*, 23:247–249.

de Beauvoir, S. (1952), *The Second Sex.* New York: Bantam Books.

—— (1966), Must we burn Sade? In: *The Marquis de Sade. The 120 Days of Sodom and Other Writings*, trans. A. Wainhouse & R. Seaver. New York: Grove Press.

DeMott, B. (1980), The pro-incest lobby. *Psychology Today*, 10:11–18.

Denko, J. D. (1973), Klismaphilia: Enema as a sexual preference. *Amer. J. Psychother.*, 27:232–250.

—— (1976), Klismaphilia—Amplification of the erotic enema deviance. *Amer. J. Psychother.*, 30:236–255.

de River, J. P. (1958), *Crime and the Sexual Psychopath.* Springfield, IL: Charles C Thomas.

Derogatis, L., Meyer, J., & Boland, P. (1981), A psychological profile of the transsexual. *J. Nerv. & Ment. Dis.*, 169:157–168.

—— —— Vazquez, N. (1978), A psychological profile of the transsexual. *J. Nerv. & Ment. Dis.*, 166:234–254.

de Sade, D. (1785), The 120 Days of Sodom. In: *The Marquis de Sade. The 120*

Days of Sodom Other Writings, trans. A. Wainhouse & R. Seaver. New York: Grove Press, 1966.

————— (1791), Justine. In: *The Marquis de Sade. The Complete Justine, Philosophy in the Bedroom and Other Writings*, trans. R. Seaver & A. Wainhouse. New York: Grove Press, 1965.

————— (1795), Philosophy in the bedroom. In: *The Marquis de Sade. The Complete Justine, Philosophy in the Bedroom and Other Writings*, trans. R. Seaver & A. Wainhouse. New York: Grove Press, 1965.

————— (1797), Julliete. In: *The Marquis de Sade. Juliette*, trans. A. Wainhouse. New York: Grove Press, 1968.

Deutsch, D. (1954), A case of transvestism. *Amer. J. Psychother.*, 8:239–242.

Dewaraja, R. (1988), Formicophilia, an unusual paraphilia, treated with counseling and behavior therapy. *Amer. J. Psychother.*, 41:593–597.

Dewhurst, C. J., & Gordon, R. R. (1963), Change of sex. *Lancet*, ii:1213–1216.

de Young, M. (1981), Siblings of Oedipus: Brothers and sisters of incest victims. *Child Welf.*, 60:561–568.

Diamond, M. (1965), A critical evaluation of the ontogeny of human sexual behavior. *Quart. Rev. Biol.*, 40:147–175.

————— (1982), Sexual identity, monozygotic twins reared in discordant sex roles and a BBC follow-up. *Arch. Sex. Behav.*, 11:181–186.

Dickes, R. (1963), Fetishistic behavior: A contribution to its complex development and significance. *J. Amer. Psychoanal. Assn.*, 11:303–330.

————— (1970), Psychodynamics of fetishism. *Med. Aspects Hum. Sexual.*, 4:39–52.

Dietz, C., & Craft, J. L. (1980), Family dynamics of incest: A new perspective. *Soc. Casework*, 61:602–609.

Dietz, P. E. (1983), Recurrent discovery of autoerotic asphyxia. In: *Autoerotic Fatalities*, ed. R. R. Hazelwood, P. E. Dietz, & A. W. Burgess. Lexington, MA: Lexington Books.

————— Burgess, A. W. (1983), Atypical autoerotic fatalities. In: *Autoerotic Fatalities*, ed. R. R. Hazelwood, P. E. Dietz, & A. W. Burgess. Lexington, MA: Lexington Books.

————— ————— Hazelwood, R. R. (1983), Autoerotic asphyxia, the paraphilias, and mental disorder. In *Autoerotic Fatalities*, ed. R. R. Hazelwood, P. E. Dietz, & A. W. Burgess. Lexington, MA: Lexington Books.

————— Evans, B. (1982), Pornographic imagery and prevalence of paraphilia. *Amer. J. Psychiat.*, 139:1493–1495.

Dinello, F. A. (1967), Stages in treatment of the case of a diaper-wearing seventeen-year-old male. *Amer. J. Psychiat.*, 123:94–96.

Dinnerstein, D. (1976), *The Mermaid and the Minotaur: Sexual Arrangements and Human Malaise*. New York: Harper & Row.

Dixen, J. M., Maddever, H., Van Maasdam, J., & Edwards, R. W. (1984), Psychosocial characteristics of applicants evaluated for surgical gender reassignment. *Arch. Sex. Behav.*, 13:269–276.

Docter, R. F. (1985), Transsexual surgery at 74: A case report. *Arch. Sex. Behav.*, 14:271–277.

————— (1988), *Transvestites and Transsexuals*. New York: Plenum Press.

Dolan, J. D. (1987), Transsexualism: Syndrome or symptom. *Can. J. Psychiat.*, 32:666–673.

Dooley, L. (1941), The relation of humor to masochism. *Psychoanal. Rev.*, 28:37–46.

Doorbar, R. R. (1969), Psychological testing of male transsexuals. In: *Transsexualism and Sex Reassignment*, ed. R. Green & J. Money. Baltimore: Johns Hopkins University Press.

Dorner, G. (1976), Hormone dependent differentiation, maturation and function of the brain and sexual behavior. In: *Progress in Sexology*, ed. R. Gemme & C. C. Wheeler. New York: Plenum Press.

———— (1988), Neuroendocrine response to estrogen and brain differentiation in heterosexuals, homosexuals, and transsexuals. *Arch. Sex. Behav.*, 17:57–75.

Drake, C. T., & McDougall, D. (1977), Effects of absence of the father and other male models on the development of boys' sex roles. *Developm. Psychol.*, 13:537–538.

Dulko, S. (1988), Sexual activity and temperament in Polish transsexuals. *Arch. Sex. Behav.*, 17:163–171.

Dupont, H. (1968), Social learning theory and the treatment of transvestite behavior in an eight-year-old boy. *Psychother: Theory, Res., & Pract.*, 5:44–45.

Dworin, W. (1984), In: *Protecting Our Children: The Fight Against Molestation. A National Symposium*. Washington, DC: U.S. Government Printing Office.

East, W. N. (1924), Observations on exhibitionism. *Lancet*, 2:370–375.

Eaton, W. O., & von Bargen, E. (1981), Asynchronous development of gender understanding in preschool children. *Child Develop.*, 52:1020–1027.

Eber, M. (1980), Gender identity conflicts in male transsexualism. *Bull. Menn. Clin.*, 44:31–38.

———— (1982), Primary transsexualism: A critique of a therapy. *Bull. Menn. Clin.*, 46:168–182.

Edelstein, E. (1960), Psychodynamics of a transvestite. *Amer. J. Psychother.*, 14:121–131.

Edgerton, M. T., Knorr, N. J., & Callison, J. R. (1970), The surgical treatment of transsexual patients: Limitations and indications. *Plastic & Reconstruct. Surg.*, 45:38–46.

Edmondson, J. S. (1972), A case of sexual asphyxia without fatal termination. *Brit. J. Psychiat.*, 121:437–438.

Ehrenreich, G. A. (1960), Headache, necrophilia, and murder: A brief hypnotherapeutic investigation of a single case. *Bull. Menn. Clin.*, 24:273–287.

Ehrhardt, A. A., Grisanti, G., & McCauley, E. A. (1979), Female to male transsexuals compared to lesbians: Behavior patterns of childhood and adolescent development. *Arch. Sex. Behav.*, 8:481–490.

———— Meyer-Bahlburg, H. F. L., Feldman, J. F., & Ince, S. E. (1984), Sex dimorphic behavior in childhood subsequent to prenatal exposure to exogenous progestogens and estrogens. *Arch. Sex. Behav.*, 13:457–477.

Eicher, W., Spoljar, M., Cleve, H., Murken, J., Richter, K., & Stangel-Rutkowski, S. (1979), H-Y antigen in trans-sexuality. *Lancet*, ii:1137–1138.

Eidelberg, L. (1959), Humiliation in masochism. *J. Amer. Psychoanal. Assn.*, 7:274–283.

Eist, H. L., & Mandel, A. U. (1968), Family treatment of ongoing incest behavior. *Family Proc.*, 7:216–232.

Eklund, P. L. E., Goorem, L. J. G., & Bezmer, P. D. (1988), Prevalence of transsexualism in the Netherlands. *Brit. J. Psychiat.*, 152:638–640.

Ellerstein, N. S., & Canavan, J. W. (1980), Sexual abuse of boys. *Amer. J. Dis. Child.*, 134:255–257.

Ellis, A. (1967), The psychology of sex offenders. In: *The Encyclopedia of Sexual Behavior*, ed. A. Ellis & A. Abarbanal. New York: Hawthorn Books.

———— Brancale, R. (1956), *The Psychology of Sex Offenders*. Springfield, IL: Charles C Thomas.

Ellis, H. (1906), Erotic symbolism. In: *Studies in the Psychology of Sex*. Vol. 2. New York: Random House, 1936.

———— (1913), Love and pain. In: *Studies in the Psychology of Sex*, Vol. 1. New York: Random House, 1936.

———— (1928), Eonism. In: *Studies in the Psychology of Sex*, Vol. 2. New York: Random House, 1936.

Ellis, L., Ames, M. A., Peckham, W., & Burke, D. (1988), Sexual orientation of human offspring may be altered by severe maternal stress during pregnancy. *J. Sex Res.*, 25:152–157.

Elwell, M. E. (1979), Sexually assaulted children and their families. *Soc. Casework*, 60:227–235.

Eme, R. F. (1979), Sex differences in childhood psychopathology: A review. *Psychol. Bull.*, 86:574–595.

Engel, W., Pfafflin, F., & Wiedeking, C. (1980), H-Y antigen in transsexuality, and how to explain testis differentiation in H-Y antigen negative male and ovary differentiation in H-Y antigen-positive females. *Hum. Genet.*, 55:315–319.

Epstein, A. W. (1960), Fetishism: A study of its psychopathology with particular reference to a proposed disorder in brain mechanism as an etiological factor. *J. Nerv. & Ment. Dis.*, 130:107–119.

———— (1961), Relationship of fetishism and transvestism to brain and particularly to temporal lobe dysfunction. *J. Nerv. & Ment. Dis.*, 133:247–253.

———— (1969), Fetishism: A comprehensive view. *Sci. & Psychoanal.*, 15:81–87.

———— (1975), The fetish object: Phylogenetic considerations. *Arch. Sex. Behav.*, 4:303–308.

———— (1980), Familial imperative ideas and actions: How encoded. *Biolog. Psychiat.*, 15:489–494.

Erickson, W. D., Walbek, N. H., & Seely, R. K. (1987), The life histories and psychological profiles of 59 incestuous stepfathers. *Bull. Amer. Acad. Psychiat. & Law*, 15:349–357.

———— ———— ———— (1988), Behavior patterns of child molesters. *Arch. Sex. Behav.*, 17:77–86.

Erikson, E. H. (1963), *Childhood and Society*, 2nd ed. New York: W. W. Norton.

Esman, A. H. (1954), A case of self-castration. *J. Nerv. & Ment. Dis.*, 120:79–82.

———— (1973), The primal scene. A review and reconsideration. *The Psychoanalytic Study of the Child*, 28:49–81. New Haven, CT: Yale University Press.

Eulenburg, A. von (1911), *Sadism and Masochism*. New York: Bell, 1984.

Evans, D. R. (1970), Subjective variables and treatment effects in aversion therapy. *Behav. Res. & Ther.*, 8:147–152.

———— (1980), Electrical aversion therapy. In: *Exhibitionism: Description, Assessment, and Treatment*, ed. D. J. Cox & R. J. Daitzman. New York: Garland STPM Press.

Everaerd, W. (1983), A case of apotemnophilia: A handicap of sexual preference. *Amer. J. Psychother.*, 37:285–293.

Faegerman, P. (1955), Fantasies of menstruation in men. *Psychoanal. Quart.*, 24:1–19.

Fagan, P. J., Wise, T. N., Derogatis, L. R., & Schmit, C. W. (1988), Distressed transvestites. *J. Nerv. & Ment. Dis.*, 176:626–632.

Fagot, B. I. (1974), Sex differences in toddler's behavior and parental reaction. *Develop. Psychol.*, 10:554–558.

——— (1977), Consequences of moderate cross-gender behavior in preschool children. *Child Develop.*, 48:902–907.

——— (1978), The influence of sex of child on parental reactions to toddler children. *Child Develop.*, 49:459–465.

Fairchild, L. (1975), On classical transvestism. Paper presented at Conference on the TV-TG-TS Phenomenon, University of Rhode Island School of Medicine.

Farrell, L. T. (1988), Factors that affect a victim's self-disclosure in father–daughter incest. *Child Welf.*, 67:462–468.

Federn, P. (1952), *Ego Psychology and the Psychoses*. New York: Basic Books.

Fedora, O., Reddon, J. R., & Yeudall, L. T. (1986), Stimuli eliciting sexual arousal in genital exhibitionists: A possible clinical application. *Arch. Sex. Behav.*, 15:417–427.

Fehrenbach, P. A., & Monastersky, C. (1988), Characteristics of female adolescent sexual offenders. *Amer. J. Orthopsychiat.*, 58:148–151.

——— Smith, W., Monastersky, C., & Deisher, R. W. (1986), Adolescent sexual offenders: Offender and offense characteristics. *Amer. J. Orthopsychiat.*, 56:225–233.

Feigen, G. M. (1972), Answers to questions: Erotic potential of enemas. *Med. Asp. Hum. Sexual.*, 6:199.

Feinbloom, D. H. (1976), *Transvestites and Transsexuals*. New York: Delta.

——— Fleming, M., Kijewski, W., & Schulter, M. (1976), Lesbian/feminist orientation among male-to-female transsexuals. *J. Homosexual.*, 2:59–71.

Fenichel, O. (1930), The psychology of transvestism. *Collected Papers*, Vol. 1. London: Routledge & Kegan Paul, 1954.

——— (1935), The scoptophilic instinct and identification. *Collected Papers*, Vol. 1. London: Routledge & Kegan Paul, 1954.

——— (1945), *The Psychoanalytic Theory of the Neuroses*. New York: W. W. Norton.

Fensterheim, H. (1974), Behavior therapy for the sexual variations. *J. Sex & Marit. Ther.*, 1:16–28.

Ferenczi, S. (1932), Confusion of tongues between adult and child. *Internat. J. Psycho-Anal.*, 30:225–230.

Finegan, J. K., Zuker, K. J., Bradley, S. J., & Doering, R. W. (1982), Patterns of intellectual functioning and spatial ability of boys with gender identity disorder. *Can. J. Psychiat.*, 27:135–139.

Finkelhor, D. (1979a), *Sexually Victimized Children*. New York: Free Press.

——— (1979b), What's wrong with sex between adults and children? *Amer. J. Orthopsychiat.*, 49:692–697.

——— Baron, L. (1986), High-risk children. In: *A Sourcebook on Child Sexual Abuse*, ed. D. Finkelhor. Beverly Hills: Sage Publications.

Finney, J. C., Brandsma, J. M., Tondow, M., & Lemaestre, G. (1975), A study of transsexuals seeking gender reassignment. *Amer. J. Psychiat.*, 132:962–964.

Fischoff, J. (1964), Preoedipal influences in a boy's determination to be "feminine" during the oedipal period. *J. Amer. Acad. Child Psychiat.*, 3:273–286.

Fisher, G. H. (1979), Psychological needs of heterosexual pedophiles. *Dis. Nerv. Syst.*, 30:419–421.

────── Howell, L. M. (1970), Psychological needs of homosexual pedophiliacs. *Dis. Nerv. Syst.*, 31:623–625.

Fisk, N. M. (1978), Five spectacular results. *Arch. Sex. Behav.*, 7:351–369.

Fleming, M. Z., Castos, D., & MacGowan, B. (1984), Ego development in female-to-male transsexual couples. *Arch. Sex. Behav.*, 13:581–594.

────── Cohen, D., Salt, P., Jones, D., & Jenkins, S. (1981), A study of pre- and post-transsexuals: MMPI characteristics. *Arch. Sex. Behav.*, 10:161–170.

────── Jenkins, S. R., & Bugarin, C. (1980), Questioning current definitions of gender identity: Implications for the Bem Sex-Role Inventory for transsexuals. *Arch. Sex. Behav.*, 9:13–26.

────── MacGowan, B. R., & Castos, D. (1985), The dyadic adjustment of female-to-male transsexuals. *Arch. Sex. Behav.*, 14:47–55.

────── ────── Salt, P. (1984), Female-to-male transsexualism: Self and spouse ratings on the PAQ. *Arch. Sex. Behav.*, 13:51–57.

────── Steinman, C., & Bocknek, G. (1980), Methodological problems in assessing sex reassignment surgery: A reply to Meyer and Reter. *Arch. Sex. Behav.*, 9:451–456.

Fookes, B. H. (1969), Some experiences in the use of aversion therapy in male homosexuality, exhibitionism and fetishism–transvestism. *Brit. J. Psychiat.*, 115:339–341.

Ford, R. (1957), Death by hanging of adolescent and young adult males. *J. Forensic Sci.*, 2:171–176.

Forel, A. (1905), *The Sexual Question.* New York: Medical Art Agency, 1922.

Forester, F. M., & Swiller, H. (1972), Transsexualism. *Internat. J. Group Psychother.*, 22:343–351.

Forgac, G. E., Cassel, C. A., & Michaels, E. J. (1984), Chronicity of criminal behavior and psychopathology in male exhibitionists. *J. Clin. Psychol.*, 40:827–832.

Fox, A. N. (1941), Psychoanalysis of a sodomist. *Amer. J. Orthopsychiat.*, 11:133–142.

Fox, R. (1980), *The Red Lamp of Incest.* New York: E. P. Dutton.

Francis, J. J., & Marcus, I. M. (1975), Masturbation: A developmental view. In: *Masturbation*, ed. I. M. Marcus & J. J. Francis. New York: International Universities Press.

Franzini, L. R., Magy, M. A., & Litrownik, A. J. (1977), Detectability and perceptions of a transsexual. *J. Homosexual.*, 2:269–279.

Fraser, M. (1981), The child. In: *Perspectives on Paedophilia*, ed. B. Taylor. London: Batsford.

Fraxi, P. (1877), *Index Librorum Prohibitorum.* New York: Documentary Books, 1962.

────── (1885), *Catena Librorum Tacendorum.* New York: Documentary Books, 1962.

Freedman, A. (1978), Psychoanalytic study of an unusual perversion. *J. Amer. Psychoanal. Assn.*, 26:749–777.

Freese, A. L. (1972), Group therapy with exhibitionists and voyeurs. *Soc. Work*, 17:44–52.

Freud, S. (1905), Three essays on the theory of sex. *Standard Edition*, 7:125–145. London: Hogarth Press, 1953.

——— (1912), Totem and Taboo. *Standard Edition*, 13:1–164. London: Hogarth Press, 1955.

——— (1915), Instincts and their vicissitudes. *Standard Edition*, 14:117–140. London: Hogarth Press, 1957.

——— (1916–1917), Introductory Lectures on Psychoanalysis. *Standard Edition*, 15. London: Hogarth Press, 1963.

——— (1919), "A child is being beaten." A contribution to the study of the origin of sexual perversions. *Standard Edition*, 17:175–204. London: Hogarth Press, 1955.

——— (1920), Beyond the pleasure principle. *Standard Edition*, 18:3–64. London: Hogarth Press, 1955.

——— (1923), The ego and the id. *Standard Edition*, 19:3–66. London: Hogarth Press, 1961.

——— (1924), The economic problem of masochism. *Standard Edition*, 19:157–170. London: Hogarth Press, 1961.

——— (1927), Fetishism. *Standard Edition*, 21:149–157. London: Hogarth Press, 1961.

——— (1932–1936), New Introductory Lectures on Psychoanalysis. *Standard Edition*, 22:3–184. London: Hogarth Press, 1964.

——— (1940), An Outline of Psychoanalysis. *Standard Edition*, 23:141–207. London: Hogarth Press, 1964.

Freund, K. (1967), Erotic preference in paedophilia. *Behav. Res. & Ther.*, 5:339–348.

——— (1981), Assessment of pedophilia. In: *Adult Sexual Interest in Children*, ed. M. Cook & K. Howells. London: Academic Press.

——— Blanchard, R. (1986), The concept of courtship disorder. *J. Sex & Marit. Ther.*, 12:79–92.

——— ——— (1987), Feminine gender identity and physical aggressiveness in heterosexual and homosexual pedophiles. *J. Sex & Marit. Ther.*, 13:25–34.

——— Heasman, G. A., Racansky, I. G., & Glancy, G. (1984), Pedophilia and heterosexuality versus homosexuality. *J. Sex & Marit. Ther.*, 10:193–200.

——— Langevin, R. (1976), Bisexuality in homosexual pedophilia. *Arch. Sex. Behav.*, 5:415–423.

——— ——— Zajac, Y., & Steiner, B. (1974), Parent–child relations in transsexual and non-transsexual homosexual males. *Brit. J. Psychiat.*, 124:22–23.

——— ——— ——— ——— Zajac, A. (1974), The transsexual syndrome in homosexual males. *J. Nerv. & Ment. Dis.*, 158:145–153.

——— McKnight, C. K., Langevin, R., & Cibiri, S. (1972), The female child as a surrogate object. *Arch. Sex. Behav.*, 2:119–133.

——— Scher, H., & Hunker, S. (1983), The courtship disorders. *Arch. Sex. Behav.*, 12:369–379.

——— ——— ——— (1984), The courtship disorders: A further investigation. *Arch. Sex. Behav.*, 13:133–139.

——— Steiner, B., & Chan, S. (1982), Two types of cross gender identity. *Arch. Sex. Behav.*, 11:49–63.

——— Watson, R., & Rienzo, D. (1987), A comparison of sex offenders against female and male minors. *J. Sex & Marit. Ther.*, 13:260–264.

Freytag, F. F. (1971), Hypnotherapeutic explorations of early enema experience. *Amer. J. Clin. Hypn.*, 14:24–31.

Friedemann, M. W. (1966), Reflection on two cases of male transvestism. *Amer. J. Psychother.*, 20:270–283.

Friend, M. R., Schiddel, L., Klein, B., & Dunaeff, D. (1954), Observations on the development of transvestism in boys. *Amer. J. Orthopsychiat.*, 24:563–574.

Fritz, G. S., Stall, K., & Wagner, N. N. (1981), A comparison of males and females who were sexually molested as children. *J. Sex & Marit. Ther.*, 7:54–59.

Frosch, J., & Bromberg, W. (1939), The sex offender—A psychiatric study. *Amer. J. Orthopsychiat.*, 9:761–776.

Furness, T. (1985), Conflict-avoiding and conflict-regulating patterns in incest and child sexual abuse. *Acta Paedopsychiat.*, 50:298–313.

Futterweit, W., Weiss, R. A., & Fagerstrom, R. M. (1986), Endocrine evaluation of forty female-to-male transsexuals: Increased frequency of polycystic ovarian disease in female transsexuals. *Arch. Sex. Behav.*, 15:69–77.

Gadpaille, W. J. (1969), Homosexual activity and homosexuality in adolescence. *Sci. & Psychoanal.*, 15:60–70.

—— (1975), *The Cycles of Sex*. New York: Charles Scribner's Sons.

—— (1980), Biological factors in the development of human sexuality. *Psychiat. Clin. N. Amer.*, 3:3–20.

Gaffney, G. R., & Berlin, F. S. (1984), Is there a hypothalamic-pituitary-gonadal dysfunction in paedophilia? *Brit. J. Psychiat.*, 145:657–660.

—— Lurie, S. F., & Berlin, F. S. (1984), Is there familial transmission of pedophilia? *J. Nerv. & Ment. Dis.*, 172:546–548.

Gagnon, J. H. (1965), Female child victims of sex offenses. *Social Prob.*, 13:176–192.

—— (1967), Sexuality and sexual learning in the child. In: *Sexual Deviance*, ed. J. H. Gagnon & W. Simon. New York: Harper & Row.

—— Simon, W. (1967), *Sexual Deviance*. New York: Harper & Row.

Galdston, R. (1978), Sexual survey #12: Current thinking on sexual abuse of children. *Med. Asp. Hum. Sexual.*, 12:44–47.

Galenson, E. (1980), Sexual development in the second year of life. *Psychiat. Clin. N. Amer.*, 3:37–44.

—— Roiphe, H. (1971), The impact of early sexual discovery on mood, defensive organization, and symbolization. *The Psychoanalytic Study of the Child*, 26:195–216. New York: Quadrangle Books.

Garma, A. (1956), The meaning and genesis of fetishism. *Internat. J. Psycho-Anal.*, 37:414–415.

Gayford, J. J. (1978), Sex magazines. *Med., Sci. & Law*, 18:44–51.

Gebhard, P. H. (1969), Fetishism and sadomasochism. *Sci. & Psychoanal.*, 15:71–80.

—— Gagnon, J. H. (1964), Male sex offenders against very young children. *Amer. J. Psychiat.*, 121:576–579.

—— —— Pomeroy, W. B., & Christenson, C. V. (1965), *Sexual Offenders*. New York: Harper & Row.

Geiser, R. J. (1979), *Hidden Victims: The Sexual Abuse of Children*. Boston: Beacon Press.

Gershman, H. (1970), The role of core gender identity in the genesis of perversions. *Amer. J. Psychoanal.*, 30:58–67.

Giarretto, H. (1981), A comprehensive child sexual abuse treatment program. In: *Sexually Abused Children and Their Families*, ed. P. Mrazek & C. Kempe. Oxford: Pergamon.

Gibson, I. (1978), *The English Vice: Beating, Sex and Shame in Victorian England and After*. London: Duckworth.

Gilberg, A. L. (1981), Treatment of young adults with sexual maladaption. *Amer. J. Psychoanal.*, 41:45–50.

Gillespie, W. H. (1940), A contribution to the study of fetishism. *Internat. J. Psycho-Anal.*, 21:401–415.

——— (1952), Notes on an analysis of sexual perversions. *Internat. J. Psycho-Anal.*, 33:397–402.

——— (1956), The structure and aetiology of sexual perversion. In: *Perversions, Psychodynamics and Therapy*, ed. S. Lorand. New York: Gramercy Books.

Gittleson, N. L., Eacott, S. T., & Mehta, B. M. (1978), Victims of indecent exposure. *Brit. J. Psychiat.*, 132:61–66.

Glasser, M. (1979), Some aspects of the role of aggression in the perversions. In: *Sexual Deviation*, 2nd ed., ed. I. Rosen. Oxford: Oxford University Press.

Glenn, J. (1984), Psychic trauma and masochism. *J. Amer. Psychoanal. Assn.*, 32:325–356.

Glueck, B. C. (1956), Psychodynamic patterns in the homosexual sex offender. *Amer. J. Psychiat.*, 112:584–590.

Glover, E. (1927), Notes on an unusual form of perversion. *Internat. J. Psycho-Anal.*, 8:10–24.

——— (1933), The relation of perversion-formation to the development of reality sense. *Internat. J. Psycho-Anal.*, 14:486–504.

Godlewski, J. (1988), Transsexualism and anatomic sex ratio reversal in Poland. *Arch. Sex. Behav.*, 17:547–548.

Goldberg, R. L., & Wise, T. N. (1985), Psychodynamic treatment of telephone scatologia. *Amer. J. Psychoanal.*, 45:291–297.

Goldberg, S., & Lewis, M. (1969), Play behavior in the year-old infant: Early sex differences. *Child Develop.*, 40:21–31.

Goldstein, M. J., & Kant, H. S. (1973), *Pornography and Sexual Deviance*. Berkeley, CA: University of California Press.

Golosow, N., & Weitzman, E. (1969), Psychosexual and ego regression in the male transsexual. *J. Nerv. & Ment. Dis.*, 149:328–336.

Goode, E., & Troiden, R. R. (1974), *Sexual Deviance and Sexual Deviants*. New York: William Morrow.

Goodwin, J. (1981), Suicide attempts in sexual abuse victims and their mothers. *Child Abuse & Neglect*, 5:217–221.

——— Shad, D., & Rada, R. T. (1978), Incest hoax: False accusations, false denials. *Bull. Amer. Acad. Psychiat. & Law*, 6:269–276.

Gordon, L. (1955), Incest as revenge against the preoedipal mother. *Psychoanal. Rev.*, 42:284–292.

Gorman, G. F. (1964), Fetishism occurring in identical twins. *Brit. J. Psychiat.*, 110:255–256.

Gosselin, C. (1979), Personality attributes of the average rubber fetishist. In: *Proceedings of the First International Conference on Love and Attraction*, ed. M. Cook & G. D. Wilson. London: Pergamon Press.

———— Eysenck, S. B. G. (1980), The transvestite double image: A preliminary report. *Pers. & Individual Diff.*, 1:172–173.

———— Wilson, G. (1980), *Sexual Variations*. New York: Simon & Shuster.

———— ———— (1984), Fetishism, sadomasochism and related behaviors. In: *The Psychology of Sexual Diversity*, ed. K. Howells. Oxford: Basil Blackwell.

Gottlieb, A. (1978), Three atypical results. *Arch. Sex. Behav.*, 7:371–375.

Grant, V. W. (1954), A problem in sex pathology. *Amer. J. Psychiat.*, 110:589–593.

———— (1960), The cross-dresser: A case study. *J. Nerv. & Ment. Dis.*, 131:149–159.

Green, A. H. (1986), True and false allegations of sexual abuse in child custody disputes. *J. Amer. Acad. Child Psychiat.*, 25:449–456.

Green, C., & Green, G. (1974), *S-M: The Last Taboo*. New York: Grove Press.

Green, R. (1974), *Sexual Identity Conflict in Children and Adults*. New York: Basic Books.

———— (1985), The gender identity disorder and later sexual orientation: Follow-up of 43 boys. *Amer. J. Psychiat.*, 142:339–341.

———— (1987), *The "Sissy Boy Syndrome" and the Development of Homosexuality*. New Haven, CT: Yale University Press.

———— Fuller, M. (1973a), Family doll play and female identity in preadolescent males. *Amer. J. Orthopsychiat.*, 43:123–127.

———— ———— (1973b), Group therapy with feminine boys and their parents. *Internat. J. Group Psychother.*, 23:54–68.

———— Money, J. (1961). Effeminacy in prepubertal boys. *Pediatrics*, 27:286–291.

———— ———— (1966), Stage-acting, role-taking and effeminate impersonation during boyhood. *Arch. Gen. Psychiat.*, 15:535–538.

———— Neuberg, D., & Finch, S. J. (1983), Sex-typed motor behaviors of "feminine" boys, conventionally masculine boys, and conventionally feminine girls. *Sex Roles*, 9:571–579.

———— Stoller, R. (1971), Two monozygotic (identical) twin pairs discordant for gender identity. *Arch. Sex. Behav.*, 1:321–327.

———— ———— MacAndrew, C. (1966), Attitudes toward sex transformation procedures. *Arch. Gen. Psychiat.*, 15:178–182.

Greenacre, P. (1953), Certain relationships between fetishism and the faulty development of the body image. *The Psychoanalytic Study of the Child*, 8:79–98. New York: International Universities Press.

———— (1955), Further considerations regarding fetishism. *The Psychoanalytic Study of the Child*, 10:187–193. New York: International Universities Press.

———— (1958), Early physical determinants in the development of the sense of identity. *J. Amer. Psychoanal. Assn.*, 6:612–627.

———— (1960), Further notes of fetishism. *The Psychoanalytic Study of the Child*, 15:191–207. New York: International Universities Press.

———— (1968), Perversions: General considerations regarding their genetic and dynamic background. *The Psychoanalytic Study of the Child*, 23:47–62. New York: International Universities Press.

———— (1979), Fetishism. In: *Sexual Deviation*, 2nd ed., ed. I. Rosen. Oxford: Oxford University Press.

Greenberg, N. H., Rosenwald, A. K., & Nielson, P. E. (1960), A study in transsexualism. *Psychiat. Quart.*, 34:203–235.

Greenson, R. R. (1964), On homosexuality and gender identity. *Internat. J. Psycho-Anal.*, 45:217–219.

——— (1966), A transvestite boy and a hypothesis. *Internat. J. Psycho-Anal.*, 47:396–403.

——— (1968), Dis-identifying from mother: Its special importance for the boy. *Internat. J. Psycho-Anal.*, 49:370–374.

Grob, C. S. (1985), Female exhibitionism. *J. Nerv. & Ment. Dis.*, 173:253–256.

Groff, M. G. (1987), Characteristics of incest offenders' wives. *J. Sex Res.*, 23:91–96.

Grossman, W. J. (1986), Notes on masochism: A discussion of the history and development of a psychoanalytic concept. *Psychoanal. Quart.*, 55:379–413.

Groth, A. N. (1977), The adolescent sexual offender and his prey. *Internat. J. Offender Ther. Compar. Criminol.*, 21:249–254.

——— (1978), Patterns of sexual assault against children and adolescents. In: *Sexual Assault of Children and Adolescents*, ed. A. W. Burgess, A. N. Groth, L. L. Homstrom, & S. M. Sgoi. Lexington, MA: Lexington Books.

——— (1979), Sexual trauma in the life histories of rapists and child molesters. *Victimol.*, 4:10–16.

——— Birnbaum, H. J. (1978), Adult sexual orientation and attraction to under-age persons. *Arch. Sex. Behav.*, 7:175–181.

——— Hobson, W. F., & Gary, T. S. (1982), The child molester: Clinical observations. *J. Soc. Work & Hum. Sexual.*, 1:129–144.

Grotjan, M. (1948), Transvestite fantasy expressed in a drawing. *Psychoanal. Quart.*, 17:340–345.

Gunderson, B. H., Melas, P. S., & Skar, J. E. (1981), Sexual behavior of preschool children: Teachers' observations. In: *Children and Sex*, ed. L. Constantine & F. Martinson. Boston: Little, Brown.

Gutheil, E. A. (1930), Analysis of a case of transvestism. In: *Stekel's Sexual Aberrations*, Vol. 2. New York: Liveright Publishing.

——— (1954), The psychologic background of transsexualism and transvestism. *Amer. J. Psychother.*, 8:231–239.

Gutheil, T. G., & Avery, N. (1977), Multiple overt incest as family defense against loss. *Fam. Proc.*, 16:105–116.

Guttmann, O. (1953), Exhibitionism: A contribution to sexual psychopathology based on twelve cases of exhibitionism. *J. Clin. & Experiment. Psychopath.*, 14:13–51.

Guyon, R. (1933), *Sex Life and Sex Ethics*. London: John Lane Bodley Head.

Guze, H. (1969), Psychosocial adjustment of transsexuals. In: *Transsexualism and Sex Reassignment*, ed. J. Green & J. Money. Baltimore: Johns Hopkins University Press.

Haberman, M. A., & Michael, R. P. (1979), Autocastration in transsexualism. *Amer. J. Psychiat.*, 136:347–348.

Hackett, T. P. (1971), The psychotherapy of exhibitionists in a court clinic setting. *Sem. Psychiat.*, 3:297–306.

Hadden, S. B. (1973), Exhibitionism. *Psychiat. Ann.*, 3:23–32.

Haire, N. (1934), *Encyclopaedia of Sexual Knowledge*. New York: Eugenics Publishing Co.

Hall, G. C., Maiuro, R. D., Vitaliano, P. P., & Proctor, W. C. (1986), The utility of the MMPI with men who have sexually assaulted children. *J. Consult. & Clin. Psychol.*, 54:493–496.

Hall Williams, J. E. (1974), The neglect of incest: A criminologist's view. *Med., Sci. & Law*, 14:64–67.

Halle, E., Schmidt, C. W., & Meyer, J. K. (1980), The role of grandmothers in transsexualism. *Amer. J. Psychiat.*, 137:497–498.

Hamburger, C. (1953), Desire for change of sex as shown by personal letters from 465 men and women. *Acta Endocrinol.*, 14:361–375.

—— Sturup, G., & Dahl-Iverson, E. (1953), Transvestism. *J. Amer. Med. Assn.*, 152:391–396.

Hamilton, J. W. (1972), Voyeurism: Some clinical and theoretical considerations. *Amer. J. Psychother.*, 26:277–287.

Hammer, E. F., & Glueck, B. C. (1957), Psychodynamic patterns of sex offenders. *Psychiat. Quart.*, 31:325–345.

Harry Benjamin International Gender Dysphoria Association (1985), Standards of care: The hormonal and surgical reassignment of gender dysphoric persons. *Arch. Sex. Behav.*, 14:147–164.

Harry, J. (1982), *Gay Children Grown Up.* New York: Praeger.

—— (1983), Defeminization and adult psychological well-being among male homosexuals. *Arch. Sex. Behav.*, 12:1–19.

Hartman, V. (1965), Notes on group psychotherapy with pedophiles. *Can. Psychiat. Assn. J.*, 10:283–289.

Hartup, W. W. (1962), Some correlates of parental imitation in young children. *Child Develop.*, 33:85–96.

—— Moore, S. G., & Sager, G. (1963), Avoidance of inappropriate sex-typing by young children. *J. Consult. Psychol.*, 27:467–473.

—— Zook, E. A. (1960), Sex role preference in three and four year-old children. *J. Consult. Psychol.*, 24:420–426.

Hass, A. (1979), *Teenage Sexuality.* Los Angeles: Pinnacle Books.

Hastings, D., & Markland, C. (1978), Post-surgical adjustment of twenty-five transsexuals (male-to-female) in the University of Minnesota study. *Arch. Sex. Behav.*, 7:327–336.

Hazelwood, R. R., Dietz, P. E., & Burgess, A. W. (1983), *Autoerotic Fatalities.* Lexington, MA: Lexington Books.

Heilbrun, A. B. (1973), Parent identification and filial sex-role behavior: The importance of biological context. In: *Nebraska Symposium on Motivation*, ed. K. Cole & R. Dienstbier. Lincoln: University of Nebraska Press.

Heilbrunn, G. (1975), On the erotization of the umbilicus. *Psychoanal. Quart.*, 44:269–273.

Heims, L. W., & Kaufman, I. (1963), Variations on a theme of incest. *Amer. J. Orthopsychiat.*, 33:311–312.

Hellman, R. E., Green, R., Gray, J. L., & Williams, K. (1981), Childhood sexual identity, childhood religiosity, and "homophobia" as influences in the development of transsexualism, homosexuality, and heterosexuality. *Arch. Gen. Psychiat.*, 38:910–915.

Hemmer, J. D., & Kleiber, D. A. (1981), Tomboys and sissies: Androgynous children? *Sex Roles*, 7:1205–1212.

Henriques, F. (1960), *Love in Action.* New York: E. P. Dutton.

Henry, G. W. (1941), *Sex Variants.* New York: Harper.

—— (1955), *All the Sexes.* New York: Rinehart.

Henry, J. (1985), Testimony before the Permanent Subcommittee on Investigations of the Committee on Governmental Affairs United States Senate on Child Pornography and Pedophilia, Part 2. Washington, DC: U.S. Government Printing Office.

Herdt, G., & Davidson, J. (1988), The Sambia "Turnim-Man": Socio-cultural and clinical aspects of gender formation in male pseudohermaphrodites with 5-alpha reductase deficiency in Papua New Guinea. *Arch. Sex. Behav.*, 17:33–56.

Herman, J., & Herschman, L. (1981), *Father–Daughter Incest*. Cambridge, MA: Harvard University Press.

Herodotus (424 B.C.), *Histories*. New York: Penguin Books, 1972.

Herold, E. E., Mantle, D., & Zemitis, O. (1979), A study of sexual offenses against females. *Adol.*, 14:65–72.

Herron, M. J., Herron, W. G., & Schultz, C. I. (1983), Sexual dominance/submission, gender and sex-role identification. *Percep. & Motor Skills*, 56:931–937.

Hertz, J., Tillinger, K. G., & Westman, A. (1961), Transvestism: Report on five hormonally and surgically treated cases. *Acta Psychiat. Scand.*, 37:288–294.

Hetherington, E. M. (1965), A developmental study of the effects of the sex of the dominant parent on sex-role preference, identification, and imitation in children. *J. Pers. & Soc. Psychol.*, 2:188–194.

―――― Deur, J. L. (1971), The effects of father absence on child development. *Young Child*, 26:233–248.

Higham, E. (1976), Case management of the gender incongruity syndrome in childhood and adulthood. *J. Homosexual.*, 2:49–57.

Hirning, L. C. (1945), Indecent exposure and other sex offenses. *J. Clin. Psychopath. & Psychother.*, 7:105–114.

―――― (1947), Genital exhibitionism, an interpretive study. *J. Clin. Psychopath.*, 8:557–564.

Hirschfeld, M. (1938), *Sexual Anomalies and Perversions*. London: Encyclopaedic Press.

―――― (1940), *Sexual Pathology*. New York: Emerson Books.

Hobbs, C. J., & Wynne, J. M. (1986), Buggery in childhood: A common syndrome of child abuse. *Lancet*, 4:792–796.

Hoenig, J. (1977a), The development of sexology during the second half of the 19th century. In: *Handbook of Sexology*, ed. J. Money & H. Musaph. Amsterdam: Excepta Medica.

―――― (1977b), Dramatis personae: Selected biographical sketches of 19th century pioneers in sexology. In: *Handbook of Sexology*, ed. J. Money & H. Musaph. Amsterdam: Excepta Medica.

―――― Duggan, E. (1974), Sexual and other abnormalities in the family of a transsexual. *Psychiat. Clin.*, 7:334–346.

―――― Kenna, J. C. (1973), Epidemiological aspects of transsexualism. *Psychiat. Clin.*, 6:65–80.

―――― ―――― (1974a), The prevalence of transsexualism in England and Wales. *Brit. J. Psychiat.*, 124:181–190.

―――― ―――― (1974b), The nosological position of transsexualism. *Arch. Sex. Behav.*, 3:272–287.

―――― ―――― (1979), EEG abnormalities and transsexualism. *Brit. J. Psychiat.*, 134:293–300.

―――― ―――― Youd, A. (1970), Social and economic aspects of transsexualism. *Brit. J. Psychiat.*, 117:163–172.

———— ———— ———— (1971), Surgical treatment for transsexuals. *Acta Psychiat. Scand.*, 47:106–133.

———— Torr, J. B. (1964), Karyotyping of transsexualists. *J. Psychosom. Res.*, 8:157–159.

Hollander, X. (1972), *The Happy Hooker*. New York: Dell.

Hoopes, J. E. (1969), Operative treatment for the female transsexual. In: *Transsexualism and Sex Reassignment*, ed. R. Green & J. Money. Baltimore: Johns Hopkins University Press.

———— Knorr, N. J., & Wolf, S. R. (1968), Transsexualism: Considerations regarding sexual reassignment. *J. Nerv. & Ment. Dis.*, 147:510–516.

Hooshmand, H., & Brawley, B. W. (1969), Temporal lobe seizures and exhibitionism. *Neurol.*, 19:1119–1124.

Hora, T. (1953), The structural analysis of transvestism. *Psychoanal. Rev.*, 40:268–274.

Hore, B. D., Nicolle, F. V., & Calnan, J. S. (1973), Male transsexualism: Two cases in a single family. *Arch. Sex. Behav.*, 2:317–321.

———— ———— ———— (1975), Male transsexualism in England: Sixteen cases with surgical intervention. *Arch. Sex. Behav.*, 4:81–88.

Housden, J. (1965), An examination of the biologic etiology of transvestism. *Internat. J. Soc. Psychiat.*, 11:301–305.

Howells, K. (1978), Some meanings of children for pedophiles. In: *Love and Attraction*, ed. M. Cook & G. Wilson. London: Pergamon.

Hucker, S., Langevin, R., Wortzman, G., Bain, J., Handy, L., Chambers, J., & Wright, S. (1986), Neuropsychological impairment in pedophiles. *Can. J. Behav. Sc.*, 18:440–448.

Hunt, D. D., Carr, J. E., & Hampson, J. L. (1981), Cognitive correlates of biologic sex and gender identity in transsexualism. *Arch. Sex. Behav.*, 10:65–77.

———— Hampson, J. L. (1980a), Transsexualism: A standardized psychosocial rating format for the evaluation of results of sex reassignment surgery. *Arch. Sex. Behav.*, 9:255–263.

———— ———— (1980b), Follow-up of 17 biological male transsexuals after sex-reassignment surgery. *Amer. J. Psychiat.*, 137:432–438.

Hunt, M. (1974), *Sexual Behavior in the 1970s*. New York: Playboy Press.

Hunter, B., Logue, V., & McMenemy, W. H. (1963), Temporal lobe epilepsy supervening on a longstanding transvestism and fetishism. *Epilepsia*, 4:60–65.

Hunter, D. (1954), Object-relation changes in the analysis of a fetishist. *Internat. J. Psycho-Anal.*, 35:302–312.

Huston, A. C. (1983), Sex-typing. In: *Carmichael's Manual of Child Psychology*, ed. P. H. Mussen. New York: John Wiley.

Huxley, P. J., Kenna, J. C., & Brandon, S. (1981a), Partnership in transsexualism. Part I. Paired and nonpaired groups. *Arch. Sex. Behav.*, 10:133–141.

———— ———— ———— (1981b), Partnership in transsexualism. Part II. The nature of the partnership. *Arch. Sex. Behav.*, 10:143–160.

Hyde, C., & Kenna, J. C. (1977), A male MZ twin pair, concordant for transsexualism, discordant for schizophrenia. *Acta Psychiat. Scand.*, 56:265–275.

Hyde, H. (1975), On transsexuality. In: *The TV-TG-TS Phenomenon*. Kingston RH: University of Rhode Island School of Nursing.

Imperato-McGinley, J., Peterson, R. E., Gautier, T., & Sturla, E. (1979), Androgens and the evolution of male gender identity among male pseudo-hermaphrodites with 5a-reductase deficiency. *N. Eng. J. Med.,* 300:1233–1237.

Ingram, M. (1981), Participating victims: A study of sexual offenses with boys. In: *Children and Sex,* ed. L. Constantine & F. Martinson. Boston: Little, Brown.

Jacklin, C. N., DiPietro, J. A., & Maccoby, E. (1984), Sex-typing behavior and sex-typing pressure in child/parent interaction. *Arch. Sex. Behav.,* 13:413–425.

———— Maccoby, E. E., & Doering, C. H. (1983), Neonatal sex-steroid hormones and timidity in 6-18-month old boys and girls. *Develop. Psychobiol.,* 16:163–168.

Jackson, T. L., & Ferguson, W. P. (1983), Attribution of blame in incest. *Amer. J. Commun. Psychol.,* 11:313–322.

Jacobi, Y. (1973), *The Psychology of C. G. Jung.* New Haven, CT: Yale University Press.

Jaffe, A. C., Dynneson, L., & ten Bensel, R. W. (1975), Sexual abuse of children: An epidemiological study. *Amer. J. Dis. Child.,* 129:689–692.

James, J., Womack, W. M., & Strauss, F. (1978), Physician reporting of sexual abuse of children. *J. Amer. Med. Assn.,* 240:1145–1146.

Janus, S., Bess, B., & Saltus, C. (1977), *A Sexual Profile of Men in Power.* Englewood Cliffs, NJ: Prentice-Hall.

Jayaram, B. N., Stuteville, O. H., & Bush, J. M. (1978), Complications and undesirable results of sex-reassignment in male-to-female transsexuals. *Arch. Sex. Behav.,* 7:337–345.

Johnson, A. M., & Robinson, D. B. (1957), The sexual deviant. *J. Amer. Med. Assn.,* 164:1559–1565.

Johnson, J. (1973), Psychopathia sexualis. *Brit. J. Psychiat.,* 122:211–218.

Johnson, W. S. (1979), *Living in Sin: The Victorian Sexual Revolution.* Chicago: Nelson-Hall.

Johnston, F. A., & Johnston, S. A. (1986), Differences between human figure drawings of child molesters and control groups. *J. Clin. Psychol.,* 42:638–647.

Johnstone, J. M., Hunt, A. C., & Ward, E. M. (1960), Plastic-bag asphyxia in adults. *Brit. Med. J.,* 2:1714–1715.

Jones, I. H., & Frei, D. (1977), Provoked anxiety as a treatment of exhibitionism. *Brit. J. Psychiat.,* 131:295–300.

———— ———— (1979), Exhibitionism—A biological hypothesis. *Brit. J. Med. Psychol.,* 52:63–70.

Jones, J. R., & Samimy, J. (1973), Plasma testosterone levels and female transsexualism. *Arch. Sex. Behav.,* 2:251–256.

Joseph, B. (1971), A clinical contribution to the analysis of a perversion. *Internat. J. Psycho-Anal.,* 52:441–449.

Jourard, S. M. (1974), *Healthy Personality.* New York: Macmillan.

Julian, V., & Mohr, C. (1979), Father daughter incest: Profile of the offender. *Victimol.,* 4:348–360.

Kahn, E. (1965), On incest and Freud's Oedipus complex. *Confinia Psychiat.,* 8:89–101.

Kahn, M., & Sexton, M. (1983), Sexual abuse of young children. *Clin. Pediat.,* 22:369–472.

Kahn, M. R. (1969), Role of the "collated internal object" in perversion-formation. *Internat. J. Psycho-Anal.,* 50:555–565.

Kahn, T. J., & Lafond, M. A. (1988), Treatment of the adolescent sexual offender. *Child & Adol. Soc. Work*, 5:135–148.

Kamel, G. W. L. (1983a), The leather career: On becoming a sadomasochist. In: *S and M*, ed. T. S. Weinberg & G. W. L. Kamel. Buffalo, NY: Prometheus Books.

——— (1983b), Leathersex: Meaningful aspects of gay sadomasochism. In: *S and M*, ed. T. S. Weinberg & G. W. L. Kamel. Buffalo, NY: Prometheus Books.

——— Weinberg, T. S. (1983), Diversity in sadomasochism four S&M careers. In: *S and M*, ed. T. S. Weinberg & G. W. L. Kamel. Buffalo, NY: Prometheus Books.

Kando, T. (1972), Role strain: A comparison of males, females, and transsexuals. *J. Marr. & Fam.*, 34:459–464.

——— (1973), *Sex Change: The Achievement of Gender Identity Among Feminized Transsexuals*. Springfield, IL: Charles C Thomas.

Kane, A. (1975), *The TV-TG-TS Phenomenon*. Kingston, RI: University of Rhode Island Medical School.

Kardiner, A. (1954), *Sex and Morality*. Indianapolis: Charter Books.

Karpman, B. (1934), The obsessive paraphilias. *Arch. Neurol. & Psychiat.*, 2:1688–1689.

——— (1947), Dream life in a case of transvestism with particular attention to the problem of latent homosexuality. *J. Nerv. & Ment. Dis.*, 106:292–337.

——— (1948), The psychopathology of exhibitionism: A review of the literature. *J. Clin. Psychopath.*, 9:179–225.

——— (1950), A case of paedophilia (legally rape) cured by psychoanalysis. *Psychoanal. Rev.*, 37:235–276.

——— (1954), *The Sexual Offender and His Offenses*. New York: Julian Press.

Katan, M. (1964), Fetishism, splitting of the ego, and denial. *Internat. J. Psycho-Anal.*, 45:237–245.

Kaufman, J., Peck, A., & Taguiri, C. (1954), The family constellation and overt incestuous relations between father and daughter. *Amer. J. Orthopsychiat.*, 24:266–279.

Kavoussi, R. J., Kaplan, M., & Becker, J. V. (1988), Psychiatric diagnosis in adolescent sex offenders. *J. Amer. Acad. Child & Adol. Psychiat.*, 27:241–243.

Keiser, S. (1949), The fear of sexual passivity in the masochist. *Internat. J. Psycho-Anal.*, 30:162–171.

Keller, A., Althof, S. E., & Lothstein, L. M. (1982), Group therapy with gender identity patients: A four year study. *Amer. J. Psychother.*, 36:223–228.

Kelly, G. (1955), *The Psychology of Personal Constructs*. New York: W. W. Norton.

Kempe, C. H. (1978), Sexual abuse, another hidden pediatric problem. *Pediat.*, 62:382–389.

Kenna, J. C., & Hoenig, J. (1978), Verbal characteristics of male and female transsexuals. *Psychiat. Clin.*, 11:233–236.

Kennedy, F., Hoffman, H. R., & Haines, W. A. (1947), A study of William Heirens. *Amer. J. Psychiat.*, 104:113–121.

Kentsmith, D. K., & Bastini, J. B. (1974), Obscene telephoning by an exhibitionist during therapy: A case report. *Internat. J. Group Psychother.*, 24:352–357.

Kernberg, O. F. (1988), Clinical dimensions of masochism. *J. Amer. Psychoanal. Assn.*, 36:1005–1029.

Kester, P. A. (1984), Effects of prenatally administered 17 alpha hydroxy-progesterone caproate on adolescent males. *Arch. Sex. Behav.*, 13:441–455.

Kestenberg, J. (1976), Psychosexual impact of childhood enemas. *Med. Asp. Hum. Sexual.*, 10:36.

Kinsey, A. C., Pomeroy, W. B., & Martin, C. E. (1948), *Sexual Behavior in the Human Male*. Philadelphia: W. B. Saunders.

———— ———— ———— Gebhard, P. H. (1953), *Sexual Behavior in the Human Female*. Philadelphia: W. B. Saunders.

Kirkland, K. D., & Bauer, C. A. (1982), MMPI traits of incestuous fathers. *J. Clin. Psychol.*, 38:645–649.

Kirkpatrick, M., & Friedman, C. T. H. (1976), Treatment of requests for sex-change surgery with psychotherapy. *Amer. J. Psychiat.*, 133:1194–1196.

Klaf, F. S., & Brown, W. (1958), Necrophilia, brief review and case report. *Psychiat. Quart.*, 32:645–652.

Knorr, N. J., Wolf, S. R., & Meyer, E. (1968), The transsexual's request for surgery. *J. Nerv. & Ment. Dis.*, 147:517–524.

———— ———— ———— (1969), Psychiatric evaluation of male transsexuals for surgery. In: *Transsexualism and Sex Reassignment*, ed. R. Green & J. Money. Baltimore: Johns Hopkins University Press.

Kockott, G., & Fahrner, E. M. (1987), Transsexuals who have not undergone surgery: A follow-up study. *Arch. Sex. Behav.*, 16:511–522.

———— ———— (1988), Male-to-female and female-to-male transsexuals: A comparison. *Arch. Sex. Behav.*, 17:539–546.

Kohlberg, L. (1969), Stage and sequence: The cognitive-developmental approach to socialization. In: *Handbook of Socialization Theory and Research*, ed. D. Goselin. Skokie, IL: Rand McNally.

Kolarsky, A., & Madlafousek, J. (1983), The inverse role of preparatory erotic stimulation in exhibitionists: Phallometric studies. *Arch. Sex. Behav.*, 12:123–148.

Kopp, S. B. (1962), The character structure of sex offenders. *Amer. J. Psychother.*, 16:64–70.

Koranyi, E. K. (1980), *Transsexuality in the Male: The Spectrum of Gender Dysphoria*. Springfield, IL: Charles C Thomas.

Kourany, R. F., Martin, J. E., & Armstrong, S. H. (1979), Sexual experimentation by adolescents while babysitting. *Adol.*, 14:283–288.

Krafft-Ebing, R. von, (1902), *Psychopathia Sexualia*. New York: G. P. Putnam's Sons, 1965.

Kronengold, E., & Sterba, R. (1936), Two cases of fetishism. *Psychoanal. Quart.*, 5:63–70.

Krueger, D. W. (1978), Symptom passing in transvestite father and three sons. *Amer. J. Psychiat.*, 135:739–742.

Kubie, L. S. (1974), The drive to become both sexes. *Psychoanal. Quart.*, 43:349–426.

———— Mackie, J. B. (1968), Critical issues raised by operations for gender transmutation. *J. Nerv. & Ment. Dis.*, 147:431–443.

Kuhn, D., Nash, S. C., & Brucken, L. (1978), Sex role concepts of two- and three-year-olds. *Child Develop.*, 49:445–451.

Kuiper, B., & Cohen-Kettenis, P. (1988), Sex reassignment surgery: A study of 141 Dutch transsexuals. *Arch. Sex. Behav.*, 17:439–457.

Kupperman, H. S. (1967), The endocrine status of the transsexual patient. *Trans. NY Acad. Sci.*, 29:434–439.

Kurland, M. L. (1960), Pedophilia erotica. *J. Nerv. & Ment. Dis.*, 131:394–403.

Kutschinsky, B. (1976), Deviance and criminality: The case of voyeur in a peeper's paradise. *Dis. Nerv. Sys.*, 37:145–151.

Kwan, M., Van Maasdam, J., & Davidson, J. S. (1985), Effects of estrogen treatment on sexual behavior in male-to-female transsexuals: Experimental and clinical observations. *Arch. Sex. Behav.*, 14:29–40.

Lamborn, L. (1978), The strange world of statutory rape. *Victimol.*, 3:205–212.

Landis, J. J. (1956), Experiences of 500 children with adult sexual deviation. *Psychiat. Quart. Suppl.*, 30:91–109.

Langer, W. C. (1972), *The Mind of Adolf Hitler*. New York: Basic Books.

Langevin, R. (1983), *Sexual Strands*. Hillsdale, NJ: Lawrence Erlbaum Associates.

————— ed. (1985), *Erotic Preference, Gender Identity and Aggression in Men*. Hillsdale, NJ: Lawrence Erlbaum Associates.

————— Bain, J., Ben-Aron, M. H., Coulthard, R., Day, D., Handy, L., Heasman, G., Hucker, S. J., Purins, J. E., Roper, V., Russon, A. E., Webster, C. D., & Wortzman, G. (1985), Sexual aggression. In: *Erotic Preference, Gender Identity, and Aggression in Men*, ed. R. Langevin. Hillsdale, NJ: Lawrence Erlbaum Associates.

————— Handy, L., Russon, A. E., & Day, D. (1985), Are incestuous fathers pedophilic, aggressive, and alcoholic? In: *Erotic Preference, Gender Identity, and Aggression in Men*, ed. R. Langevin. Hillsdale, NJ: Lawrence Erlbaum Associates.

————— Huncker, S. J., Ben-Aron, M. H., Purins, J. E., & Hook, H. J. (1985), Why are pedophiles attracted to children? Further studies of erotic preferences in heterosexual pedophiles. In: *Erotic Preference, Gender Identity, and Aggression in Men*, ed. R. Langevin. Hillsdale, NJ: Lawrence Erlbaum Associates.

————— ————— Handy, L., Hook, H. J., Purins, J. E., & Russon, A. E. (1985), Erotic preference and aggression in pedophilia: A comparison of heterosexual, homosexual, and bisexual types. In: *Erotic Preference, Gender Identity and Aggression in Men*, ed. R. Langevin. Hillsdale, NJ: Lawrence Erlbaum Associates.

————— Paitich, D., & Russon, A. E. (1985), Voyeurism: Does it predict sexual aggression or violence in general? In: *Erotic Preference, Gender Identity and Aggression in Men*, ed. R. Langevin. Hillsdale, NJ: Lawrence Erlbaum Associates.

————— ————— Steiner, E. (1977), The clinical profile of male transsexuals living as females vs. those living as males. *Arch. Sex. Behav.*, 6:143–154.

Langfeldt, T. (1981), Processes in sexual development. In: *Children and Sex*, ed. L. Constantine & F. Martinson. Boston: Little, Brown.

Langlois, J., & Downs, C. (1980), Mothers, fathers and peers as socialization agents of sex-typed play behavior in young children. *Child Develop.*, 51:1237–1247.

LaTorre, R. A. (1980), Devaluation of the human love object: Heterosexual rejection as a possible antecedent to fetishism. *J. Abnorm. Psychol.*, 89:295–298.

Laub, D., & Fisk, N. (1974), A rehabilitation program for gender dysphoria syndrome by surgical sex change. *Plastic & Reconstruct. Surg.*, 53:388–403.

Laufer, M. (1968), The body image, the function of masturbation, and adolescence: Problems of the ownership of the body. *The Psychoanalytic Study of the Child*, 23:114–137. New York: International Universities Press.

———— (1976), The central masturbation fantasy, the final sexual organization, and adolescence. *The Psychoanalytic Study of the Child*, 31:297–316. New York: International Universities Press.

Laws, D. R. (1984), The assessment of diverse sexual behavior. In: *The Psychology of Sexual Diversity*, ed. K. Howells. Oxford: Basil Blackwell.

Lazarus, A. A. (1968), A case of pseudonecrophilia treated by behavior therapy. *J. Clin. Psychol.*, 24:113–115.

Leavitt, F., Berger, J., Hoepner, H. J., & Northrop, G. (1980), Presurgical adjustment in male transsexuals with and without hormonal treatment. *J. Nerv. & Ment. Dis.*, 168:693–697.

Lebovitz, P. (1972), Feminine behavior in boys. Aspects of its outcome. *Amer. J. Psychiat.*, 128:1283–1289.

Lederer, W. (1968), *The Fear of Women*. New York: Harcourt, Brace, Jovanovich.

Lee, J. A. (1983), The social organization of sexual risk. In: *S and M*, ed. T. S. Weinberg & G. W. L. Kamel. Buffalo, NY: Prometheus Books.

Leitenberg, H., & Slavin, L. (1983), Comparison of attitudes toward transsexuality and homosexuality. *Arch. Sex. Behav.*, 12:337–346.

Lenzer, G. (1975), On masochism: A contribution to the history of a phantasy and its theory. *Signs: J. Women in Cult. & Soc.*, 1:277–324.

Lenznoff, M., & Westley, W. A. (1956), The homosexual community. *Soc. Prob.*, 3:257–263.

Leser, H. (1967), The Hirschfeld Institute for Sexology. In: *The Encyclopedia of Sexual Behavior*, ed. A. Ellis & A. Abarbanel. New York: Hawthorn Books.

Levine, E. M. (1976), Male transsexuals in the homosexual subculture. *Amer. J. Psychiat.*, 133:1318–1321.

———— Grunewald, D., & Shaiova, C. H. (1976), Behavioral differences and emotional conflict among male-to-female transsexuals. *Arch. Sex. Behav.*, 5:81–85.

———— Shaiova, C. H., & Mihailovic, M. (1975), Male to female: The role transformation of transsexuals. *Arch. Sex. Behav.*, 4:173–186.

Levine, S. B. (1980), Psychiatric diagnosis of patients requesting sex reassignment surgery. *J. Sex & Marit. Ther.*, 6:164–173.

———— Shumaker, R. (1983), Increasingly Ruth. *Arch. Sex. Behav.*, 12:247–261.

Levitan, H. L. (1963), The exhibitionist. *Psychoanal. Quart.*, 32:246–248.

Lev-Ran, A. (1974), Gender role differentiation in hermaphrodites. *Arch. Sex. Behav.*, 3:391–424.

Lewinsky, H. (1944), On some aspects of masochism. *Internat. J. Psycho-Anal.*, 25:150–155.

Lewis, M. D. (1963), A case of transvestism with multiple body–phallus identification. *Internat. J. Psycho-Anal.*, 44:345–351.

Lewis, V. G. (1976), Androgen insensitivity syndrome: Erotic component of gender identity in nine women. In: *Progress in Sexology*, ed. R. Gemme & C. C. Wheeler. New York: Plenum Press.

Liakos, A. (1967), Familial transvestism. *Brit. J. Psychiat.*, 113:49–51.

Liben, L. S., & Signorella, M. L. (1980), Gender related schemata and constructive memory in children. *Child Develop.*, 51:11–18.

Lichtenstein, H. (1961), Identity and sexuality. *J. Amer. Psychoanal. Assn.*, 9:179–260.

Lief, H. I., Dingman, J. F., & Bishop, M. P. (1962), Psychoendocronologic studies in a male with cyclic changes in sexuality. *Psychosom. Med.*, 24:357–368.

Lihn, H. (1971), Sexual masochism: A case report. *Internat. J. Psycho-Anal.*, 52:469–478.

Lim, M. H., & Bottomley, V. (1983), A combined approach to the treatment of effeminate behavior in a boy: A case study. *J. Child Psychol. & Psychiat.*, 24:469–479.

Lindemalm, G., Korlin, D., & Uddenberg, N. (1986), Long-term follow-up of "sex change" in 13 male-to-female transsexuals. *Arch. Sex. Behav.*, 15:187–210.

Lindgren, T. W., & Pauly, I. B. (1975), A body image scale for evaluation of transsexuals. *Arch. Sex. Behav.*, 4:639–656.

Lindzey, G. (1967), Some remarks concerning incest, the incest taboo, and psychoanalytic theory. *Amer. Psychol.*, 22:1051–1059.

Linebaugh, P. (1984), In: *Protecting Our Children: The Fight Against Molestation. A National Symposium.* Washington, DC: U.S. Government Printing Office.

Litin, E. N., Griffin, M. E., & Johnson, A. M. (1956), Parental influence in unusual sexual behavior in children. *Psychoanal. Quart.*, 25:37–56.

Litman, R. E., & Swearingen, C. (1972), Bondage and suicide. *Arch. Psychiat.*, 27:80–85.

Lloyd, R. (1976), *For Money or Love.* New York: Vanguard Press.

Loeb, L., & Shane, M. (1982), The resolution of a transsexual wish in a five-year-old boy. *J. Amer. Psychoanal. Assn.*, 30:419–434.

Loewenstein, R. M. (1957), A contribution to the psychoanalytic theory of masochism. *J. Amer. Psychoanal. Assn.*, 5:197–234.

London, L. S. (1957), *Sexual Deviations in the Male and in the Female.* New York: Bell Publishing Co.

——— Caprio, F. S. (1950), *Sexual Deviations.* Washington, DC: Linacre Press.

Longo, R. E., & Groth, A. N. (1983), Juvenile sexual offenses in the histories of adult rapists and child molesters. *Internat. J. Offender Ther. & Compar. Criminol.*, 27:150–155.

Lorand, S. (1930), Fetishism in statu nascendi. *Internat. J. Psycho-Anal.*, 11:419–427.

Lothstein, L. M. (1977), Countertransference reactions to gender dysphoric patients: Implications for psychotherapy. *Psychother. Theory, Res. & Pract.*, 14:21–31.

——— (1978), The psychological management and treatment of hospitalized transsexuals. *J. Nerv. & Ment. Dis.*, 166:255–262.

——— (1979a), The aging gender dysphoria (transsexual) patient. *Arch. Sex. Behav.*, 8:431–444.

——— (1979b), Psychodynamics and sociodynamics of gender dysphoric states. *Amer. J. Psychother.*, 33:214–238.

——— (1980a), The postsurgical transsexual: Empirical and theoretical considerations. *Arch. Sex. Behav.*, 9:547–564.

——— (1980b), The adolescent gender dysphoric patient: An approach to treatment and management. *J. Pediat. Psychol.*, 5:93–109.

——— (1982a), Amphetamine abuse and transsexualism. *J. Nerv. & Ment. Dis.*, 170:568–571.

——— (1982b), Sex reassignment surgery: Historical, bioethical, and theoretical issues. *Amer. J. Psychiat.*, 139:417–426.

——— (1983), *Female-to-Male Transsexualism: Historical, Clinical, and Theoretical Issues.* Boston: Routledge & Kegan Paul.

——— Levine, S. B. (1981), Expressive psychotherapy with gender dysphoric patients. *Arch. Gen. Psychiat.*, 38:924–929.

Lowy, F. H., & Kolivakis, T. L. (1971), Autocastration by a male transsexual. *Can. Psychiat. Assn. J.*, 16:399–405.

Lukianowicz, N. (1959), Survey of various aspects of transvestism in the light of our present knowledge. *J. Nerv. & Ment. Dis.*, 128:36–64.

——— (1960a), Two cases of transvestism. *Psychiat. Quart.*, 34:517–537.

——— (1960b), Imaginary sexual partners. *Arch. Gen. Psychiat.*, 3:429–449.

——— (1962), A rudimentary form of transvestism. *Amer. J. Psychother.*, 16:665–675.

——— (1965), Symbolic self-strangulation in a transvestite schizophrenic. *Psychiat. Quart.*, 39:244–257.

——— (1972), Incest. *Brit. J. Psychiat.*, 120:301–313.

Lundstrom, B. (1981), *Gender Dysphoria: A Social-Psychiatric Follow-up Study of 31 Cases Not Accepted for Sex Reassignment.* Goteborg, Sweden: University of Goteborg.

——— Pauly, I., & Walinder, J. (1984), Outcome of sex reassignment surgery. *Acta Psychiat. Scand.*, 70:289–294.

Lustig, N., Dresser, J., Spellman, S., & Murray, T. (1966), Incest: A family group survival pattern. *Arch. Gen. Psychiat.*, 14:31–40.

Lutz, D. J., Roback, H. B., & Hart, M. (1984), Feminine gender identity and psychological adjustment of male transsexuals and male homosexuals. *J. Sex Res.*, 20:350–362.

Lynn, D. B. (1969), *Parental and Sex-role Identification. A Theoretical Formulation.* Berkeley, CA: McCutchan.

——— (1974), *The Father: His Role in Child Development.* Monterey, CA: Brooks/Cole.

MacCulloch, M. J., Snowden, P. R., Wood, P. J. W., & Mills, H. E. (1983), On the genesis of sadistic behavior: The sadistic fantasy syndrome. *Brit. J. Psychiat.*, 143:20–29.

MacDonald, J. M. (1973), *Indecent Exposure.* Springfield, Il: Charles C Thomas.

MacDonald, M. W. (1938), Criminally aggressive behavior in passive effeminate boys. *Amer. J. Orthopsychiat.*, 8:70–78.

MacFarlane, D. F. (1984), Transsexual prostitution in New Zealand: Predominance of persons of Maori extraction. *Arch. Sex. Behav.*, 13:301–309.

MacFarlane, K., & Waterman, J. (1986), *Sexual Abuse of Young Children.* New York: Guilford Press.

Machotka, P., Pittman, F. S., & Flomenhaft, K. (1967), Incest as a family affair. *Fam. Proc.*, 6:98–116.

MacKenzie, K. R. (1978), Gender dysphoria syndrome: Towards standardized diagnostic criteria. *Arch. Sex. Behav.*, 7:251–262.

MacLean, G., & Robertson, S. B. (1976), Self-enucleation and psychosis: Report of two cases and discussion. *Arch. Gen. Psychiat.*, 33:242–249.

Mahler, M. S. (1972), On the first three subphases of separation-individuation process. *Internat. J. Psycho-Anal.*, 53:333–338.

Maisch, H. (1972), *Incest*. New York: Stein & Day.

Maleson, F. G. (1984), The multiple meanings of masochism in psychoanalytic discourse. *J. Amer. Psychoanal. Assn.*, 32:325–356.

Maletzky, B. M. (1980), Assisted covert sensitization. In: *Exhibitionism: Description, Assessment, and Treatment*, ed. D. J. Cox & R. J. Daitzman. New York: Garland STPM Press.

Malinowski, B. (1929), *The Sexual Life of Savages in North-Western Melanesia*. New York: Harcourt, Brace.

Malitz, S. (1966), Another report of the wearing of diapers and rubber pants by an adult male. *Amer. J. Psychiat.*, 122:1435–1437.

Marcus, D. E., & Overton, W. F. (1978), The development of cognitive gender constancy and sex role preferences. *Child Develop.*, 49:434–444.

Marcus, S. (1966), *The Other Victorians*. New York: Basic Books.

Marks, I. M. (1972), Phylogenetic and learning in the acquisition of fetishism. *Dan. Med. Bull.*, 19:307–310.

——— Gelder, M. G., & Bancroft, J. H. (1970), Sexual deviants two years after electric aversion. *Brit. J. Psychiat.*, 117:173–185.

Markus, H. (1977), Self-schemata and processing information about the self. *J. Pers. & Soc. Psychol.*, 35:63–78.

——— Crane, M., Bernstein, S., & Saladi, M. (1982), Self-schemas and gender. *J. Pers. & Soc. Psychol.*, 42:38–50.

Marshall, W. L. (1974), A combined treatment approach to the reduction of multiple fetish-related behaviors. *J. Consult. & Clin. Psychol.*, 42:613–616.

——— (1988), The use of sexually explicit stimuli by rapists, child molesters, and nonoffenders. *J. Sex Res.*, 25:267–288.

Marshall, W. N., Puls, T., & Davidson, C. (1988), New child abuse spectrum in an era of increased awareness. *Amer. J. Dis. Child.*, 142:664–667.

Martin, C. L., & Halverson, C. F. (1981), A schematic processing model of sex typing and stereotyping in children. *Child Develop.*, 52:1119–1134.

Martin, M. J., & Walters, J. (1982), Familial correlates of selected types of child abuse and neglect. *J. Marr. & Fam.*, 44:267–276.

Martino, M. (1977), *Emergence: A Transsexual Autobiography*. New York: Crown Publishers.

Masica, D. N., Money, J., & Ehrhardt, A. A. (1971), Fetal feminization and female gender identity in the testicular feminizing syndrome of androgen insensitivity. *Arch. Sex. Behav.*, 1:131–142.

Maslow, A. H. (1942), Self-esteem (dominance-feeling) and sexuality in women. *J. Soc. Psychol.*, 16:259–294.

——— (1954), *Motivation and Personality*, 2nd ed. New York: Harper & Row, 1970.

——— (1971), *The Farther Reaches of Human Nature*. New York: Viking Press.

Masters, W. H., & Johnson, V. E. (1966), *Human Sexual Response*. New York: Bantam Books.

Mathis, J. L. (1980), Group therapy. In: *Exhibitionism: Description, Assessment and Treatment*, ed. D. J. Cox & R. J. Daitzman. New York: Garland STPM Press.

——— Collins, M. (1970), Progressive phases in the group therapy of exhibitionists. *Internat. J. Group Psychother.*, 20:163–169.

May, R. (1969), *Love and Will.* New York: W. W. Norton.

McCaghy, C. H. (1968), Drinking and deviance disavowal: The case of child molesters. *Soc. Problems*, 16:43–49.

McCauley, E. A., & Ehrhardt, A. A. (1977), Role expectations and definitions: A comparison of female transsexuals and lesbians. *J. Homosex.*, 3:137–147.

————— ————— (1980), Sexual behavior in female transsexuals and lesbians. *J. Sex Res.*, 16:202–211.

McCawley, A. (1965), Exhibitionism and acting out. *Comprehen. Psychiat.*, 6:396–409.

McCreary, C. P. (1975), Personality profiles of persons convicted of indecent exposure. *J. Clin. Psychol.*, 31:260–262.

McCully, R. S. (1963), An interpretation of projective findings in a case of female transsexualism. *J. Project. Techniques & Pers. Assess.*, 27:436–446.

————— (1964), Vampirism: Historical perspective and underlying process in relation to a case of auto-vampirism. *J. Nerv. & Ment. Dis.*, 139:440–451.

————— (1976), A Jungian commentary on Epstein's case (wet-shoe) fetish. *Arch. Sex. Behav.*, 5:185–188.

McDougall, J. (1972), Primal scene and sexual perversions. *Internat. J. Psycho-Anal.*, 53:371–384.

McGeorge, J. (1964), Sexual assaults on children. *Med. Sci. & Law*, 4:245–253.

McGuire, R. J., Carlisle, J. M., & Young, B. G. (1965), Sexual deviations as conditioned behaviour: A hypothesis. *Behav. Res. & Ther.*, 2:185–190.

McKee, E. A., Roback, H. B., & Hollender, M. H. (1976), Transsexualism in two male triplets. *Amer. J. Psychiat.*, 133:334–337.

Meerloo, J. A. M. (1967), Change of sex and collaboration with psychosis. *Amer. J. Psychiat.*, 124:263–264.

Meiselman, K. C. (1978), *Incest.* New York: Jossey Bass.

Meyer, J. K. (1971), Clinical variants among applicants for sex reassignment. *J. Sex Res.*, 7:35–41.

————— (1974a), Clinical variants among applicants for sex reassignment. *Arch. Sex. Behav.*, 3:527–558.

————— (1974b), Psychiatric considerations in the sexual reassignment of non-intersex individuals. *Plastic & Reconstruct. Surg.*, 1:275–283.

————— (1980), Body ego, selfness, and gender sense: The development of gender identity. *Psychiat. Clin. N. Amer.*, 3:21–36.

————— (1982), The theory of gender disorders. *J. Amer. Psychoanal. Assn.*, 30:381–448.

————— Dupkin, C. (1985), Gender disturbance in childhood. *Bull. Menn. Clin.*, 49:236–269.

————— Hoopes, J. E. (1974), The gender dysphoria syndromes. *Plastic & Reconstruct. Surg.*, 54:447–451.

————— Knorr, N. J., & Blumer, D. (1971), Characteristics of a self-designated transsexual population. *Arch. Sex. Behav.*, 1:219–231.

————— Reter, N. (1979), Sex reassignment follow-up. *Arch. Gen. Psychiat.*, 36:1010–1015.

Meyer, W. J., Finkelstein, J. W., Stuart, C. A., Webb, A., Smith, E. R., Payer, A. F., & Walker, P. A. (1981), Physical and hormonal evaluation of trans-sexual patients during hormonal therapy. *Arch. Sex. Behav.*, 10:357–370.

————— Walker, P. A., & Suplee, Z. R. (1981), A survey of transsexual hormonal treatment in twenty gender-treatment centers. *J. Sex Res.*, 17:344–349.

Meyer-Bahlburg, H. F. (1977), Sex hormones and male homosexuality in comparative perspective. *Arch. Sex. Behav.*, 6:297–325.

———— (1980), Hormones and homosexuality. *Psychiat. Clin. N. Amer.*, 3:349–364.

Meyers, R. G., & Berah, E. F. (1983), Some features of Australian exhibitionists compared with pedophiles. *Arch. Sex. Behav.*, 12:541–548.

Migeon, C. J., Rivarola, M. A., & Forest, M. G. (1968), Studies on androgens in transsexual subjects. *Johns Hopkins Med. J.*, 123:128–133.

Mitchell, W., Falconer, M., & Hill, D. (1954), Epilepsy with fetishism relieved by temporal lobectomy. *Lancet*, 2:626–630.

Mittelmann, B. (1955), Motor patterns and genital behavior: Fetishism. *The Psychoanalytic Study of the Child*, 10:241–263. New York: International Universities Press.

Mohr, J. W. (1981), Age structures in pedophilia. In: *Adult Sexual Interest in Children*, ed. M. Cook & K. Howells. New York: Academic Press.

———— Turner, R. E., & Jerry, M. B. (1964), *Pedophilia and Exhibitionism*. Toronto: University of Toronto Press.

Moll, A. (1906), *Libido Sexualis*. New York: American Ethnological Press, 1933.

———— (1912), *The Sexual Life of the Child*. New York: Macmillan.

Molner, G., & Cameron, P. (1975), Incest syndrome: Observations in a general hospital psychiatric unit. *J. Can. Psychiat. Assn.*, 20:373–377.

Money, J. (1971), Prefatory remarks on outcome of sex reassignment in 24 cases of transsexualism. *Arch. Sex. Behav.*, 1:163–165.

———— (1974), Two names, two wardrobes, two personalities. *J. Homosex.*, 1:65–70.

———— (1984a), Gender-transposition theory and homosexual genesis. *J. Sex & Marit. Ther.*, 10:75–82.

———— (1984b), Paraphilias: Phenomenology and classification. *Amer. J. Psychother.*, 38:164–179.

———— Block, D. (1971), Speech, sexuality and the temporal lobe: An analysis of spontaneous speech of thirteen male transsexuals. *J. Sex Res.*, 7:35–41.

———— Brennan, J. G. (1969), Sexual dimorphism in the psychology of female transsexuals. In: *Transsexualism and Sex Reassignment*, ed. R. Green & J. Money. Baltimore: Johns Hopkins University Press.

———— ———— (1970), Heterosexual vs. homosexual attitudes: Male partners' perception of the feminine image of male transsexuals. *J. Sex Res.*, 6:193–209.

———— dePriest, M. (1976), Three cases of genital self-surgery and their relationship to transexualism. *J. Sex Res.*, 12:283–294.

———— Ehrhardt, A. A. (1972), *Man and Woman, Boy and Girl*. Baltimore: Johns Hopkins University Press.

———— Epstein, R. (1967), Verbal aptitude in eonism and prepubertal effeminacy—A feminine trait. *Trans. NY Acad. Sci.*, 29:448–454.

———— Hampson, J. G., & Hampson, J. L. (1955), An examination of some basic sexual concepts: The evidence of human hermaphroditism. *Bull. Johns Hopkins Hosp.*, 97:301–319.

———— ———— ———— (1957), Imprinting and the establishment of gender role. *Arch. Neurol. & Psychiat.*, 77:333–336.

———— Joboris, R., & Furth, G. (1977), Apotemnophilia: Two cases of self-demand amputation as a paraphilia. *J. Sex. Res.*, 13:115–125.

———— Lamacz, M. (1984), Gynemimesis and gynemimetophilia: Individual and cross-cultural manifestations of a gender-coping strategy hitherto unnamed. *Comprehen. Psychiat.*, 25:392–403.

——— Primrose, C. (1969), Sexual dimorphism and dissociation in the psychology of male transsexuals. In: *Transsexualism and Sex Reassignment*, ed. R. Green & J. Money. Baltimore: Johns Hopkins University Press.

——— Russo, A. J. (1981), Homosexual vs. transvestite or transsexual gender-identity/role: Outcome study in boys. *Internat. J. Fam. Psychiat.*, 2:139–145.

——— Schwartz, M., & Lewis, V. (1984), Adult erotosexual status and fetal hormonal masculinization and demasculinization. *Psychoneuroendocrinol.*, 9:405–414.

——— Simcoe, K. W. (1986), Acrotomophilia, sex and disability: New concepts and case report. *Sex. & Disabil.*, 7:43–50.

——— Wolff, G. (1973), Sex reassignment: Male to female to male. *Arch. Sex. Behav.*, 2:245–250.

Morgan, A. J. (1978), Psychotherapy for transsexual candidates screened out of surgery. *Arch. Sex. Behav.*, 7:273–283.

Morin, S. F., & Schultz, S. J. (1978), The gay movement and the rights of children. *J. Soc. Iss.*, 34:137–148.

Morris, J. (1974), *Conundrum*. New York: Harcourt Brace Jovanovich.

Moulton, R. W., Liberty, P. G., Burnstein, E., & Altucher, N. (1966), Patterning of parental affection and disciplinary dominance a determinant of guilt and sex typing. *J. Pers. & Soc. Psychol.*, 4:356–363.

Mrazek, P. B., & Bentovim, A. (1981), Incest and the dysfunctional family system. In: *Sexually Abused Children and Their Families*, ed. P. B. Mrazek & C. Kempe. Oxford: Pergamon Press.

Munroe, R. L., Whiting, J. W. M., & Hally, D. J. (1969), Institutionalized male transvestism and sex distinctions. *Amer. Anthropol.*, 71:87–91.

Murray, H. A. (1938), *Explorations in Personality*. New York: Science Editions.

Mussen, P. H., & Distler, L. (1960), Child-rearing antecedents of masculine identification in kindergarten boys. *Child Develop.*, 31:89–100.

——— Rutherford, E. (1963), Parent–child relations and parental personality in relation to young children's sex-role preferences. *Child Develop.*, 34:589–607.

M'Uzan, M. de (1973), A case of masochistic perversion and an outline of a theory. *Internat. J. Psycho-Anal.*, 54:455–467.

Nabokov, V. (1970), *The Annotated Lolita*. New York: McGraw-Hill.

Nacht, S., Diatkine, R., & Favreau, J. (1956), The ego in pleasure relationships. *Internat. J. Psycho-Anal.*, 37:404–413.

Nadler, R. P. (1968), Approach to psychodynamics of obscene telephone call. *NY State J. Med.*, 68:521–526.

Nagler, S. H. (1957), Fetishism: A review and a case study. *Psychiat. Quart.*, 31:713–741.

Nakashima, I. I., & Zakus, G. E. (1977), Incest: Review and clinical experience. *Pediat.*, 60:696–701.

Nedoma, K., Mellan, J., & Pondelickova, J. (1971), Sexual behavior and its development in pedophilic men. *Arch. Sex. Behav.*, 1:267–271.

Newcomb, M. D. (1985), The role of perceived relative parent personality in the development of heterosexuals, homosexuals, and transvestites. *Arch. Sex. Behav.*, 14:147–164.

Newman, L. E. (1976), Treatment for the parents of feminine boys. *Amer. J. Psychiat.*, 133:683–687.

———— Stoller, R. J. (1971), The oedipal situation in male transsexualism. *Brit. J. Med. Psychol.*, 44:295–303.

———— ———— (1974), Nontranssexual men who seek sex reassignment. *Amer. J. Psychiat.*, 131:437–441.

Newton, D. E. (1978), Homosexual behavior and child molestation: A review of the evidence. *Adol.*, 13:29–54.

Newton, E. (1972), *Mother Camp: Female Impersonators in America.* Chicago: University of Chicago Press.

Nixon, E. (1964), The Chevalier D'Eon: A case of double identity. *History Today*, 14:126–134.

Noguchi, T. T. (1983), *Coroner.* New York: Pocket Books.

Nordyke, N. S., Baer, D. M., Etzel, B. C., & LeBlanc, J. M. (1977), Implications of the stereotyping and modification of sex role. *J. Appl. Behav. Anal.*, 10:553–557.

Nydes, J. (1950), The magical experience of the masturbation fantasy. *Amer. J. Psychother.*, 4:303–310.

O'Brien, S. (1983), *Child Pornography.* Dubuque: Kendall/Hunt.

Olkon, D., & Sherman, I. (1944), Eonism with added psychopathic features. *J. Nerv. & Ment. Dis.*, 99:159–164.

Oppenheim, G., & Robbin, F. (1974), The male transvestite (A Confide cassette). Tappan, NY: Confide.

Ostow, M. (1953), Transvestism. *J. Amer. Med. Assn.*, 152:1553.

Ovesey, L. (1969), *Homosexuality and Pseudohomosexuality.* New York: Science House.

———— Person, E. (1973), Gender identity and sexual psychopathology in men: A psychodynamic analysis of homosexuality, transsexualism and transvestism. *J. Amer. Acad. Psychoanal.*, 1:54–72.

———— ———— (1976), Transvestism: A disorder of the sense of self. *Internat. J. Psychoanal. Ther.*, 5:219–236.

Paitich, E., Langevin, R., Freeman, R., Mann, K., & Handy, L. (1977), The Clarke SHQ: A clinical sex biography questionnaire for males. *Arch. Sex. Behav.*, 6:421–436.

Panel (1956), The problem of masochism in the theory and technique of psychoanalysis. M. N. Stein, reporter. *J. Amer. Psychoanal. Assn.*, 4:526–538.

———— (1981), Masochism: Current concepts. N. Fisher, reporter. *J. Amer. Psychoanal. Assn.*, 29:673–688.

———— (1984), The relation between masochism and depression. J. Caston, reporter. *J. Amer. Psychoanal. Assn.*, 32:603–614.

Panken, S. (1967), On masochism: A re-evaluation. *Psychoanal. Rev.*, 54:527–541.

———— (1973), *The Joy of Suffering: Psychoanalytic Theory and Therapy of Masochism.* New York: Jason Aronson.

Panton, J. H. (1979), MMPI profile configurations associated with incestuous and non-incestuous child molesting. *Psychol. Rep.*, 45:335–338.

Parker, G., & Barr, R. (1982), Parental representations of transsexuals. *Arch. Sex, Behav.*, 11:221–230.

Parker, H., & Parker, S. (1986), Father daughter sexual abuse: Emerging perspectives. *Amer. J. Orthopsychiat.*, 56:531–549.

Parkin, A. (1963), On fetishism. *Internat. J. Psycho-Anal.*, 44:352–361.

Parsons, T. (1954), The incest taboo in relation to social structure and the socialization of the child. *Brit. J. Sociol.*, 5:101–117.

Partridge, B. (1960), *A History of Orgies*. New York: Bonanza Books.

Pauly, I. B. (1965), Male psychosexual inversion: Transsexualism. A review of 100 cases. *Arch. Gen. Psychiat.*, 13:172–181.

—— (1968), The current status of the change of sex operation. *J. Nerv. & Ment. Dis.*, 147:460–467.

—— (1969a), Adult manifestations of male transsexualism. In: *Transsexualism and Sex Reassignment*, ed. R. Green & J. Money. Baltimore: Johns Hopkins University Press.

—— (1969b), Adult manifestations of female transsexualism. In: *Transsexualism and Sex Reassignment*, ed. R. Green & J. Money. Baltimore: Johns Hopkins University Press.

—— (1974a), Female transsexualism: Part I. *Arch. Sex. Behav.*, 3:487–507.

—— (1974b), Female transsexualism: Part II. *Arch. Sex. Behav.*, 3:509–526.

Payne, S. M. (1939), Some observations on the ego development of the fetishist. *Internat. J. Psycho-Anal.*, 20:161–170.

Peabody, G. A., Rowe, A. T., & Wall, J. H. (1953), Fetishism and transvestism. *J. Nerv. & Ment. Dis.*, 118:339–350.

The Pearl (1879–1880), New York: Ballantine Books, 1968.

Pennington, V. M. (1960), Phrenotopic medication in transvestism. *J. Neuropsychiat.*, 2:35–40.

Perlmutter, L. H., Engel, T., & Sager, C. J. (1982), The incest taboo: Loosened sexual boundaries in remarried families. *J. Sex & Marit. Ther.*, 8:83–96.

Perry, D. G., & Bussey, K. (1979), The social learning theory of sex differences: Imitation is alive and well. *J. Pers. & Soc. Psychol.*, 37:1699–1712.

Person, E., & Ovesey, L. (1974a), The transsexual syndrome in males I: Primary transsexualism. *Amer. J. Psychother.*, 28:4–20.

—— —— (1974b), The transsexual syndrome in males: II. *Amer. J. Psychother.*, 28:174–193.

—— —— (1978), Transvestism: New perspectives. *J. Amer. Acad. Psychoanal.*, 6:301–323.

—— —— (1983), Psychoanalytic theories of gender identity. *J. Amer. Acad. Psychoanal.*, 11:203–226.

—— —— (1984), Homosexual cross-dressers. *J. Amer. Acad. Psychoanal.*, 12:167–186.

Peskin, H. (1967), Pubertal onset and ego functioning. *J. Abnorm. Psychol.*, 72:1–15.

Peters, J. J. (1976), Children who are victims of sexual assault and the psychology of offenders. *Amer. J. Psychother.*, 30:398–421.

—— Sadoff, R. L. (1970), Clinical observations on child molesters. *Med. Asp. Hum. Sexual.*, 4:20–32.

Peto, A. (1975), The etiological significance of the primal scene perversions. *Psychoanal. Quart.*, 44:177–190.

Petritzer, B. K., & Forster, J. (1955), A case study of a male transvestite with epilepsy and juvenile diabetes. *J. Ment. & Nerv. Dis.*, 121:557–563.

Pettit, I., & Burr, R. (1980), Temporal lobe epilepsy with diaper fetishism and gender dysphoria. *Med. J. Austral.*, 2:208–209.

Philbert, M. (1971), Male transsexualism: An endocrine study. *Arch. Sex. Behav.*, 1:91–93.

Pleck, J. H. (1981), *The Myth of Masculinity*. Cambridge, MA: MIT Press.

Plummer, K. (1981), The paedophile's progress: A view from below. In: *Perspectives on Paedophilia*, ed. B. Taylor. London: Batsford.

Pomeroy, J. C., Behar, D., & Stewart, M. A. (1981), Abnormal sexual behavior in pre-pubescent children. *Brit. J. Psychiat.*, 138:119–125.

Pomeroy, W. B. (1967), A report on the sexual histories of twenty-five transsexuals. *Trans. NY Acad. Sci.*, 29:444–447.

———— (1975), The diagnosis and treatment of transvestites and transsexuals. *J. Sex & Marit. Ther.*, 1:215–228.

Power, D. J. (1976), Sexual deviation and crime. *Med., Sci. & Law.*, 16:111–128.

Prince, C. V. (1957), Homosexuality, transvestism and transsexualism. *Amer. J. Psychother.*, 11:80–85.

———— (1978), Transsexuals and pseudotranssexuals. *Arch. Sex. Behav.*, 7:263–272.

———— (1981), *Understanding Cross Dressing*. Tulare, CA: Chevalier.

———— Bentler, P. M. (1972), Survey of 504 cases of transvestism. *Psychol. Rep.*, 31:903–917.

Prins, H. (1985), Vampirism—A clinical condition. *Brit. J. Psychiat.*, 146:666–668.

Pruett, K. D., & Dahl, K. (1982), Psychotherapy of gender identity conflict in young boys. *J. Amer. Acad. Child Psychiat.*, 21:65–70.

Rachman, S. (1966), Sexual fetishism: An experimental analog. *Psychol. Rec.*, 16:293–296.

———— Hodgson, R. J. (1968), Experimentally induced "sexual fetishism." *Psychol. Rec.*, 18:25–27.

Rada, R. T. (1976), Alcoholism and the child molester. *Ann. NY Acad. Sci.*, 273:492–496.

———— Kellner, R., Laws, D. R., & Winslow, W. W. (1978), Drinking, alcoholism and the mentally disordered sex offender. *Bull. Amer. Acad. Psychiat. & Law*, 6:296–300.

———— Laws, D. R., & Kellner, R. (1976), Plasma testosterone levels in the rapist. *Psychosom. Med.*, 38:257–268.

Rader, C. M. (1977), MMPI profiles of exposers, rapists and assaulters in a court service population. *J. Consult. & Clin. Psychol.*, 45:61–69.

Rado, S. (1940), A critical examination of the concept of bisexuality. *Psychosom. Med.*, 2:459–467.

Randell, J. B. (1959), Transvestism and trans-sexualism. *Brit. Med. J.*, 2:1448–1452.

———— (1969), Preoperative and postoperative status of male and female transsexuals. In: *Transsexualism and Sex Reassignment*, ed. R. Green & J. Money. Baltimore: Johns Hopkins University Press.

———— (1971), Indications for sex reassignment surgery. *Arch. Sex. Behav.*, 1:153–161.

———— (1975), Transvestism and trans-sexualism. *Brit. J. Psychiat. Spec. Suppl.* No. 9:201–205.

Raphling, E., Carpenter, B., & Davis, A. (1967), Incest. *Arch. Gen. Psychiat.*, 16:505–511.

Raymond, J. (1979), *The Transsexual Empire: The Making of the She-Male*. Boston: Beacon Press.

Raymond, M. J. (1956), Case of fetishism treated by aversion therapy. *Brit. Med. J.*, 2:854–857.

Redmount, R. S. (1953), A case of a female transvestite with marital and criminal complications. *J. Clin. Experiment. Psychopath.*, 14:95–111.

Regestein, O. R., & Reich, P. (1978), Pedophilia occurring after onset of cognitive impairment. *J. Nerv. & Ment. Dis.*, 166:794–798.

Reich, W. (1949), *Character-Analysis*, 3rd ed. New York: Orgone Institute Press.

Reik, T. (1941), *Masochism and Modern Man*. New York: Farrar, Straus & Rinehart.

Reinisch, J. M., & Karow, W. G. (1977), Prenatal exposure to synthetic progestins and estrogens: Effect on human development. *Arch. Sex. Behav.*, 6:257–288.

Rekers, G. A. (1975), Stimulus control over sex-typed play in cross-gender identified boys. *J. Experiment. Child Psychol.*, 20:136–148.

——— (1977), Atypical gender development and psychological development. *J. Appl. Behav. Anal.*, 10:559–571.

——— Bentler, P. M., Rosen, A. C., & Lovaas, O. I. (1978), Child gender disturbances: A clinical rationale for intervention. *Psychother.: Theory, Res., & Pract.*, 14:2–11.

——— Lovaas, O. I. (1974), Behavioral treatment of deviant sex-role behaviors in a male child. *J. Appl. Behav. Anal.*, 7:173–190.

——— Mead, S. L., Rosen, A. C., & Brigham, S. L. (1983), Family correlates of male childhood gender disturbance. *J. Genet. Psychol.*, 142:31–42.

——— Varni, J. W. (1977), Self-monitoring and self-reinforcement processes in a pre-transsexual boy. *Behav. Res. & Ther.*, 15:177–180.

Renvoize, J. (1982), *Incest: A Family Pattern*. London: Routledge & Kegan Paul.

Resnik, H. L. P. (1972), Erotized repetitive hangings: A form of self-destructive behavior. *Amer. J. Psychother.*, 26:4–21.

——— Peters, J. J. (1967), Outpatient group therapy with convicted pedophiles. *Internat. J. Group Psychother.*, 17:151–158.

Restak, R. M. (1979), The sex-change conspiracy. *Psychology Today*, 20:20–25.

Revitch, E. (1965), Sex murder and the potential sex murderer. *Dis. Nerv. Syst.*, 26:640–648.

——— Weiss, R. (1962), The pedophilic offender. *Dis. Nerv. Syst.*, 23:73–78.

Rhinehart, J. W. (1961), Genesis of overt incest. *Comprehen. Psychiat.*, 2:338–349.

Rhodes, J. M. (1980), Theoretical and therapeutic integration. In: *Exhibitionism: Description, Assessment, and Treatment*, ed. D. J. Cox & R. J. Daitzman. New York: Garland STPM Press.

Rickles, N. K. (1950), *Exhibitionism*. Philadelphia: J. B. Lippincott.

Riemer, S. (1940), A research note on incest. *Amer. J. Sociol.*, 45:566–575.

Righton, P. (1981), The adult. In: *Perspectives on Paedophilia*, ed. B. Taylor. London: Batsford.

Rimza, M., & Niggeman, E. (1982), Medical evaluation of sexually abused children: A review of 311 cases. *Pediat.*, 69:8–14.

Ritchie, G. G. (1968), The use of hypnosis in a case of exhibitionism. *Psychother.: Theory, Res. & Pract.*, 5:40–43.

Roback, H. B., McKee, E., Webb, W., Abramowitz, C. V., & Abramowitz, S. I. (1976), Psychopathology in female sex-change applicants and two help-seeking controls. *J. Abnorm. Psychol.*, 85:430–432.

——— Strassberg, D. S., McKee, E., & Cunningham, J. (1977), Self-concept and psychological adjustment differences between self-identified male transsexuals and male homosexuals. *J. Homosex.*, 3:15–20.

Roberto, L. G. (1983), Issues in diagnosis and treatment of transsexualism. *Arch. Sex. Behav.*, 12:445–473.

Roiphe, H., & Galenson, E. (1973), The infantile fetish. *The Psychoanalytic Study of the Child*, 28:147–166. New Haven, CT: Yale University Press.

Romm, M. E. (1942), Compulsion factors in exhibitionism. *J. Crim. Psychopath.*, 3:585–596.

———— (1949), Some dynamics of fetishism, *Psychoanal. Quart.*, 13:137–153.

Rook, K. S., & Hammen, C. L. (1977), A cognitive perspective on the experience of sexual arousal. *J. Soc. Iss.*, 33:7–29.

Rooth, G. (1970), Some historical notes on indecent exposure and exhibitionism. *Medico-Legal J.*, 38:135–139.

———— (1973), Exhibitionism outside Europe and America. *Arch. Sex. Behav.*, 2:352–363.

Rosen, A. C. (1974), Brief report of MMPI characteristics of sexual deviation. *Psychol. Rep.*, 35:73–74.

———— Rekers, G. A., & Friar, L. R. (1977), Theoretical and diagnostic issues in child gender disturbances. *J. Sex Res.*, 13:89–103.

———— Teague, J. (1974), Case studies in development of masculinity and femininity in male children. *Psychol. Rep.*, 34:971–983.

Rosen, I. (1979), Exhibitionism, scopophilia, and voyeurism. In: *Sexual Deviation*, 2nd ed., ed. I. Rosen. Oxford, UK: Oxford University Press.

Rosen, R. C., & Kople, S. A. (1977), Penile plethysmography and biofeedback in the treatment of a transvestite–exhibitionist. *J. Consult. & Clin. Psychol.*, 45:908–916.

Rosenbaum, S., & Faber, M. (1979), The adolescent sexual asphyxia syndrome. *J. Amer. Acad. Child Psychiat.*, 17:546–558.

Rosenfeld, A. (1979), Endogamic incest and the victim-perpetrator model. *Amer. J. Dis. Child.*, 133:406–410.

———— Bailey, R., Siegel, B., & Bailey, G. (1986), Determining incestuous contact between parent and child: Frequency of children touching parents' genitals in a nonclinical population. *J. Amer. Acad. Child Psychiat.*, 25:481–484.

Ross, M. W., Walinder, J., Lundstrom, B., & Thuwe, I. (1981), Cross-cultural approaches to transsexualism. A comparison between Sweden and Australia. *Acta Psychiat. Scand.*, 63:75–82.

Rossman, G. P. (1976), *Sexual Experience Between Men and Boys*. New York: Association Press.

Rousseau, J. J. (1778), *Confessions of J. J. Rousseau*. New York: Modern Library, 1945.

Rubenfine, D. L. (1965), On beating fantasies. *Internat. J. Psycho-Anal.*, 46:315–322.

Rubin, J. Z., Provenzano, F. J., & Luria, Z. (1974), The eye of the beholder: Parents' view on sex of new-borns. *Amer. J. Orthopsychiat.*, 44:512–519.

Rubin, R. T., Reinish, J. M., & Haskett, R. F. (1981), Postnatal gonadal steroid effects on human behavior. *Science*, 211:1318–1324.

Rubins, J. L. (1969), Sex perversion: Some dynamic considerations. *Amer. J. Psychoanal.*, 29:94–105.

Rush, F. (1980), *The Best Kept Secret: Sexual Abuse of Children*. New York: McGraw-Hill.

Russell, D. H. (1972), Treatment of adult exhibitionists. *Internat. J. Offender Ther. & Compar. Criminol.*, 16:121–124.

Rutter, M. (1971), Normal psychosexual development. *J. Child Psychol. & Psychiat.*, 11:259–283.

Sabalis, R. F., Frances, A., Appenzeller, S. N., & Moseley, W. B. (1974), Three sisters: Transsexual male siblings. *Amer. J. Psychiat.*, 131:907–909.

——— Staton, M. A., & Appenzeller, S. N. (1977), Transsexualism: Alternate diagnostic and etiological considerations. *Amer. J. Psychoanal.*, 37:223–228.

Sacher-Masoch, L. von. (1870), *Venus in Furs*. n.p.: Nesor Publishing Co.

Sachs, H. (1923), On the genesis of perversions. *Psychoanal. Quart.*, 55:477–488, 1986.

Sadger, J. (1926), A contribution to the understanding of sado-masochism. *Internat. J. Psycho-Anal.*, 7:484–491.

Sadoughi, W., Jayaram, B., & Bush, I. (1978), Postoperative changes in self concept of transsexuals as measured by the Tennessee Self Concept Scale. *Arch. Sex. Behav.*, 7:347–349.

Saghir, M. T., & Robins, E. (1973), *Male and Female Homosexuality. A Comprehensive Investigation*. Baltimore: Williams & Wilkins.

Sanford, L. T. (1980), *The Silent Children*. New York: McGraw-Hill.

Sandfort, T. G. (1984), Sex in pedophiliac relationships: An empirical investigation among a nonrepresentative group of boys. *J. Sex Res.*, 20:123–142.

Sapolsky, B. S. (1984), Arousal effect and the aggression-moderating effect of erotica. In: *Pornography and Sexual Aggression*, ed. N. M. Malamuth & E. Donnerstein. New York: Academic Press.

Sarafino, E. (1979), An estimate of nationwide incidence of sexual offenses against children. *Child Welf.*, 58:127–134.

Sarrel, P. M., & Masters, W. H. (1982), Sexual molestation of men by women. *Arch. Sex. Behav.*, 11:117–123.

Sass, F. (1975), Sexual asphyxia in the female. *J. Forensic Sci.*, 20:181–185.

Savage, M. O., Preece, M. A., Jeffcoate, S. L., Ransley, P. G., Rumsby, G., Mansfield, M. D., & Williams, D. I. (1980), Familial male pseudohermaphroditism due to deficiency of 5 alpha-reductase. *Clin. Endocrinol.*, 12:397–406.

Schachter, S., & Singer, J. E. (1962), Cognitive, social and physiological determinants of emotional state. *Psychol. Rev.*, 69:379–399.

Schad-Somers, S. P. (1982), *Sadomasochism*. New York: Human Sciences Press.

Schilder, P. (1936), The analysis of ideologies as a psychotherapeutic method. *Amer. J. Psychiat.*, 93:601–617.

Schmideberg, M. (1956), Delinquent acts as perversions and fetishes. *Internat. J. Psycho-Anal.*, 37:422–424.

Schneider, S. F., Harrison, S. I., & Siegel, B. L. (1965), Self-castration by a man with cyclic changes in sexuality. *Psychosom. Med.*, 27:53–70.

Schrenk-Notzing, A. von. (1895), *The Use of Hypnosis in Psychopathia Sexualis*. New York: Julian Press, 1956.

Schwartz, M. F. (1976), Pair-bonding experience of 26 early treated adrenogenital females ages 17–27. In: *Progress in Sexology*, ed. R. Gemme & C. C. Wheeler. New York: Plenum.

Scott, E. M. (1977), The sexual offender. *Internat. J. Offender Ther. & Compar. Criminol.*, 21:255–263.

Scott, G. G. (1983), *Dominant Women Submissive Men*. New York: Praeger.

Segal, M. M. (1965), Transvestism as an impulse and as a defense. *Internat. J. Psycho-Anal.*, 46:209–217.

Segal, Z. V., & Marshall, W. L. (1985), Heterosexual social skills in a population of rapists and child molesters. *J. Consult. & Clin. Psychol.*, 53:55–63.

Sepher, J. (1971), Mate selection among second generation kibbutz adolescents and adults: Incest avoidance and negative imprinting. *Arch. Sex. Behav.*, 1:293–307.

Seyler, L., Canalis, E., Spare, S., & Reichlin, S. (1978), Abnormal gonadotrophin secretory responses to LRH in transsexual women after diethylstilbestrol priming. *J. Clin. Endocrinol. & Metabol.*, 47:176–183.

Shankel, L. W., & Carr, A. C. (1956), Transvestism and hanging episodes in a male adolescent. *Psychiat. Quart.*, 30:478–493.

Shapiro, H. A. (1974), Answers to questions: Enemas as sexual stimulants. *Med. Asp. Hum. Sexual.*, 8:159.

Shave, D. (1976), Transsexualism as a concretized manifestation of orality. *Amer. J. Psychoanal.*, 36:57–66.

Sheehan, W., & Garfinkel, B. D. (1988), Case study: Adolescent autoerotic deaths. *J. Amer. Acad. Child & Adol. Psychiat.*, 27:367–370.

Sheldon, H. (1988), Childhood sexual abuse in adult female psychotherapy referrals. *Brit. J. Psychiat.*, 148:107–111.

Shelton, W. R. (1975), A study of incest. *Internat. J. Offender Ther. & Compar. Criminol.*, 19:139–153.

Shoor, M., Speed, M. H., & Bartlet, C. (1966), Syndrome of the adolescent child molester. *Amer. J. Psychiat.*, 122:783–789.

Shore, E. R. (1984), The former transsexual: A case study. *Arch. Sex. Behav.*, 13:277–285.

Shore, M. F., Clifton, A., Zelin, M., & Myerson, P. G. (1971), Patterns of masochism: An empirical study. *Brit. J. Med. Psychol.*, 44:59–66.

Siegel, L., & Zitrin, A. (1978), Transsexuals in the New York city welfare population: The function of illusion in transsexuality. *Arch. Sex. Behav.*, 7:285–290.

Silver, R. L., Boon, C., & Stones, M. H. (1983), Searching for meaning in misfortune: Making sense of incest. *J. Soc. Iss.*, 39:81–101.

Silverman, D. (1941), The treatment of exhibitionism: An experiment in cooperation between police and psychiatric clinic. *Bull. Menn. Clin.*, 5:85–93.

Simon, R. (1967), A case of female transsexualism. *Amer. J. Psychiat.*, 123:1598–1601.

Siomopoulos, V. (1974), Transsexualism: Disorder of gender identity, thought disorder, or both? *J. Amer. Acad. Psychoanal.*, 2:201–213.

——— Goldsmith, J. (1976), Sadism revisited. *Amer. J. Psychother.*, 30:631–640.

Sipova, L., & Starke, L. (1977), Plasma testosterone values in transsexual women. *Arch. Sex. Behav.*, 6:477–481.

Skrapec, C., & MacKenzie, K. R. (1981), Psychological self-perception in male transsexuals, homosexuals, and heterosexuals. *Arch. Sex. Behav.*, 10:357–370.

Smirnoff, V. N. (1969), The masochistic contract. *Internat. J. Psycho-Anal.*, 50:665–671.

Smith, R., Rhoades, J. M., & Llewellyn, C. E. (1961), Exhibitionism. *NC Med. J.*, 22:261–267.

Smith, S. M., & Braun, C. (1978), Necrophilia and lust murder: Report of a rare occurrence. *Bull. Amer. Acad. Psychiat. & Law*, 6:259–268.

Smukler, A. J., & Schiebel, D. (1975), Personality characteristics of exhibitionists. *Dis. Nerv. Syst.*, 36:600–602.

Snow, E., & Bluestone, H. (1969), Fetishism and murder. *Sci. & Psychoanal.*, 15:88–97.

Socarides, C. W. (1959), Meaning and content of pedophiliac perversion. *J. Amer. Psychoanal. Assn.*, 7:84–94.

——— (1960), The development of a fetishistic perversion: The contribution of preoedipal phase conflict. *J. Amer. Psychoanal. Assn.*, 8:281–311.

——— (1969), The desire for sexual transformation: A psychiatric evaluation of transsexualism. *Amer. J. Psychiat.*, 125:1419–1425.

——— (1988), *The Preoedipal Origin and Psychoanalytic Therapy of Sexual Perversions*. Madison, CT: International Universities Press.

Solomon, R. L., & Corbit, J. D. (1974), An opponent-process theory of motivation. *Psychol. Rev.*, 81:119–145.

Sorensen, R. C. (1973), *Adolescent Sexuality in Contemporary America*. New York: World Publishing.

Sorensen, T. (1981a), A follow-up study of operated transsexual males. *Acta Psychiat. Scand.*, 63:486–503.

——— (1981b), A follow-up study of operated transsexual females. *Acta Psychiat. Scand.*, 64:50–64.

——— Hertoft, P. (1980a), Transsexualism as a nosological unity in men and women. *Acta Psychiat. Scand.*, 61:135–151.

——— ——— (1980b), Sexmodifying operations in Denmark in the period 1950–1977. *Acta Psychiat. Scand.*, 61:56–66.

——— ——— (1982), Male and female transsexualism: The Danish experience with 37 patients. *Arch. Sex. Behav.*, 11:133–155.

Speaker, T. J. (1986), *Psychosexual Infantilism in Adults: The Erotization of Regression*. Unpublished doctoral dissertation, Columbia Pacific University.

Spencer, M. J., & Dunklee, P. (1986), Sexual abuse of boys. *Pediat.*, 78:133–138.

Spengler, A. (1977), Manifest sadomasochism in males. Results of an empirial study. *Arch. Sex. Behav.*, 6:441–456.

Spensley, J., & Barter, J. T. (1971), The adolescent transvestite on a psychiatric service: Family patterns. *Arch. Sex. Behav.*, 1:347–356.

Sperber, M. A. (1973), The 'as if' personality and transvestism. *Psychoanal. Rev.*, 60:605–612.

Sperling, M. (1947), The analysis of an exhibitionist. *Internat. J. Psycho-Anal.*, 28:32–45.

——— (1963), Fetishism in children. *Psychoanal. Quart.*, 32:374–392.

Sperling, O. (1956), Psychodynamics of group perversions. *Psychoanal. Quart.*, 25:56–65.

Spiro, M. E. (1975), *Children of the Kibbutz*, rev. ed. Cambridge, MA: Harvard University Press.

Spitz, R. (1962), Autoerotism re-examined: The role of early sexual behavior patterns in personality formation. *The Psychoanalytic Study of the Child*, 17:283–315. New York: International Universities Press.

Stack, A. (1983), *Lust Killer*. New York: Signet.

Starka, L., Sipova, L., & Hynie, J. (1975), Plasma testosterone in male trans-sexuals and homosexuals. *J. Sex Res.*, 11:134–138.

Steiner, B. W., Sanders, R. M., & Langevin, R. (1985), Crossdressing, erotic preference, and aggression: A comparison of male transvestites and trans-sexuals. In: *Erotic Preference, Gender Identity, and Aggression in Men*, ed. R. Langevin. Hillsdale, NJ: Lawrence Erlbaum Associates.

———— Satterberg, J. A., & Muir, C. F. (1978), Flight into femininity. The male menopause. *Can. Psychiat. Assn. J.*, 23:405–410.

Stekel, W. (1929a), *Sadism and Masochism*, Vol. 1. New York: Liveright.

———— (1929b), *Sadism and Masochism*, Vol. 2. New York: Liveright.

———— (1930a), *Sexual Aberrations*, Vol. 1. New York: Liveright.

———— (1930b), *Sexual Aberrations*, Vol. 2. New York: Liveright.

Stern, M. (1979), *Sex in the U.S.S.R.* New York: Times Books.

Stoller, R. J. (1964a), The hermaphroditic identity of hermaphrodites. *J. Nerv. & Ment. Dis.*, 139:453–457.

———— (1964b), A contribution to the study of gender identity. *Internat. J. Psycho-Anal.*, 45:220–226.

———— (1967), Transvestites' women. *Amer. J. Psychiat.*, 124:333–339.

———— (1968), *Sex and Gender: On the Development of Masculinity and Femininity.* New York: Science House.

———— (1969a), Parental influences in male transsexualism. In: *Transsexualism and Sex Reassignment*, ed. R. Green & J. Money. Baltimore: Johns Hopkins University Press.

———— (1969b), A biased view of "sex transformation" operations. *J. Nerv. & Ment. Dis.*, 149:312–317.

———— (1970), Pornography and perversion. *Arch. Gen. Psychiat.*, 22:490–500.

———— (1971), The term "transvestism." *Arch. Gen. Psychiat.*, 24:230–237.

———— (1972), Etiological factors in female transsexualism: A first approxi-mation. *Arch. Sex. Behav.*, 2:47–64.

———— (1973), Male transsexualism: Uneasiness. *Amer. J. Psychiat.*, 130:536–539.

———— (1974), Symbiosis anxiety and the development of masculinity. *Arch. Gen. Psychiat.*, 30:164–172.

———— (1975), *Perversion: The Erotic Form of Hatred.* New York: Delta.

———— (1979), Fathers of transsexual children. *J. Amer. Psychoanal. Assn.*, 27:837–866.

———— (1980), Gender identity disorders. In: *Comprehensive Textbook of Psy-chiatry*, Vol. 2, 3rd. ed., ed. H. I. Kaplan, A. M. Freedman, & B. J. Sadock. Baltimore: Williams & Wilkins.

———— (1982), Transvestism in women. *Arch. Sex. Behav.*, 11:99–115.

———— (1985a), *Observing the Erotic Imagination.* New Haven, CT: Yale Uni-versity Press.

———— (1985b), *Presentation of Gender.* New Haven, CT: Yale University Press.

———— Baker, H. J. (1973), Two male transsexuals in one family. *Arch. Sex. Behav.*, 2:323–328.

———— Herdt, G. H. (1982), The development of masculinity: A cross-cultural contribution. *J. Amer. Psychoanal. Assn.*, 39:29–59.

Stolorow, R. D. (1975), The narcissistic function of masochism (and sadism). *Internat. J. Psycho-Anal.*, 56:441–448.

———— Grand, H. (1973), A partial analysis of a perversion involving bugs. *Internat. J. Psycho-Anal.*, 54:349–350.

Storms, M. D. (1980), Theories of sexual orientation. *J. Pers. & Soc. Psychol.*, 38:783–792.

Storr, A. (1957), The psychopathology of fetishism and transvestism. *J. Anal. Psychol.*, 2:153–166.

Strassberg, D. S., Roback, H., Cunningham, J., McKee, E., & Larsen, P. (1979), Psychopathology in self-identified female-to-male transsexuals and heterosexuals. *Arch. Sex. Behav.*, 6:491–496.

Stricker, G. (1967), Stimulus properties of the Blacky to a sample of pedophiles. *J. Gen. Psychol.*, 77:35–39.

Strindberg, J. A. (1913), *Confession of a Fool*, trans. E. Schlenssner. Boston: Small, Maynard.

Sturup, G. K. (1976), Male transsexuals. A long term follow-up after sex reassignment operations. *Acta Psychiat. Scand.*, 53:51–63.

Summit, R., & Kryso, J. (1978), Sexual abuse of children: A clinical spectrum. *Amer. J. Orthopsychiat.*, 48:237–251.

Swanson, D. W. (1968), Adult sexual abuse of children: The man and circumstances. *Dis. Nerv. Syst.*, 29:677–683.

——— (1971), Who violates children sexually? *Med. Asp. Hum. Sexual.*, 5:184–197.

Swift, C. (1979), The prevention of sexual child abuse: Focus on the perpetrator. *J. Clin. Child Psychol.*, 8:133–136.

Symons, N. J. (1927), Does masochism necessarily imply the existence of a death instinct? *Internat. J. Psycho-Anal.*, 8:38–46.

Talamini, J. T. (1982), *Boys will be Girls*. Washington, DC: University Press.

Tauber, M. A. (1979), Sex differences in parent–child interaction styles during a free play session. *Child Develop.*, 50:981–988.

Taylor, A. J. W., & McLachlan, D. G. (1962), Clinical and psychological observations on transvestites. *NZ Med. J.*, 61:496–506.

——— ——— (1964), Transvestism and psychosexual identification. *NZ Med. J.*, 63:369–372.

Taylor, F. H. (1947), Observations of some cases of exhibitionism. *J. Ment. Sci.*, 93:631–638.

Thompson, S. K. (1975), Gender labels and early sex role development. *Child Develop.*, 46:339–347.

True Baby Letters & Experiences (1985a), Book 1. Seattle, WA: Infantae Press.

True Baby Letters & Experiences (1985b), Book 2. Seattle, WA: Infantae Press.

Tsoi, W. F. (1988), The prevalence of transsexualism in Singapore. *Acta Psychiat. Scand.*, 78:501–504.

——— Kok, L. P., & Long, F. Y. (1977), Male transsexualism in Singapore. *Brit. J. Psychiat.*, 131:405–409.

Tsushima, W. T., & Wedding, D. (1979), MMPI results of male candidates for transsexual surgery. *J. Pers. Assess.*, 43:385–387.

Tuchman, W. W., & Lachman, J. H. (1964), An unusual perversion: The wearing of diapers and rubber pants in a 29-year-old male. *Amer. J. Psychiat.*, 120:1198–1199.

Turner, R. E. (1964), The sexual offender. *Can. Psychiat. Assn. J.*, 9:533–540.

Tuteur, W. (1963), Child molesters and men who expose themselves—Anthropological approach. *J. Foren. Sci.*, 8:515–525.

Uddenberg, N. J., Walender, J., & Hojerback, T. (1979), Parental contact in male and female transsexuals. *Acta Psychiat. Scand.*, 60:113–120.

Ullerstram, L. (1966), *The Erotic Minorities*. New York: Grove Press.

Vanden Bergh, R. L., & Kelly, J. F. (1964), Vampirism: A review with new observations. *Arch. Gen. Psychiat.*, 11:543–547.

Vander Mey, B. B., & Neff, R. L. (1982), Adult–child incest: A review of research and treatment. *Adol.*, 17:717–735.

Van de Velde, T. H. (1926), *Ideal Marriage*, 3rd ed. New York: Random House, 1965.

Van Kammen, D. P., & Money, J. (1977), Erotic imagery and self-castration in transvestism/transsexualism: A case report. *J. Homosex.*, 2:359–366.

Van Putten, T., & Fawzy, F. I. (1976), Sex conversion surgery in a man with a severe gender dysphoria. A tragic outcome. *Arch. Gen. Psychiat.*, 33:751–753.

Verner, A., & Snyder, C. (1966), The pre-school child's awareness of anticipation of adult sex roles. *Sociometry*, 29:159–168.

Verschoor, A. M., & Poortinga, J. (1988), Psychosocial differences between Dutch male and female transsexuals. *Arch. Sex. Behav.*, 17:173–178.

Videla, E., & Prigoshin, N. (1976), Female trans-sexualist with abnormal karyotype. *Lancet*, 2:1081.

Virkkunen, M. (1974), Incest offenses and alcoholism. *Med., Sci. & Law*, 14:124–128.

——— (1976), The pedophilic offender with antisocial character. *Acta Psychiat. Scand.*, 53:401–405.

Vogt, J. H. (1968), Five cases of transsexualism in females. *Acta Psychiat. Scand.*, 44:62–88.

Volkan, V., & Berent, S. (1976), Psychiatric aspects of surgical treatment for problems of sexual identification (transsexualism). In: *Modern Perspectives in the Psychiatric Aspects of Surgery*, ed. J. G. Howells. New York: Brunner/Mazel.

——— Bhatti, T. (1973), Dreams of transsexuals awaiting surgery. *Comprehen. Psychiat.*, 14:269–279.

Wachtel, S., Green, R., Simon, N. G., Reichart, A., Cahill, L., Hall, J., Nakamura, D., Wachtel, G., Futterweit, W., Biber, S. H., & Ihlenfeld, C. (1986), On the expression of H-Y antigen in transsexuals. *Arch. Sex. Behav.*, 15:51–68.

Waggoner, R. W., & Boyd, D. A. (1941), Juvenile aberrant sexual behavior. *Amer. J. Orthopsychiat.*, 11:275–291.

Wakeling, A. (1979), A general psychiatric approach to sexual deviation. In: *Sexual Deviation*, 2nd ed., ed. I. Rosen. Oxford, UK: Oxford University Press.

Walinder, J. (1969), Transsexuals. In: *Transsexualism and Sex Reassignment*, ed. R. Green & J. Money. Baltimore: Johns Hopkins University Press.

——— (1971), Incidence and sex ratio of transsexualism in Sweden. *Brit. J. Psychiat.*, 119:195–196.

——— Lundstrom, B., & Thuwe, I. (1978), Prognostic factors in the assessment of male transsexuals for sex reassignment. *Brit. J. Psychiat.*, 132:16–20.

——— Thuwe, I. (1976), A law concerning sex reassignment of transsexuals in Sweden. *Arch. Sex. Behav.*, 5:255–258.

——— ——— (1977), A study of consanguinity between the parents of transsexuals. *Brit. J. Psychiat.*, 131:73–74.

Ward, J. (1972), Prenatal stress feminizes and demasculinizes the behavior of males. *Science*, 175:82–84.

Ward, N. (1975), Successful treatment of transvestism associated with manic-depression. *J. Nerv. & Ment. Dis.*, 161:204–207.

Warner, G., & Lahn, M. (1970), A case of female transsexualism. *Psychiat. Quart.*, 44:476–487.

Weinberg, M. S., Williams, C. J., & Moser, C. (1984), The social constituents of sadomasochism. *Soc. Prob.*, 31:379–389.

Weinberg, S. K. (1955), *Incest Behavior*. New York: Citadel Press.

Weinberg, T. S. (1978), Sadism and masochism sociological perspectives. *Bull. Amer. Acad. Psychiat. & Law*, 6:284–295.

——— (1987), Sadomasochism in the United States: A review of recent sociological literature. *J. Sex Res.*, 23:50–69.

Weiner, I. (1962), Father–daughter incest. *Psychiat. Quart.*, 36:601–632.

——— (1964), On incest: A survey. *Excerpta Criminol.*, 4:137–155.

Weinrich, J. D. (1985), Transsexuals, homosexuals, and sissy boys. On the mathematics of follow-up studies. *J. Sex Rex.*, 21:322–328.

Weiss, J., Rogers, E., Darwin, M. R., & Dutton, C. B. (1955), A study of girl sex victims. *Psychiat. Quart.*, 29:1–26.

Weissman, P. (1957), Some aspects of sexual activity in a fetishist. *Psychoanal. Quart.*, 15:450–471.

Weitzman, E. L., Shamoian, C. A., & Golosow, N. (1970), Identity diffusion and the transsexual resolution. *J. Nerv. & Ment. Dis.*, 151:295–302.

——— ——— ——— (1971), Family dynamics in male transsexualism. *Psychosom. Med.*, 33:289–299.

Wells, L. A. (1981), Family pathology and father–daughter incest. *J. Clin. Psychiat.*, 42:197–202.

Westermeyer, J. (1978), Incest in psychiatric practice: A description of patients and incestuous relationships. *J. Clin. Psychiat.*, 39:643–648.

Whitam, F. L. (1977), Childhood indicators of male homosexuality. *Arch. Sex. Behav.*, 6:89–98.

White, L. A. (1948), The definition and prohibition of incest. *Amer. Anthropol.*, 50:416–435, 1963.

Wiedman, G. H. (1953), Letter. *J. Amer. Med. Assn.*, 152:1167.

Wild, N. J., & Wynne, J. M. (1986), Child sex rings. *Brit. Med. J.*, 293:183–185.

Wilson, G. D., & Cox, D. N. (1983), Personality of paedophile club members. *Pers. & Individ. Diff.*, 4:323–329.

Wilson, G. W. (1948), A further contribution to the study of olfactory repression with particular reference to transvestism. *Psychoanal. Quart.*, 17:322–339.

Wilson, J. D., George, F. W., & Griffin, J. E. (1981), The hormonal control of sexual development. *Science*, 211:1278–1284.

Windham, D. (1965), *Two People*. London: Michael Joseph.

Winkler, R. C. (1977), What types of sex-role behavior should behavior modifiers promote? *J. Appl. Behav. Anal.*, 10:549–552.

Winnicott, D. W. (1953), Transitional objects and transitional phenomena. *Internat. J. Psycho-Anal.*, 34:89–97.

Wise, T. N., & Meyer, J. K. (1980), The border area between transvestism and gender dysphoria: Transvestitic applicants for sex reassignment. *Arch. Sex. Behav.*, 9:327–342.

Wittels, F. (1937), The mystery of masochism. *Psychoanal. Rev.*, 24:139–149.

Witzig, J. S. (1968), The group treatment of male exhibitionists. *Amer. J. Psychiat.*, 125:179–185.

W. L.-E. (1902), Book reviews. *Brit. Med. J.*, 1:339–341.

Wojdowski, P., & Tebor, I. B. (1976), Social and emotional tensions during transexual passing. *J. Sex Res.*, 12:193–205.

Wolf, A. P. (1966), Childhood association and sexual attraction: A further test of the Westermarck hypothesis. *Amer. Anthropol.*, 72:503–515.

Wolf, S. R., Knorr, N. J., Hoopes, J. E., & Meyer, E. (1968), Psychiatric aspects of transsexual surgery management. *J. Nerv. & Ment. Dis.*, 147:525–531.

Wolfe, B. E. (1979), Behavioral treatment of childhood gender disorders: A conceptual and empirical critique. *Behav. Mod.*, 3:550–575.

Wolfe, L. (1981), *The Cosmo Report*. New York: Arbor House.

Wolff, V. (1977), *Bisexuality*. London: Quartet Books.

Woodbury, J., & Schwartz, E. (1971), *The Silent Sin: A Case History of Incest*. New York: Signet.

Woody, R. H. (1973), Integrated aversion therapy and psychotherapy: Two sexual deviation case studies. *J. Sex Res.*, 9:313–324.

Worden, F. C., & Marsh, J. T. (1955), Psychological factors in men seeking sex transformation: Preliminary report. *J. Amer. Med. Assn.*, 157:1292–1298.

Wright, R. (1980), Rape and physical violence. In: *Sex Offenders in the Criminal Justice System*, ed. D. J. West. Cambridge, UK: University of Cambridge Press.

Wulff, M. (1946), Fetishism and object choice in early childhood. *Psychoanal. Quart.*, 15:450–471.

Yalom, I. (1960), Aggression and forbiddenness in voyeurism. *Arch. Gen. Psychiat.*, 3:305–319.

———— Green, R., & Fisk, N. (1973), Prenatal exposure to female hormones: Effect on psychosexual development in boys. *Arch. Gen. Psychiat.*, 28:554–561.

Yates, A. (1982), Children eroticized by incest. *Amer. J. Psychiat.*, 139:482–484.

Yawger, N. S. (1940), Transvestism and other cross-sex manifestations. *J. Nerv. & Ment. Dis.*, 92:41–48.

Zavitzianos, G. (1971), Fetishism and exhibition in the female and their relationship to psychopathy and kleptomania. *Internat. J. Psycho-Anal.*, 52:297–305.

———— (1977), The object in fetishism, homeovestism and transvestism. *Internat. J. Psycho-Anal.*, 58:487–495.

———— (1982), The perversion of fetishism in women. *Psychoanal. Quart.*, 51:405–425.

Zechnich, R. (1971), Exhibitionist: Genesis, dynamics and treatment. *Psychiat. Quart.*, 45:70–75.

Zucker, K. J. (1985), Cross-gender identified children. In: *Gender Dysphoria*, ed. B. W. Steiner. New York: Plenum Press.

———— Doering, R. W., Bradley, S. J., & Finegan, J. K. (1982), Sex-typed play in gender-disturbed children: A comparison to sibling and psychiatric controls. *Arch. Sex. Behav.*, 11:309–321.

———— Finegan, J. K., Doering, R. W., & Bradley, S. J. (1983), Human figure drawings of gender-problem children: A comparison to sibling, psychiatric, and normal controls. *J. Abnorm. Child Psychol.*, 11:287–298.

———— ———— ———— ———— (1984), Two subgroups of gender-problem children. *Arch. Sex. Behav.*, 13:27–39.

Zuger, B. (1966), Effeminate behavior present in boys from early childhood I. The clinical syndrome and follow-up studies. *J. Pediat.*, 69:1098–1107.

——— (1970), The role of familial factors in persistent effeminate behavior in boys. *Amer. J. Psychiat.*, 126:1167–1170.

——— (1974), Effeminate behavior in boys: Parental age and other factors. *Arch. Gen. Psychiat.*, 30:173–177.

——— (1978), Effeminate behavior present in boys from childhood: Ten additional years of follow-up. *Comprehen. Psychiat.*, 19:363–369.

——— (1984), Early effeminate behavior in boys outcome and significance of homosexuality. *J. Nerv. & Ment. Dis.*, 172:90–97.

——— (1988), Is early effeminate behavior in boys early homosexuality? *Comp. Psychiat.*, 29:509–519.

——— Taylor, P. (1969), Effeminate behavior present in boys from early childhood. II. Comparison with similar symptoms in non-effeminate boys. *Pediat.*, 44:375–380.

NAME INDEX

SUBJECT INDEX

473